ROVER
3 & 3·5 litre
Gold Portfolio
1958-1973

Compiled by
R.M. Clarke

ISBN 1 85520 0899

Brooklands Books Ltd.
'Holmerise', Seven Hills Road,
Cobham, Surrey, England

Printed in Hong Kong

BROOKLANDS BOOKS

BROOKLANDS ROAD TEST SERIES
AC Ace & Aceca 1953-1983
Alfa Romeo Alfasud 1972-1984
Alfa Romeo Alfetta Coupes GT. GTV. GTV6 1974-1987
Alfa Romeo Giulia Berlinas 1962-1976
Alfa Romeo Giulia Coupes 1963-1976
Alfa Romeo Giulietta Gold Portfolio 1954-1965
Alfa Romeo Spider 1966-1990
Allard Gold Portfolio 1937-1958
Alvis Gold Portfolio 1919-1967
American Motors Muscle Cars 1966-1970
Armstrong Siddeley Gold Portfolio 1945-1960
Aston Martin Gold Portfolio 1972-1985
Austin Seven 1922-1982
Austin A30 & A35 1951-1962
Austin Healey 100 & 100/6 Gold Portfolio 1952-1959
Austin Healey 3000 Gold Portfolio 1959-1967
Austin Healey Sprite 1958-1971
Avanti 1962-1983
BMW Six Cylinder Coupes 1969-1975
BMW 1600 Col. 1 1966-1981
BMW 2002 1968-1976
Bristol Cars Gold Portfolio 1946-1985
Buick Automobiles 1947-1960
Buick Muscle Cars 1965-1970
Buick Riviera 1963-1978
Cadillac Automobiles 1949-1959
Cadillac Automobiles 1960-1969
Cadillac Eldorado 1967-1978
High Performance Capris Gold Portfolio 1969-1987
Chevrolet Camaro SS & Z28 1966-1973
Chevrolet Camaro & Z-28 1973-1981
High Performance Camaros 1982-1988
Camaro Muscle Cars 1966-1972
Chevrolet 1955-1957
Chevrolet Corvair 1959-1969
Chevrolet Impala & SS 1958-1971
Chevrolet Muscle Cars 1966-1978
Chevelle and SS 1964-1972
Chevy Blazer 1969-1981
Chevy EL Camino & SS 1959-1987
Chevy II Nova & SS 1962-1973
Chrysler 300 1955-1970
Citroen Traction Avant Gold Portfolio 1934-1957
Citroen DS & ID 1955-1975
Citroen SM 1970-1975
Citroen 2CV 1949-1988
Shelby Cobra Gold Portfolio 1962-1969
Cobras and Cobra Replicas Gold Portfolio 1962-1989
Cobras & Replicas 1962-1983
Chevrolet Corvette Gold Portfolio 1953 1962
Corvette Stingray Gold Portfolio 1963-1967
High Performance Corvettes 1983-1989
Daimler SP250 Sport & V-8250 Saloon Gold Portfolio 1959-1969
Datsun 240Z 1970-1973
Datsun 280Z & ZX 1975-1983
De Tomaso Collection No.1 1962-1981
Dodge Charger 1966-1974
Dodge Muscle Cars 1967-1970
Excalibur Collection No.1 1952-1981
Facel Vega 1954-1964
Ferrari Cars 1946-1956
Ferrari Dino 1965-1974
Ferrari Dino 308 1974-1979
Ferrari 308 & Mondial 1980-1984
Ferrari Collection No.1 1960-1970
Fiat-Bertone X1/9 1973-1988
Fiat Pininfarina 124 + 2000 Spider 1968-1985
Ford Automobiles 1949-1959
Ford Bronco 1966-1977
Ford Bronco 1978-1988
Ford Consul. Zephyr Zodiac MkI & II 1950-1962
Ford Cortina 1600E & GT 1967-1970
Ford Fairlane 1955-1970
Ford Falcon 1960-1970
Ford GT40 Gold Portfolio 1964-1987
Ford RS Escorts 1968-1980
Ford Zephyr Zodiac Executive MkIII & MkIV 1962-1971
High Performance Escorts Mk1 1968-1974
High Performance Escorts Mk II 1975-1980
High Performance Escorts 1980-1985
High Performance Escorts 1985-1990
High Performance Capris Gold Portfolio 1969-1987
High Performance Mustangs 1982-1988
Holden 1948-1962
Honda CRX 1983-1987
Hudson & Railton 1936-1940
Jaguar and SS Gold Portfolio 1931-1951
Jaguar XK120 XK140 XK150 Gold Portfolio 1948-1960
Jaguar MkVII VIII IX X 420 Gold Portfolio 1950-1970
Jaguar Cars 1961-1964
Jaguar Mk2 1959-1969
Jaguar E-Type Gold Portfolio 1961-1971
Jaguar E-Type 1966-1971
Jaguar E-Type V-12 1971-1975
Jaguar XJ12 XJ5.3 V12 Gold Portfolio 1972-1990
Jaguar XJ6 Series II 1973-1979
Jaguar XJ6 & Series III 1979-1986
Jaguar XJS Gold Portfolio 1975-1988
Jeep CJ5 & CJ6 1960-1976
Jeep CJ5 & CJ7 1976-1986
Jensen Cars 1946-1967
Jensen Cars 1967-1979
Jensen Interceptor Gold Portfolio 1966-1986
Jensen Healey 1972-1976
Lamborghini Cars 1964-1970
Lamborghini Cars 1970-1975
Lamborghini Countach Col No.1 1971-1982
Lamborghini Countach & Urraco 1974-1980
Lamborghini Countach & Jalpa 1980-1985
Lancia Stratos 1972-1985
Land Rover 1948-1973 - A Collection
Land Rover Series I 1948-1958
Land Rover Series II & IIa 1958-1971
Land Rover Series III 1971-1985
Land Rover 90 & 110 1983-1989
Lincoln Gold Portfolio 1949-1960
Lincoln Continental 1961-1969
Lotus and Caterham Seven Gold Portfolio 1957-1989
Lotus Cortina Gold Portfolio 1963-1970
Lotus Elan Gold Portfolio 1962-1974
Lotus Elan Collection No.2 1963-1972
Lotus Elite 1957-1964
Lotus Elite & Eclat 1974-1982
Lotus Turbo Esprit 1980-1986
Lotus Europa Collection No.1 1966-1974

Marcos Cars 1960-1988
Maserati 1965-1970
Maserati 1970-1975
Mazda RX-7 Collection No.1 1978-1981
Mercedes 190 & 300SL 1954-1963
Mercedes 230/250/280SL 1963-1971
Mercedes Benz SLs & SLCs Gold Portfolio 1971-1989
Mercedes Bens Cars 1949-1954
Mercedes Bens Cars 1954-1957
Mercedes Bens Cars 1957-1961
Mercedes Bens Competition Cars 1950-1957
Mercury Muscle Cars 1966-1971
Metropolitan 1954-1962
MG TC 1945-1949
MG TD 1949-1953
MG TF 1953-1955
MG Cars 1959-1962
MGA & Twin Cam Gold Portfolio 1955-1962
MGA Roadsters 1955-1962
MGA Collection No.1 1955-1982
MGB MGC & V8 Gold Portfolio 1962-1980
MGB Roadsters 1962-1980
MGB GT 1965-1980
MG Midget 1961-1980
Mini Cooper Gold Portfolio 1961-1971
Mini Moke 1964-1989
Mini Muscle Cars 1961-1979
Mopar Muscle Cars 1964-1967
Mopar Muscle Cars 1968-1971
Morgan Three-Wheeler Gold Portfolio 1910-1952
Morgan Cars 1960-1970
Morgan Cars Gold Portfolio 1968-1989
Morris Minor Collection No.1
Mustang Muscle Cars 1967-1971
Oldsmobile Automobiles 1955-1963
Old's Cutlass & 4-4-2 1964-1972
Oldsmobile Muscle Cars 1964-1971
Oldsmobile Toronado 1966-1978
Opel GT 1968-1973
Packard Gold Portfolio 1946-1958
Pantera Gold Portfolio 1970-1989
Plymouth Barracuda 1964-1974
Plymouth Muscle Cars 1966-1971
Pontiac Tempest & GTO 1961-1965
Pontiac GTO 1964-1970
Pontiac Firebird 1967-1973
Pontiac Firebird and Trans-Am 1973-1981
High Performance Firebirds 1982-1988
Pontiac Fiero 1984-1988
Pontiac Muscle Cars 1966-1972
Porsche 356 1952-1965
Porsche Cars in the 60's
Porsche Cars 1960-1964
Porsche Cars 1964-1968
Porsche Cars 1968-1972
Porsche Cars 1972-1975
Porsche Turbo Collection No.1 1975-1980
Porsche 911 1965-1969
Porsche 911 1970-1972
Porsche 911 1973-1977
Porsche 911 Carrera 1973-1977
Porsche 911 Turbo 1975-1984
Porsche 911 SC 1978-1983
Porsche 914 Gold Portfolio 1969-1976
Porsche 914 Collection No.1 1969-1983
Porsche 924 Gold Portfolio 1975-1988
Porsche 928 1977-1989
Porsche 944 1981-1985
Range Rover Gold Portfolio 1970-1988
Reliant Scimitar 1964-1986
Riley 11/2 & 21/2 Litre Gold Portfolio 1945-1955
Rolls Royce Silver Cloud 1955-1965
Rolls Royce Silver Shadow 1965-1981
Rover P4 1949-1959
Rover P4 1955-1964
Rover 3 & 3.5 Litre Gold Portfolio 1958-1973
Rover 2000 + 2200 1963-1977
Rover 3500 1968-1977
Rover 3500 & Vitesse 1976-1986
Saab Sonett Collection No.1 1966-1974
Saab Turbo 1976-1983
Shelby Mustang Muscle Cars 1965-1970
Stubebaker Gold Portfolio 1947-1966
Stubebaker Hawks & Larks 1956-1963
Sunbeam Tiger & Alpine Gold Portfolio 1959-1967
Thunderbird 1955-1957
Thunderbird 1958-1963
Thunderbird 1964-1976
Toyota Land Cruiser 1956-1984
Toyota MR2 1984-1988
Triumph 2000. 2.5. 2500 1963-1977
Triumph GT6 1966-1974
Triumph Spitfire 1962-1980
Triumph Spitfire Col No.1 1962-1982
Triumph Stag 1970-1980
Triumph Stag Collection No.1 1970-1984
Triumph TR2 & TR3 1952-60
Triumph TR4-TR5-TR250 1961-1968
Triumph TR6 1969-1976
Triumph TR6 Collection No.1 1969-1983
Triumph TR7 & TR8 1975-1982
Triumph Herald 1959-1971
Triumph Vitesse 1962-1971
TVR Gold Portfolio 1959-1990
Volkswagen Cars 1936-1956
VW Beetle Collection No.1 1970-1982
VW Golf GTi 1976-1986
VW Karmann Ghia 1955-1982
VW Kubelwagen 1940-1975
VW Scirocco 1974-1981
VW Bus. Camper. Van 1954-1967
VW Bus. Camper. Van 1968-1979
VW Bus. Camper. Van 1979-1989
Volvo 120 1956-1970
Volvo 1800 1960-1973

BROOKLANDS ROAD & TRACK SERIES
Road & Track on Alfa Romeo 1949-1963
Road & Track on Alfa Romeo 1964-1970
Road & Track on Alfa Romeo 1971-1976
Road & Track on Alfa Romeo 1977-1989
Road & Track on Aston Martin 1962-1990
Road & Track on Auburn Cord and Duesenburg 1952-1984
Road & Track on Audi & Auto Union 1952-1980
Road & Track on Audi 1980-1986

Road & Track on Austin Healey 1953-1970
Road & Track on BMW Cars 1966-1974
Road & Track on BMW Cars 1975-1978
Road & Track on BMW Cars 1979-1983
Road & Track on Cobra, Shelby & GT40 1962-1983
Road & Track on Corvette 1953-1967
Road & Track on Corvette 1968-1982
Road & Track on Corvette 1982-1986
Road & Track on Datsun Z 1970-1983
Road & Track on Ferrari 1950-1968
Road & Track on Ferrari 1968-1974
Road & Track on Ferrari 1975-1981
Road & Track on Ferrari 1981-1984
Road & Track on Fiat Sports Cars 1968-1987
Road & Track on Jaguar 1950-1960
Road & Track on Jaguar 1961-1968
Road & Track on Jaguar 1968-1974
Road & Track on Jaguar 1974-1982
Road & Track on Jaguar 1983-1989
Road & Track on Lamborghini 1964-1985
Road & Track on Lotus 1972-1981
Road & Track on Maserati 1952-1974
Road & Track on Maserati 1975-1983
Road & Track on Mazda RX7 1978-1986
Road & Track on Mercedes 1952-1962
Road & Track on Mercedes 1963-1970
Road & Track on Mercedes 1971-1979
Road & Track on Mercedes 1980-1987
Road & Track on MG Sports Cars 1949-1961
Road & Track on MG Sprots Cars 1962-1980
Road & Track on Mustang 1964-1977
Road & Track on Nissan 300-ZX & Turbo 1984-1989
Road & Track on Peugeot 1955-1986
Road & Track on Pontiac 1960-1983
Road & Track on Porsche 1961-1967
Road & Track on Porsche 1968-1971
Road & Track on Porsche 1972-1975
Road & Track on Porsche 1975-1978
Road & Track on Porsche 1979-1982
Road & Track on Porsche 1982-1985
Road & Track on Porsche 1985-1988
Road & Track on Rolls Royce & B'ley 1950-1965
Road & Track on Rolls Royce & B'ley 1966-1984
Road & Track on Saab 1955-1985
Road & Track on Toyota Sports & GT Cars 1966-1984
Road & Track on Triumph Sports Cars 1953-1967
Road & Track on Triumph Sports Cars 1967-1974
Road & Track on Triumph Sports Cars 1974-1982
Road & Track on Volkswagen 1951-1968
Road & Track on Volkswagen 1968-1978
Road & Track on Volkswagen 1978-1985
Road & Track on Volvo 1957-1974
Road & Track on Volvo 1975-1985
Road & Track - Henry Manney at Large and Abroad

BROOKLANDS CAR AND DRIVER SERIES
Car and Driver on BMW 1955-1977
Car and Driver on BMW 1977-1985
Car and Driver on Cobra, Shelby & Ford GT 40 1963-1984
Car and Driver on Corvette 1956-1967
Car and Driver on Corvette 1968-1977
Car and Driver on Corvette 1978-1982
Car and Driver on Corvette 1983-1988
Car and Driver on Datsun Z 1600 & 2000 1966-1984
Car and Driver on Ferrari 1955-1962
Car and Driver on Ferrari 1963-1975
Car and Driver on Ferrari 1976-1983
Car and Driver on Mopar 1956-1967
Car and Driver on Mopar 1968-1975
Car and Driver on Mustang 1964-1972
Car and Driver on Pontiac 1961-1975
Car and Driver on Porsche 1955-1962
Car and Driver on Porsche 1963-1970
Car and Driver on Porsche 1970-1976
Car and Driver on Porsche 1977-1981
Car and Driver on Porsche 1982-1986
Car and Driver on Saab 1956-1985
Car and Driver on Volvo 1955-1986

BROOKLANDS PRACTICAL CLASSICS SERIES
PC on Austin A40 Restoration
PC on Land Rover Restoration
PC on Metalworking in Restoration
PC on Midget/Sprite Restoration
PC on Mini Cooper Restoration
PC on MGB Restoration
PC on Morris Minor Restoration
PC on Sunbeam Rapier Restoration
PC on Triumph Herald/Vitesse
PC on Triumph Spitfire Restoration
PC on VW Beetle Restoration
PC on 1930s Car Restoration

BROOKLANDS MOTOR & THOROUGHBRED & CLASSIC CAR SERIES
Motor & T & CC on Ferrari 1966-1976
Motor & T & CC on Ferrari 1976-1984
Motor & T & CC on Lotus 1979-1983

BROOKLANDS MILITARY VEHICLES SERIES
Allied Mil. Vehicles No.1 1942-1945
Allied Mil. Vehicles No.2 1941-1946
Dodge Mil. Vehicles Col. 1 1940-1945
Military Jeeps 1941-1945
Off Road Jeeps 1944-1971
Hail to the Jeep
US Military Vehicles 1941-1945
US Army Military Vehicles WW2-TM9-2800

BROOKLANDS HOT ROD RESTORATION SERIES
Auto Restoration Tips & Techniques
Basic Bodywork Tips & Techniques
Basic Painting Tips & Techniques
Camaro Restoration Tips & Techniques
Custom Painting Tips & Techniques
Engine Swapping Tips & Techniques
How to Build a Street Rod
Mustang Restoration Tips & Techniques
Performance Tuning - Chevrolets of the '60s
Performance Tuning - Ford of the '60s
Performance Tuning - Mopars of the '60s
Performance Tuning - Pontiacs of the '60s

BROOKLANDS BOOKS

CONTENTS

5	The New Rover 3 litre	*Autosport*	Sept.	26 1958
8	It'a Here . . . the Big Rover	*Wheels*	May	1959
10	Rover 3 litre Road Test	*Autocar*	Aug.	21 1959
14	The Heavenly Bath Chair Road Test	*Modern Motor*	Sept.	1959
18	Rover 3 litre Road Test	*Sports Cars Illustrated*	May	1960
21	The 3 litre Rover	*Motor Sport*	April	1961
24	The 3 litre Rover with Overdrive Road Test	*Motor*	Nov.	22 1961
28	Rover 3 litre Road Test	*Track & Traffic*	Nov.	1961
31	Rover 3 litre Automatic Road Test	*Autocar*	Dec.	1 1961
34	Brain Beats Brainbox	*Modern Motor*	March	1962
36	Rover 3 litre Road Test	*Road & Track*	June	1962
40	More Power for Rovers	*Autocar*	Sept.	28 1962
46	Mk. 2 Rover 3 litre Saloon	*Motor*	Oct.	3 1962
50	Rover 3 litre – That Viking Tenacity Road Test	*Wheels*	Jan.	1963
54	Rover 3 litre Coupé Road Test	*Autocar*	July	5 1963
59	Rover 3 litre – Buying Secondhand	*Motor*	July	24 1965
60	Rover 3 litre Automatic Road Test	*Autocar*	Nov.	13 1964
66	Rover 3 litre Coupé Mk. 3 Road Test	*Autocar*	May	6 1966
72	For Older Men	*Motor Sport*	Oct.	1966
73	The New Rover 3.5 V8 Road Test	*Autosport*	Sept.	29 1967
75	Power with Pomp – Rover 3.5 litre Coupé Road Test	*Motor*	Oct.	7 1967
82	A Week of Luxury	*Motor Sport*	Nov.	1967
84	Rover Goes V8	*Modern Motor*	Nov.	1967
87	Group Test Comparison Test	*Motor*	Oct.	19 1968
93	Personal Choice	*Motor*	Oct.	26 1968
95	1967 Rover 3.5 litre Used Car Test	*Autocar*	June	11 1970
97	Classic Choice – 1960's Range	*Thoroughbred & Classic Cars*	July	1979
98	1970 Rover 3.5 litre Coupé Used Car Test Part 2	*Autocar*	Mar.	23 1972
102	The Finest Rover of All	*Autosport*	July	17 1959
104	The Rover 3 litre Saloon Road Test	*Car – South Africa*	Sept.	1959
109	Rover 3 litre Road Test	*Road & Track*	Dec.	1959
112	Specifications	*World Car Catalogue*		1963
113	The 3 litre Rover Road Test	*Car Life*	March	1960
118	German Journey	*Motor*	April	20 1960
122	The Rover 3 litre Road Test	*Autosport*	Sept.	16 1960
124	Rover Refinements	*Motor*	Sept.	28 1960
127	A Rover on the Continent	*Autosport*	April	27 1962
128	Rover 3 litre Road Test	*Motor Trend*	June	1962
134	Rover 3 litre Mark 1A Road Test	*Cars Illustrated*	April	1962
139	New Rovers	*Motor*	Oct.	3 1962
142	For Rover Buyers – A High Performance Coupé	*Wheels*	Dec.	1962
144	Rover with a Bite	*Autocar*	Feb.	15 1963
147	Rover 3 litre Road Test	*Car and Driver*	Oct.	1963
150	Rover Coupé Road Test	*Road & Track*	Oct.	1963
154	1962 Rover 3 litre – Used Car on Test	*Autocar*	Feb.	4 1966
156	Panelcraft Rover 3 litre	*Autocar*	May	15 1964
157	Armchair Luxury Road Test	*Motor*	Mar.	19 1966
163	V for the Rover	*Motor*	Sept.	28 1967
166	Rover 3.5 litre Road Test	*Autocar*	Sept.	28 1967
171	Rover Go V	*Motor*	Oct.	7 1967
174	Rovers Return	*Old Motor*	Nov.	1981
178	Behind the Scenes	*Thoroughbred & Classic Cars*	Oct.	1984

BROOKLANDS BOOKS

ACKNOWLEDGEMENTS

Since the first Brooklands Book on these big Rovers appeared a few years ago, we have been able to track down a large quantity of material which did not appear in the original volume. Much of this new material comes from countries outside Great Britain, and sheds a new light on the way overseas markets responded to these typically British motor cars. We were sure that enthusiasts would wish to see it and so, when the time came to reprint the original volume, we decided instead to expand it into one of our larger Gold Portfolios.

All the Brooklands Books depend for their very existence upon the generosity and under-standing of those who hold the copyright to the articles and features they reproduce. For permission to use the material in this volume, we are indebted to the managements of Autocar, Autosport, Car and Driver, Car Life, Car – South Africa, Cars Illustrated, Modern Motor, Motor, Motor Sport, Motor Trend, Old Motor, Road & Track, Sports Cars Illustrated, Thoroughbred & Classic Cars, Canada Track & Traffic, Wheels and The World Car Catalogue.

Our thanks also go to motoring writer James Taylor for the few words of introduction which follow, and we recommend to all Rover enthusiasts his two standard works on these cars: The Classic Rovers, 1934-1977 and The Post-War Rover, P4 and P5.

R.M. Clarke

I confess to extreme bias here: the Rover P5 3-litre and P5B 3½-litre models have been my favourite classic cars for fifteen years, and there has usually been at least one of these big Rovers sitting in the Taylor garage. For their combination of discreet luxury with simple mechanical components, I believe they have no equals; and what very few people realise is just how quickly they can be driven with safety.

The first 3-litre models were introduced at the 1958 Earls Court Motor Show, and could be had with four-speed, overdrive, or automatic transmissions. They were well-received, but there could be little doubt that they were underpowered. So, on the Mark II models launched in 1962, Rover introduced an uprated engine, its new cylinder head developed in conjunction with tuning consultant Harry Weslake. The original interior trim, very 'Fifties in inspiration, had meanwhile disappeared when a number of cosmetic revisions were made for the Mk. IA models in 1961. Transmission options were by now limited to overdrive or automatic.

Along with the Mark II came the Coupé, originally conceived as a high-performance derivative but in practice simply an alternative body style which featured an attractive lowered and tapering roof-line. Detail development of these models continued right through to 1965, when the final 3-litre variants were introduced. The Mark III models had heavily revised interiors and some exterior changes, all of which anticipated the forthcoming V8-engined cars.

The light-alloy 3½-litre V8 engine was a General Motors design which had been used in that company's "compact" cars in the early 1960s. Made redundant largely by cheaper manufacturing technology, it still had plenty of development life left in it when Rover acquired it for their own use in 1965. The P5 was the Rover most urgently in need of a new engine, and in autumn 1967 it was relaunched with V8 power as the 3.5-litre Saloon and Coupé, or P5B (the "B" stood for Buick, the GM division which had originated the engine). Even though only automatic transmission was available, performance was quite dramatically improved, and sales exceeded Rover's own expectations by a huge margin. Production continued for a further six years, during which time the P5B earned the distinction of becoming both Prime Ministerial and Royal transport.

These big Rovers are at last being recognised by the classic car movement, and are now catered for by several specialists and by their own enthusiasts' club – the Rover P5 Owners' Club. In many ways, it is easier now to run one than it was fifteen years ago, when they were simply obsolete models as far as British Leyland garages were concerned. It is a matter of great personal satisfaction to me that interest in them is sufficient to encourage Brooklands Books to produce this fascinating collection of reprinted articles; and I am sure that P5 and P5B enthusiasts everywhere will welcome it as essential reading to further the enjoyment of their cars.

James Taylor

RECOGNIZABLE immediately as a Rover, the new car is very well proportioned indeed, and is much sleeker and more modern in appearance than its predecessors, as well as being roomier. Notable are the slim screen pillars, brought well back to improve visibility.

THE Rover car possesses a reputation which must be almost unique. Other makes may be faster, or have more exciting design features, but the Rover is revered throughout the world for sheer quality. It is almost taken for granted nowadays that any new car will cause its owner a good deal of trouble, but a Rover is expected to be 100 per cent. reliable from the start, and to continue so indefinitely. All this is no accident, for each car goes through such a series of inspections and quality checks that any failure would be unthinkable.

It is thus of extreme interest that the Rover Co., Ltd., are producing an entirely new car. This is the most powerful Rover yet, having a 3-litre engine developing 115 b.h.p., and although it is lower, wider, and longer than previous models, the ancestry is still obvious. This machine is an addition to the existing range, which is continued with the exception of the 105R (automatic).

JOHN BOLSTER LOOKS AT *The New Rover 3-litre*

... and discovers a completely new 100 m.p.h. saloon. built to very high standards of quality. at a far from astronomical price.

★

The 3-litre Rover is first of all a more roomy car than its predecessors. It is as fast as, or a little faster than, the 105S, and has greater acceleration. It combines this with the silence and smoothness of the 90, and much greater

flexibility than has yet been offered. It will be appreciated, therefore, that the 3-litre is a high-quality, 5/6-seater saloon of superb refinement, with a genuine 100 m.p.h. performance in addition.

An entirely new engine has the traditional overhead inlet valves in the light alloy head, and side exhaust valves in the cast iron block. The most important feature is a sturdy crankshaft in E.N. 110 steel, running on seven copper-lead bearings. This permits a compression ratio as high as 8.75 to 1 to be used without any diminution of smoothness, and speeds up to 5,000 r.p.m. are easily encompassed. Roller-type tappets, borrowed from the latest Rover diesel engine, ensure a long life for the camshaft, while the timing chain has an hydraulically operated tensioner.

Although two carburetters are employed on the 105S, the manufacturers have a preference for the simplicity and easy maintenance of a single unit. Accordingly, Harry Weslake has developed a design which gives twin-carburetter performance from one large instrument. This is a 2 ins. horizontal S.U., and of course the air filtering and silencing are very thorough.

A Borg-Warner automatic transmission may be specified, or the excellent Rover four-speed gearbox in conjunction with a 10 ins. Borg and Beck clutch. In either case, the final drive ratio is 3.9 to 1, or 4.3 to 1 when the optional Laycock-de Normanville overdrive is fitted. The open propeller shaft is divided, with a central steady bearing, and the rear axle has a hypoid drive.

An entirely new system of chassis construction is adopted. In brief, there is a box-section forward extension which carries the front suspension, steering, and power unit. This is attached to the main chassis-cum-body structure through six rubber-mounted anchorages. The floor pressings incorporate girder sections to take the main stresses, and the rear springs are isolated through extra large rubber bushes, and a novel triangular rubber mounting which avoids side float. It will thus be seen that road noise is insulated with great thoroughness.

The front suspension is also new, with wishbones and laminated torsion bars, which are anchored to a cross-member

INTERIOR comfort has been given careful consideration. A bench front seat is standard furniture, but separate seats may be ordered, and there is a choice of synchromesh gearbox, with or without overdrive, or Borg-Warner automatic transmission.

of the forward chassis extension. The top swivel pivot is a plain ball joint, but the lower load-carrying one incorporates a ball and anti-friction bearing. The Burman recirculating ball steering box operates through a forward-mounted three-piece track rod, and there is an anti-roll torsion bar. Telescopic dampers are used all round.

As on previous Rovers, the front brakes are of the two trailing shoe pattern, but the hydrostatic feature has been dropped in favour of an automatic clearance adjustment. The front drums are 11 ins. x 3 ins. in size, and at the rear the leading and trailing shoe brakes operate in 11 ins. x 2¼ ins. drums. The adoption of pendant pedals has made it possible to mount the master cylinder and Girling vacuum servo in a high and completely sheltered position.

The body is of all-steel construction, and features an elaborate built-in heating and ventilation system, with a large air inlet in the centre of the scuttle. This has permitted the deletion of the ventilating panels at the front of the side windows, which, in conjunction with the narrow screen pillars, is most beneficial to visibility. Anti-draught louvres are also fitted to the windows. Bench-type seats are standard, but individual front seats may be ordered. The body appointments and equipment are of the highest Rover quality, and of course the finish is superb. Suffice it to say that the comfort of the passengers has been studied in the most minute detail.

The wheelbase of the 3-litre is 9 ft. 2½ ins., and the track 4 ft. 7 ins. in front and 4 ft. 8 ins. at the rear. The ground clearance is exceptional at 7½ ins. and the weight is rather over 30 cwt. The price, including British P.T., is £1,763 17s. with synchromesh gearbox, or £1,921 7s. with Borg-Warner automatic transmission.

This car is bound to create a furore, both at home and abroad.

An exclusive "Autosport" cutaway drawing by Theo Page

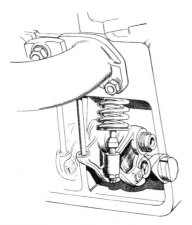

ENGINE accessibility (right) is good, electrical components being particularly easy to reach. The unconventional side-exhaust and overhead-inlet valve arrangement gives the engine an unusual "shape". Roller-type tappets (above) are also unusual and were originally used in Rover diesel engines.

FRONT SUSPENSION is shown here. Upper wishbones are conventional, but the lower ones are extended rearwards for greater rigidity. Springing medium is a gaitered laminated torsion bar running longitudinally and visible in the right-hand picture.

It's here . . . the BIG

More than enough to ruffle the hair of that Viking warrior perched out front.

Back view shows Italian grace of line, British solidity. Good visibility is one of Three Litre's outstanding design features. No mucking about in this department.

Overhead inlet, side exhaust motor has tons of beef, and silence as well. Note subframe supporting front suspension and engine. Rest of body is one unit.

WE seem to remember having said before that there's something about a Rover.

The same applies to the new Three Litre, but it's a different something. If you've seen it, you'll agree with us. If you haven't, the happy event will probably come about this way . . .

You'll be standing on a street corner in town somewhere, scouring the traffic for the missus in the Holden. Suddenly there'll be a whisper beside you, a semi-silent squish of tyres, and the most exotic piece of sculptured steel you've seen in many a year will disappear around the corner.

"Lancia!" you'll scream hysterically as you leap into a taxi (wifey and the family chariot forgotten), "Follow that car!"

But you'll be in for a shock, for your Italian-looking dreamboat of an automobile will be a Rover. Yes, really. Big brother and lineal descendent of those beautifully made but rather British looking 90s and 105s.

The Three Litre is nothing like any other Rover. Its lines are as modern as the day, high waisted and clean in the classic manner. Under the bonnet purrs a new six-cylinder, 2,995 c.c. motor, still with the uniquely silent overhead inlet/side exhaust valve gear favoured by the Solihull firm since just after the war.

Important engine changes include a substitution of a seven-bearing crankshaft for the old four-prop and roller tappets for the directly operated type.

Biggest news of all, though, is that the new car has no chassis. A readily detachable sub-assembly carries the motor and front suspension, and the rest of the body is built as a single unit.

The front end itself is thoroughly 1959. Laminated torsion bars with adjustable anchorage points support the car, and spherical joints carry the wishbones and links. Top wishbones are canted downwards towards the rear — a clever way of stopping nose dive under braking.

Rear springs are longer and wider than those of the smaller Rovers, and they have no shackles. Thick rubber blocks look after location instead. The steering column has a universal joint to allow for relative movement of the half-chassis and the body shell.

Typical of Rover is the use of a stainless steel handbrake cable running over die cast pulleys. No lubrication, no sticking, no worries.

Body is all steel, without the usual aluminium panels. Inside, it is superbly planned. Instruments and toggle switches are grouped in a big binnacle right in front of the driver, a hefty crash pad extends across the car and around the sides, and polished wood is used only where

Rover

Big 'un from Rover has grace as well as polish. Screen wraps right around in '59 fashion, yet window-top louvres exclude draughts nineteen thirties-style — truly the best of two worlds!

Inside, adjustable armrests, crash padding, full three-abreast seating plus precision gearshifting. Big instrument binnacle is sound sense, we're thinking.

sun and weather won't damage it. Another crash pad runs across the front compartment at knee level, with a parcels shelf behind it.

The gear lever in manual shift cars is on the floor, but it's cranked to clear a middle passenger's legs. Genuine hide, pile carpet and grain walnut are the trim materials. All the doors have adjustable armrests, and there are individually adjustable fresh air units on both sides of the car. They can be controlled to direct a blast of air anywhere inside a given range. An elaborate heating and demisting system is standard equipment.

Altogether a lovely car, which should have performance to match its styling and engineering appeal.

Australia's first Three Litre was on show at Sydney's Royal Easter Show, but supplies will be short for some time. Price £2,590.

Borg Warner automatic transmission costs £205 more.   #

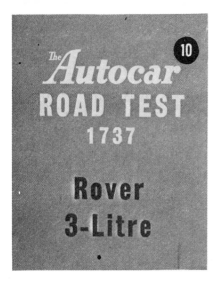

A high waistline and large radiator grille are features of the 3-Litre Rover. The side lamps have small red markers visible to the driver

FOR many years the Rover Company has enjoyed a well deserved reputation for producing cars to a very high standard of finish, comfort and silence at a price, in world markets, within the upper limits of the medium range. The new 3-Litre, added to the company's programme in October 1958, enhances this character, for it is much roomier than previous models, has a style which transforms traditional to modern thought without being bizarre, has a sufficiently high performance for the majority of owners, and road manners which, without being outstanding, are in the main, satisfactory. These qualities are supported by a newly introduced system of Girling brakes having servo-assistance with front discs and rear drums, which results in an extremely high standard of braking safety at all speeds.

Compared with the P.4 Rover models, which share a common body shell but have engines of differing capacities and ratings, the 3-Litre (known as the P.5 within the works) is a completely new design with important differences from its predecessors, each contributing to a change in characteristics. It is 3½in lower and the track is 3in wider at the front and 4in at the rear; these two features, in conjunction with a much lower floor level, have reduced roll considerably. The lower floor has been achieved by using integral body and chassis construction for the first time in a Rover car. Another important change is the use of an orthodox wishbone type of front suspension with laminated torsion bars. These units, and the engine-gear box assembly, are carried on an individual sub-frame, connected to the body hull at six points with rubber-insulated attachments.

The engine is similar in basic layout to the other four- and six-cylinder models, but its capacity is raised to 2,995 c.c. The crankshaft has seven main bearings to increase stiffness and improve quietness of running. For a unit of this size the power output at 115 b.h.p. gross is modest. Undoubtedly, in using a single carburettor and arranging for the peak torque to occur as low as 1,500 r.p.m., the aim has been to provide flexibility over a wide range rather than a maximum performance infrequently used in a car of this type. With a 3cwt load, the car will climb a 1 in 7.7 gradient at a steady speed in top gear; similarly laden, it will take off in bottom gear on a 1 in 3 hill and continue to accelerate smoothly.

This model can be supplied with either a Borg-Warner fully automatic transmission or a manual four-speed box having synchromesh on the upper three ratios and a central gear change. The model tested had the manual control and in addition was equipped with Laycock de Normanville overdrive—an optional extra. For a car in this class the majority of owners would specify this extra, which operates on top gear only and improves the mechanical refinement at high cruising speeds. When the overdrive is fitted the axle gearing is lowered (4.3 to 1 as against 3.9 to 1 in standard form).

By making full use of the engine power, surprisingly good performance figures were achieved, bearing in mind that the car has a kerb weight of 32½cwt. Mean figures were 20.3sec for the standing quarter mile; from rest to 60 m.p.h., 16.2sec, and to 80 m.p.h., 31.5sec; and a maximum of 96.4 m.p.h.

In recording the standing start performance figures the car was subjected to much more severe treatment than it would be likely to encounter in the hands of the average owner. Clutch take-up was always smooth, but axle hop was difficult to avoid, and in the worst conditions there was a succession of thumps of the axle against its rubber bump stop before the wheels established unbroken contact with the ground. Fairly high loads are required to operate the clutch pedal, which has a long movement and needs to be fully depressed for clean engagement of the gears.

The long central gear lever can be adjusted in its relationship to the wheel to suit the individual driver, but has rather a springy action and notchy operation which make it a far from pleasant mechanism. This action appears to result from relatively heavy spring loads on the selector shaft. The ratios are well chosen, though third gear could be raised slightly with advantage. First gear was consistently difficult to engage and the synchromesh on the other gears could be beaten during very fast changes.

In most main road conditions in this country the ride, fully or lightly laden, is very good indeed, and the handling characteristics do not change noticeably between extremes of load. Suspension is excellent over unmade roads, and the damping is firm for these conditions, when the unsprung portions are subjected to rather violent movements. A succession of slight bumps and hollows taken at a speed which matched the frequency of the suspension did produce some pitching; this did not reach severe proportions, but with the slower wheel movements the damping did not appear so effective. These features were confirmed by the car's behaviour during cornering. Taken round a bend very fast, roll was firmly resisted; on the same corner at a much lower speed, passengers were aware of the increase in roll.

At speed the steering is reasonably light and accurate, with no trace of kick-back at the wheel. Below approximately

The boot has a low floor with the spare wheel beneath. A flap conceals the more bulky tools and the protruding battery (right) has a detachable cover

35 m.p.h. it feels heavier, and some lost movement around the straight ahead position was noticed, with a corresponding lack of precision.

Two tyre sizes can be specified; those on this particular car were of the smaller section—6.70-15in. When they were inflated to the pressures recommended for full load there was considerable squeal on corners. With the pressures set to the maker's recommendations for normal loads, this noise was often quite embarrassing at speeds as low as 20 m.p.h., particularly on polished tarred surfaces.

On very rough surfaces such as the worst type Belgian pavé or ripply corrugations, the car rode comfortably and the body appeared to be rigid, with no scuttle shake. Some roads with a slightly rough surface produced a trace of front-end tremor, presumably attributable to the rubber-mounted front suspension and engine sub-unit. Switch-back, winding roads in France, with typical poor surface, accentuated these front-end effects and brought a lack of steering precision, the car straying somewhat from its intended course if hurried though a succession of such bends. But there was no sliding of the rear wheels.

Adhesion in the dry is very good, the steering characteristics being neutral for all practical purposes. In the wet the tendency is for the front end to lose adhesion first, but cornering speeds need to be high for this to happen.

Braking on either a wet or dry surface reached a very high standard indeed, particularly in the wet. The low pedal loads, with a maximum effort of 75lb locking the wheels with two aboard, were praised by all who drove the car. The best stop of 0.94g was achieved with 70lb pedal load. These new front disc, rear drum brakes were progressive throughout their range, without a trace of servo delay, and from speeds of 90 m.p.h. they could be used repeatedly and remained stable for each of the four wheels, so that the car never pulled aside from a straight line. Simulated Alpine tests produced no fade; in these conditions the increase in pedal travel was negligible, and there was no smell of hot linings. If the first brake application was heavy after the car had been standing for some time the rear wheels locked first, but once the drums had become warm this did not recur. The hand brake, operated by a pull-out, umbrella-type handle to the right of the steering wheel, was efficient and light in operation. In its "on" position there was some interference with the winding handle of the driver's window.

Fuel consumption for the 1,721 miles of the test, which included measurement of performance figures, averaged 19.2 m.p.g.; the total quantity of oil used was 6 pints—equal to 2,300 m.p.g. The fuel consumption is reasonable for the size of the car and the performance which it offers. In hard driving or in continuous traffic, the figure will drop to 18 m.p.g., but without too much restraint on the part of the driver consumption can be raised to 24 m.p.g. with frequent use of the overdrive, which reduces engine speed by 22 per cent in relation to road speed compared with direct top.

For normal use the fuel tank provides a range of 250 miles before the main supply runs out; there is, in addition, a reserve capacity of 1½ gallons, controlled by a facia-mounted switch which brings into circuit a second electric feed pump. The fuel filler, mounted high on the left side, flush with the bodywork, is of the hinged flap type. It can be locked with a key, but on pressing the key button in its unlocked position the flap springs open and it can then be slammed shut. Unfortunately the filler pipe does not take the full flow from a modern pump without blowback.

Overdrive operated very sweetly in all conditions, in part because of its special linkage. There is an inhibitor switch which prevents changes taking place when the column-mounted selector lever is moved, if the engine is on overrun or at very light throttle openings. Another

Individual front seats were fitted in the test car and arm rests on the front doors are adjustable for height. Tools are carried in rubber in a tray beneath the facia. Each back rest has a flap pocket

refinement is a kick-down switch situated beneath the throttle pedal; this enables normal top to be obtained by full depression of the pedal for rapid acceleration. Overdrive is reselected automatically when the accelerator pedal is partially lifted, if the column control switch is left in its overdrive position.

During the period of this test ambient temperatures were invariably above 70deg F, and often around 80deg F. In these conditions the rich mixture control, operated by a firm T-handle mounted below the full width parcel shelf, was needed for the first start each day. The engine required rich mixture for the first mile, and another mile passed before it became fully responsive. This particular car had its fast idle set too high for easy manœuvring, and the rich mixture warning lamp on the dash did not stay alight with the control partially out, where most people would be likely to leave it. The engine is well insulated from the passenger compartment and is smooth throughout its range, except for a slight resonance on the overrun from high speeds.

A feature of the car is that it has no hinged quarter vents, and each door window has a plastic draught excluder along its top edge. A minor criticism of these is that they resulted in some distortion, and prevented one reading high-mounted signposts through the top 3in of the windows. With all the windows closed there was negligible wind noise at all speeds; with them wound down fully, there was draught-free ventilation at speeds up to 75 m.p.h. Even in this condition the extra noise did not interfere with normal conversation.

Ventilation is assisted by a very good supply of fresh air, with four individual controls, the driver and front passenger each having two. There is a separate vent at each side on the top edge of the facia, a neat swivelling handle controlling the quantity of air; a deflector plate on the outside of the grille directs the fresh air either into the face, or over the head for the benefit of the rear passengers also. These

The well-filled engine compartment has a counter-balanced lid. The single carburettor has an oil bath air cleaner and large silencer; plugs and distributor are readily accessible

Rover
3-litre . . .

Perspex louvres over the door windows are an aid to air circulation; no quarter vents are fitted. The fuel filler is behind the rear window

controls were very effective at speeds above 45 m.p.h. when a side window—preferably a rear one—was kept open to relieve internal pressure. There are two additional cold air vents with a pull-out control knob which locks in any one of four positions, and they direct cool air over the legs of the front occupants.

If the heating system (controlled by two vertically operating levers in the middle of the facia) with an output equivalent to 4 kilowatts, works as efficiently as the fresh air system—and we have no reason to doubt it—it would also be a very cosy car in wintry conditions.

In the matter of internal appointments the Rover is outstanding, and more luxuriously appointed than most of its competitors in world markets. Natural leather and thick pile carpets with underlay are used.

This particular car was equipped with the optionally extra bucket seats, which are well shaped and deeply upholstered. By suitably positioning the securing bolts at the base, individual settings for height and rake are obtainable; a minor criticism is that the fore and aft adjustment could, with advantage, be more finely pitched. The cushions are high relative to the scuttle; the pleasantly small-diameter steering wheel is well raked and its rim is comfortably thin. Screen pillars are slim in the line of vision, of constant thickness throughout their height, joining the roof with a very small radius to avoid beetle-brow effects.

Foot space around the pedals is plentiful, and the dip switch is operated by an organ-type pedal on which the left foot can be rested. This foot is used also to operate the windscreen washers, the plunger for which is mounted above and to the left of the dip switch pedal.

All instruments are contained in a cowling raised from the main facia. There are two circular dials—on the left is the speedometer, with trip and distance recorder; that to the right contains three segments for water temperature, dynamo charge rate, fuel and oil levels. Beside this instrument panel are vertical rows each of three switches. On the right, from top to bottom, they control lights, petrol reserve, and combined ignition and starter; on the left they switch panel lights (with rheostat control); oil level, with

There is an organ pedal for operation of the dip switch on the left of the clutch pedal. All instruments are close to eye level and there is a wide tray beneath the facia. On the doors are adjustable armrests and map pockets

indication of sump level reading on the fuel contents gauge; and wipers. Sensibly, each of these switches operates outwards, so there is never any confusion as to which way an individual switch should be moved.

Beneath the two-spoked wheel there are three lever controls. On the left is that for the overdrive, and on the right the turn indicator and head lamp switch; this selects side lamps or main beams. It would be more convenient if the shorter of the two switches were uppermost, and the distance between them were reduced.

The mahogany facia, of fine, straight grain, is very tasteful. On the passenger's side there is a well-proportioned, deep, lockable glove compartment, the lid of which forms a rigid tray in its open position. Beneath the facia is a full-width parcel shelf with a front retaining ledge, sponge-covered for safety. This tray would be better if it were surfaced with a nap cloth instead of leather, for then there would be less likelihood of objects sliding from side to side during cornering.

Rear passengers receive particular consideration. The seats are very comfortable with a folding central armrest in addition to a fixed one on each door. Knee room is generous, and the feet can be placed well forward beneath the radiused bottom edges of the front seat squabs. The ride is even more comfortable than that experienced by front passengers. In fact, because of its size and characteristics, this car is better suited to be chauffeur-driven than any of its predecessors.

Space for oddments and parcels is outstandingly good. In addition to the front parcels shelf there is one behind the rear seats, with a recess in the middle to accommodate deep objects without interfering with rearward vision; there are also elastic-closed magazine pockets in the front doors and behind each front seat. Above each front door is a courtesy lamp which lights up when any door is opened, and an overriding switch is provided for individual operation. There is also a light in each rear quarter, for use by rear passengers; these are metal framed, flush fitting, but are placed just where a passenger might rest his head when dozing. It would be an advantage if they were recessed.

Much thought has been given to safety provision, for foam rubber underlay is provided beneath the leather cloth at many points, including the top rim of the rear window above the passengers' heads. Typical of the detail thought put into the appointments is a neat tray beneath the parcel shelf on the passenger's side, containing a fine set of hand tools, each with its own moulded recess in foam rubber. Larger tools such as wheel brace, jack, tyre pump and starting handle are clipped in position behind the left rear wheel arch, and covered by a leathercloth curtain. There are two jacking points beneath the sill at each side of the car, and the wheel brace is used to lower the spare wheel from a tray beneath the luggage boot floor. There is sufficient space for a normal complement of holiday luggage for five people if care is taken with the packing; the battery, protected by a loose cover, is mounted on the right-hand side of the boot.

All suspension joints and steering pivots on the Rover are sealed to retain the lubricant put in by the manufacturers, and routine servicing, apart from the usual check of oil, water and brake fluid levels, is confined to four points on the two-piece propeller shaft. These require attention at recommended intervals of 3,000 miles.

Head lamps are fully up to the car's performance, having good spread and penetration for maximum speed, yet are well diffused when dipped. Side lamps are mounted high on the wings and include red tell-tales on the top, visible from the driving seat.

Traditionally Rover have always been conservative rather than radical in their engineering design; they have never made changes for change's sake. New ideas are always being considered, but are thoroughly investigated before being introduced into a new model. The 3-Litre epitomises this thinking, for it has been evolved from a sound line of antecedents. In the standard of comfort, appointments and silence of running it has few equals in the world, and certainly none in its price range.

ROVER 3-LITRE

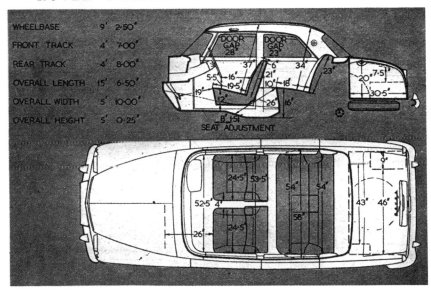

WHEELBASE	9' 2.50"
FRONT TRACK	4' 7.00"
REAR TRACK	4' 8.00"
OVERALL LENGTH	15' 6.50"
OVERALL WIDTH	5' 10.00"
OVERALL HEIGHT	5' 0.25"

Scale ¼in to 1ft. Driving seat in central position. Cushions uncompressed.

PERFORMANCE

ACCELERATION:
Speed range, Gear Ratios and Time in sec.

M.P.H.	3.35 to 1*	4.3 to 1	5.92 to 1	8.79 to 1	14.52 to 1
10—30	—	—	6.9	4.7	—
20—40	12.1	8.8	6.3	4.8	—
30—50	12.7	9.2	6.7	—	—
40—60	14.6	10.3	8.2	—	—
50—70	17.4	12.4	—	—	—
60—80	19.6	15.7	—	—	—
70—90	24.1	—	—	—	—

*Overdrive

From rest through gears to:

M.P.H.	sec.
30	5.0
40	7.5
50	11.7
60	16.2
70	22.7
80	31.5
90	46.8

Standing quarter mile, 20.3 sec.

MAXIMUM SPEED IN GEARS:

Gear		M.P.H.	K.P.H.
O.D.	(mean)	96.4	155.3
	(best)	97.5	156.9
Top	(mean)	90.8	146.1
	(best)	92.0	148.1
3rd		66	106.2
2nd		44	70.8
1st		26	41.8

TRACTIVE EFFORT:

	Pull (lb per ton)	Equivalent Gradient
O.D.	210	1 in 10.6
Top	285	1 in 7.7
Third	374	1 in 5.9
Second	545	1 in 3.8

SPEEDOMETER CORRECTION: M.P.H.

Car speedometer:	10	20	30	40	50	60	70	80	90
True speed:	9	19	29	39	49	59	69	79	88

BRAKES: (at 30 m.p.h. in neutral)

Pedal load in lb	Retardation	Equivalent stopping distance in ft
25	0.34g	89
50	0.66g	46
70	0.94g	32.2

FUEL CONSUMPTION:

Constant Speeds	M.P.G.	
M.P.H.	Direct Top	O.D. Top
30	32.1	36.1
40	29.2	34.5
50	25.4	30.8
60	22.2	27.2
70	20.0	23.5
80	17.1	20.5
90	13.8	17.3

Overall fuel consumption for 1,721 miles, 19.2 m.p.g. (14.4 litres per 100 km.). Approximate normal range 16–24 m.p.g. (17.7–11.8 litres per 100 km). Fuel: premium grade.

TEST CONDITIONS: Weather: dry, no wind.
Air temperature: 69 deg. F.
Acceleration figures are the means of several runs in opposite directions.
Tractive effort obtained by Tapley meter.
Model described in *The Autocar* of 26 September 1958.

DATA

PRICE (basic), with saloon body, including heater, £1,210 0s. 0d.
British purchase tax, £505 5s 10d.
Total (in Great Britain), £1,715 5s 10d.
Extras: Radio £46 3s 8d (with tax).
Overdrive £68 0s 0d (with tax).
Bucket seats £17 0s 0d (with tax).

ENGINE: Capacity, 2,995 c.c. (183 cu in).
Number of cylinders, 6.
Bore and stroke, 77.8 × 105mm. (3.063 × 4.134in.).
Valve gear, overhead inlet, side exhaust, pushrods.
Compression ratio, 8.75 to 1.
B.H.P. 115 (gross) at 4,500 r.p.m. (B.H.P. per ton laden 64.8).
Torque, 164 lb ft at 1,500 r.p.m.
M.P.H. per 1,000 r.p.m. in top gear, 18.26; in overdrive, 23.44.

WEIGHT: (With 5 gals. fuel), 32.5 cwt (3,633 lb).
Weight distribution (per cent); F, 53.5; R, 46.5.
Laden as tested, 35.5 cwt (3,970 lb).
Lb per c.c. (laden), 1.32.

BRAKES: Type: Girling disc front, drum rear.
Method of operation: hydraulic, vacuum servo assisted.
Dimensions: F, 10.8in diameter; R, 11in diameter; 2¼in wide.
Swept area: F, 246 sq in; R, 173 sq in.

TYRES: 6.70-15in Dunlop Gold Seal.
Pressures (lb sq in): F, 24; R, 26 (normal); F, 28; R, 30 (fast driving).

TANK CAPACITY: 12.5 Imperial gallons, plus 1.5 gals. reserve.
Oil sump, 10 pints.
Cooling system, 22.5 pints (including heater).

STEERING: Turning circle.
Between kerbs: R, 38ft 10in; L, 39ft 4.5in.
Between walls: R, 40ft 8in; L, 41ft 2.5in.
Turns of steering wheel from lock to lock, 4.2.

DIMENSIONS: Wheelbase, 9ft 2.5in.
Track: F, 4ft 7in; R, 4ft 8in.
Length (overall): 15ft 6.5in.
Width: 5ft 10in.
Height: 5ft 0.25in.
Ground clearance: 7.8in.

ELECTRICAL SYSTEM: 12-volt; 57 ampère-hour battery.
Head lights: Double dip; 60–40 watt bulbs.

SUSPENSION: Front, independent, laminated torsion bars and anti-roll bar.
Rear: Semi-elliptic leaf-springs.

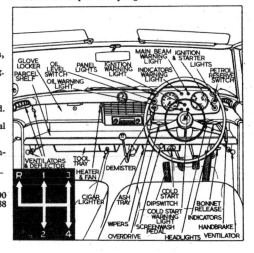

THE HEAVENLY

modern MOTOR ROAD TEST

BATH-CHAIR

Bryan Hanrahan tests new Rover Three-litre with automatic drive — finds it smooth, decorous, relaxingly luxurious

AS a self-confessed Roverphile, I am bound to tell you that I've driven Rovers which I liked better than the new Three-litre.

Mainly, I'm thinking of the 1947 straight-six sportsman's saloon with beam front axle, and the current high-compression 105S. Then there was the 1951 "75" I owned from 23,000 to 78,000 miles of its life that literally never had a spanner on the engine, and went better and better as the miles rolled on.

I don't mean that there's anything crook about the Three-litre—it's a beautiful bit of machinery—but it hasn't got quite the old Rover personality.

For instance, on test I couldn't get it to oil a plug or cut a shocker rubber . . . there wasn't even a squeal from brakes or tyres.

Why, my old '51 at times would actually select two gears at once!

Where are those endearing little features of yore? You always knew that you couldn't be driving anything but a Rover.

And the appearance. Side-on, the Three-litre looks like a rather obese Ford Zephyr; the old waistline and classical flow of the vestigial mudguard profiles are gone.

Aside from that—a matter of taste, anyway—the Three-litre is so smooth that it's almost sickly, and so decorous it's almost dull.

Bath-chair motoring de-luxe. I don't mean to say that the Three-litre isn't both lively and rapid so far as sheer performance is concerned—the

INTERIOR is a picture of expensive dignity: high-grade leather upholstery, touches of walnut trim. Arrow points to automatic drive control.

car's almost on a par with the new Humber Snipe. But I expected more.

It's not all the car's fault—nor the Rover Company's. Our harsh petrol is the trouble.

Britain and all the other main countries to which the Three-litre is going have 100-octane fuel or thereabouts, and they get the car as designed—with 8.75 to 1 compression. We have to set for 7.5 to 1.

Same thing happened with the 105 models, except that they were cut from only 8.5 to 7.5. A great shame, because I think the Three-litre would normally be a genuine 100 m.p.h. car instead of the 95 m.p.h. job we get.

Interesting Engine

Maximum power of the 2995 c.c. engine on 7.5 compression is estimated at 105 b.h.p. gross at 4250 r.p.m. against 115 on 8.75. And the engine will gladly spin at 5000 in top with the slightest encouragement from wind or grade.

The engine is not just a bored-out 105; it's a new block casting with several interesting new features.

Main ones are the use of roller cam followers, which should considerably increase the life of the camshaft and messy overhead-and-side valve train; and seven instead of four copper-lead main bearings, to take the increased compression loads and cut down any tendency to crank-bending vibrations.

These two innovations should deal with the main weaknesses of the postwar Rover engine—camshaft and main-bearing wear.

Inherent design of the roller tappets allows higher valve lifts and better breathing. There should be a lot of development potential in the engine.

Carburation is by one big two-inch SU—another indication of big development potential.

Against the 105 engine's 138lb./ft. torque at 1750 r.p.m., the Three-litre gives 138lb./ft. at only 1500.

Transmission

The Rover Three-litre is available in three transmission forms—fully automatic three-speed Borg Warner (as tested); four-speed manual box; and four-speed manual box with overdrive.

The automatic and standard models have a 3.9 to 1 back axle; the overdrive (top gear only) has a lower 4.3 to 1 ratio for better acceleration in the indirect gears, but still with a rev-saving overdrive top cruising ratio.

Basically the Borg Warner box is standard on the Three-litre. But two intelligent Rover mods (sometimes they surprise you) give the driver the whip-hand.

First, there's an intermediate gear hold which keeps intermediate engaged till 64 m.p.h. The advan-

FAST cornering induces little roll, steering is beautifully responsive. Note huge rear window. BELOW: Tools are housed under boot lining.

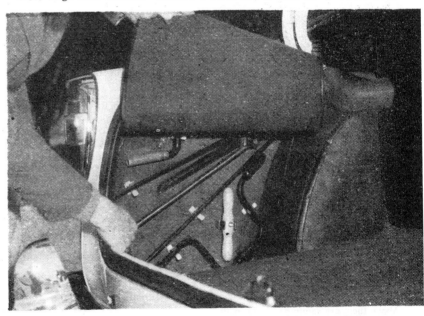

tages of this in traffic, fast cornering and braking on long grades were discussed in the Snipe and automatic Vanguard tests, so I won't go into them again.

Second Rover mod does away with part-throttle downward changes by using a kick-down switch on the accelerator pedal. This cuts that annoying flicking up and down in the normal drive range when mixed up in traffic which is alternating between 20 and 50 m.p.h.

You stay in top gear right down to 17 m.p.h.—unless you deliberately

press the accelerator to the floorboards.

For slower alternating traffic (9 a.m. in Collins Street), the intermediate hold is engaged—and until your speed drops below 4 m.p.h., in intermediate you stay.

In both cases the transmission works smoothly and efficiently in only one gear with the torque available. Only in extreme circumstances does a lower ratio come into play.

As I've said before, anything that makes an automatic less automatic improves it.

New Body Structure

Now for the body. Rover have returned to something close to their 1949-style construction. Basis of the body is a pressed-steel hull, with a half-length chassis that carries front suspension, engine and gearbox. Back suspension is carried by welded box reinforcements.

The idea, I think, is to get the lightness of unit construction, combined with the extra rigidity of a chassis to localise road shocks and accident damage.

Having studied a workshop manual, I don't think there will be much saving in labor costs for maintenance just because the engine, suspension and transmission can be taken out in one unit. The Three-litre, like all Rovers, is a swine to work on. But perhaps in extremes like a bad crash, big work savings could be made (more likely they'd benefit the insurance company rather than the owner).

Anyway, I won't shoot off my mouth on that one too soon. But I did like the old full-length box-chassis—many a life it has saved in murderous prangs.

Body panels are now all-steel. Gone are the non-corroding alloy doors, boot-lid and mudguard-skirts of the previous models. Rust-proofing, though, is said to be meticulous, so we'll wait and see on that one, too.

Lush Interior

The big, wide interior is fitted out for six with a luxury that no Roman emperor enjoyed.

Normal equipment in the front is a luxuriously upholstered bench-type seat with central folding armrest, but separate bucket-type seats are available if required. Quickly adjustable armrests are fitted to the doors.

At the back, the wide bench-type seat has the usual folding centre armrests. Leg and knee room are generous with the new low-level floor, which has also increased headroom by 1¼in., despite the lower overall height.

Upholstery and trim are done in high-grade leather, and walnut is used on gloveboxes and also for fillets on the doors, just below window level. Above them are safety pads, and pads are also provided above the fascia and across the full-width front parcel shelf.

Map pockets are fitted to the front doors, and there is a recessed parcel shelf below the rear window.

Instruments are concentrated in a binnacle in front of the driver. One large dial accommodates the speedo, and another the thermometer, ammeter and fuel gauge—the fuel gauge also serving to show the engine-oil level when a switch is operated.

Warning lights for the flashing indicators, headlamp main beam,

NEW 3-litre engine retains Rover's traditional overhead-and-side valve layout but features several interesting innovations. Output is 105 b.h.p.

MAIN SPECIFICATIONS

ENGINE: 6-cylinder, overhead inlet and side exhaust valves; bore 77.8mm., stroke 105mm., capacity 2995 c.c.; compression ratio 7.5 to 1; maximum b.h.p., estimated 105 gross at 4250 r.p.m.; maximum torque, 164lb./ft. at 1500 r.p.m.; S.U. horizontal carburettor, electric fuel pump; 12v. ignition.

TRANSMISSION: Borg Warner three-speed automatic with 10in. single dry-plate clutch; ratios — 1st, 9.0-18.9; 2nd, 5.6-11.75; top, 3.9 to 1; spiral-bevel final drive, 3.9 to 1 ratio.

SUSPENSION: Front independent, by swinging links and laminated torsion bars, with anti-roll bar; semi-elliptics at rear; telescopic hydraulic shock-absorbers all round

STEERING: Burman recirculating-ball type; 3½ turns lock-to-lock, 38ft. 6in turning circle.

WHEELS: Pressed-steel discs with 6.70 by 15in. tyres.

BRAKES: Girling servo-assisted hydraulic, 2 trailing shoes front; lining area 176 sq. in.

CONSTRUCTION: Unitary, with sub-frames.

DIMENSIONS: Wheelbase 9ft. 2½in.; track, front 4ft. 7in., rear 4ft. 8in.; length 15ft. 6½in., width 5ft. 10in., height 5ft. 0¼in.; ground clearance (unladen) 7½in

WEIGHT (as tested): 34½cwt.

FUEL TANK: 14 gallons.

PERFORMANCE ON TEST

CONDITIONS: Cold, slight cross-wind; dry bitumen; two occupants, premium fuel.

BEST SPEED: 96 m.p.h.

FLYING quarter-mile: 94.5 m.p.h.

STANDING quarter-mile: 20.9s.

SPEED range in gears: Low, 0-28 m.p.h.; intermediate, 8-64; top, 20-96.

ACCELERATION from rest through gears, using fixed Low and Intermediate hold: 0-30, 5.3s.; 0-40, 7.6s.;

0-50, 11.2s.; 0-60, 16.0s.; 0-70, 20.1s.; 0-80, 28.1s.; 0-90, 40.0s.

ACCELERATION in Drive range: 10-30, 4.1s.; 20-40, 4.9s.; 30-50, 6.4s.; 40-60, 7.4s.; 50-70, 10.0s.; 60-80, 14.9s.; 70-90, 25.1s.

BRAKING: 31ft. 8in. to stop from 30 m.p.h.

FUEL CONSUMPTION: 33 m.p.g. at steady 30 m.p.h.; 26 at 60; 22.8 overall for 200-mile test.

PRICE: £2850 including tax

THE HEAVENLY BATH-CHAIR

ignition, oil pressure and choke are disposed in the centre of the binnacle, which is flanked by a series of positive toggle switches; these are indirectly illuminated and control the variable instrument lighting, oil-level indicator, wiper, fuel reserve and side lights.

Headlamps are operated by a finger-tip steering-column switch next to the direction-indicator, and there's an organ-pedal type of dipper which also makes a rest for the left foot. Also on the binnacle is the combined ignition-and-starter switch.

In addition to all the normal items, the equipment includes a cigar lighter, windscreen-washers, child-proof safety locks, four interior lights, and a fitted tool-drawer under the fascia panel.

All doors are at last hinged on their leading edges—about time Rover adopted this safety measure!

Window arrangements are unusual in that hinged ventilating panels are not used. Instead, draughtless ventilation is provided by means of a high-level air intake in the scuttle, with ducts to face-level air vents located in the corners of the wrap-around screen.

These are purely fresh-air ducts, and both the quantity of air admitted and its direction can be controlled. Exit is allowed by lowering the side windows slightly, the openings being protected by external louvres. These louvres are made of peculiar-looking plastic and strike a distinctly "ersatz" note.

This fresh-air supply is independent of the elaborate heating-and-demisting system of four-kilowatt output, which also takes its air supply from the scuttle intake.

The luggage boot is big, and its floor is flat and unobstructed. Its lid, like the bonnet, is counter-balanced.

Big tools are housed on the left-hand side, and the battery (completely insulated by a plastic cover, and drained through a tray) on the right. The transverse fuel tank is isolated from the passenger compartment by a steel bulkhead and separated from the boot by a detachable panel. Alongside the tank is the SU electric fuel pump.

Suspension, Steering

Front suspension is interesting. Long, laminated torsion bars carry upper and lower links independently for each wheel. At the top, a plain ball-joint does universal duty for steering and riding; at the bottom, the extra load is carried by a ball-bearing and ball-joint.

Very cunningly and effectively, the upper wishbone is inclined so that the nose tends to lift rather than dip under braking. A neat and simple way of countering weight transference.

A roll-bar ties the two wheels together.

The rear is carried on conventional semi-elliptic leafsprings, but with bonded rubber bobbins in place of shackles. This set-up is claimed to reduce sideways movement of the springs.

Steering is conventional Rover-style—a three-piece track rod with idler shaft, and a Burman recirculating-ball box.

Gearing is reasonably quick at $3\frac{1}{2}$ turns lock-to-lock, and the turning circle of 38ft. 6in. is about average for this size of car.

Take the Three-litre out on the road, and you immediately discover that the steering is superb—as with the Mercedes 190 I tested recently, the wheel is so light and responsive that it seems to be intelligent. The brain's messages are instantly sent to the front wheels, as if they were an extension of your mind.

Handling, Performance

Having fitted into the driving-seat as if it had been done up for me in Savile Row, I didn't need much encouragement to try out the handling on the way to the test strip.

The way the Three-litre takes corners—even tight ones—and brakes at any old time on any old surface is a piece better than the Rover 105 performs.

Reason is that there's less under-steer; in fact, when you're trying hard in the sixties, the steering characteristics are nearly neutral.

The car is safe as houses—and it could gainfully employ the extra steam the designers intended it to have.

The brakes are servo-assisted Girlings with two trailing shoes at the front and leading-and-trailing shoes at the back. This arrangement does away with any tendency to grab at the front, because the shoes are pushed off the drums by wheel rotation as soon as the pedal is relaxed.

Though 176 square inches of lining area doesn't sound overmuch to deal with a test weight of $34\frac{1}{2}$ cwt., the brakes did not fade or protest. Average of six consecutive stops from 30 m.p.h. in neutral was 31ft. 8in.— a remarkable figure. Tapley meter reading was 96 percent.

Main acceleration figures, changing from fixed low to intermediate hold and keeping the foot down hard, were 0-30 m.p.h. in 5.3sec., 0-60 in 16.0, and then something of a wait for 0-90 in 40sec. flat.

True top speed was 94.5 m.p.h. The standing-start quarter-mile was covered in 20.9sec.

The car was viceless throughout, taking the most callous right foot with a muffled suck from the SU (like a politely concealed burp). It has the heels of the current 105S (manual-box), despite being a bigger car, with two extra cwt. to lug around.

Almost as good as the steering is the ride, on all but very broken surfaces.

I think that with its 15-inch wheels and 6.70 tyres, it gives a far superior ride to a Mercedes 220 on all average going. The Merc's 13-inch wheels find every depression, and only on really rough stuff or in hair-raising cornering does the independent back end show up better.

That doesn't mean that I think the Three-litre is better off with a solid back end. Why can't it have an independent one? The price, as tested, is £2850!

So there's the latest Rover. Still as smooth and quiet as anything on wheels, still suffering from some archaic mechanical design features . . . still without the steam that is its designers' due.

"A very elegant carriage, Modom, Sir!"

●●●

SCI Road Test: ROVER 3 LITER

ROAD TEST

ROVER 3 LITER

Price as tested: $4775
Importer: Rover Motor Co. of North America, Ltd.
36-12 37th Street
Long Island City 1, N. Y.

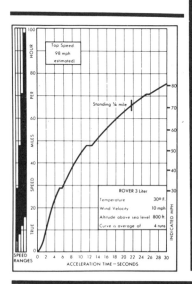

ENGINE:

Displacement ....182.6 cu in, 2995 cc
Dimensions ....Six cyl, 3.06 x 4.13 in
Compression Ratio ....8.75 to one
Power (SAE) ....115 bhp @ 4250 rpm
Torque ....164 lb-ft @ 1500 rpm
Usable rpm Range ....800-4800 rpm
Piston Speed $\div \sqrt{s/b}$
@ rated power ....2525 ft/min
Fuel Recommended ....Premium
Mileage ....18-23 mpg
Range ....300-380 miles

CHASSIS:

Wheelbase ....110.5 in
Tread, F,R ....55, 56 in
Length ....186.5 in
Suspension: F, ind., wishbones, lam. torsion
bars; R. rigid axle, leaf springs.
Turns to Full Lock 2¼
Tire Size ....6.70 x 15
Swept Braking Area — drum ....364 sq in
Curb Weight (full tank) ....3640 lbs
Percentage on Driving Wheels 47%
Test Weight ....3900 lbs

DRIVE TRAIN:

Gear	Synchro?	Ratio	Step	Overall	Mph per 100 rpm
Rev	No	2.97	—	11.58	6.9
1st	No	3.37		13.17	6.1
			65%		
2nd	Yes	2.04		7.97	10.0
			48%		
3rd	Yes	1.38		5.37	14.9
			38%		
4th	Yes	1.00		3.90	20.5

Final Drive Ratios: 3.90 to one,
4.30 with 78% O.D.

Graph:
Top Speed 98 mph (estimated)
Standing ¼ mile
ROVER 3 Liter
Temperature 30° F
Wind Velocity 10 mph
Altitude above sea level 800 ft
Curve is average of 4 runs
ACCELERATION TIME — SECONDS

► One of the last things a driver thinks about while threading through today's frenetic traffic is how long the manufacturer of his choice has been in business. This little nugget of information, on first thought, would seem to have little to do with how well the car goes. On reflection, however, and in connection with the Rover 3 Liter to be examined here, it has a great deal to do with the performance and appearance of an auto firm's end product.

Only two other U.S. car builders — Ford and Olds — can match the Rover Company's 56 continuous years of designing and fabricating automobiles. In many ways the newest Rover reflects traditional thinking — solid rear axle, chair-high seating, F-head engine — while in others — laminated torsion bar front suspension, monocoque chassis, disc brakes — it is abreast of, if not ahead of, contemporary engineering. A modern aspect of the 3 Liter is its body shape. Externally it owes much to the Italian school of design, suitably worked around in front to retain — though faintly — some flavor of the traditional Rover grille. This marriage of the Latin line and British conservatism has been tried on one or two other English luxury cars in the past. The results, unfortunately, have not produced a lasting union. The 3 Liter, however, seems to be a happy combination of both schools of thought, one that we think will wear well. Attaining a modern appearance that would not offend old-line Rover owners must have been one of the more difficult jobs faced by the engineering staff when they laid out the new car. Down through the years Rover cars have been adopted by some of Britain's better families. A new model in vulgar taste would be tantamount to having a young son sent down from Oxford for slovenly dress. This deference to the tastes of past Rover buyers gives a clue to the type of car that the company has been building for the past half century. Rovers have been solid, dependable, unostentatious automobiles that quietly inform driver and passengers alike that they are riding in a luxury car. This same impression is given onlookers as the Rover goes silently by.

The new 3 Liter in no way differs from this established approach. Entrance through the 36-inch wide front door opening can be accomplished without loss of dignity or breath. The first thing that strikes a neophyte Rover driver when he gets behind the wheel is that this is a big car. Its wheelbase is only 7.5 inches less than the latest Plymouth, yet overall length is 22.5 inches less than the same be-finned U.S. sedan. The next thing that one notices is the quality of workmanship displayed in the interior trim. For one attuned to the vagaries of production-line techniques employed on small economy sedans, the Rover interior impresses by its lack of sharp points, ragged edges, and short-measure head linings. Adding to this feeling of richness are the real leather upholstery and walnut-faced door fillets.

The pleasantly thick-rimmed steering wheel is set at just about the right angle and does not project into the driver's line of sight, while the instrument binnacle is positioned high enough to allow readings to be taken without consciously having to take one's eyes from the road. This instrument pod, cowled to eliminate reflections, contains dials for speed, water temperature, fuel and oil levels, switches for panel lights (with brightness control) main lights, oil level and key start ignition lock. Warning lights, placed between the two big dials, are used to indicate lack of oil pressure and sparks. With the exception of the cold start device — manual choke with an amber light that warns when it's in use, and the oil level gadget that utilizes the fuel gauge pointer when the right switch is flicked to give a rough estimate of the amount of oil in the sump — all of these instruments can be found on many other cars. What you don't find, however, is the quality of workmanship that makes everything on the Rover work with such a degree of smoothness that you find yourself clicking things on and off just to look and listen. ►

Only the intake valves are topside on the Rover 3 Liter. Exhaust valves are in the side of the block. Muffler quiets air rushing into the carb.

Rover trunk is large by any standard. Battery is mounted on right of compartment away from engine heat. Tire tools are clipped to left side.

Fuel filler is integral with hinged lid. Cover is chromed and lockable. Tank is mounted in dead space behind rear seat.

Road Test
Rover 3 Liter

The seating position (our test car had the bench seat — bucket seats can be had as optional extras) is very comfortable with the emphasis on giving a driver of more than average size plenty of room. Distaff drivers (that most American women drive is a fact that has to be faced) might find the driving seat just a little too commodious. The fold-down arm rest cuts the 55-inch-wide front seat roughly in half, thus limiting the distance that the smaller driver will slide on the smooth leather, but it still leaves a generous space for the small-derriered to rattle around in. Gears are shifted in the four-speed box by a crooked lever that projects, after suitable bends, from under the car-wide parcel shelf. It is shaped so as not to discommode a central passenger. After getting the gear shift lever very neatly out of the way it seems a shame that the rather large transmission tunnel does encroach on the foot room of the middle passenger. In use the gearbox fits the temperament of the Rover to a T. Strong, blocker-type synchromesh prevents ultra-fast shifts, while making normal shifts simple and silent. On our test car the detent spring that prevents accidental engagement of reverse when one is going for first gear was a little weak. This proved a minor embarrassment on one occasion. Rover drivers should never appear flustered to people in lesser vehicles.

With a twist of the ignition key the 182-cubic-inch six is ready to go. When cold there is just the slightest amount of valve noise. After the engine is warm you have to use the ignition warning light to find out whether or not you've stalled. (An aside on the amount of time it takes for the 3 Liter to warm up: Apparently Rover owners are not expected to ride in cold cars. Within blocks the very comprehensive heating system is pouring out warm air.) Under way the Rover impresses by its silence. Up to 45 or 50 mph you can hear the electric clock ticking. At speeds over that, wind noise — right around the center door post — muffles the sound of the clock, but doesn't intrude on conversation carried on at a living room level of pitch and volume.

On the open road the Rover reveals its reason for being. At speed the steering that seemed heavy in slow crawling traffic is light and precise, while the big, roomy seats allow plenty of fidgeting space. It is easy to visualize a captain of industry hurrying from one end of England to the other on important business in the comfort of his Rover. Ride is just a little firmer than on domestic sedans, which does away with that floating sensation you sometimes get in softly sprung cars at turnpike speeds. Bumps, with the stiffer suspension of the 3 Liter, are over and done with without the series of diminishing oscilla-

tions familiar to users of American-built luxury cars. Cornering — or just plain handling — is good for any situation that a Rover user might find himself in. Tires do howl on tight corners if recommended pressures are adhered to, and the car understeers to a greater and greater degree as speeds into turns are increased.

The Rover brakes are more than a little responsible for the car's ability to put up high averages. When first tried we thought they were a little puny to cope with the 3 Liter's 4,000-odd pounds of bulk. This, however, was a case of familiarity breeding satisfaction. It was also an interesting case of how preconditioned senses can mislead. In 90 percent of the automobiles being built today one sign of husky brakes doing their job is the sight of the nose of the car dipping violently. This is not what happens with the Rover, however. When the stop pedal is pushed the car simply stops — without dipping, swaying or swerving — it just stops. Few of the effects of deceleration are transmitted to the occupants. One simple way to achieve this non-dipping quality is by tipping the front wishbones up slightly, which is what the Rover people have done. All of the above commentary was based on the brakes of our test car, which were drum-type all around. Newer 3 Liter cars are equipped with Girling discs on the front which should make braking capabilities that much better.

The empathy between buyers and builder is nowhere better displayed than in the very comprehensive owner's manual that accompanies every Rover car. Its tone is that of two old friends having a chat over a good dinner. One page in particular comes to mind. The first paragraph reads thus: "The Rover Company feels that there are many owners who may not be fully aware of certain changes which have come about in engine design and manufacturing technique, and the characteristics of modern engine lubricants." What follows is a compact, but comprehensive, discussion of multi-weight oils, and oil consumption in modern engines. The writer assumed two things: 1. That the reader hadn't owned anything but Rovers in the past. 2. That the acquisition of a new 3 Liter would be the first time a reader would have need for — or come to know about — multi-grade oils, his other Rovers having been designed before these lubricants were placed on the market. The nice thing about all this is that the writer's assumptions were probably correct.

Lastly. If the unthinkable should happen and a Rover owner came to an unscheduled halt, ten well-made hand tools reside in a form-fitting sponge rubber-lined tray that slides out from under the parcel shelf. If it's only a flat tire, however, a jack, lug wrench, tire pump and spare tire valve in a little lidded depression can be found in the trunk — all securely fastened to prevent rattles, of course. For a flat battery a crank is also clipped on the side of the trunk. All of these things, along with the very well-written owner's manual, should make a Rover driver fairly self-sufficient. A delivered price of over $5000 makes the 3 Liter Rover an expensive car to buy. However, purchase of a Rover is the nearest an individual can come to buying a friend.   —SCI

The 3-Litre Rover

A Fine Car in the Solihull Tradition, providing Notable Comfort and Silence at High Cruising Speeds

GOOD CAR, PLEASANT PLACE.—The 3-litre Rover photographed by the statue of Charles Kingsley, author of " The Water Babies," " Westward Ho," etc., at Bideford in N. Devon. Kingsley was born in Devon in 1819.

THE 3-litre Rover has a good deal in common with a pair of shoes or a favourite cap—it improves on long acquaintance. When the Solihull Company brought out their 3-litre they took their biggest step since the war, in breaking away from their well-established but somewhat old-fashioned cars. Of unitary construction, the biggest of the current range of Rovers at first seems to be merely a quite pleasant rather bulky, softly sprung car. It takes a couple of hundred miles or so before the true worth, and a few minor shortcomings, of the 3-litre are revealed.

To die-hard Rover addicts—and who shall gainsay the very great worth of the longer-established 80 and 100 models ?—there may be initial disappointment in finding that the neat black instrument panel and the r.h. brake lever with its individual " shepherd's crook " handle have gone, while the external appearance of this big 3-litre is very different from that of the other Rover models.

On longer acquaintance one finds many of the well-liked Rover features continued in the 3-litre, which very soon emerges as a particularly spacious, comfortable saloon, very nicely appointed, of ample performance, and a car capable of covering the ground unobstrusively, largely because of the notably low level of mechanical, road and wind noise and also because the Girling disc front brakes give confidence in " press-on " driving.

It has been said that the post-war Rover is the poor-man's Rolls-Royce and the aforesaid silent running is certainly complimentary to this sentiment, while under the bonnet of the 3-litre the 77.8 × 105 mm. 115 b.h.p. six-cylinder engine has in common with those six-cylinder Rolls-Royce and Bentley cars made before the introduction of the new V8 engine, overhead inlet and side exhaust valves, a valve arrangement found also in the Rover 100, whereas normal o.h.v. are used for the four-cylinder Rover 80. It is also true of both Rolls-Royce and Rover that the noisiest item (at low speeds) is the clock!

The 3-litre is a spacious car, which will seat three in comfort on its broad back seat if the central arm-rest is folded and which *can* accommodate the same number on its bench front seat, although a broad transmission tunnel and the central gear lever make the Rover a five-seater for the longer journeys. The back compartment floor is also bisected by the prop. shaft tunnel. All occupants, however, have plenty of leg, head and elbow room and although the seats do not appear to be specially shaped, they are comfortable and well-sprung even when occupied for many hours at a stretch. Height and rake of the front seat can be varied by repositioning the securing bolts and a lever provides

easy fore and aft adjustment. The front seat, too, has a broad folding centre arm-rest and there are useful side arm-rests cum pulls, those at the front easily adjustable for height by operating a press-button. Separate front seats are available as an extra. Upholstery is in high-quality hide and good floor carpets over felt underlays enable the Rover's owner to feel as at-home in his car as in the board room. A very pleasing item is the provision of neat interior lights, two on each side, each with its own sliding switch and courtesy action from the adjacent door, so that individual passengers can have light by which to read without involving the others. The Rover has heavy doors which, if they do not shut with the double-action " clonk " beloved by vintage-car enthusiasts, at least shut very nicely as modern doors go. They have good-quality handles, lever type with safety locks for those on the rear doors, push-button external locks, and window winders with rotating finger-grips calling for just under three turns to lower the front, two turns to lower the back windows. Visibility is good on account of a semi-wrap-round windscreen with slender pillars, which does not intrude on ease of entry but does have the shortcoming that the wipers leave unswept areas at the extreme sides of this wide screen.

Reference has already been made to the quiet running of the

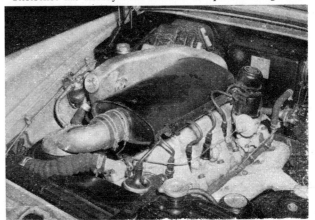

The engine of the 3-litre shares, with the Rover 100, overhead inlet and side exhaust valves.

NEAR HOME AGAIN.—The Rover poses outside the church at Eversley, in Hampshire, where Charles Kingsley was rector and where he was buried in 1875. In the Rover the journey from Bideford to Eversley can be made effortlessly in some 3½ hours under winter road conditions.

3-litre Rover and this is due in no small measure to the fact that such efficient ventilation is provided that the car can be occupied comfortably, even in hot weather, with every window shut. On each side of the facia simple fresh-air vents, in the form of holes normally covered by pivotted flaps, direct a stream of cool air into the car past the faces of the front-seat occupants, and knobs on the scuttle sides, with four settings, send cool air along the floor of the car. Thus the windows do not need to be opened and, indeed, the usual openable ¼-lights are dispensed with. Instead, rain gutters are provided over each window. Very neat vertical quadrant levers, one each side of the radio panel, control the efficient Smiths heater/demister/defroster unit, these simple controls having their functions clearly labelled. A knob on the extremity of the l.h. lever brings in a quiet booster fan. Except for a little disturbance round the windows, wind-noise is extremely low, even at an 80 m.p.h. cruising speed, and the liberal use of rubber and other sound-deadening expedients has brought road-noise to a very low level. As the engine runs extremely quietly (being inaudible when idling, incidentally) and as only bottom gear emits any appreciable hum, motoring in the 3-litre Rover is a very restful means of fast travel. The Avon tyres contribute to this peaceful progression, protesting hardly at all and then only mildly under considerable provocation, although we ran them at somewhat higher pressures than the handbook recommends. This is all the more creditable as two tyre sizes are available and the smaller Avons were on the test-car.

Reverting to interior details, Rover owners are endowed with very generous parcels stowage. There is not only a deep, lipped full-width under-facia shelf, into which only the steering column intrudes, giving the driver his separate section, but each front door has a big pull-out pocket, which normally lies flush. Then the back shelf is wide and the lockable cubby hole, its lid of polished wood to match the rest of the *decor*, is of fairly generous dimensions, although only just deep enough to take a Rolleiflex camera placed on its side. The cubby lid drops down to make a shelf but is locked with the ignition key, not the best arrangement if the car is left in a public garage. To lock the car another key is needed but the ignition key opens the boot, which, again, is an arrangement that could be improved. The doors can be locked from inside the car so that they cannot be opened from outside or, alternatively, it is possible to lock the doors from outside the car without recourse to a key; in fact, the Rover has something in common with a combination safe and it is possible to get locked out unless a spare key is carried. Locks in both front doors enable the final locking to be done at the kerbside, no matter at which side of the road the Rover is parked. The back door handles incorporate safety locks to prevent all but very observant children opening them from inside and the handles pull backwards to open the doors.

Convenience seems to have been the aim of whoever planned the equipment of this fine car. Thus twin pull-out ash-trays are fitted to the back of the front seat squab, the front-seat occupants have a drawer-type ash-tray on the driver's side of the gear lever with a lighter on the other side under the centre of the facia, and the twin smoked-glass vizors swivel sideways, the passenger's having a vanity mirror. The stowage of small tools and touching-

up paint, etc., in a rubber-lined pull-out shelf over the front passenger's knees, is retained, larger tools and jacking equipment are carried beneath a trimmed flap in the side of the boot, and here the battery is kept where it is cool, under a metal cover.

A driver of average height can just see the nearside front wing and each front wing incorporates a side lamp tell-tale. The steering wheel, which has good finger grips on the underside of its rim, is set sensibly low and close to it is the raised, hooded instrument panel. This has a 100 m.p.h. speedometer, with a steady, white-tipped needle, calibrated every 10 m.p.h. It incorporates trip with decimal and total milometers and is matched by a dial showing dynamo charge, water temperature (normally about 80 deg. C.) and fuel contents, but a separate oil pressure dial would be appreciated. All the instruments carry the snob Jaeger label. Down each side of this square panel are tapered flick-switches. On the left the top switch controls panel lighting with rheostat action, a job done better by a rotatable switch, although this is a very trivial criticism. Below it is a switch that causes the fuel gauge to indicate sump oil level—a welcome refinement—while the bottom switch looks after the screen wipers. These are efficient but before self-parking the blades do a frenzied jig, which can leave a strip of water in the line of vision, especially if the washers have just been used. These very powerful Lucas electric " screenjet " washers are controlled by a tiny press-button on the left side of the steering-column. Two matching switches to those on the left occupy the right of the panel, the top one selecting the lamps, that beneath bringing in the reserve petrol supply.

It takes some time to become accustomed to the location of these identical switches at different levels and although each is labelled, the lettering is not easily read while driving. A further complication is seen in the lights controls, for after switching on with the aforesaid flick-switch a short stalk-lever on the r.h. side of the steering column, which tends to be masked by the longer flashers-control stalk lever above it, has to be moved downwards to select headlamps, yet to dip the headlamps a foot control is involved. There is no means of flashing full-beam warnings without recourse to the foot dipper and only the tell-tales on the wings remind the driver to switch off the sidelamps when leaving the car. However, this cluster of switches leaves the facia clear for a second lidded cubby hole or a radio installation—the latter a good H.M.V. on the test car, with roof aerial.

Below the r.h. flick-switches is the ignition-key aperture, the key turning to work the starter. There is only one position, as the radio is wired separately. Crash-padding along the top of the facia is broken for an electric clock, lit from the instrument lighting, to be incorporated. There is also crash-padding along the lower edge of the facia but this safeguard is offset by many jagged handles and controls about the driving compartment.

The Rover has well-placed pedals, with plenty of room for the left foot to rest on the floor between the clutch pedal and a small treadle-pedal that depresses the dipper button. The accelerator is also of treadle type. The steering wheel has a small diameter horn ring which is convenient without getting in the way and provides full instrument visibility, but which blasts a rather blatant horn. The hand-brake lever has become one of the cheap pull-

The comfortable front compartment of the 3-litre Rover. Note the hooded instrument panel, long cranked gear-lever, spacious under-facia shelf and arm-rest on front door, adjustable by operating a push-button.

out variety set rather far forward above the facia shelf, for operation by the right hand. Somewhat difficult to release if fully applied, it is quite well placed and held the car on steep hills.

Under the facia is a toggle lever actuating the S.U. cold-start control; another, functioning very easily, opens the bonnet lid. The instrument panel contains a lower cluster of three warning lamps telling of low oil pressure, ignition on or cold-start left out—the last-named being inoperative on the test car. Two smaller lights at the top of the panel are for flashers and main-beam in use, respectively, the latter rather embarrassingly at eye level. There is a good quality, useful rear-view mirror, of the diminishing variety, however, which can be dangerous.

That about concludes a survey of the Rover's interior layout, except to remark that " pulls " are fitted to aid back-seat occupants, and that coat-hooks are provided, four in all, on each side of the car.

The gear-lever is the long, cranked, central lever used for some years by Rover. It selects the ratios with more precision than its shape, curving upwards from beneath the facia shelf to a small, lettered knob, would suggest but can swing past bottom-gear position and select reverse inadvertently. A short remote lever would be a welcome refinement to a refined motor car. However, the action is quite pleasant, the lever can be adjusted to left or right, and the clutch is smooth and light. But if gear changes are hurried the synchromesh can be beaten and bottom gear sometimes engages somewhat brutally.

On the test-car a left-hand stalk lever operated overdrive and the Rover has such ample power that it can be regarded very largely as a top-gear car, overdrive being frequently employed and direct top being resorted to for extra acceleration. In bottom gear an indicated 30 m.p.h. is the limit, with 48 m.p.h. possible in second and 70 m.p.h. in third gear before sudden valve crash intrudes. In overdrive top gear 80 is a silent, effortless cruising speed and, given its head, the 3-litre Rover will go on to a genuine 97 m.p.h. Acceleration is smooth rather than vivid, although the smooth silent flow of power can be deceptive and high average speeds are returned without the driver being conscious of having been trying at all hard. From rest 60 m.p.h. is reached in 16 seconds, for example. The Girling brakes, disc on the front wheels, aided by a vacuum servo, give powerful retardation for extremely low pedal pressures, and in every way these brakes proved entirely acceptable.

In respect of suspension, which is by square-section torsion-bars (as on a VW) and wishbones in conjunction with an anti-roll bar at the front and by ½-elliptic leaf-springs (with check leaves) at the back, the Rover shows that it is intended primarily as a sedate rather than a very fast car, for there is some roll when cornering and rather too much up-and-down motion over all but the smoothest roads. Sudden bumps remind one that a rigid back axle is used and the body shell transmits some of the wheel movement, in the form of mild shake and some minor body rattles. Over unmade roads the Rover becomes very lively but remains comfortable.

This somewhat supple and casually damped suspension is all the greater pity because the power steering functions so well, being light as soon as the wheel is turned, providing the engine is running, and still enabling the driver to enjoy a fair degree of " feel " through the front wheels, while it is geared as high as just over 2½ turns, lock-to-lock, and transmits slight vibration but no kick-back if the road is rough. There is mild castor-return action and one is only conscious that this is power steering when it becomes very light on making a sudden swerve. The once-pronounced Rover understeer has been largely eliminated and for all practical purposes the car takes corners on a nearly neutral line.

The Rover engine " pinked " very faintly on super-grade fuels but does not normally require 100-octane petrol. Tested under arduous conditions varying from long-distance fast motoring fully loaded to a great deal of pottering about congested towns (such as Barnstaple!) and up Devon hills, petrol consumption was 19.7 m.p.g. It would be normal to refuel as soon as the reserve supply has been switched in; this represents a range of 241 miles. The reserve supply sufficed for a further 30 miles. The filler is under a lockable flap (released by a press-button so that pump attendants sometimes call for the key when, in fact, it isn't locked) on the near side, replenishable from a can with a spout. In a total of 820 miles a pint of Castrol was sufficient to restore the sump-level.

A key is required to open the luggage boot, the lid of which stays open automatically. On the test-car it tended to stick. The luggage space is best described as vast and the boot floor is flat, the only obstruction being the battery box. The spare wheel is under the floor and a refinement, typical of Rover, is a valve extension

THE 3-LITRE ROVER SALOON

Engine : Six cylinders, 77.8 × 105 mm. (2,995 c.c.). Push-rod-operated overhead inlet valves, side exhaust valves. 8.75-to-1 compression-ratio. 115 b.h.p. at 4,500 r.p.m.

Gear ratios : First, 14.52 to 1; second, 8.78 to 1; third, 5.92 to 1; top, 4.3 to 1; overdrive top, 3.35 to 1.

Tyres : 6.70 × 15 Avon H.M. Ribbed 4-ply tubeless, on bolt-on steel disc wheels.

Weight : 1 ton 12 cwt. 1 qtr. 0 lb. (without occupants but ready for the road, with approximately half-a-gallon of petrol).

Steering ratio : 2¼ turns, lock-to-lock (power steering).

Fuel capacity : 14 gallons (plus 1½ gallons in reserve). (Range, not including reserve supply, 241 miles.)

Wheelbase : 9 ft. 2½ in.

Track : Front, 4 ft. 7⅝ in.; rear, 4 ft. 8 in.

Dimensions : 15 ft. 6½ in. × 5 ft. 10 in. × 5 ft. 0¼ in. (high).

Price : £1,258 (£1,783 5s. 10d. inclusive of purchase tax). With extras, as tested : £1,920 2s. 10d.

Makers : The Rover Company Limited, Meteor Works, Solihull, Warwickshire, England.

enabling pressure to be checked with the wheel *in situ*.

The bonnet lid, which carries sound-damping material on its underside, is also self-propping and opens to reveal the impressive power unit, with its big S.U. carburetter and six-branch exhaust manifold on which is cast the firing order. There is a big A.C. air-cleaner along the off-side but dip-stick, plugs, coil, hydraulic reservoirs, in fact all under-bonnet services are readily accessible, although the dip-stick is rather awkward to replace, and the spring-clipped lid to the oil filler orifice difficult to remove. This is a fine engine, with 7-bearing crankshaft, copper/lead-lined steel shell bearings and alloy cylinder head, which develops maximum power at the modest speed of 4,500 r.p.m., giving maximum torque of 164 lb./ft. at 1,500 r.p.m. and a b.m.e.p. of 136 lb./ft. at the same speed. Cooling is by pump and 4-blade fan, the system holding 22½ pints and the lubrication system incorporates an A.C.-Delco full-flow filter and circulates 10 pints of oil. In overdrive form the gearbox holds 5 pints of lubricant and the drive goes *via* a 2-piece propeller shaft with centre bearing to a semi-floating spiral-bevel back axle containing 3 pints of oil.

It is a significant selling point that the Rover chassis requires no lubrication except for the propeller shaft joints and inspection of the steering-box oil level every 3,000 miles. Rover claim a high degree of rust-prevention and dust exclusion, and from what I saw of their manufacturing methods some years ago I have every reason to regard the 3-litre as extremely durable and thoroughly sound and dust-proofed. The carpet felting, for instance, is laid over a bitumen sealing compound and the external finish is faultless.

For night driving the Lucas lamps give excellent illumination.

In conclusion, the 3-litre Rover is a very fine car. Its weak points are flexible suspension giving too much up-and-down motion and some roll on corners, while the unitary construction is not entirely free from shake over bad roads. Otherwise this is a beautifully appointed and fully-equipped car, capable of quiet and effortless cruising in the very high top and overdrive gears. The lower gears are so quiet that it is possible to stay in third gear under the impression that top gear has been selected. It competes with a certain twin-cam Coventry-built car in price but offers more spacious accommodation and will undoubtedly appeal to connoisseurs of good cars, particularly those who have had a long line of Rovers.

Overdrive is included in the price but two-tone finish, power steering and radio inflate the £1,783 5s. 10d. to a total of £1,920 2s. 10d. inclusive of purchase tax. At this price the 3-litre Rover, a car very much in the best English tradition, cannot be regarded as an expensive luxury.—W.B.

The Motor Road Test No. 41/61—

Make: Rover — Type: 3-Litre Saloon

Makers: The Rover Co., Ltd., Solihull, Warwickshire

Test Data

World copyright reserved; no unauthorised reproduction in whole or in part.

CONDITIONS: *Weather: Cool, mainly fine, little wind. (Temperature 46°-48° F., barometer 28.8-28.9 in. Hg.) Surface: Damp tar macadam and concrete. Fuel: Premium grade pump petrol (approx. 97 Research Method Octane Rating).*

INSTRUMENTS

Speedometer at 30 m.p.h.	2% fast
Speedometer at 60 m.p.h.	3% fast
Speedometer at 90 m.p.h.	2% fast
Distance recorder	Accurate

WEIGHT

Kerb weight (unladen, but with oil, coolant and fuel for approx. 50 miles) ...	32½ cwt.
Front/rear distribution of kerb weight	55/45
Weight laden as tested	36 cwt.

MAXIMUM SPEEDS

Overdrive Top Gear

Mean of two laps of banked circuit	96.9 m.p.h.
Best one-way quarter-mile	97.8 m.p.h.

Direct Top Gear

Lap of banked circuit	92.7 m.p.h.
Best one-way quarter-mile	94.7 m.p.h.

"Maximile" Speed. (Timed quarter-mile after one mile accelerating from rest.)

Mean of opposite runs	90.0 m.p.h.
Best one-way time equals	92.8 m.p.h.

Speed in gears

Max. speed in 3rd gear	70 m.p.h.
Max. speed in 2nd gear	44 m.p.h.
Max. speed in 1st gear	27 m.p.h.

FUEL CONSUMPTION

Overdrive top gear

35½ m.p.g. at constant 30 m.p.h. on level.
32 m.p.g. at constant 40 m.p.h. on level.
28½ m.p.g. at constant 50 m.p.h. on level.
25 m.p.g. at constant 60 m.p.h. on level.
22½ m.p.g. at constant 70 m.p.h. on level.
19½ m.p.g. at constant 80 m.p.h. on level.
16½ m.p.g. at constant 90 m.p.h. on level.

Direct top gear

31 m.p g. at constant 30 m.p.h. on level.
27 m.p.g. at constant 40 m.p.h. on level.
24 m.p.g. at constant 50 m.p.h. on level.
21¼ m.p.g. at constant 60 m.p.h. on level.

Overall Fuel Consumption for 728.2 miles, 38.1 gallons, equals 19.1 m.p.g. (14.8 litres/100 km.).

Touring Fuel Consumption (m.p.g. at steady speed midway between 30 m.p.h. and maximum, less 5% allowance for acceleration), 23.0.

Fuel tank capacity (maker's figure), 14 gallons.

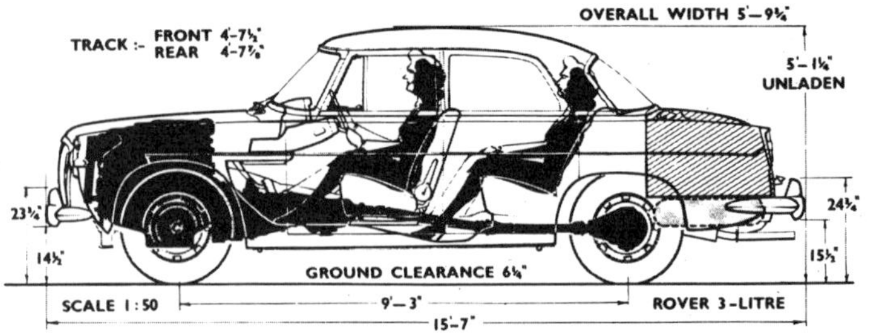
OVERALL WIDTH 5'—9¼"
TRACK :- FRONT 4'-7½" REAR 4'-7⅞"
5'-1⅛" UNLADEN
23¾"
14½"
24¾"
15½"
GROUND CLEARANCE 6¼"
SCALE 1:50
9'—3"
ROVER 3-LITRE
15'-7"

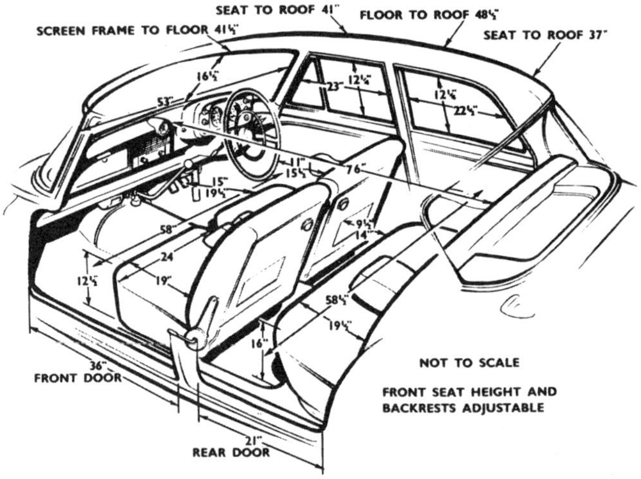
SEAT TO ROOF 41"
FLOOR TO ROOF 48½"
SCREEN FRAME TO FLOOR 41½"
SEAT TO ROOF 37"
16½"
53"
23"
12¼"
12¼"
22½"
11"
15½"
76"
15"
19½"
58"
9½"
14"
24
12½"
19"
58½"
19½"
16"
36"
FRONT DOOR
21"
REAR DOOR
NOT TO SCALE
FRONT SEAT HEIGHT AND BACKRESTS ADJUSTABLE

STEERING

Turning circle between kerbs: Left, 40 ft.; right, 38 ft.

Turns of steering wheel from lock to lock, 2½.

ACCELERATION TIMES from standstill

0-30 m.p.h.	5.2 sec.
0-40 m.p.h.	8.3 sec.
0-50 m.p.h.	12.2 sec.
0-60 m.p.h.	17.3 sec.
0-70 m p.h.	24.7 sec.
0-80 m.p.h.	32.2 sec.
Standing quarter-mile	21.0 sec.

ACCELERATION TIMES on upper ratios

	Over-drive top gear	Direct top gear	Third gear
10-30 m.p.h. ...	—	8.8 sec.	6.3 sec.
20-40 m.p.h. ...	11.8 sec.	9.0 sec.	6.8 sec.
30-50 m.p.h. ...	13.0 sec.	9.5 sec.	7.3 sec.
40-60 m.p.h. ...	15.2 sec.	10.6 sec.	8.8 sec.
50-70 m.p.h. ...	18.2 sec.	13.1 sec.	—
60-80 m.p.h. ...	23.5 sec.	17.8 sec.	—

HILL CLIMBING at sustained steady speeds

Max. gradient on overdrive top gear	1 in 12.4 (Tapley 180 lb./ton)
Max. gradient on direct top gear	1 in 8.9 (Tapley 250 lb./ton)
Max. gradient on 3rd gear ...	1 in 6.3 (Tapley 350 lb./ton)
Max. gradient on 2nd gear ...	1 in 4.6 (Tapley 480 lb./ton)

BRAKES from 30 m.p.h.

0.94 g retardation (equivalent to 32 ft. stopping distance) with 75 lb. pedal pressure.
0.69 g retardation (equivalent to 43½ ft. stopping distance) with 50 lb. pedal pressure.
0.28 g retardation (equivalent to 117 ft. stopping distance) with 25 lb. pedal pressure.

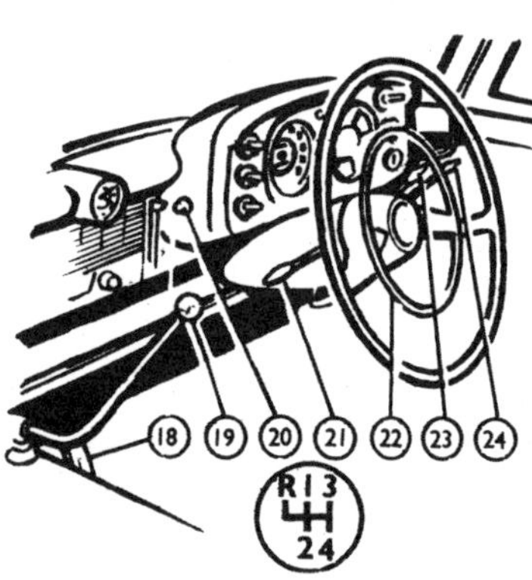
18
19
20
21
22
23
24
R 1 3
2 4

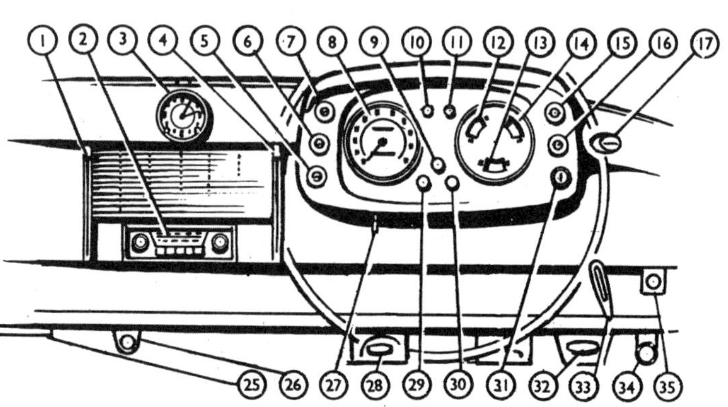
1
2
3
4
5
6
7
8
9
10
11
12
13
14
15
16
17
25
26
27
28
29
30
31
32
33
34
35

1. Heater. 2, Radio (extra). 3, Clock. 4. Heater demisting control. 5, Screen-wiper switch, 6, Oil-level indicator switch. 7, Panel light switch. 8, Speedometer and distance recorder. 9, Dynamo charge warning light. 10, Direction indicator warning light. 11, Main beam warning light. 12, Water temperature gauge. 13, Petrol and oil level gauge. 14, Ammeter. 15, Lights master switch. 16, Fuel reserve switch. 17, cold air vent (one each side). 18, Dip switch. 19, Gear lever. 20, Screen washer control. 21, Overdrive switch. 22, Horn ring. 23, Headlamp switch. 24, Direction indicator switch. 25, Fitted tool drawer. 26, Cigar lighter. 27, Trip adjuster. 28, Choke control. 29, Oil pressure warning light. 30, Choke warning light. 31, Ignition and starter switch. 32, Bonnet catch release. 33, Handbrake. 34, Cold air control. 35, Brake fluid level warning light.

—The 3-litre Rover (with overdrive)

Roominess, Refinement, and a Brisk Performance

INTRODUCED three years ago, the 3-litre Rover supplemented the company's long-standing policy of having two or three models virtually identical apart from their power units. This policy is still exemplified in the four-cylinder, 2¼-litre "80" and six-cylinder, 2.6-litre "100" saloons, whereas the 3-litre is both a bigger and more powerful car. It has nearly 6 in. more internal width, much more luggage room, and a generally lower build and lines which, although in the Rover tradition, are more up to date.

The result is a car that gives a high degree of comfort and refinement, with a brisk yet flexible performance.

Extremes of performance or economy are not primary aims of a model of this type, but the Rover, for a comfortable six-seater car, offers a most acceptable blend of both these qualities. A maximum speed of nearly 100 m.p.h. (two laps of a banked circuit were covered at 96.9 m.p.h.) goes with the ability to reach 50 m.p.h. and 70 m.p.h. from a standstill in 12.2 sec. and 24.7 sec. respectively and to climb gradients of 1 in 12.4 in overdrive top gear or of 1 in 8.9 in direct top. Fuel consumption, over 728.2 miles of varied running, was 19.1 m.p.g., with constant-speed consumption figures in overdrive ranging from 35½ m.p.g. at a steady 30 m.p.h. to 16½ m.p.g. at a steady 90 m.p.h.

The six-cylinder engine—which is happy on normal premium pump fuels despite a moderately high compression ratio of 8.75 to 1—has overhead inlet and side exhaust valves. This layout, with the aluminium-alloy cylinder head mounted at an angle to the block, results in a bulky unit. Although the space in the engine compartment is well filled by the engine and auxiliaries, details are planned so that all points requiring regular attention are easy to reach when the wide bonnet, which is counter-balanced and lined with insulating material, is lifted.

The engine starts easily and warms up sufficiently quickly for the choke soon to be dispensed with; a thermostatically controlled warning light comes on as a

The latest 3-litre Rover is distinguished from earlier versions by its stainless steel wheel trims and front quarter lights which replace the original ventilation louvres.

In Brief

Price (including power-assisted steering as tested) £1,342 plus purchase tax £616 6s. 5d. equals £1,958 6s. 5d.
Price without power steering (including purchase tax) £1,879 11s. 5d.

Capacity	2,995 c.c.
Unladen kerb weight ...	32¼ cwt.
Acceleration:	
20-40 m.p.h. in direct top gear	9.0 sec.
0-50 m.p.h. through gears	12.2 sec.
Maximum direct top-gear gradient	1 in 8.9
Maximum speed	96.9 m.p.h.
"Maximile" speed ...	90.0 m.p.h.
Touring fuel consumption	23.0 m.p.g.

Gearing: 18.3 m.p.h. in top gear at 1,000 r.p.m. (overdrive, 23.4 m.p.h.); 26.6 m.p.h. at 1,000 ft./min. piston speed (overdrive, 34.1 m.p.h.).

The 3-litre Rover

reminder if the choke is left in action when the engine is warm. Smooth and quiet at all speeds, the engine gives an easy cruising speed of 75-80 m.p.h. in overdrive, which is applied to top gear only; at the other end of the scale, overdrive can also be used in built-up areas when the traffic is light. In direct top, on the other hand, the engine pulls smoothly at well below 20 m.p.h., and this is also a suitable gear for cross-country work on winding lanes. In third gear an easy 60 m.p.h. is available when rapid acceleration is required.

Overdrive Operation

The Laycock de Normanville overdrive, which is a standard fitment on Rover 3-litres with synchromesh gearboxes (automatic transmission is an extra), is operated by a control on the left of the steering column. In addition, a "kick-down" arrangement on the accelerator pedal enables direct top to be engaged when the car is in overdrive by pressing the pedal beyond the normal throttle range, the necessary additional pressure being nicely graded to call for a positive movement of the foot but no undue effort.

Another overdrive refinement is the provision of an inhibitor that cuts out transmission shocks if the overdrive control is operated in inappropriate circumstances; the control is arranged so that a slight easing of the throttle is necessary before the overdrive can engage, while, at the other end of the scale, reversion to direct top is prevented in over-run conditions. Although the latter arrangement has worked well on previous Rovers tested, it was not infallible on this particular model, which would, at times, accept direct drive from overdrive on a closed throttle.

The cranked central gear lever is a compromise between a central floor change and a steering-column control, the aim being to combine the positive action of the former with three-abreast seating. It works moderately well, but it is less positive than a normal floor change. A further point of criticism is that reverse gear can be engaged in mistake for first. There is very little noise from the transmission, third gear, in particular, being almost inaudible.

Built-in Hydrosteer power-assisted steering was fitted to the test model; it provides a good blend of light action and a fair degree of "feel." Although no normal road shocks are felt at the wheel, the car is sensitive to longitudinal road defects of the "tramline" class, whilst most drivers may take a little while to play themselves in to the sensitivity of the steering on the straight. On the other hand only 2½ turns of the wheel are required from lock to lock, a valuable advantage in the event of a skid. The self-centring action is strong enough for ordinary driving, but hard acceleration in a lower gear coming out of a right-angle turn calls for some assistance from the driver in straightening up. In the main, the power steering is a great asset, especially for those who drive extensively in town and have to park in confined spaces.

On corners the 3-litre Rover has no vices, a moderate degree of understeer never being disconcerting. Roll is well controlled and the suspension provides a comfortably soft yet firm ride on normal surfaces; bad roads cause no discomfort but make one conscious that the wheels are having a rough time.

The driving compartment has been laid out with awareness of a driver's needs, all the controls being placed conveniently and without any risk of their being confused; a possible exception is the side/headlamp lever switch which is below the longer direction indicator switch on the right of the steering column and is therefore not easy to reach in a hurry. The lighting switches are unusual; a toggle switch on the instrument panel brings the lights into operation, the switch just mentioned provides a change from side to head, and a foot dipper gives beam control. While not offering the full advantages of a finger-tip switch for signalling in daytime, the headlamps can easily be flashed by using the instrument panel switch if the column switch is left in the headlamp position.

Some good details include variable instrument lighting, a reserve petrol switch (which also brings a reserve pump into action), a switch for converting the fuel gauge to an engine oil level indicator, and a handbrake warning light which (if it fails to operate) indicates that the brake fluid level is low. The servo-assisted disc-front/drum-rear brakes are powerful and require little effort, and the pistol-grip hand-brake will hold the car on a 1 in 4 gradient.

Vision is very good, points of note including the wide arcs swept by the wipers, visibility of the front wing tips (and also the indicator pips which show when the side lamps are alight), and a panoramic mirror which covers the whole area of the wide rear window.

There is plenty of room inside the car, and six people can be carried in comfort. The car tested was fitted with the individual front seats which are available as an extra at £18 19s. 2d., including tax. Deep, comfortably upholstered and adjustable for height with a spanner, these have individual centre arm rests, and there are also adjustable arm rests on the doors. The rear seating is equally comfortable and

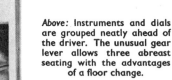

Above: Instruments and dials are grouped neatly ahead of the driver. The unusual gear lever allows three abreast seating with the advantages of a floor change.

Left: Offered as an option to a bench, the individual front seats are deep and generously upholstered.

Right: Safety belts can be fitted to all four seats at a cost of £19. Pockets are provided in the back of the front seats.

Spring-loaded pockets for maps and other flat articles are provided beneath the front door arm rests.

The large boot has a flat floor and is lined throughout. A robust set of tools is clipped neatly to the side.

there are fixed side arm rests and a wide, central, folding rest.

Ventilation and heating are well thought out. The main heater controls are easy and positive to operate and provide both a good volume of air and enough heat when required; in addition, face-level ventilators at each end of the facia panel provide an adjustable supply of unwarmed air which helps to keep the interior fresh. Further fresh-air ventilators for hot weather are arranged in the sides of the scuttle. New for 1962 are hinged ventilators on the front doors; these are of the extractor type and do not allow rain to drip into the interior in bad weather.

Provision for the paraphernalia of motoring is practical. There is a very large flat-floored boot, and the interior is well provided for the sort of small items that so often make for untidiness. A moderate-sized glove locker (with lock), has beneath it a full width parcel shelf (which would be better with a rather deeper retaining ledge). The front doors have large spring-loaded pockets for flat objects such as maps; further pockets are provided on the backs of the front squabs, and there is the usual parcel shelf at the rear.

Other details include transparent tinted vizors, child-safety locks on the rear doors, safety padding for the scuttle and front

parcel shelf, four interior lights located above the doors and controlled both individually and by courtesy switches, a boot light, and a fitted tool-drawer beneath the front parcel shelf. An extra (at £19 inclusive) on the car tried was a set of Irving safety harness at both front and rear.

In all, this improved New Series model offers a satisfactory performance, a high degree of silence and comfort, and above all, a combination of good engineering, high-grade finish and careful attention to detail.

Specification

Engine
Cylinders	6
Bore	77.8 mm.
Stroke	105 mm.
Cubic capacity	2,995 c.c.
Piston area	44.2 sq. in.
Valves: Overhead inlet (push-rod operated) and side exhaust.	
Compression ratio	8.75/1
Carburetter ... S.U. horizontal (type HD8)	
Fuel pump ... ... Two S.U. electric	
Ignition timing control: Centrifugal and vacuum.	
Oil filter ... ... AC-Delco full-flow	
Max. power (gross) 115 b.h.p. (net 108 b.h.p.)	
at	4,500 r.p.m.
Piston speed at max. b.h.p.: 3,100 ft./min.	

Transmission
Clutch ... Borg and Beck, 10-in. s.d.p.	
Top gear (s/m) ... 4.3 (overdrive, 3.35)	
3rd gear (s/m)	5.923
2nd gear (s/m)	8.785
1st gear	14.516
Reverse	12.762
Overdrive: Laycock de Normanville with manual control and kick-down.	
Propeller shaft ... Divided open, Hardy Spicer	
Final drive ... ... Spiral bevel	
Top gear m.p.h. at 1,000 r.p.m.: 18.3 (overdrive, 23.4).	
Top gear m.p.h. at 1,000 ft./min. piston speed: 26.6 (overdrive, 34.1).	

Chassis
Brakes: Girling hydraulic with vacuum servo; discs at front and drums at rear.
Brake diameters:
Front discs	10¾ in.
Rear drums	11 in.

Friction areas: 104.9 sq. in. of lining area working on 401.5 sq. in. rubbed area of discs and drums.
Suspension:
Front: Independent by ball-jointed transverse wishbones and laminated torsion bars; anti-roll bar.
Rear: Semi-elliptic leaf springs with progressive rate and rubber-cushion rear shackles.
Shock absorbers: Woodhead Monroe, telescopic.
Steering gear (as tested): Hydrosteer with built-in power assistance.
Tyres (as tested) ... 6.70-15 Dunlop RS5

Coachwork and Equipment

Starting handle ... ... Yes	
Battery mounting ... ... In luggage boot	
Jack ... ... Bipod screw type	
Jacking points ... 4 sockets under body sides	

Standard tool kit: Jack, wheelbrace, wheel-trim remover, in boot. Fitted tool drawer under facia containing 3 double-ended spanners, adjustable spanner, 2 box spanners and tommy bar, screwdriver, tyre gauge and 2 touch-up pencils.
Exterior lights: 2 headlamps, 2 side lamps, 2 stop/tail lamps, reversing lamp, rear number-plate lamp.
Number of electrical fuses	2

Direction indicators: Self-cancelling amber flashers.
Windscreen wipers: Electrical, two-blade, self-parking.
Windscreen washers ... Twin-jet electric	
Sun vizors ... Two (tinted transparent type)	

Instruments: Speedometer with total and decimal trip distance recorders, combined fuel/oil level gauge, water thermometer, ammeter and clock.
Warning lights: Dynamo charge, mixture enrichment, oil pressure, direction indicators, headlamp main beam and combined handbrake/brake-fluid level.

Locks: With ignition key—ignition/starter and front doors; with other keys—boot, glove locker and petrol filler.	
Glove lockers ... One on facia (with lock)	
Map pockets: In front doors (and in backs of optional extra separate front seats).	
Parcel shelves: One below facia and one behind rear seat.	
Ashtrays: Two in front (with optional positions) and two in backs of front seats.	
Cigar lighters ... ... One on facia	
Interior lights: Four (above doors, with individual and courtesy switches).	
Interior heater: Fresh-air heater and screen demister; also separate unheated-air ducts on facia and at sides of scuttle.	
Car radio ... ... Optional extra	
Extras available: Separate front seats and also fully-reclining separate front seats, safety harness (front and rear), radio, power-assisted steering, two-tone finish, removable limousine division. RS5 tyres.	
Upholstery material ... ... Leather	
Floor covering ... Carpets with underfelt	
Exterior colours standardized: Ten (two-tone combinations available at £14 11s. 8d. inclusive).	
Alternative body styles ... ... None	

Maintenance

Sump ... ... 10 pints, S.A.E. 20	
Gearbox ... ... 5 pints, S.A.E. 90 E.P.	
Rear axle ... ... 3 pints, S.A.E. 90 E.P.	
Steering-gear lubricant ... S.A.E. 90 E.P.	
Cooling system capacity: 22½ pints (2 drain taps)	
Chassis lubrication: By grease gun every 3,000 miles to 2 points.	
Ignition timing ... 3 degrees before t.d.c.	
Contact-breaker gap ... 0.014-0.016 in.	
Sparking-plug type ... Champion N5	
Sparking-plug gap 0.029-0.032	
Valve timing: Inlet opens 17 deg. before t.d.c. and closes 41 deg. after b.d.c.; exhaust opens 45 deg. before b.d.c. and closes 13 deg. after t.d.c.	

Tappet clearances (hot): Inlet, 0.006 in.; exhaust, 0.010 in.	
Front wheel toe-in ... Plus or minus 1/16 in.	
Camber angle ... ... 2 deg.	
Castor angle ... ... Zero	
Steering swivel-pin inclination ... 4 deg.	
Tyre pressures: Front, 24-26 lb.; rear, 22-30 lb. (Increase 6 lb. per sq. in. for sustained speeds over 80 m.p.h.)	
Brake fluid ... ... Girling	
Battery type and capacity: Lucas 12-volt, 57 amp. hr., type BT9A.	

CT&T ROAD TEST

Rover 3-Litre *Sound, Solid and highly Satisfying*

The Car

SINCE 1904 a series of quietly elegant, impeccably built motor cars have issued forth from the Rover Motor Company at Solihull, England. Current doyen of the Rover line is the stately 3-Litre, introduced in 1959.

Rovers are respected as much for stamina as smoothness; the rugged Land Rover cross-country vehicle is another product of the same company. Though obviously fine cars, Rovers haven't let luxury become a fetish.

Mechanically the 3-Litre is interesting if not dar-

ing. Body is of unit construction, with a sub-frame carrying engine, transmission, front suspension and steering. Suspension at front is by laminated torsion bars with Thompson ball joints and rubber-bushed wishbone pivots. Rear suspension is by conventional semi-eliptic leaf springs attached by rubber-bushed bearings and rubber cushion shackles. The six-cylinder, 2995 cc in-line engine carries seven main bearings and its chief characteristic is astounding smoothness.

Rovers aren't likely to attract people interested in keeping up with the Joneses. They blend unobtrusively into the background.

Styling

A squarish over-all shape and proportionately small cabin area lend the 3-Litre a solid look while the traditional Rover radiator quickly identifies the marque. There isn't a "stylist's" trick anywhere. No gimmicks are used to deliver this car's message. Thus if you like the conservative approach styling is eminently successful. If you don't, you're probably not a Rover customer.

Rovers can be had in several muted colors besides a few "recommended two-tone combinations". In other words, the customer who wants a red and yellow Rover will just have to paint it himself.

Workmanship need hardly be discussed with Rovers; if this firm didn't invent the word as applied to cars they probably had a large hand in setting the standards. The 3-Litre follows suit from bonnet to boot.

Interior

Our test car was fitted with individual front bucket-type seats. These are firm and capacious, upholstered in prime quality leather as are all door panels. Occupants find themselves cradled to the shoulder blades with ample room to slide or stretch laterally. Folding armrests lend armchair comfort for driver and passenger.

Instruments — and there is a staggeringly full complement of these — are well positioned in a cowl protruding from the walnut-panelled facia. Manual controls work via crisp toggle switches.

Floors are carpeted and there is generous footroom fore and aft. A parcel tray runs beneath the facia while pockets in both front doors and two glove compartments carry small extras. A small tool tray slides out from beneath the instrument panel. There are even two self-emptying ashtrays provided up front and two more in back.

Driving

Our test car was equipped with optional four-speed manual transmission with overdrive. The shift lever angles up crookedly from the transmission tunnel and has a remote, rather wobbly action which had us shifting into first when we'd aimed at third. This isn't recommended since bottom gear isn't synchromesh.

Somewhat heavy steering in city traffic became lighter as speeds increased. In combination with a firm yet supple ride, and almost enough silence to hear your heart beat at cruising speeds, the 3-Litre is a relaxing car to drive and especially on long jaunts where fatigue is unknown. At speeds of 70-90 mph there is almost no noise and no vibration, and the feeling of isolation from the world rushing past outside is almost eerie. It's easily possible to read the fine print of a newspaper at these speeds.

Takeoff is brisk but hardly torrid, and first gear—useful for little more than starting—sets up a decidedly un-Roverlike whine. The throw to third with the somewhat imprecise gearshift lever is long. In a straight line the 3-Litre lopes rather than gallops, working up to a shade over 100 mph in no particular hurry but seemingly content to stay there once maximum speed has been gained.

Manoeuverability is better than the loud and long tire squeal while cornering would indicate. No driver in his right mind would play leadfoot with a Rover but the car will track decently and understeers more and more as more throttle is applied in hard cornering. Overdrive serves to cut revs by 22% and doesn't boost power at all. It's merely intended to let the engine breathe a little easier at cruising speed and is better left for use on long runs in the higher ranges.

Should emergencies arise, the servo-assisted front disc brakes do a commendable job of hauling the car down without pitching occupants forward or dipping the front end. For a car whose test weight tipped the

below — Instrument panel · functional yet elegant.
right — Rear view conveys solid look.

Road's-eye view of Rover prow

Heater and Ventilation

Individual foot-level and face-level fresh air vents can be fiddled with for almost any combination of ventilation required. An opening below the windscreen feeds air to the heater, and three slots on the inside give ample defrosting power.

Last word

To describe the Rover 3-Litre as an excellent car would indeed be gilding the lily. That is already proven. But considering the fact that it sells, fully equipped, for several thousand dollars less than other cars in the luxury class the Rover shapes up as a truly outstanding automobile. It's mortal and as with any man-made objects has its faults but these are totally outweighed by the car's comfort, smoothness, soundness of design and awesome attention to detail.

scales at over 4,000 lb. these brakes are comfortingly capable.

The word that occurs to us in describing the Rover's road behaviour is serene; its refined character and plentiful creature comfort could easily create a superiority complex in the driver. We found ourselves placid even in heavy traffic jams.

Economy

The Rover shoudn't be expensive to run. Average consumption in city driving on premium fuel was 21 mpg, while steady 50-70 mph cruising yielded 24.5 mpg. Frequent use of overdrive could conceivably boost this figure considerably on trips.

Storage space

Trunk is large despite carrying both spare tire and battery, each of which is discreetly covered and tucked out of the way. The interior is full of nooks and crannies for stowing small packages.

No frills, no gimmicks · but good looking anyway

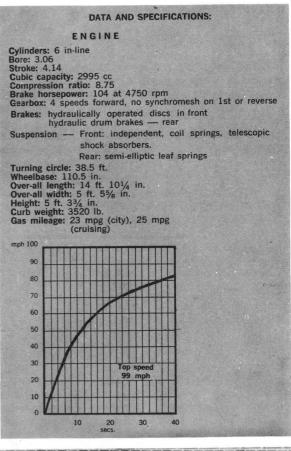

DATA AND SPECIFICATIONS:

ENGINE

Cylinders: 6 in-line
Bore: 3.06
Stroke: 4.14
Cubic capacity: 2995 cc
Compression ratio: 8.75
Brake horsepower: 104 at 4750 rpm
Gearbox: 4 speeds forward, no synchromesh on 1st or reverse
Brakes: hydraulically operated discs in front
hydraulic drum brakes — rear
Suspension — Front: independent, coil springs, telescopic shock absorbers.
Rear: semi-elliptic leaf springs
Turning circle: 38.5 ft.
Wheelbase: 110.5 in.
Over-all length: 14 ft. 10¼ in.
Over-all width: 5 ft. 5⅝ in.
Height: 5 ft. 3¾ in.
Curb weight: 3520 lb.
Gas mileage: 23 mpg (city), 25 mpg (cruising)

Top speed 99 mph

1849

ROVER 3-LITRE Automatic

Swivelling quarter-windows now fitted to the front doors of the 3-litre are hinged on their leading edges, and may be kept partially open at high speed without spoiling the low level of wind noise

CHANGES to Rover cars are made infrequently, and only after careful assessment and trial; their owners are assured of a design which will not quickly become dated. Thus, production of the Rover 3-litre ran for three years with no major visible alterations from the original specification announced at the London Show in 1958. Last September, however, the time came for a number of valuable improvements to be incorporated in this largest car of the range, making it even more refined and pleasant to drive.

Of these, the most significant is certainly the repositioning of the rear engine mountings. Earlier models suffered from a tendency to engine shake, described in our Road Test as a "front-end tremor on roads with a slightly rough surface." This has now been eliminated completely, so that the car feels thoroughly taut and rigid, even when driven fast over stretches of really bad road.

Useful benefit is also derived from the development work which Rover have undertaken on the Borg-Warner automatic transmission available for the 3-litre, and to enable us to assess this as well an automatic model was supplied for this Road Test. Immediately apparent is the revision of the hold control, as the mechanical T-shaped handle mounted below the parcels shelf is now replaced by an electric switch with long lever, conveniently placed for finger-tip operation just below the steering wheel rim. There has also been a change in its function, for it now acts in the same way as the full-throttle kickdown switch which remains below the accelerator pedal, but it is independent of the throttle.

When the car was first tried, operation of this switch brought in the lowest of the three transmission ratios unless the car speed was above 30 m.p.h., and this could be inconvenient if the control was used in hilly country. The effect was that if, when climbing on a light throttle, the engine began to labour slightly and the control was used to change down, the transmission would go through intermediate straight into low, producing unnecessarily high engine revs. However, the settings for this manual hold control are adjustable, and it was arranged that a Rover engineer should reset the solenoid control to its lower limit. Using a ramp, the job took him less than a minute.

As altered, the effect of this switch was far more satisfactory. In the original high setting, the change-up speeds when the hold control was used were 30 m.p.h. for low to intermediate, and 60 m.p.h. for the change to direct, and the appropriate change down would be made if the switch was used when the car was travelling at less than these two speeds. After adjustment, however, down changes with the hold in use occurred at 17 and 35 m.p.h., respectively, while the full-throttle kick-down speeds remained unaltered.

Well-matched Transmission

Any intermediate settings of the solenoid may be used, and it is to the credit of the Rover engineers that this choice has been offered, to enable the transmission to be adjusted to suit different drivers. As applied to the 3-litre Rover, and particularly as readjusted, the Borg-Warner automatic transmission proved more suitable and well-married to the engine characteristics than in any of the many cars we have yet tried with this unit.

Naturally, the familiar characteristics of the Borg-Warner automatic transmission are retained, and upward changes when the hold control is not used occur at increasingly high speeds (according to extent of throttle opening) to maxima of 20 m.p.h. (out of low) and 45 m.p.h. (into direct) when full throttle is used without depressing the accelerator to kick-down point. On a very light throttle opening, the car moves off from rest in intermediate range without using low ratio at all. The L position on the selector, of course, holds low regardless of speed at the driver's discretion, and provides overrun engine braking.

Take-offs from rest are always very smooth without being sluggish, but the automatic model loses progressively on acceleration throughout the speed range in comparison with the manual gearbox and overdrive version which we tested on 21 August 1959. Thus more time is required for overtaking. Acceleration to 60 m.p.h. was achieved in 20·2sec, and occupied little short of the quarter-mile, for which the standing start time was just 22·0sec. There is reasonably rapid acceleration to 70 m.p.h. and through to 80 m.p.h., but the car then tends to hang fire slightly. Up to maximum speed, however, the Rover will cruise with the almost total absence of mechanical noise which is one of its greatest delights.

Reclining and fully adjustable bucket seats, fitted to the test car, are an optional extra. Two front ashtrays are provided and slides are fitted for either to be repositioned to the left of the steering column

Rover 3-litre Automatic . . .

Starting is always instantaneous, but when thoroughly cold the engine does like use of the choke for the first few seconds; this also prevents the dead cold engine from stalling when the transmission selector is moved initially to Drive. Within the first mile or so the engine warms up to its work rapidly, and the thermometer needle soon mounts to its normal position at 75 deg. C.

In assessing the fuel consumption of the 3-litre it is fair to remember that this is a big car with a kerb weight of more than 33cwt, and one in which silence and refinement have been given first place. It is creditable indeed that by using reasonably restrained acceleration, and seldom exceeding 50 m.p.h. on a main road run, we had no difficulty in obtaining 25 m.p.g., while in brisk driving on a cross-country route 20·3 m.p.g. was returned. Sustained high cruising speeds and frequent use in heavy traffic have had an unfavourable influence on the overall consumption figure of 17·4 m.p.g.

As a comparison, a manual transmission model used recently on the Continent by the Technical Editor returned an overall consumption of 18·9 m.p.g. for 1,806 miles. Oil consumption of both cars worked out at approximately

2,500 m.p.g. for the automatic test car, and just under 4,000 m.p.g. for the overdrive model. An unusually accurate running check on oil level is provided by a facia switch, giving the reading on the fuel gauge. The fuel tank holds 14 gallons, and as a positive 1½-gallon reserve is supplied one feels confident to run the tank lower than on cars fitted only with a fuel gauge, thus extending the range between refuelling stops. As on all Rover models now, the reserve supply is drawn by a separate pump, available as a standby in case of failure of the main pump.

Also new as far as this test is concerned is the power steering, which Rover offer as optional equipment on the 3-litre at £79 extra including purchase tax. It derives its power from a pump at the rear of the dynamo shaft; in case of failure of the hydraulic system full control of the car remains without power assistance. The dynamo and water pump are driven by separate belts.

As applied to the test car, the steering is light to the point of requiring negligible effort, and the ease with which the steering can be turned at manœuvring speeds goes a long way towards compensating for the somewhat restricted locks and consequently large turning circle.

In addition to the lower effort at the wheel rim which power assistance provides, the number of turns from lock to lock have also been reduced to 2·6 from 4·2 with the fully mechanical type. Understeer is quite pronounced at high cornering speeds but it is substantially disguised and more easily countered with the aid of the power assistance; there is a limited initial response to steering wheel movement and because of the light effort involved this results in some drivers taking corners and altering course with rather sharp and abrupt changes. On the other hand this low response around the straight ahead position contributed to very good directional stability even in a strong cross wind at high speeds, in which conditions it maintained a very straight course. The steering retains adequate self-centring. Even in hard cornering there is little body roll.

Tyre Squeal Reduced

In the wet, the adhesion is reassuring, and the wheels showed no tendency to slide unless a skid was provoked deliberately. A marked improvement in this 3-litre compared with the earlier one tested two years ago is in the almost complete elimination of tyre squeal.

Pressure increases of 6 p.s.i. are recommended for sustained high speeds, and in fact these settings were retained for most of the test mileage, since the extra hardness did not seem to spoil in any way the commendable comfort of the suspension. The wheel actions are well damped so that the car gives a pleasantly stable ride, yet the resilience of the suspension allows most minor irregularities of road surface to pass practically unnoticed. Only on a severe pothole is a fairly firm vertical movement noticed. A repetition of surface characteristics, however, does tend to catch the suspension "out of phase" and on washboard and short, successive undulations the vertical travel of the wheels appears to be too restricted for full absorption.

Girling vacuum servo-assisted brakes are fitted, using 10·8in. dia. discs at the front wheels. On the automatic car a large foot pedal allows easy left foot braking. One could scarcely wish for brakes to be better since response is smoothly progressive to the point where the theoretical 1g maximum deceleration is produced at the relatively low pedal effort of 75 pounds. At high speed the brakes quickly tug the car's speed down if the need arises, while on wet roads it is remarkable how hard the brakes may be used without fear of locking the wheels and inducing a slide. Repeated applications on a long mountain descent in North Wales did not provoke any detectable loss of efficiency even at the extreme degree where unnecessary over-use made the brakes so hot that smoke was issuing from the front pads. The handbrake is controlled by a convenient pull handle

Useful pockets are provided on the backs of the front seats. Irvin diagonal and lap-strap safety harness fitted to the test car proved convenient to use once operation of the fastenings had been mastered

The fuel filler cap is lockable, but may be secured without the key if this is preferred. One key serves for the ignition and door locks, and the fuel filler key also locks the boot and the facia locker. The car can also be locked without the key

beneath the facia, and will hold the car securely on a 1-in-3 gradient. On the same test hill, incidentally, the automatic transmission allowed an easy restart.

The list of new features on this Rover is still not exhausted, because the test car also has the latest type of optional reclining bucket seat made available only last month. It provides limited lateral support on cornering, but is well padded for anatomically correct seating without forcing the occupants to slump forward. Similarly, the cushions are well padded and extend well under the thighs, and no discomfort is experienced after sitting in the car for many hours in succession on a long journey. An excellent feature is that with these special seats a small winding handle is provided just in front of the cushion, allowing one and a half inches of vertical adjustment of the framework. This supplements the reclining backrest provision and the normal fore-and-aft movement, so that both front occupants may set their seats individually for personal comfort. In the rear compartment, even when the front seats are fully back, there is really generous leg room, and indeed there are few cars in production today which can offer rear seat comfort to equal that provided by the 3-litre Rover.

All-round visibility is good, and the steering wheel does not intrude at all into the driver's line of vision. Relatively slender windscreen pillars are correctly angled and sited to form the minimum obstruction to visibility. In rain, large areas of the screen are swept by the wipers, but on the test car they tended to drag on a partially damp screen and then to sweep a much diminished arc, suggesting that too much wind-up is permitted in the drive from the motor; also,

although the familiar self-parking two-speed pattern of wiper is used, only the slower speed is available. Electrically operated windscreen washers are standard. The new quarter lights are hinged along their leading edges, so that rain water does not drip into the car when they are open in wet weather. Push-button locks on their catches ensure that they will not serve as an invitation to car thieves.

Fresh-air inlets are still provided in the upper edge of the facia on each side, and now have a small circular trap-door which can be used to deflect air on to one's face, or to decrease and cut off the air bleed as required. Cool air may also be admitted through the heater, as well as through a vent (with an individual pull control) on each side just below the parcels shelf. In winter, powerful fresh-air heating and demisting is available soon after a cold start.

Ample illumination both on main and dipped beams is given by the headlamps, and the dipswitch has an organ-pedal to serve as a rest for the driver's left foot. Little red tell-tales on the tops of the sidelamps are visible from the driving seat, showing when these lights are on and, as is usual Rover practice, the lights are controlled by a facia master switch, with steering column selector lever for choice of side or headlamps. The panel lamps are wired through the ignition circuit, and are independent of the sidelamps; variable brightness control is neatly incorporated in the switch. Melodious but powerful horns are controlled by a small diameter horn ring on the steering wheel.

Four bright interior lamps are turned on individually or as courtesy lights when the respective door is opened; two of them on together provide ample illumination for map

CONTINUED ON PAGE 43

Generously roomy, the luggage locker has an unobstructed flat floor, with the spare wheel mounted underneath in a wind-down cradle. The battery is under the cover on the right of the boot, while the large tools and starting handle are covered by the flap on the left. Right: The engine compartment shows the same high standard of finish as the rest of the car, and although it is well filled, access to most routine service components is good

BRAIN BEATS BRAINBOX

ONE of the things everyone wants to know about an automatic is how it compares with the manual-gearbox version of the same model.

I'd been wanting to find that out myself in the case of the 3-litre Rover ever since testing the automatic car, back in September 1959. But manual 3-litres were scarcer than hen's teeth in this country for a long time — and I had to wait until now to satisfy my curiosity.

By then the 3-litre had received several modifications—not obvious to

as a caveman's skull, even over the worst of going.

A lot of work has been done on the three-speed Borg Warner automatic gearbox. It now has a throttle kickdown switch as well as a manual intermediate gear hold.

Instead of always starting in first as it used to, a light throttle foot pedals off the car in intermediate. But if you're in a hurry, just floor the pedal and it kicks down to first.

On the test car, change-up speeds with the hold in use were 30 m.p.h. for low and 60 for intermediate.

and suspension joints are sealed for life at the factory and there is only ONE grease nipple. This is on the sliding joint of the propeller shaft and needs attention at only 3000-mile intervals.

What Tests Showed

Pitting the two cars against the clock, I soon found that — in the Rover's case, anyway—human control is still superior to the robot.

That Borg Warner transmission was always smooth, and up to 50 m.p.h. it bade fair to match the

the eye, but having an important bearing on performance and comfort —so I found myself re-testing the automatic as well to ensure a true comparison.

Here's the general picture:

Both cars have a 2995c.c. six-cylinder engine with pushrod-operated overhead inlet and side exhaust valves which gives 115 b.h.p. on a compression ratio of 8.75 to 1; both have had the back engine mounts repositioned to stop engine shake.

This was a sort of tremor in the front-end which was set up by broken road surfaces. It has been completely cured now—the car is as solid-feeling

Down-changes took place at 55 and 10 m.p.h.

I would prefer higher maximums for intermediate and first. Performance, particularly at the top end, could be much improved. The auto gets up and goes quite nicely to 80—but after that things happen pretty slowly.

But let it be said for Rover that their development of the Borg Warner allows the solenoids governing change-points to be adjusted—in a matter of minutes.

Let's have none of that tosh about Rovers being messy to adjust and maintain. With both cars, all steering

manual car. But then the manual took over with a vengeance . . .

Compare the 0-60 m.p.h. figures— 20.8sec. for the automatic and only 17.8 for the manual. The 0-90 times hardly bear any sort of comparison— 53.4sec. against 46.3.

On maximum speed runs, the manual did a mean 98.2 m.p.h. against 95.3 for the auto.

But the chief delight in a Rover is not what it will do—it's how it does it. Mechanical noise has been practically banished and wind noise is unusually low up to 90 m.p.h.

In fact, tyre roar—not more than you'd get from the same tyres on an-

modern
MOTOR
TWIN TEST

Rover 3-litre automatic is no match for the manual-gearbox model, reports Bryan Hanrahan

NEW kickdown and "hold" arrangements give driver more control over automatic (above); but it still can't beat manual car (left)..

other car—is a big part in the overall noise factor. I suppose the Rover is as quiet as any car made.

Fuel consumption was pretty good for cars weighing in at over 35cwt. on test. Over 240 miles, the auto just scraped into the 20 m.p.g.-plus bracket by two-tenths of a gallon; the manual-gearbox model (with overdrive) gave 23.4 over the same distance.

Considering that both 3-litres are not exactly slow motor cars and that they carry every bit of furniture and equipment you can imagine, the figures are outstanding.

The 14-gallon tank gives a reasonable range of well over 200 miles.

Handling is traditionally British: distinct understeer at all cornering speeds, right up to the limit.

The wheel has a medium ratio of 4.2 turns lock-to-lock. I have the feeling that the lightness this ratio gives would be preferable to the heaviness of a quicker gearing with a car of this weight.

Self-centring is smart. The 3-litre goes round a corner accurately and without wallowing.

All average road surfaces are planed neatly by the suspension—long torsion bars and wishbones up front, conventional semi-elliptics and rigid axle at the back. Rough stuff is handled well because wheel travel is long. *Continued on page 81*

Continued on page 81

MAIN SPECIFICATIONS

ENGINE: 6-cylinder, overhead inlet and side exhaust valves; bore 77.8mm., stroke 105mm., capacity 2995c.c.; compression ratio 8.75 to 1; maximum b.h.p. 115 at 4500 r.p.m.; maximum torque 164ft./lb. at 1500 r.p.m.; S.U. carburettor, twin electric fuel pumps; 12v. ignition.
TRANSMISSION: Single dry-plate clutch; 4-speed gearbox, synchromeshed on top three; overdrive optional; normal final ratio 3.9 to 1; with overdrive (as tested) 4.3 to 1.
SUSPENSION: Front independent, by swinging links and laminated torsion bars, with anti-roll bar; semi-elliptics at rear; telescopic hydraulic shock-absorbers all round.
STEERING: Burman recirculating-ball type; 3¼ turns lock-to-lock, 38ft. 6in. turning circle.

WHEELS: Pressed-steel discs with 6.70 by 15in. tyres.
BRAKES: Servo-assisted hydraulic, discs at front and drums at rear.
CONSTRUCTION: Unitary, with subframes.
DIMENSIONS: Wheelbase 9ft. 2½in.; track, front 4ft. 7½in., rear 4ft. 8in.; length 15ft. 6½in., width 5ft. 10in., height 5ft. 0½in.; clearance 7½in.
KERB WEIGHT: 31½cwt.
FUEL TANK: 14 gallons.
AUTOMATIC MODEL: Same as for manual, except for Borg-Warner three-speed automatic transmission with 10in. single dry-plate clutch; ratios—1st, 2.308; 2nd, 1.435; top, 1.0 to 1; reverse, 2.009 to 1; solenoid-operated intermediate hold; kerb weight, 32cwt.

PERFORMANCE ON TEST

CONDITIONS (both tests): Fine, warm; no wind; smooth bitumen; two occupants; premium fuel.
BEST SPEED: automatic, 98 m.p.h.; manual, 102.1 m.p.h.
FLYING quarter-mile: automatic, 95.3 m.p.h.; manual, 98.2 m.p.h.
STANDING quarter-mile: automatic, 21.9s.; manual, 20.5s.
MAXIMUM in indirect gears: automatic, 1st, 30 m.p.h.; 2nd, 60; manual, 1st, 25; 2nd, 48; 3rd, 68.
ACCELERATION from rest through gears: automatic—0-30, 6.4s.; 0-40, 9.9s.; 0-50, 14.1s.; 0-60, 20.8s.; 0-70, 28.0s.; 0-80, 37.8s.; 0-90, 53.4s. Manual—0-30, 5.2s.; 0-40, 8.0s.; 0-50, 11.6s.; 0-60, 17.8s.; 0-70, 24.1s.; 0-80, 33.4s.; 0-90, 46.3s.

PASSING ACCELERATION: automatic (using kickdown and intermediate hold), 10-30, 4.8s.; 20-40, 7.1s.; 30-50, 8.5s.; 40-60, 10.3s.; 50-70, 15.9s.; 60-80, 19.1s.; 70-90, 36.0s. Manual (using appropriate gears), 10-30, 4.2s.; 20-40, 6.8s.; 30-50, 8.0s.; 40-60, 8.6s.; 50-70, 10.9s.; 60-80, 17.2s.; 70-90, 25.9s.
BRAKING: automatic, 31ft. 2in. to stop from 30 m.p.h. in neutral; manual, 31ft. 8in.
FUEL CONSUMPTION: automatic, 20.2 m.p.g. overall for 250-mile test; manual, 23.1 m.p.g.
SPEEDO (both cars): accurate at 30 m.p.h., 3 m.p.h. fast at 90.

PRICE (with tax): automatic, £2975; manual, £2760

ROVER 3-LITER

THERE'S SOMETHING ABOUT A ROVER that's hard to put into words. Over the years, the staff at *Road & Track* has experienced the usual changes, but the strange love affair with this automobile continues.

This attitude would be understandable if the Rover, for example, offered high performance. But it doesn't: the performance can best be described as satisfactory but hardly inspiring. Possibly we could say that the Rover's styling is responsible for its charm; but to most of us its over-all appearance, though refined, is still pretty mundane, if not almost dowdy. No one in this country ever gives it a second look.

Many of the best automotive writers have tried to explain the insidious charm of the Rover and we think the sentence by Denise McCluggage, who writes the automobile column for *Town & Country,* sums things up properly. She wrote, "It is simply a well-engineered, beautifully constructed automobile that appeals to people who want well-engineered, beautifully constructed automobiles."

Designed more for the buyer who is interested in quality and comfort than in neck-snapping acceleration and guided-missile styling, the Rover 3-liter has pretty well bridged the gap between the ultra expensive few (Rolls-Royce, Bentley and Mercedes 300-SE) and the multitude of inexpensive family-type cars.

The interior can be described as "British traditional," having leather-upholstered seats, carpeted floors and highly polished wood trim. We are not enamored of wood in an automobile in any form, structural or decorative, but are forced to concede that it looks elegant—in the manner of an exclusive men's club.

Both a bench-type front seat (our test car was so equipped) and individual front seats are optional, the individual seats costing $75 extra. For Rover owners who intend to be chauffeur-driven, a sliding glass partition mounted between the backrest of the front seat and the roof is available—for $594. This partition, once installed, can be removed in a matter of minutes. Air conditioning, that mobile form of emancipation from the elements, costs another $595 and we've seen occasions when it was worth every penny of the price.

The instruments are grouped in a panel, projecting from the main "dashboard" in front of the driver, to be viewed through the steering wheel. The steering wheel is large enough, and the horn ring small enough so that the instruments are seldom obscured; actual instrumentation is provided by the speedometer, fuel level (which, by flipping a switch, shows oil level in the sump), water temperature and ammeter gauges. Oil pressure, ignition on/off, direction signals and high beam are indicated by lights on the panel. In addition, a light indicates when the cold-start lever (choke) is pulled out and a handbrake warning light is combined with a brake fluid light, which indicates when brake fluid in the reservoir (not the master cylinder) drops below a safe level.

A vertical row of switches on each side of the instrument cluster controls the windshield wipers, oil level indicator, headlights, panel lights and main/reserve fuel tank switch.

The Rover's interior includes many niceties not found elsewhere in production cars: The front door-pull/arm rests are adjustable for height; storage for the inevitable odds and ends accumulated by automobile owners is provided for by a pocket in each front door, a shallow but full-width package tray under the dash and *two* "glove" compartments. One of these compartments is usurped by the radio when it is factory installed. On the passenger's side, under the package shelf, is a pull-out tray with tools set into molded rubber inserts. This unit fell onto our female passenger's shins the first time we tried to demonstrate its use. Both the upper edge of the dash and the front of the package tray are padded for safety. Face-level air vents are mounted on each side of the panel and are individually controlled by driver and passenger.

Like all current Rovers (the special T-4 Gas Turbine excepted), the 3-liter is propelled by an in-line engine with

the so-called "F" cylinder head; i.e., the intake valves are in the head, operated by pushrods and rocker arms, while the exhaust valves are in the block and operated directly off the camshaft. This system was used for many years by Rolls-Royce and Bentley on the in-line sixes, and in the early Twenties by Hudson, Essex (4-cyl) and Reo in the U.S.

The cylinder block is cast integrally with the crankcase, and the crankshaft, which carries a harmonic vibration damper, runs in seven copper/lead-lined bearings. The cylinder head is aluminum alloy.

The transmission on our test car was a Borg-Warner unit built to Rover specifications, with the control lever mounted on the steering column. Transmission ratios are 2.308, 1.435 and 1:1; the torque converter stall ratio in 1st, 2nd and reverse is 2.1:1. A finger-tip switch allows the driver to retain

2nd gear up to 60-65 mph or 1st gear up to 30 mph. On cars equipped with manually shifted transmissions a 4-speed unit of Rover manufacture is used with synchromesh on 2nd, 3rd and 4th gears. Laycock de Normanville overdrive is standard and the gear ratios are 3.376, 2.043, 1.377 and 1:1 with an o/d step-up to 0.778.

Power is transmitted through a two-piece driveshaft to a live rear axle positioned by semi-elliptic springs. Both ends of the springs are rubber-mounted to reduce road noise; they require no maintenance. Rear axle motion is controlled by tubular dampers.

The front suspension is independent, with an upper A-arm on each side and lower radius links connected to laminated torsion bars. An anti-roll bar is utilized and, as on the rear, tubular hydraulic dampers are installed.

Body construction is of the unit frame/body type but a separate welded structure, much like the front of a standard frame, is attached to the body assembly (by six rubber mountings) to carry the engine, front suspension and steering assemblies.

There is nothing radical or unique about the suspension of the Rover, but it is a well-tried and extremely well developed system which results in satisfactory, if not outstanding, road behavior. The car does not handle like a sports car, and was not designed to do so, but the steering is accurate and reasonably quick, the springing gives a soft but well-controlled ride and sedulous attention to sound insulation has insured quiet.

With a combination of disc brakes in front and large (11 by 2.5 in.) drums at the rear, the circumstances when a Rover would run out of brakes would be extraordinary.

Since our last test and appraisal of the Rover 3-liter (December 1959), opening wind wings have been added to the front doors and the little "awnings" over the side windows have been cast into oblivion. We can't say we're sad to see them go, although opinion seems to be divided on the end result in regard to passenger comfort. Wind buffeting with the

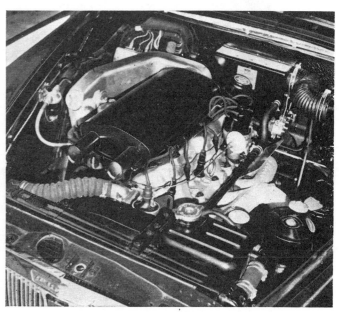

ROVER 3-LITER *continued*

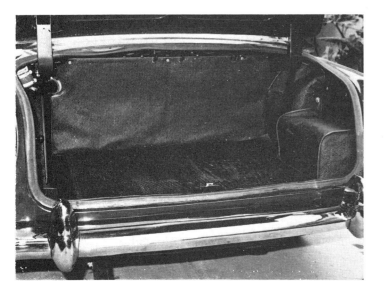

windows partially open has been reduced, but the chance of water dripping in has been increased.

Rover offers 10 single-color paint choices and six two-tone combinations. None of our staff liked the two-tone arrangement, as recorded in our previous report, and we still prefer a single color for the Rover.

A potential buyer who compares performance with price will be disappointed in the Rover but a buyer who equates quality with price will be pleased. We found no compromise with quality on our test car—everything fit, everything worked (too easily in the case of the tool tray) and was beautifully finished.

As for the transmission options, the manually shifted 4-speed will undoubtedly out-perform the 3-speed automatic but other than that there is little to choose between them. We were disappointed in the hill climbing ability of the 3-liter with automatic transmission but, then, we are used to cars with automatic transmissions having *circa* 300 bhp to propel them along. Even with its moderate 115 bhp, the power seemed adequate for all driving conditions except starting from near rest on a grade exceeding 10%.

A car like the Rover has a very strong appeal for a very limited group of automobile buyers. The size of this group is further diminished by the elimination of those who can't afford the rather steep price. Therefore, we will never see a great number of Rovers on the roads of the U.S. (just under 700 were sold in the U.S. in 1961), but those who choose a Rover will find that it serves them well.

ROAD TEST
ROVER 3-LITER

SCALE: 10" DIVISIONS

DIMENSIONS

Wheelbase, in	110.5
Tread, f and r	55.6/56.0
Over-all length, in	186.5
width	70.0
height	60.2
equivalent vol, cu ft	455
Frontal area, sq ft	23.4
Ground clearance, in	7.8
Steering ratio, o/a	n.a.
turns, lock to lock	2.5
turning circle, ft	40
Hip room, front	58
Hip room, rear	58.5
Pedal to seat back, max	39.0
Floor to ground	10.0

CALCULATED DATA

Lb/hp (test wt)	35.0
Cu ft/ton mile	78.4
Mph/1000 rpm (3rd)	20.2
Engine revs/mile	2980
Piston travel, ft/mile	2050
Rpm @ 2500 ft/min	3630
equivalent mph	73
R&T wear index	61.0

SPECIFICATIONS

List price	$5495
Curb weight, lb	3670
Test weight	4020
distribution, %	55/45
Tire size	6.70-15
Brake swept area	419
Engine type	6 cyl, F-head
Bore & stroke	3.06 x 4.13
Displacement, cc	2995
cu in	182.7
Compression ratio	8.75
Bhp @ rpm	115 @ 4500
equivalent mph	91
Torque, lb-ft	164 @ 1500
equivalent mph	32

GEAR RATIOS

3rd (1.00)	3.90
2nd (1.44)	5.61
1st (2.31)	9.01
1st (2.31 x 2.1)	18.9

SPEEDOMETER ERROR

30 mph	actual, 30.6
60 mph	58.9

PERFORMANCE

Top speed (3rd), mph	100
best timed run	n.a.
3rd ( )	
2nd (4200)	59
1st (3550)	31

FUEL CONSUMPTION

Normal range, mpg	16/20

ACCELERATION

0-30 mph, sec	5.8
0-40	9.1
0-50	13.0
0-60	18.6
0-70	25.8
0-80	36.0
0-100	
Standing ¼ mile	21.6
speed at end	65

TAPLEY DATA

3rd, lb/ton @ mph	210 @ 50
2nd	300 @ 38
1st	450 @ 27
Total drag at 60 mph, lb	155

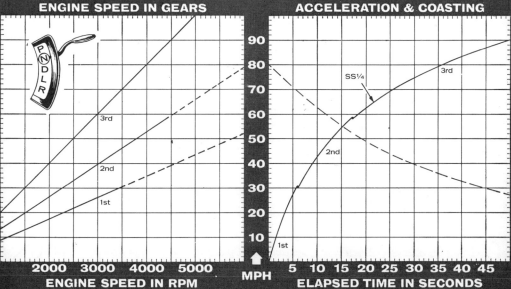

ENGINE SPEED IN GEARS

ACCELERATION & COASTING

3rd

2nd

1st

SS¼

3rd

2nd

1st

2000 3000 4000 5000

ENGINE SPEED IN RPM

MPH

5 10 15 20 25 30 35 40 45

ELAPSED TIME IN SECONDS

MORE POWER FOR ROVERS

Underslung bi-metal instruments for fuel and oil level, water temperature, oil pressure and battery current are fitted beneath the main instrument dials on the Coupé. The rev counter reads up to 5,500 r.p.m., with red at 5,300

AN additional model called the 3-Litre Coupé joins the Rover range for the 1963 season, and the three existing cars—the 80, 100 and 3-litre—are continued in improved form and with greatly increased power in each case. The new Coupé model is a four-seater—not a two-seater, which is the general interpretation of the term "coupé"—and is based on the new 3-litre Mark II saloon. All the improvements made to the 3-litre are incorporated in the Coupé as well.

This new Coupé is listed at £1,499 basic with manual transmission and £50 more with automatic, the respective prices with purchase tax being £2,062 2s 9d and £2,130 17s 9d. Prices for the 95 and 110 are somewhat higher than those for the models they replace, the 95 at £1,373 (basic £998) being £18 more than the 80, and the 110, at £1,534 (basic £1,115), £27 more than the 100. For the 3-litre, the full prices, with purchase tax, for manual and automatic models are £50 and £54 more respectively.

The Rover four-cylinder 2¼-litre engine

is discontinued for passenger cars, but will remain as a power unit for the Land-Rover. The new 80 model, called the 95, now has the 2·6-litre engine with overhead inlet and side exhaust valves which previously powered the 100. It is a six-cylinder unit, and its compression ratio is increased from 7·8 to 8·8 to 1. This change, which raises the power output from 93 b.h.p. (net) at 4,750 r.p.m., to 102 b.h.p., developed at the same crankshaft speed, was introduced in the latter stages of production of the 100. A few detail alterations are made to the car also, including the use of toggle switches, and the addition of a handbrake warning light on the dash, serving also as a warning for low level of brake fluid.

For both the 110 and the 3-litre Mark II models, revised induction designed by Weslake has resulted in increased power, particularly at the top end of the range. There is little alteration to the cylinder head, though the area behind the inlet valves is relieved and contoured. The main change is that the manifold is no longer cast in unit with the cylinder head.

It is now a separate casting, bolted to the head. The effect has been to change the two abrupt corners into a gradual S-bend. The result is much improved breathing, and more even filling. In the case of the 2·6-litre engine in the 110 the power is increased from the original 93 b.h.p. to 123 b.h.p., developed at 5,000 r.p.m. The compression ratio is 8·8 to 1, as for the new Rover 95. In the 3-litre engine, these induction changes have raised the power from 115 b.h.p. to 134 b.h.p. (gross), again developed at 5,000 r.p.m. As previously, there is a slight reduction in compression ratio (8·0 instead of 8·8 to 1) for the 3-litre when automatic transmission is specified.

With the 110 and 3-litre, there is no change in final drive ratio, and overdrive remains standard equipment on both cars. However, overdrive is now regarded as an essential fifth gear, and to prevent accidental disengagement of this at high speed, which could have disastrous effects with the increased crankshaft speed available, the overdrive kickdown switch beneath the accelerator is no

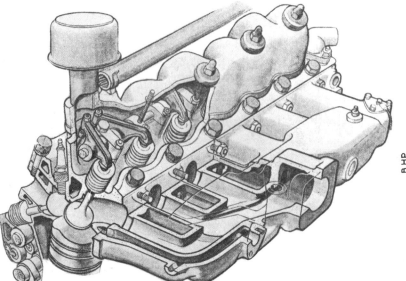

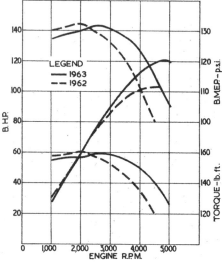

It is above 3,500 r.p.m. that the increased power of the 3-Litre Mark II and Coupé engine is particularly appreciated. Left: New cylinder head and manifold for the 110 and 3-litre engines

Prices

	Basic	U.K. List		
	£	£	s	d
95	998	1,373	5	3
110	1,115	1,534	2	9
3-Litre Mark II	1,325	1,822	17	9
(Automatic)	1,375	1,891	12	9
3-Litre Coupé	1,499	2,062	2	9
(Automatic)	1,549	2,130	17	9

▲

Zero-torque locks are fitted on the Coupé, and a new ratchet mechanism ensures that the key can be turned only in the correct direction, whether to lock or unlock the doors

Although a much faster car, featuring many interior improvements, the new 3-litre Mark II saloon is unidentifiable from its predecessor externally ▶

longer fitted; a part-throttle inhibitor, which prevents engagement of overdrive at small throttle openings, is still provided. For the 95, overdrive is no longer available, and this car now has a 3-9 to 1 axle ratio giving 19 m.p.h. per 1,000 r.p.m.

For further changes to the 3-litre are the replacement of the central gear change, previously mounted well forward, with a new vertical lever remote-control change much farther back, within easy reach of the driver's left hand; and the raising of both second and third gear ratios, enabling the driver to obtain very real advantage from the increase in engine performance.

For improved road holding, the suspension, front and rear, has been lowered by one inch on the 3-litre, and there are revised damper settings calculated to give a much more level ride as well as better road adhesion. The bump stops are reduced in height by half an inch. New rear springs with nylon separators, and different dampers are used. A slightly lower-geared but very much more sturdy and accurate steering gearbox by Burman is now fitted on the 3-litre. Power assistance is an optional extra as before.

Borg-Warner automatic transmission continues to be available at extra cost on this model, and only when this transmission is specified can a bench seat be supplied in the front; with the manual transmission model the new positioning of the gear lever makes individual seats essential. Vertical adjustment of the whole seat through a range of one-and-a-half inches is available by means of an adjusting handle when the Rover Hallam, Sleigh and Cheston reclining seats are specified.

Detail improvements to the interior include the use of African cherry wood for the facia and window surrounds instead of walnut, switches with " spade " knobs in place of the previous pointed pattern, and a two-speed heater fan instead of the previous single-speed unit. The indicator switch now does double duty also as headlamps flasher. Ammeters, temperature and fuel gauges on all models are now of bi-metal type, and there is a switch for turning on one side and tail lamp for parking use. A more vigorous rate for the windscreen wipers, still single-speed, has been chosen for this car, and on all models, except the 95, there is an electric windscreen washer which works when its switch is pressed and held down, without any preset timing. The 95 has a plunger-type washer. Bulbless

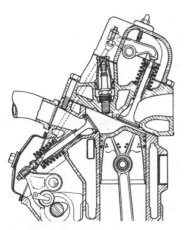

As before, the Rover 3-litre inlet manifold is water-heated, but is manufactured as a unit separate from the cylinder head. This longitudinally cut manifold shows the passageways. Left: Revised inlet port

A cigarette lighter and ashtray are built into the division between the individual rear seats of the 3-litre Coupé

ROVER CHANGES . . .

The replacement for the Rover 100 is the 110, with power output increased from 102 to 123 b.h.p. Only the altered name strips distinguish the new car from its predecessor in external view, though there are several interior refinements. A remote-control floor change for the four-speed gearbox is the most significant interior revision on the 3-litre saloon. Individual front seats are fitted on all manual gearbox models (below)

SPECIFICATION

ENGINE

No. of cylinders ...	6 in line
Bore and stroke ...	77·8 x 105mm (3·06 x 4·13in.)
Displacement ...	2,995 c.c. (183 cu. in.)
Valve position ...	Overhead inlet, side exhaust
Compression ratio	8·75 to 1 (8·0 with automatic)
Max. b.h.p. (net)...	121 at 5,000 r.p.m. (119 at 4,750 r.p.m. with automatic)
Max. b.m.e.p. (net)	132 p.s.i. at 2,650 r.p.m. (133 p.s.i. at 2,500 r.p.m. with automatic)
Max. torque (net)	169 lb.ft. at 1,750 r.p.m. (161 lb.ft. at 2,000 r.p.m. with automatic)
Carburettor ...	One S.U.
Fuel pump ...	Dual S.U., alongside tank
Tank capacity ...	14 Imp. gallons (63·7 litres) including 1·5-gal reserve
Sump capacity ...	10 pints (5·7 litres)
Oil filter ...	Full flow, renewable element
Cooling system ...	23 pints including heater (13 litres)
Battery ...	12-volt, 57-amp-hr.

TRANSMISSION

Clutch ...	Single dry plate, 10in. dia. Rover-modified Borg-Warner automatic transmission optional
Gearbox ...	Four speeds, synchromesh on 2nd, 3rd and top
Overall gear ratios	O.D. Top 3·3, top 4·3, 3rd 5·5, 2nd 8·1, 1st 14·5, reverse 12·8 to 1
Final drive ...	Semi-floating spiral bevel, 4·3 to 1 (3·9 to 1 with automatic)

CHASSIS

Brakes ...	Girling hydraulic, servo-assisted, disc front, drum rear
Disc dia. ...	10·8in.
Drum dia., shoe width ...	11 x 2·25in.
Suspension: front	Independent, laminated torsion bars, anti-roll bar
rear	Live beam axle with half-elliptic leaf springs
Dampers ...	Telescopic, front and rear
Wheels ...	Steel disc; 5 studs
Tyre size ...	6·70 x 15in.
Steering ...	Burman recirculating ball. Power assisted with Coupé, optional with saloon
Turns lock to lock	4·75 (2·5 with power assistance)

DIMENSIONS (Manufacturer's figures):

Wheelbase ...	9ft. 2·5in. (281cm)
Track ...	F, 4ft. 7·3in. (141cm); R, 4ft. 8in. (142cm)
Overall length ...	15ft. 6·5in. (474cm)
Overall width ...	5ft. 10in. (178cm)
Overall height (unladen) ...	4ft. 11·5in. (150cm); 4ft. 9in. (145cm) for Coupé
Ground clearance (unladen) ...	7·9in. (20cm)
Turning circle ...	40ft. (12·4m)
Kerb weight ...	32·5 cwt (1,650 kg)

PERFORMANCE DATA

Top gear m.p.h. per 1,000 r.p.m.	18·7 (24·1 in O.D. top; 20·8 with automatic)
Torque lb. ft. per cu. in. engine capacity...	0·92
Brake surface area swept by linings ...	F, 260 sq. in.; R, 156 sq. in. (256 sq. in. per ton)
Weight distribution ...	F, 55 per cent; R, 45 per cent

sealed beam headlamps are fitted on all models. Dunlop Road Speed RS5 or Avon Turbo speed IV tyres are standard on all models except the 95.

3-litre Coupé

With a body similar in essentials to that of the 3-litre Mark II, the new coupé model is designed to seat four only, and power-assisted steering is standard. The roof is lowered by 2½in. compared with the saloon, and this, in addition to the reduced height of the suspension setting, gives the car a pleasantly low and sporting appearance. To the rear, the roof-line is more sharply curved, and the rear window lies nearer to the horizontal than on the saloon. The rear seat is moved forward and is divided into two spacious individual seats designed to keep their occupants well located.

Above the waistline, the doors are neatly blended with chrome window surrounds which are considerably narrower than the fixed frames of the saloon, and the windows are larger. In place of the

combined circular instrument matching the speedometer, the Coupé has a 4⅝in dia. rev counter. The displaced instruments —ammeter, fuel gauge and coolant thermometer—are fitted in separate binnacles beneath the main instrument nacelle. A fourth instrument—an oil pressure gauge—is provided, making the 3-litre Coupé the first Rover saloon for many a year to feature an oil pressure gauge.

Other detail improvements which help to make the Coupé specially attractive are zero torque door locks and simplified key operation, so that the key can only be turned in the correct direction; improved door seals; a cigarette lighter in the rear fixed armrest in addition to that on the facia; and revised electrical details. The individual front seats, with Rover Hallam, Sleigh and Cheston vertical adjustment as well as rake and fore-and-aft settings, are standard equipment on both manual and automatic transmission versions of the Coupé. Under-bonnet and boot interior illumination is provided.

Suspension lowered by 1in., and roof line by 2½in., give the Coupé a low and purposeful appearance; narrow window frames of stainless steel are fitted, and there is an opening quarter window in each of the four doors

CONTINUED FROM PAGE 33

reading. When the luggage locker lid is raised with the tail-lamps in use a boot interior light comes on. There is also a bright automatic reversing lamp, and at night the transmission selector quadrant is illuminated. Three facia warning lights grouped together refer to oil pressure, ignition and the choke—when the choke is in use with a hot engine. There is also a warning light near the handbrake, wired through the ignition circuit to indicate either that the handbrake is on, or that the fluid level in the master cylinder reservoir is seriously low.

Instruments grouped neatly in front of the driver include the coolant thermometer and combined fuel or oil level gauge mentioned earlier, with an ammeter and trip mileometer, and mounted centrally in the facia there is a clock, which kept perfect time throughout the test.

Features for the convenience and enjoyment of those who travel in the Rover are unusually comprehensive, and include centre and adjustable side armrests; transparent tinted sun vizors, with a vanity mirror on the left one; full-width parcels shelf and lockable facia compartment; front door pockets; childproof safety devices on the rear door handles; and four ashtrays. All steering and suspension joints are sealed on manufacture, and the only grease nipple, on the sliding joint of the propeller shaft, requires attention at the 3,000-mile service intervals.

With both this car and the overdrive model taken to the Continent we have amassed some 3,500 miles in the latest version of Rover's 3-litre. The many staff members who drove either or both of them all agreed that this is quite the best model yet produced by the Solihull factory, which is praise indeed for a company whose vehicles have always set a high standard. The outstanding characteristics of the 3-litre are its comfort and spaciousness, and its silence of running almost regardless of speed.

ROVER 3-LITRE AUTOMATIC

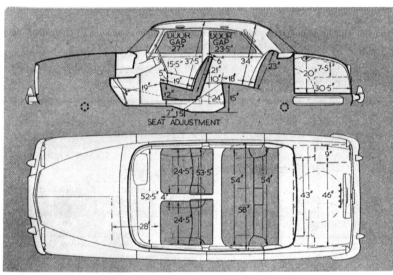

Scale ⅛in. to 1ft. Driving seat in central position. Cushions uncompressed.

DATA

PRICE (basic), automatic transmission, £1,335.
British purchase tax, £613 2s 3d.
Total (in Great Britain), £1,948 2s 3d.
Extras including tax: Radio, £42 5s 10d.
Power steering, £78 15s 0d.
Reclining seats, £33 10s 0d per pair.
Individual front seats, £18 19s 2d.
Two-tone finish, £14 11s 8d.
Removable division, £120.
Safety harness, £28 (set of four)

ENGINE: Capacity, 2,995 c.c. (183 cu. in.).
Number of cylinders, 6.
Bore and stroke, 77·8 × 105mm (3·1 × 4·1in.)
Valve gear, pushrod overhead inlet, side exhaust.
Compression ratio, 8·75 to 1.
B.h.p. 108 net at 4,500 r.p.m. (b.h.p. per ton laden 59·5).
Torque, 164 lb. ft. at 1,500 r.p.m.
M.p.h. per 1,000 r.p.m. in top gear, 20·1.

WEIGHT (with 5 gal fuel): 33·3 cwt (3,724lb).
Weight distribution (per cent); F, 54·9; R, 45·1.
Laden as tested, 36·3 cwt (4,060 lb).
Lb per c.c. (laden), 1·4.

BRAKES: Girling hydraulic, vacuum servo-assisted.
Disc dia. F, 10·8in.
Drum dimensions: R, 11in. dia.; 2·25in. wide.
Swept area: F, 260 sq. in.; R, 156 sq. in.
(230 sq. in. per ton laden).

TYRES: 6·70—15in. Dunlop Gold Seal tubeless.
Pressures (p.s.i.): F, 24; R, 22 (normal).
F, 30; R, 28 (fast driving).

TANK CAPACITY: 14 Imperial gallons.
Oil sump, 10 pints.
Cooling system, 22·5 pints.

DIMENSIONS: Wheelbase, 9ft 2·5in.
Track, F, 4ft 7·3in.; R, 4ft 8in.
Length (overall), 15ft 6·5in.
Width, 5ft 10in.
Height, 5ft 0·3in.
Ground clearance, 7·9in.
Frontal area, 23·6 sq. ft. (approx.).
Capacity of luggage space: 16 cu. ft. (approx.).

ELECTRICAL SYSTEM: 12-volt; 57 ampère-hour battery.
Headlamps, 60-40 watt bulbs.

SUSPENSION: Front, independent, laminated torsion bars and anti-roll bar.
Rear, semi-elliptic leaf springs.

PERFORMANCE

ACCELERATION TIMES (mean):
Speed range, Gear Ratios, and Time in Sec.
m.p.h.

m.p.h.	Top	Intermediate	Low
10—30 ..	—	—	4·9
20—40 ..	—	7·0	—
30—50 ..	—	8·3	—
40—60 ..	12·8	10·2	—
50—70 ..	15·5	—	—
60—80 ..	19·3	—	—
70—90 ..	35·6	—	—

Gear ratios: Top, 3·9 to 1; Intermediate, 11·8 to 5·6; Low, 18·9 to 9·0.

From rest through gears to:

30 m.p.h.	..	6·2 sec.
40 "	..	9·8 "
50 "	..	14·3 "
60 "	..	20·2 "
70 "	..	27·9 "
80 "	..	38·5 "

Standing quarter mile 22·0 sec.

MAXIMUM SPEEDS ON GEARS:

Gear		m.p.h.	k.p.h.
Top ..	(mean)	93·6	150
	(best)	94	151
Intermediate	..	60	96
Low ..	..	30	48

TRACTIVE EFFORT (by Tapley meter):

	Pull (lb per ton)	Equivalent gradient
Intermediate ..	305	1 in 7·2

SPEEDOMETER CORRECTION: m.p.h.

Car speedometer	..	..	..	10	20	30	40	50	60	70	80	90
True speed	..	..	..	12	21	30	39	48	57	67	77	87

BRAKES (at 30 m.p.h. in neutral):

Pedal load in lb	Retardation	Equiv. stopping distance in ft
25	0·25g	125
50	0·68g	44
75	1·0g	30

FUEL CONSUMPTION (at steady speeds in top gear):

30 m.p.h.		33·0 m.p.g.
40 "		29·1 "
50 "		25·8 "
60 "		22·5 "
70 "		18·9 "
80 "		16·1 "
90 "		12·7 "

Overall fuel consumption for 1,657 miles, 17·4 m.p.g. (16·0 litres per 100 km.).
Approximate normal range 16—25 m.p.g. (17·7-11·3 litres per 100 km.).
Fuel: Premium grades.

TEST CONDITIONS: Weather: Dry, clear sky, little wind.
Air temperature, 45 deg. F.

STEERING: Turning circle.
Between kerbs, L, 41ft 11in.; R, 41ft 3in.
Between walls, L, 43ft 9in.; R, 43ft 1in.
Turns of steering wheel from lock to lock, 2·6

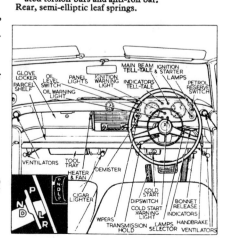

ROVER 1963

new Coupé leads new, more powerful range of swift and silent cars

New — the sleek and stylish 3-Litre high-performance Coupé. The Mark II 3-Litre Saloon: swifter version of a widely acclaimed car. The 110: faster, more powerful replacement for the 100. The 95: luxury six-cylinder motoring for the family.

One of the world's best engineered cars

Every Rover improvement is made with the whole engineering of the car in mind: hence the nicely-calculated balance between power and handling qualities, between performance and comfort, in every Rover ever built. The new engine modification for 1963 is a typical example. Rover engineering has developed the two 3-Litre models and the 110 to give substantial-ly more power. And because of careful Rover planning, this extra performance is achieved well within the cars' road-holding capacity. Balanced developments like this confirm the Rover claim to be one of the world's best engineered cars.

Rover success in 1962 Liège Rally

Rover 3-Litre Saloons came 1st and 3rd in their class in the Liège-Sofia-Liège Rally this year, described by the Sunday Times correspondent as "without doubt the most gruelling endurance test for both crews and cars. To finish the Liège is equivalent to gaining a class win in any other European rally."

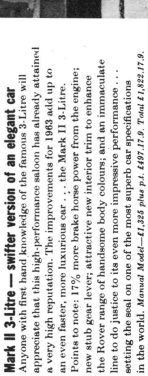

Mark II 3-Litre — swifter version of an elegant car

Anyone with first hand knowledge of the famous 3-Litre will appreciate that this high-performance saloon has already attained a very high reputation. The improvements for 1963 add up to an even faster, more luxurious car . . . the Mark II 3-Litre. Points to note: 17% more brake horse power from the engine; new stub gear lever; attractive new interior trim to enhance the Rover range of handsome body colours; and an immaculate line to do justice to its even more impressive performance . . . setting the seal on one of the most superb car specifications in the world. *Manual Model—£1,325 plus p.t. £497.17.9. Total £1,822.17.9. Automatic Model—£1,375 plus p.t. £516.12.9. Total £1,891.12.9.*

The new Rover 3-Litre Coupé

combines all the outstanding features of the internationally acclaimed Saloon with a new sleekness of line and fleetness of foot. The low and elegant shape is quite new yet unmistakably Rover. The controls and interior layout—with its four deeply-moulded bucket seats—are planned specifically for motorway driving. And note the new stub gear lever. Yet, here again, the comfort and attention to detail are entirely in the Rover tradition. Under the bonnet, the new high-output engine has been further developed to make this the fastest Rover in the range—and thanks to Rover engineering principles, this extra power can be enjoyed well within the car's masterly road-holding and braking capacity. The new Coupé quietly carries the individual qualities of Rover motoring into a new world of faster achievement. *Manual Model £1,499 plus p.t. £563.2.9. Total £2,062.2.9. Automatic Model—£1,549 plus p.t. £581.17.9. Total £2,130.17.9.*

The new 110—faster replacement for the 100

Pleasantly formal and dignified without, uncommonly comfortable within, the new Rover 110 has a performance that belies its deceptively quiet looks. The familiar Rover 100 six-cylinder engine has been given more power, so that the Rover 110 will quietly attain—and surpass—the magic 100 mph. *Basic price—£1,115 plus p.t. £419.2.9. Total £1,534.2.9.*

The new 95—luxury six-cylinder family motoring

The new 95 offers you six-cylinder Rover luxury, replacing the four-cylinder 80 for very little extra cost. Its advanced engine produces an abundance of silk-smooth power and there are front wheel disc brakes (as on all Rover models) to curb it effortlessly. The highest Rover standards of finish and technical excellence are fully maintained. Altogether the 95 is the ideal introduction for the family to swift and comfortable Rover motoring. *Basic price—£998 plus p.t. £375.5.3. Total £1,373.5.3.*

NEW 3-LITRE COUPÉ

BY APPOINTMENT TO
HER MAJESTY QUEEN ELIZABETH II
MANUFACTURERS OF MOTOR CARS AND LAND-ROVERS
THE ROVER COMPANY LIMITED

THE ROVER COMPANY LIMITED *Solihull · Warwickshire*
London offices and showrooms : Devonshire House, Piccadilly.
MAKERS OF FINE CARS AND THE WORLD-FAMOUS LAND-ROVER

ROVER—ONE OF THE WORLD'S BEST ENGINEERED CARS

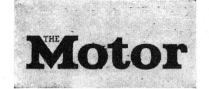

MAKE: *Rover* *TYPE:* *3 Litre Mark II*

MAKERS: *The Rover Co., Ltd., Solihull, Warwickshire, England*

THE Motor

ROAD TEST • No. 40/62

DATA

CONDITIONS: *Weather: Dry, fine, with little wind. (Temperature 50°-54° F., Barometer 29.6 in. Hg.) Surface: Dry macadam and smooth concrete. Fuel: Premium grade pump petrol (98 Octane Rating by Research Method.)*

INSTRUMENTS

Speedometer at 30 m.p.h.	3% fast
Speedometer at 60 m.p.h.	1% fast
Speedometer at 90 m.p.h.	2% fast
Distance recorder	1% fast

WEIGHT

Kerb weight (unladen, but with oil, coolant and fuel for approximately 50 miles)	33½ cwt.
Front/rear distribution of kerb weight	54/46
Weight laden as tested	37¼ cwt.

MAXIMUM SPEEDS

Flying Quarter Mile (Overdrive)

Mean of four opposite runs	108.0 m.p.h.
Best one-way ¼-mile time equals	110.4 m.p.h.

"Maximile" Speed. (Timed quarter mile after one mile accelerating from rest.)

Mean of four opposite runs	101.1 m.p.h.
Best one-way time equals	103.4 m.p.h.

Speed in gears

Max. speed in 4th gear	96 m.p.h.
Max. speed in 3rd gear	77 m.p.h.
Max. speed in 2nd gear	50 m.p.h.
Max. speed in 1st gear	29 m.p.h.

FUEL CONSUMPTION

(Overdrive top gear)

30½ m.p.g. at constant 30 m.p.h. on level
30½ m.p.g. at constant 40 m.p.h. on level
28 m.p.g. at constant 50 m.p.h. on level
25 m.p.g. at constant 60 m.p.h. on level
23 m.p.g. at constant 70 m.p.h. on level
20½ m.p.g. at constant 80 m.p.h. on level
18 m.p.g. at constant 90 m.p.h. on level

(Direct top gear)

28 m.p.g. at constant 30 m.p.h. on level
26½ m.p.g. at constant 40 m.p.h. on level
24 m.p.g. at constant 50 m.p.h. on level
22 m.p.g. at constant 60 m.p.h. on level
20 m.p.g. at constant 70 m.p.h. on level
18 m.p.g. at constant 80 m.p.h. on level
15¾ m.p.g. at constant 90 m.p.h. on level

Overall Fuel Consumption for 2,002 miles, 114.35 gallons, equals 17.5 m.p.g. (16.2 litres/100 km.)

Touring Fuel Consumption (m.p.g. at steady speed midway between 30 m.p.h. and maximum, less 5% allowance for acceleration) 22 m.p.g.

Fuel tank capacity (maker's figure) 14 gallons, including 1½ gallons in reserve.

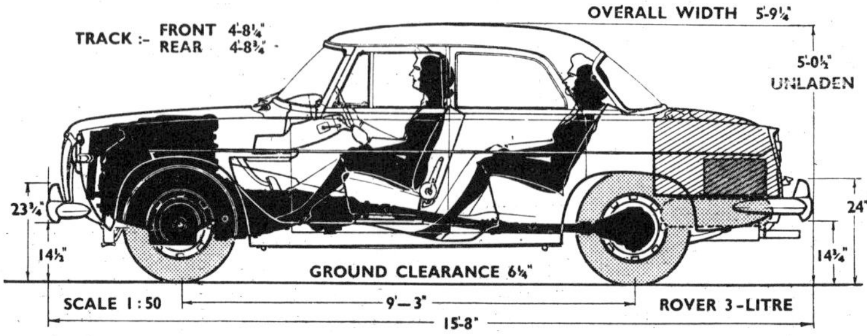
OVERALL WIDTH 5'-9¼"
TRACK :- FRONT 4'-8½" REAR 4'-8¾"
5'-0½" UNLADEN
23¾"
24"
14½"
14¾"
GROUND CLEARANCE 6¼"
SCALE 1:50
9'-3"
ROVER 3-LITRE
15'-8"

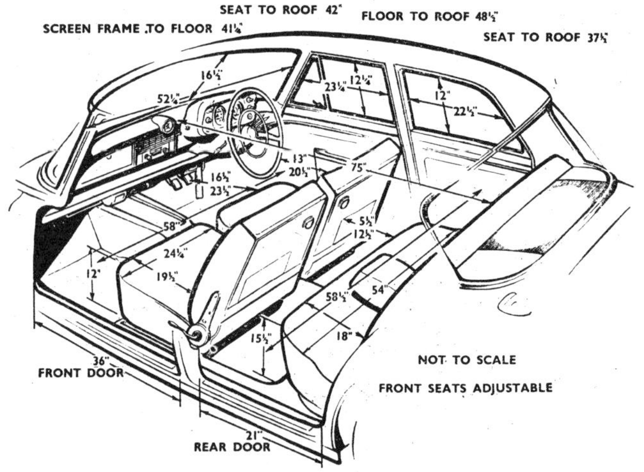
SEAT TO ROOF 42"
FLOOR TO ROOF 48½"
SCREEN FRAME TO FLOOR 41¼"
SEAT TO ROOF 37½"
16½"
52½"
12¼"
23¾"
12"
22½"
13"
20½"
75"
16½"
23½"
5½"
12½"
58"
24½"
19½"
12"
58½"
54"
18"
15½"
36"
FRONT DOOR
NOT TO SCALE
FRONT SEATS ADJUSTABLE
21"
REAR DOOR

BRAKES from 30 m.p.h.

0.97 g retardation (equivalent to 31 ft. stopping distance) with 125 lb. pedal pressure.
0.93 g retardation (equivalent to 32½ ft. stopping distance) with 100 lb. pedal pressure.
0.86 g retardation (equivalent to 35 ft. stopping distance) with 75 lb. pedal pressure.
0.75 g retardation (equivalent to 40 ft. stopping distance) with 50 lb. pedal pressure.
0.35 g retardation (equivalent to 86 ft. stopping distance) with 25 lb. pedal pressure.

HILL CLIMBING at sustained steady speeds

Max. gradient on overdrive top	1 in 12.0 (Tapley 185 lb./ton)
Max. gradient on top gear	1 in 8.6 (Tapley 260 lb./ton)
Max. gradient on 3rd gear	1 in 6.5 (Tapley 340 lb./ton)
Max. gradient on 2nd gear	1 in 4.4 (Tapley 500 lb./ton)

ACCELERATION TIMES from standstill

0-30 m.p.h.	4.5 sec.
0-40 m.p.h.	7.3 sec.
0-50 m.p.h.	10.1 sec.
0-60 m.p.h.	14.5 sec.
0-70 m.p.h.	19.0 sec.
0-80 m.p.h.	26.4 sec.
0-90 m.p.h.	33.9 sec.
Standing quarter mile	19.8 sec.

ACCELERATION TIMES on upper ratios

	O/drive Top	Top gear	3rd gear
10-30 m.p.h.	11.9 sec.	8.8 sec.	6.9 sec.
20-40 m.p.h.	11.4 sec.	8.5 sec.	6.4 sec.
30-50 m.p.h.	12.6 sec.	9.2 sec.	6.5 sec.
40-60 m.p.h.	15.0 sec.	10.1 sec.	7.9 sec.
50-70 m.p.h.	16.1 sec.	10.8 sec.	8.9 sec.
60-80 m.p.h.	17.0 sec.	11.6 sec.	—
70-90 m.p.h.	21.9 sec.	13.4 sec.	—

STEERING

Turning circle between kerbs:

Left	38¾ ft.
Right	40¼ ft.
Turns of steering wheel from lock to lock	2¾

Specification

Engine

Cylinders	6
Bore	77.8 mm.
Stroke	105 mm.
Cubic capacity	2,995 c.c.
Piston area	44.2 sq. in.
Valves	Overhead inlet (pushrod operated) side exhaust
Compression ratio	8.75/1 (alternative 8.0/1)
Carburetter	Single S.U. H.D.8
Fuel pump	two S.U. electric
Ignition timing control	Centrifugal and vacuum
Oil filter	AC-Delco full flow
Maximum power (net)	121 b.h.p.
at	4,800 r.p.m.
Piston speed at maximum b.h.p.	3,307 ft./min.

Transmission

Clutch	Borg & Beck single dry plate 10 in. dia., hydraulically actuated
Top gear (s/m)	4.30 (Overdrive, 3.345)
3rd gear (s/m)	5.478
2nd gear (s/m)	8.12
1st gear	14.516
Reverse	12.762
Overdrive	Laycock-de Normanville
Propeller shaft	Hardy Spicer, divided
Final drive	Spiral bevel
Top gear m.p.h. at 1,000 r.p.m.	18.3 (Overdrive, 23.4)
Top gear m.p.h. at 1,000 ft./min. piston speed	26.6 (Overdrive, 34.1)

Chassis

Brakes	Girling, disc and drum with vacuum servo
Brake dimensions	Front discs 10¾ in. dia. Rear drums 11 in. dia.
Friction areas	104.9 sq. in. of lining working on 405.5 sq. in. rubbed area of discs and drums
Suspension: Front	Independent by ball jointed transverse wishbones and laminated torsion bars, anti-roll bar
Rear	Semi-elliptic leaf springs with nylon anti-friction buttons and grease gaiters
Shock absorbers	Woodhead Monroe telescopic
Steering gear	Burman F3 recirculating ball (Optional power assistance on test car)
Tyres	6.70—15 Dunlop R.S.5. or Avon Turbospeed Mk IV

Rover 3-litre Saloon

Better Performance Added to Traditional Rover Virtues

FOR many years silence, luxury, and smoothness have been associated with Rover cars. Now the 3-Litre has been provided with more power giving it better acceleration and a higher top speed. While the quietness has not been impaired, more petrol is consumed if the full potential of this large, spacious saloon is used. Speeds substantially over 100 m.p.h. can easily be attained. With more sporting appeal comes a greatly improved gearchange and better roadholding but lavish trim and a tasteful roomy interior firmly emphasize that it remains an impressively quiet saloon in which initial cost is secondary to sound engineering and meticulous attention to detail. The new Mark II Rover 3-Litres are fully described on page 329 of this issue.

Alterations

THE conservative lines of the 3-Litre saloon are unaltered from the previous model. The 2,995 c.c., six-cylinder i.o.e. engine has, however, been considerably modified to produce 16% more power, and to cope with this increase suitable alterations have also been made to the suspension. This has been lowered and Dunlop RS5 or Avon Turbospeed Mark IV tyres are now fitted as original equipment. The new cylinder head and manifolding give 121 net b.h.p., compared with the 108 b.h.p. of the Mark I, resulting in an increase in maximum speed from 96.9 m.p.h. to 108 m.p.h., and all the acceleration and hill-climbing figures show an improvement despite an increase in weight from 32½ cwt. to 33½ cwt. "Maximile" speed is also up, from 90.0 m.p.h. to 101.1 m.p.h.

Quality Trim

THE standard of the interior trim in the Rover 3-Litre is matched by very, very few cars which might conceivably be termed "series production." Hide upholstery and solid African Cherrywood combine with really effective sound insulation and mechanical parts that are themselves quiet to provide luxury and refinement. The interior is spacious, with a "bay window" effect as a result of the scuttle being well forward. Visibility through the wrap-round windscreen is good, the fast, single-speed wipers clean it effectively, and two tinted sun visors (the passenger's with a vanity mirror) are provided.

The remoteness of the facia results in the instruments being placed in a separate nacelle on top of the steering column housing. In a bold, but effective compromise between the practical and the decorative, practicality comes off best, showing the driver in two large, round dials and no fewer than seven warning lights all he might reasonably want to know. The clock is the only fugitive from this panel, mounted in the centre of the scuttle visible to everyone.

The speedometer has decimal trip and total mileage recorders and the minor switchgear is grouped neatly round the sides of the nacelle. All the switches, except the ignition/starter, are

Almost indistinguishable from earlier 3-Litres, the Mark II has practical and not unfashionable lines. A recognition point is a longer exhaust tailpipe.

In Brief

Price (including power steering as tested) £1,379 plus purchase tax £518 2s. 9d. = £1,897 2s. 9d.	
Price without power steering (including purchase tax), £1,822 17s. 9d.	
Capacity	2,995 c.c.
Unladen kerb weight	33½ cwt.
Acceleration:	
20-40 m.p.h. in top gear	8.5 sec.
0-50 m.p.h. through gears	10.1 sec.
Maximum top gear gradient	1 in 8.6
Maximum speed	108 m.p.h.
"Maximile" speed	101.1 m.p.h.
Touring fuel consumption	22 m.p.g.
Gearing: 18.3 m.p.h. in top gear at 1,000 r.p.m. (overdrive 23.4 m.p.h.)	

Rover 3-Litre

of the toggle type, one in the middle operating an oil level indicator combined with the fuel gauge, and the choke control is below the facia. Three stalks, sprouting rather confusingly from the steering column, operate overdrive, indicators/headlamp flasher, and headlamps on/off, respectively. The exterior lights are worked by a master switch in the nacelle, the headlamps by the third stalk and a foot-operated dipswitch. Side and tail lights on one side of the car only may be left on for prolonged parking and there is a reversing light operated by engagement of reverse gear.

The new gear lever, while a great improvement over the previous device feels rather ponderous and the clutch travel is long. The synchromesh is good and inadvertent engagement of reverse is prevented by a positive stop button on top of the knob. Care has to be taken to avoid jerky gear changes and the unsynchronized first gear emits a loud whine. The remainder of the transmission with a divided propeller shaft is quiet and vibrationless. During the rather unnatural conditions of our performance testing, first gear failed under fierce acceleration from a standstill.

Overdrive works on top gear and has an inhibitor switch to prevent downward changes being made on the overrun. The arrangement Rovers use enables the internal clutches in the overdrive to be set for top gear torque only, instead of for third or even second gear torque, which automatically makes for greater freedom from jerky operation. The kick-down system of the Mark I 3-Litre has been discontinued in view of

the danger of it coming into play at the higher speeds of which the new car is capable.

Braking is by servo-assisted discs on the front and drums on the rear wheels. The foot pedal is spongy and the help given by the servo does not appear consistent throughout a heavy application, resulting in jerky operation. Prolonged use results in fade and squealing from the discs although Rovers point out that the test car was equipped with Don 105 linings which they claim, are for " average " use, whereas DS5S linings may be specified for harsher treatment. The handbrake held the car on a 1 in 3 test hill from which it was also possible to start off in first gear. To warn against moving away with the handbrake on, there is a very bright amber light shining from below the facia straight into the driver's eyes—a sensible warning, equally effective by day or night.

Well-bred

ROVER horse-power has always seemed particularly well-bred and the 121 horses of the Mark II 3-Litre have come from the same stable. The six-cylinder engine is smooth throughout the speed range, and can only be heard from inside the car when going quickly in the indirect gears. When idling, it is quite inaudible and detectable only by the winking of the ignition warning light and a very gentle rocking of the gear lever. When travelling fast, the silence is spoiled only by slight

Above : The instrument panel, covered in non-reflecting black is directly behind the steering wheel. *Top right :* Rear passengers have ashtrays and map pockets in the backs of the front seats. *Right :* The unusually-shaped aluminium cover conceals the rockers for the overhead inlet valves. Air goes through the flat air cleaner to a single S.U. carburetter.

wind noise and even this is not enough to make the occupants raise their voices or turn up the radio at any speed right up to the maximum.

Although the overall fuel consumption has fallen from 19.1 to 17.5 m.p.g., the steady speed figures show a different story. While the new car is certainly less economical at low speeds, higher in the range, the difference diminishes until the positions are reversed. At 30 m.p.h. in direct top gear, for example, the Mark I gave 31 m.p.g. and the Mark II, 28 m.p.g.; at 40 m.p.h. in overdrive top, the Mark I gave 35½ m.p.g. and the Mark II only 30½ m.p.g. But at 90 m.p.h. in overdrive the new car does 18 m.p.g. while the Mark I could only manage 16½ m.p.g. The difference at 60 in direct top is only ½ m.p.g., but still in favour of the new car. Long inlet manifolds particularly suited to high gas speeds account for the improvements. The increased acceleration, however, and the better handling of the new car encourage the use of higher speeds and as a result, the overall figure suffers.

The provision of cool air ducts means that only in very hot weather would it be necessary to have a Rover's windows open. A stream of cool air can be directed to the driver or front passenger at face or feet level from small openings controlled by a butterfly valve in the top rail of the facia or handle-controlled openings below. The heating and demisting system is effective and silent. An optional extra fitted to the test car and costing £22 10s. including tax is an electrically heated panel in the rear window which will not mist or freeze up.

Standard steering on the Rover 3-Litre is Burman recirculating ball type, but for an extra £74 5s. including tax this may be assisted by a higher geared power system. The road test car had the equipment and although many people found it desirable

The boot is rectangular and is illuminated after dark. The box on the right houses the battery and there are tools clamped to the left side behind the lining material

on this fairly heavy car, some disliked the loss of road feel. Appreciated in city traffic conditions it made the Rover easy to handle and particularly easy to park despite its bulk. Out of town, however, it became all too simple to turn on too much lock when entering a corner owing to the inability to judge the behaviour of the front wheels. This, combined with the deceptive speed and silence of the car proved unpleasant.

Within the limits of a large saloon with suspension soft enough to provide a comfortable ride, cornering was good. There is some roll but this did not materially affect control of the car. The handling is much better than the Mark I 3-Litre partly owing to the suspension changes, but partly also to the new tyres running at 26 p.s.i. (30 for sustained high speeds) instead of 22-24 p.s.i. There is consistent understeer and the rigid back axle behaves well, even on bumpy corners. There is a little whine from the tyres on smooth surfaces, but they are quiet under most conditions of straight running or cornering.

For Others

THE British manufactured Lyback seats were optional extras fitted to the test car. They cost £24 15s. with tax, adjust for height as well as reach and, of course, the back folds almost flat at the touch of a lever.

Parcel accommodation is good with a rather shallow, lockable compartment in the facia and another in the centre when the radio is not fitted. There is a useful little tray on top of the gearbox hump, a large parcel shelf below the facia running the full width of the car and another behind the rear seats. Map pockets are provided in the front doors, but all four operate individual courtesy lights. The boot is fully lined and the only encroachment on its conveniently rectangular space is the battery under a cover on the right. A comprehensive array of tools stowed on the left supplements the small tools in a rubber-lined tray under the facia. The spare wheel is in a separate compartment below the boot floor, a typical piece of Rover detail planning being an opening with a lid giving access to the tyre valve so that pressure can be checked without removing the wheel. Safety arrangements for the passengers include "child-proof" locks on the rear doors, provision for the optional seat belts, and mild crash padding.

Boot and bonnet have counterbalanced lids and access through the latter to the well-finished engine is good. The dip-stick and oil filter are situated quite near the exhaust manifold and care has to be taken to avoid touching this when checking the level or replenishing. Only two pints of oil were added during our 2,000-mile test.

The higher speeds attainable by the 3-Litre Rover and its recent success in the Liège-Sofia-Liège Rally indicate that legendary strength has been allied to a new, higher standard of roadworthiness appealing to the fast, even sporting driver. The image of the Rover as a comfortable means of transport for the elderly is no longer accurate. Nevertheless, with the high-quality execution of a design which lays stress on silence, luxury, and roominess it consolidates its place as de luxe, executive-style transport.

Coachwork and Equipment

Starting handle .. .. .. Yes	
Battery mounting .. .. Luggage locker, R.H. side	
Jack .. .. Bipod pillar	
Jacking points .. .. 4 external sockets at sides	
Standard tool kit .. .. jack, wheelbrace, starting handle, tyre pump, pliers, screwdriver, three double-ended spanners, adjustable spanner, plug spanner, box spanner and bar, wheel trim removal tool, tyre pressure gauge, luggage strap, two touch-up pencils.	
Exterior lights : 2 head, 2 side, 2 stop/tail, reversing lamp, rear number plate.	
Number of electrical fuses 4	
Direction indicators Self-cancelling amber flashers	
Windscreen wipers .. .. Lucas electrical self parking, 2-blade	
Windscreen washers .. Lucas electrical, type 4SJ	

Sun visors .. .. .. 2, tinted transparent, universally pivoted	
Instruments : Speedometer with total and decimal trip mileage recorders, clock, fuel and oil level gauge water thermometer, ammeter.	
Warning lights: Dynamo charge, choke, oil pressure, handbrake, turn indicators. main beam.	
Locks .	
With ignition key .. Ignition, both front doors	
With other keys .. Luggage locker, glove box, petrol filler	
Glove lockers .. One lockable on left of facia, one, not lockable, in centre when optional radio not fitted.	
Map pockets . One inside each front door	
Parcel shelves : One below facia, one behind rear seat	
Ashtrays .. One below facia, one in back of each front seat	

Cigar lighters .. One, below parcel She	
Interior lights .. 4, above doors with courtesy and manual switches.	
Interior heater : Fresh-air heater and demister with separate cool air ducts on screen rail and below scuttle.	
Car radio .. .. Optional extra	
Extras available .. .. Lyback fully adjustable reclining seats, heated backlight, power assisted steering, safety belts, radio (H.M.V. or Pye).	
Upholstery material .. .. Prime quality hide	
Floor covering .. .. Carpets with underfelt over bitumastic compound.	
Exterior colours standardized .. Ten single tone Ten duotone available at extra cost.	
Alternative body styles .. .. Coupé	

Maintenance

Sump .. .. .. 12 pints, S.A.E. 20/30	Contact breaker gap .. .. .014-.016 in.	Camber angle .. .. 1½ deg.	
Gearbox .. .. .. 3 pints, S.A.E. 90 Hypoid	Sparking plug type .. Champion H5. 14mm.	Castor angle .. .. .. ¼ deg. positive	
Overdrive .. .. .. 1½ pints, S.A.E. 90 Hypoid	Sparking plug gap .. .. .. .029-.031 in.	Steering swivel pin inclination .. .. 4½ deg.	
Rear axle .. .. .. 3 pints, S.A.E. 90 Hypoid	Valve timing : Inlet opens 13 deg. b.t.d.c. and closes 45 deg. a.b.d.c. ; Exhaust opens 48 deg. b.b.d.c., and closes 16 deg. a.t.d.c.	Tyre pressures :	
Steering gear lubricant, power 3-3½ pints Castrol TQ manual 1¼ pints, 90 Hypoid		Front 26 lb. plus 4 p.s.i. for high-speed cruising	
Cooling system capacity .. 24 pints (2 drain taps)	Tappet clearances (hot) :	Rear .. .. 26 lb.	
Chassis lubrication .. by grease gun every 6,000 miles to 1 point	Inlet .. .. .006 in.	Brake fluid .. .. Girling	
	Exhaust .. .. .010 in.	Battery type and capacity Lucas BT9A 12-volt, 57 amp.-hr.	
Ignition timing .. 3 deg. b.t.d.c. (fully retarded)	Front wheel toe-in .. zero plus or minus 1/16 in.		

Rover styling has not changed much over the last few years, even though there have been a number of details improvements.

ROVER 3-litre –

Conservative, handsome, rugged and highly desirable, the

In keeping with a car of its type, the Rover has a large luggage compartment, which is very accessible. Although heavy, car is not particularly big.

Dashboard layout in the 3-litre is outstandingly good. Everything is grouped in front of the driver. Note the padded parcel shelf.

By PETER HALL

that viking tenacity

Rover 3-litre is one of the top cars, says tester Peter Hall.

WRITING about really good automobiles, built for a price class way beyond the means of a man who writes about motor cars — a class in which cost is not the maker's primary concern — is a very difficult assignment.

The writer feels that the quality car — if it has been successfully designed, and it rarely hasn't been — is almost beyond criticism. Hence he might tend to rave about it and write what seems to be just another advertisement.

On the other hand, he is dedicated professionally to the proposition that the perfect car has not been and probably never will be made, so he must criticise. Often the criticism seems to concentrate on unimportant details — the placing of ash trays, the color of the brake pedal rubber, and so on. These inflated criticisms of minor aspects of the good car usually tend to emphasise the overall impression that the car is exceptionally good, and the rave review is thus accentuated. One feels one is whirling around in a vicious circle.

The Rover is a case in point. I cannot remember seeing the writings of any road test on any Rover model since the second World War that gave any impression other than he was totally impressed by the model under test.

So I found the current version of the newest Rover model—the 3-litre.

Actually, the 3-litre has been in production since 1958 and, although the current model has the addition to its name of Mark 1a, it differs only in minor detail. Another version was released in Britain at the October London Motor Show, but its changes are so insignificant, except for the addition of the slightly jazzier coupe model, that a full test of the 1962 Mark 1a gives a complete impression of what the latest style of Rover motoring is like.

Briefly, it is utterly luxurious and deeply satisfying to anyone with an appreciation of well-designed superbly built automobiles.

Appearance is the same as all the other 3-litres built in the last four years, with only a couple of minor changes.

The small, plastic cantilever-type verandas that jutted out over each of the four side windows have gone. Their main purpose was to compensate for the lack of front quarter panel vent windows, prevent draughts and keep out rain when Roverites drove about with the windows down.

WHEELS FULL ROAD TEST

Engine uses overhead inlet and side exhaust valve cylinder head. It is notable for its smoothness, lively performance.

The quarter vent panels are now fitted to the front doors and they seemed to be quite effective in reducing draughts. They also helped to take a little of the load off the front window winding mechanism.

Chrome plated hub caps and separate trim rings have been dropped in place of better looking and tougher stainless steel discs which combine the functions (?) of both cap and trim ring.

From the outside, there is nothing else to distinguish the current 3-litre from last year's model, or, for that matter, from next year's.

There are, however, other changes and they are quite important in that they make a fine car finer.

Earlier three-litres tended to suffer from some front end shake when driven hard over rough roads —they even developed it when cruised at near top speed on good surfaces. This wasn't really surprising (nor a severe case of front-end shake, either) considering that the 3-litre was the old Rover firm's first essay into the manufacture of a chassis-less car. Indeed, Rover still builds cars with chassis, such as the Rover 100 that is sold here and the four-cylinder 80 that is available in England, but is not imported here except on special order.

On the Mark 1a, important modifications have been made to the design of the sub-frame that holds the engine and front suspension.

The assembly is stronger, more rigid and heavily insulated at the six attachment points than on earlier models, and showed a worthwhile improvement on the road.

Front end shake has been entirely eliminated on rough roads and, on the open highway, the Rover sat down firmly and smoothly.

Appearance of the Rover gives an excellent idea of its real nature.

The lines are clean and uncluttered and the overall impression is of a big and comfortable car, modern but conservatively so, and likely to look just as good in 10 years time, whatever the fashion of the day, as it does now.

Yet, from some angles, especially side-on, the Rover has a faintly sporting aura—a lean crouched look that gives the impression of a wild one in tame clothes that can really show a hairy leg when it wants.

It can, too, as the performance figures show. The test car was fitted with automatic transmission, as are most Rovers sold in this country, and was barely run in. Worse, from the performance point of view, the car had hardly ever been over 30 mph before I got my hands on it.

Yet, acceleration was swift and sure and the best top speed run exceeded 94 mph. More miles on the speedo and a better tune (the test car was running quite rich) would take the potential maximum closer to 100.

Power comes from as fine a six cylinder engine as the motor industry boffins have yet designed. With a capacity of 2995 cc and such fancy items as overhead inlet and side exhaust valves, aluminium head, seven bearing crankshaft and roller-type cam followers contribute to its 115 brake horsepower and a smooth flexibility throughout its revving range that has to be sampled to be properly appreciated.

The automatic transmission is basically the familiar three-speed Borg Warner type. However, the unit has been extensively modified to Rover's specifications, and a couple of changes have been made since the early days of the 3-litres.

Now, the transmission, in normal driving, starts off in second or intermediate. Previously, it always started in first and went right through the box, both ways.

You can still get first, if you want a really quick start, merely by flooring the accelerator. But for normal driving, intermediate is utterly smooth and provides adequate acceleration without sign of strain.

Another change is relocation of the admirable intermediate hold switch from low down in the centre of the dashboard to the steering column.

The switch protrudes from the column on the right amid a whole bunch of similar switches that control the turning light indicators and headlight dipping. It is a bit confusing at first, but you soon get to learn the position of the appropriate switch.

In addition to the overriding switch, you can always drop the transmission from drive to intermediate up to about 60 mph, and from intermediate to low up to about 35, by flooring the accelerator. Of course, there is also a Low position on the hand selector on the left of the steering column.

Brakes were one of the highlight features of the Rover. Big discs and big drums at the front, all with power assistance, gave the car tremendous stopping power. Throughout the acceleration tests, I spared the brakes not one jot—yet they stood up remarkably well with no sign of fade or loss of effectiveness whatever.

On fast cruising runs through hilly and winding country, the brakes were superb. No matter how fast you travelled, how frequently you needed to press hard on the broad, well-placed pedal, the 33 cwt of Rover (and test crew) reacted immediately in just the right way. *Continued on Page* 81

wheels ROAD TEST

TECHNICAL DETAILS OF THE ROVER 3-LITRE

HOY·429

PERFORMANCE

TOP SPEED:

Fastest run .... 94.4 mph
Average of all runs .... 93.8 mph

MAXIMUM SPEED IN GEARS:

Low .... 45 mph
Intermediate .... 66 mph
Drive .... 94.4 mph

ACCELERATION:

Standing Quarter-mile:

Fastest run .... 21.5 sec
Average of all runs .... 21.7 sec
0 to 30 mph .... 6.1 sec
0 to 40 mph .... 8.8 sec
0 to 50 mph .... 13.7 sec
0 to 60 mph .... 19.3 sec
0 to 70 mph .... 26.6 sec
20 to 40 mph .... 8.0 sec
30 to 50 mph .... 7.4 sec
40 to 60 mph .... 6.8 sec

GO-TO-WHOA:

0-60-0 mph .... 23.3 sec

SPEEDO ERROR:

Indicated	Actual
30 mph	29.1 mph
50 mph	48.4 mph
70 mph	67.2 mph

FUEL CONSUMPTION:

16.3 mpg over 156 hard miles (car running rich, see text)

PRICE: £2811

SPECIFICATIONS

ENGINE:

Cylinders .... six, in-line
Bore and stroke .... 77.8 mm by 105 mm
Cubic capacity .... 2995 cc
Compression ratio .... 8.75 to 1
Valves .... overhead inlet, side exhaust
Carburettor .... Single SU
Power at rpm .... 115 bhp at 4500
Torque .... 164 lb/ft at 1500 rpm

TRANSMISSION:

Type .... Borg-Warner automatic

SUSPENSION:

Front .... independent, torsion bars
Rear .... leaf springs, solid axle
Shockers .... telescopic

STEERING:

Type .... recirculating ball
Turns, 1 to 1 .... 4½
Circle .... 40 ft

BRAKES:

Type .... disc front, drums rear. Power assisted

DIMENSIONS:

Wheelbase .... 9 ft 2½ in
Track, front .... 4 ft 7 5-16 in
Track, rear .... 4 ft 8 in
Length .... 15 ft 6½ in
Width .... 5 ft 10 in
Height .... 5 ft 0½ in

TYRES:

Size .... 6.70 by 15

WEIGHT:

Kerb .... 32¾ cwt

Rover 3-litre Coupé 2,995 c.c.

BY reputation, the established Rover image is predominately directed towards durability and quality of construction, rather than performance and speed. High standards of enginering have been maintained consistently, and even if recent designs have been conservatively progressive rather than ambitious and exciting, they have always been soundly executed.

It was, therefore, something of a departure from their traditional practice when Rover introduced a more sporting version of their 3-litre saloon for last year's Motor Show. Although termed a coupé, this model has all the mechanical features of the saloon and only details distinguish it. In justification of its name, the coupé has a lowered roof-line and more sloping rear window, which give a measure of sleekness to the body at the expense of rear seat accommodation and window height.

Unsporting in its specification and characteristics, the familiar six-cylinder engine (with overhead inlet and side exhaust valves) now develops 121 b.h.p. net at 5,000 r.p.m., and a maximum torque of 169 lb. ft. at only 1,750 r.p.m. Power-assisted steering is standard and the test car had the manual four-speed gearbox. One has the choice of Borg-Warner automatic transmission for £62 **extra**.

Although we tested an automatic saloon in *Autocar* 1 December 1961, the last manual 3-litre road test appeared almost four years ago in *Autocar* 21 August 1959. Performance comparisons with the automatic model would be unrealistic, since not only are there power losses in the transmission but the engine runs on a lower compression ratio. Development over four years has added a hundredweight to the 3-litre cars; to offset this there is a 16·5 per cent power increase.

In terms of maximum speed the test car was somewhat indeterminate; at the red sector on the rev counter (5,300 r.p.m.) in top, the true road speed was 93 m.p.h., so overdrive was necessary for the ultimate. This ratio is intended primarily as a cruising gear, showing only just over 4,000 r.p.m. at 100 m.p.h. This means that a lot of open road is needed before a true maximum is reached. When the performance figures were first measured we could do no better than a mean of 104 m.p.h., equivalent to a speedometer reading of 111 m.p.h. Since this was below expecta-

PRICES		£	s	d
Four-door Coupé		1,536	10	0
Purchase Tax		320	13	4
	Total (in G.B.)	**1,857**	**3**	**4**
Extras (including P.T.)				
Two-tone finish		12	1	8
Heated rear window		28	7	11

Window-sill stalks for locking the doors are new to Rovers. The reclining mechanism of the front seats can be seen, but not the screw jacks that adjust height over a range of 1·5in.

Rover 3-litre Coupé...

tions, the car was returned to the manufacturers for investigation, and when re-tested under still-air conditions this was raised to the mean we have printed of nearly 109 m.p.h.

Strict handbook instructions warn the driver not to go beyond the amber sector (5,300 r.p.m.) of the rev counter at the risk of serious engine damage, so we naturally observed this restriction. Scaling the measured road speeds in the gears, however, revealed our true maximum revs to have been only 5,000 r.p.m.—indicating a 7 per cent error in the instrument.

Although the tarmac road surface was dry for the standing-start acceleration measurements, the quickest times were achieved by the most un-Roverlike technique of spinning the wheels. Letting the clutch in smartly at not more than 3,000 r.p.m. caused marked rear axle tramp, and gave a 0 to 50 m.p.h. time of 11·7sec—the same as for the 1959 car. By increasing the take-off engine speed to 3,500 r.p.m. there was more wheelspin, which helped to provide a clean getaway without losing revs—lowering the time to 10·3sec.

First gear has a Vintage whine to it, which is not

The single large S.U. carburettor draws its air through a flat AC air cleaner, and alongside on the left is a separate filter for the fuel system. The dipstick is on the right under the exhaust manifold, where it gets hot

unpleasant, and unless one is really in a hurry second gear starts can be made as a normal practice. There was a pronounced engine vibration around 3,700 r.p.m. mainly on the overrun which could be felt and heard in all gears. This is quite out of character with the refined nature of the car, but on most roads one can still hustle along without exceeding 3,500 r.p.m.

Last time we tested a 3-litre with power-assisted steering it was geared to give 2·6 turns lock to lock. Although this car needed 3·2 turns, its turning circle was about 2ft less so the ratio would appear to be the same. It took time for a driver new to the car to feel at ease, the initial tendency being to take a late and consequently too big swing on the wheel. When this happens the outside front tyre digs in suddenly and one then has to back-off to keep to the chosen line. With familiarity, though, one soon appreciates the small efforts required, especially at town speeds when the wheel literally can be wound round with one finger.

Safe Cornering

Cornering characteristics are of the "fail safe" understeering variety. If a bend is taken too fast, the car simply slows itself with the aid of front tyre scrub, to the accompaniment of protesting squeals from the Dunlop RS5s. Under these extreme conditions there is appreciable body roll, most noticeable at the front, which reminds one that after all the Rover is a 34cwt saloon.

On most surfaces the ride comfort is good. Shocks from ruts and bumps are well damped, but sometimes small movements of the rubber-mounted front sub-frame can be felt through the steering wheel. Heavy braking and even sudden gear changes cause the front end to dive, but on gentle undulations there is no marked pitching to upset the passengers. Considering the large mass of unsprung weight the suspension was a very good compromise. On *pavé* there were no rattles, but some shake, especially in the steering column and instrument binnacle. At speeds above 45 m.p.h. the corrugations of a washboard surface were well smoothed inside the car.

On good roads such as the main *routes nationales* of France, long distances can be covered fast in a very comfortable and relaxed manner, so that one finishes a day's run fresh.

Controls for the driver are generally well positioned, the two vertical rows of electrical switches being practically at fingertip reach with the hands on the wheel. The most distant of the levers on the steering column (that for dipping the lamps) is the shorter. The reverse would be an improvement—or even to have both the same length. Concealed lamps give a subtle glow to the switches at night, but even on full power the variable instrument lighting seemed a bit dim. Contrary to previous Rover practice, all lamps are now wired through the main lighting switch, which has an extra position for parking that extinguishes the nearside lamps. Little ruby prisms on the top wing

Without the saloon alongside it is difficult to distinguish the coupe version, which has a lower roof line and a more sloping rear window. Small stainless steel plates bearing the Rover crest adorn the rear quarters of the roof just above the waistline

surfaces refract light to show the driver which sidelamps are lit.

The instruments have matt black bezels and are housed in and below a large hooded binnacle. It might be an improvement to slope these away from the vertical to avoid reflections from their glasses.

Lucas sealed-beam headlamps with 60-watt main filaments give tremendous spread of light with a long throw. Dipping causes a sharp cut-off which in contrast seems more abrupt than it really is. Pulling the indicator lever towards the wheel flashes the main beams—an essential for fast cars on motorways. However, to alert narcoleptic dawdlers the melodious horns had insufficient penetration.

Both front seats have exceptionally versatile adjusting mechanisms that are an object lesson in themselves. In addition to sliding and reclining adjustments, there is a screw jack that lifts the whole seat over a range of 1·5in. All shapes and lengths of drivers can settle within comfortable reach of steering wheel and pedals, and still see the tops of the front wings. On the test car, which was fairly new, the cushioning of the seats felt too firm, but experience with older examples shows this to be intentional to allow for the slight sagging that comes as the hide covering settles; and, after all, Rovers are meant to be kept for several years. On corners, though, there is little lateral support even with the central armrest down, the seat being so wide.

The geometry of the pedals is first class, and harmonizes well with natural ankle movements. It was easy to heel-and-toe with the large treadle-type throttle, which has a smooth and progressive action, and one can swivel between the brake and throttle pedals without lifting one's heel.

Pre-war Rover practice has been revived in the short, remote-control gear lever with its press-button guard for reverse. Provided one pushes the clutch pedal right to the floor, changes are silent and smooth-feeling, although 1st to 2nd cannot be hurried. When selecting 1st from rest there is a "crunch" unless one waits a few seconds with the clutch out, or pulls back very lightly towards 2nd before moving the lever forwards into 1st, thus letting the synchromesh cones stop the layshaft spinning.

To make sure that the overdrive always takes up or releases without jerking, an inhibitor switch is fitted that overrides the manual selector and prevents it operating unless there is a predetermined throttle opening. While convenient for changing into overdrive, it is annoying to have to accelerate in order to change down out of overdrive into direct top, for one normally does this to increase the engine braking when slowing down.

With vacuum servo assistance and generous rubbed areas the brakes were always reassuringly powerful. From 30 m.p.h. in neutral a pedal load of 100lb gave 1·0g retardation and the pistol-grip handbrake had much more purchase than early examples of this type, a 1-in-3 hill presenting no problems with two up and test gear on board.

By lowering the height of the cushion in the back, no headroom has been lost on the coupé, but passengers now sit with their knees up and cannot see out quite as well as in the saloon. The seats are shaped separately, making the car strictly a four-seater, although the central armrest still folds away. Between the seats is a "smokers' companion" with ashtray and electric lighter. In the front

Below: The boot is fully lined and has its own lamp. The hump on the right is the battery box, and the larger tools are clipped to a panel on the left; small tools are in a drawer under the parcel shelf inside the car. Right: The small horn-ring does not restrict the view of the large dials, or the warning lamps. The smaller instruments are under the main binnacle

Rover 3-litre Coupé...

there is another cigarette lighter under the parcel shelf alongside the twin ashtrays, which thoughtfully have false bottoms so that each time they are pulled out they appear empty.

Despite the full-width shelf and a wide, locking glove box, there was nowhere of the right shape to tuck a twin-lens reflex camera away out of sight. There are four elastic-sided map pockets, one in each front door, and two in the seat backs.

Most of the test mileage was carried out during a particularly warm spell of weather, and therefore gave us a chance to try, and appreciate, the excellent ventilation arrangements. At either end of the facia is a cool air outlet with a butterfly flap across it that can be set to direct and vary the flow to one's face or hands. Additional ducts with variable valves feed air to the feet, and a boosted draught can be supplied by the heater when set to "cold." With all the windows shut the interior can be kept refreshingly cool and airy without any wind noise at all. Even at speeds of 100 m.p.h. there is only a whisper, and conversation or the radio can be heard without straining.

Cruising at a steady 90 m.p.h. in overdrive consumed fuel at the same rate as our overall figure of 17·6 m.p.g.

Although a proportion of our 1,255 miles was on motorways at about this speed, a good deal more was across country roads in the thick of Bank Holiday traffic, so under more average conditions something approaching 20 m.p.g. would be possible.

There is much about the coupé that is traditionally Rover, and some that is new. Adjustable armrests on the front doors, high-geared window winders, a fully equipped tray of small tools under the parcels shelf—all these have been retained. New are the door locks, the best system now available, with stalks on the window sills for locking and a ratchet arrangement that stops one from turning the key the wrong way. Throughout the car the fruits of painstaking development are obvious, and the attention to detail is satisfying and surprising to an observer conditioned to modern cost-paring techniques. A nice touch is the way the rubber mouldings for gear lever gaiter and heel mat exactly match the colour of the carpets, and most of our staff also liked the unglazed finish of the dark African cherrywood.

Some cars, of which Rover is one, seem to emit an aura that manages to instil itself into the driver and passengers until they take on a measure of this character and reflect it in their driving and treatment of the car. Even the exuberance of youth would be quickly tempered after a brief spell at the wheel. Yet when a fast mood takes one the car responds eagerly, and covers distances rapidly and with inconspicuous efficiency.

Specification

Scale: 0·3in. to 1ft.

Cushions uncompressed.

ENGINE

Cylinders	... 6 in-line, water cooled
Bore	... 77·8mm (3·06in.)
Stroke	... 105mm (4·13in.)
Displacement	... 2,995 c.c. (183 cu. in.)
Valve gear	... Overhead inlet, side exhaust
Compression ratio	8·75-to-1
Carburettor	... One S.U. H.D.8
Fuel pump	... S.U. high pressure electric
Oil filter	... External full flow, renewable element
Max. power	... 121 b.h.p. (net) at 5,000 r.p.m.
Max. torque	... 169lb. ft. at 1,750 r.p.m.

TRANSMISSION

Clutch	... Borg and Beck, single dry plate, 10in. dia.
Gearbox	... Four speeds, synchromesh on upper three ratios, central floor change
Overall ratios	... O.D. Top 3·35, Top 4·3, 3rd 5·48, 2nd 8·11, 1st 14·52, reverse 12·76
Final drive	... Hypoid bevel 4·3 to 1

CHASSIS

Construction	... Integral steel body

SUSPENSION

Front	... Independent, wishbones with torsion bars, telescopic dampers, anti-roll bar
Rear	... Live axle, half-elliptic leaf-springs, telescopic dampers
Steering	... Hydrosteer, power-assisted. Wheel dia. 17in

BRAKES

Type	... Girling, vacuum servo, discs front, drums rear
Dimensions	... F, 10·75in. dia., R. 11in. dia., 2·25in. wide shoes
Swept area	... F. 260 sq. in. R. 155 sq. in. Total: 415 sq. in. (228 sq. in. per ton laden)

WHEELS

Type	... Pressed steel, 5 studs, 4·5in. wide rim
Tyres	... 6·70—15in. Dunlop RS5

EQUIPMENT

Battery	... 12-volt 57-amp. hr.
Headlamps	... Lucas 60-45-watt
Reversing lamp	... Standard, one
Electric fuses	... Four
Screen wipers	... Single-speed, self-parking
Screen washer	... Standard, Lucas electric
Interior heater	... Standard, fresh air
Safety belts	... Extra, no anchorages
Interior trim	... Hide seats, p.v.c. headlining
Floor covering	... Carpet
Starting handle	... Standard
Jack	... Screw pillar
Jacking points	... Two each side of body
Other bodies	... Saloon

MAINTENANCE

Fuel tank	... 14 Imp. gallons (inc. 1·5 reserve)
Cooling system	... 24·5 pints (inc. heater)
Engine sump	... 10 pints. Change oil every 3,000 miles. Change filter element every 6,000 miles
Gearbox and over-drive	... 4·5 pints SAE 90. Change oil every 9,000 miles
Final drive	... 3 pints SAE 90. Change oil every 9,000 miles
Grease	... 1 point every 3,000 miles
Tyre pressures	... F. and R. 26 p.s.i. (normal driving), F. and R. 30 p.s.i. (fast driving), F. 26, R. 30 p.s.i. (full load)

OVERALL LENGTH 15' 6·5"
OVERALL WIDTH 5' 0·3"
OVERALL HEIGHT 4' 11"
GROUND CLEARANCE 7·9"
WHEELBASE 9' 2·5"
FRONT TRACK 4' 7·3"
REAR TRACK 4' 8"

Make · ROVER   Type · 3-litre Coupé

Manufacturer : The Rover Co. Ltd., Solihull, Warwickshire.

Test Conditions
Weather ... Dry and sunny, with 8-17 m.p.h. wind
Temperature ... 24 deg. C. (76 deg. F.). Barometer
29·65in. Hg.
Dry concrete and tarmac surfaces.

Weight
Kerb weight (with oil, water and half-full fuel tank)
33·5cwt (3,752lb–1,702kg.)
Front-rear distribution, per cent F, 54; R, 46.
Laden as tested .... 36·5cwt (4,088lb–1,854kg.)

Turning Circles
Between kerbs .... L, 38ft 0in.; R, 40ft 9in.
Between walls .... L, 40ft 0in.; R, 42ft 9in.
Turns of steering wheel lock to lock .... 3·2

Performance Data
Overdrive top gear m.p.h. per 1,000 r.p.m. ... 23·8
Top gear m.p.h. per 1,000 r.p.m. .... 18·7
Mean piston speed at max. power ... 3,445ft/min.
Engine revs. at mean max. speed ...... 4,570 r.p.m.
B.h.p. per ton laden .... 66·3

FUEL AND OIL CONSUMPTION

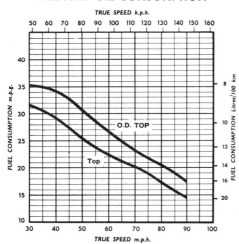

FUEL................................Premium Grade
(95-97 octane RM)
Test Distance .... 1,255 miles
Overall Consumption .... 17·6 m.p.g.
(16·1 litres/100 km.)
Normal Range .... 16-22 m.p.g.
(17·7–12·8 litres/100 km.)
OIL: S.A.E. 20W ... Consumption 4,000 m.p.g.

HILL CLIMBING AT STEADY SPEEDS

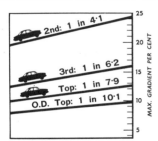

GEAR PULL	O.D. Top	Top	3rd	2nd
(lb per ton)	220	280	355	530
Speed range (m.p.h.)	48–53	46–49	43–47	35–38

MAXIMUM SPEEDS AND ACCELERATION (mean) TIMES

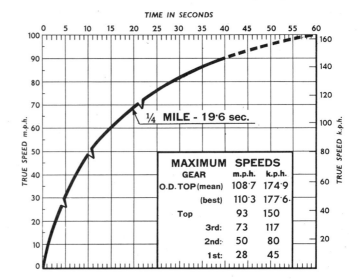

MAXIMUM	SPEEDS	
GEAR	m.p.h.	k.p.h.
O.D. TOP (mean)	108·7	174·9
(best)	110·3	177·6
Top	93	150
3rd:	73	117
2nd:	50	80
1st:	28	45

¼ MILE - 19·6 sec.

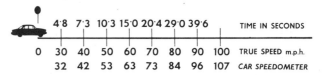

		4·8	7·3	10·3	15·0	20·4	29·0	39·6		TIME IN SECONDS
0	30	40	50	60	70	80	90	100		TRUE SPEED m.p.h.
	32	42	53	63	73	84	96	107		CAR SPEEDOMETER

Speed range and time in seconds

m.p.h.	O.D. Top	Top	3rd	2nd	1st
10—30	—	9·7	7·6	4·8	—
20—40	12·8	9·4	7·4	5·1	—
30—40	14·4	9·7	7·7	5·5	—
40—60	14·8	9·9	8·0	—	—
50—70	16·1	11·1	9·0	—	—
60—80	20·5	12·8	—	—	—
70—90	30·8	17·4	—	—	—

BRAKES (from 30 m.p.h. in neutral)	Pedal Load	Retardation	Equiv. distance
	25lb	0·22g	137ft
	50lb	0·53g	57ft
	75lb	0·88g	34ft
	100lb	1·0g	30·1ft
Handbrake		0·34g	88ft

CLUTCH   Pedal load and travel—40lb and 5in.

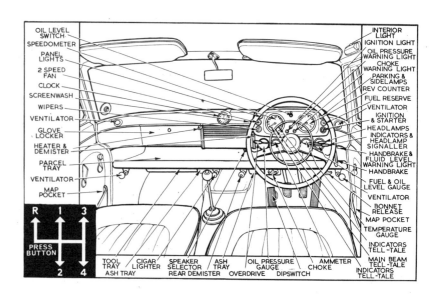

The used car buyer's guide

SPOT CHECK

The Rover 3-litre

SOME people, especially those who had run Rovers before, found the 3-litre Rover a slightly disappointing car when it first appeared. Despite its more modern design, better performance and roomier body in comparison with the classic P4 family of models, it lacked some of the niceties that many years of development and production brought to that classic series. It also suffered from a few teething troubles of the type almost inevitable with an entirely new design.

Typical of the kind of thing involved were the petrol filler arrangements. A moulded rubber hose between the tank and the filler cap seemed a neat idea; but slight porosity produced fumes in the boot and the makers reverted to the more conventional metal tube with rubber hoses at each end.

Another feature of early Mk. I cars which was soon changed was the braking system; drums were used all round and these were apt to squeal, as well as being hardly in keeping with the rest of the car. Discs were therefore adopted at the front and many of the early cars were converted.

Twelve to 18 months of intensive development work served to put these and similar things right and make the 3-litre a typical Rover—"one of Britain's fine cars" to borrow the sales depart-

ment's apt phrase. The main changes are set out in the data panel.

Today, the 3-litre takes its place as a high-grade, roomy, family car offering good handling, a maximum speed in excess of 100 m.p.h. and the smoothness and refinement synonymous with the name Rover. Unusual features include an overhead-inlet/side-exhaust valve arrangement of the type used successfully by Rover for many years, and a combination of unitary and separate chassis construction in which the engine-gearbox unit is carried on a separate, rubber-mounted sub-frame at the front, mated to a stressed hull in which girder sections are welded to the base of the shell to provide the main structure.

Bodywork

The body has no particular weak points but second-hand buyers should, of course, watch for tell-tale signs of rust. If they exist, they are likely to take the form of blisters under the paint-work round the headlamps or at the rear of the front wings and "A" posts, as these signify corrosion working through from the underside.

A point worth mentioning at this stage is that door hinges are deliberately arranged to provide some apparent play so that they can seal correctly when closed; this should not be mistaken for

worn hinges, provided that the doors obviously close satisfactorily.

On early Mk. I models some troubles were experienced with water leaks. If the front carpets show signs of having been soaked, water may have been finding its way in from the channel into which the bonnet top closes; leakage from this point can seep into the back of the glove box and so on to the floor. Liberal use of sealing compound wherever there are signs of trouble in the channel should provide a cure. If it does not, it may be necessary to remove the front wing and to attend to the drain pipe from the heater air box.

Alternatively, the source of trouble may originate in the windscreen surround. In this case the cure lies in removing the stainless-steel beading, and sealing the screen surround with compound; a new beading should then be fitted. Another occasional source of trouble lies in missing or perished rubber grommets which are used to seal unused control apertures (provided to allow for right-, or left-hand drive).

If water leaks occur in the boot, these, most likely, will be due to defective seals which prevent the lid seating properly or, on Mk. I models, to defective sealing of the wheel-arches; treatment with a suitable compound should deal with the latter.

The engine

The 3-litre engine has an excellent reputation for good service, but condition will naturally depend upon mileage and usage. On early Mk. I models, it was not possible to obtain a very even, slow tick-over because a high-lift camshaft was used, but this is not detrimental.

With the bonnet lifted, valve noise can be heard, but should not be obtrusive, and there should be no noticeable clatter from the timing chain. If the

CONTINUED ON PAGE 65

BRIEF SPECIFICATION

Engine: 6-cyl., 2,995 c.c., o.h. inlet and side exhaust valves. Net outputs: Mk. I, 108 b.h.p.; Mk. II, 121 b.h.p.

Transmission: Single dry-plate clutch, 4-speed gearbox (with synchromesh on 2, 3 and 4) and overdrive; Borg-Warner automatic transmission available as extra; divided open propshaft.

Dimensions: Length, 15 ft. 6½ in.; width, 5 ft. 9½ in.; kerb weight, approx. 33 cwt.

PERFORMANCE

Maximum speed: Mk. I (auto*), 95.0 m.p.h.; Mk. IA (O/D†), 96.9 m.p.h.; Mk. II saloon (O/D),

108.0 m.p.h.; Mk. II Coupé (auto), 102.4 m.p.h. Acceleration: 0-50 m.p.h. through gears; Mk. I (auto), 12.4 sec.; Mk. IA (O/D), 12.2 sec.; Mk. II saloon (O/D), 10.1 sec.; Mk. II Coupé (auto), 13.4 sec. 20-40 m.p.h. in direct top or kick-down range; Mk. I (auto), 5.5 sec.; Mk. IA (O/D), 9.0 sec.; Mk. II saloon (O/D), 8.5 sec.; Mk. II Coupé (auto), 5.8 sec.

Touring fuel consumption: Mk. I (auto), 20.5 m.p.g.; Mk. IA (O/D), 23.0 m.p.g.; Mk. II saloon (O/D), 22.0 m.p.g.; Mk. II Coupé (auto), 19.15 m.p.g.

Braking: From 30 m.p.h.; 31 to 33½ ft.
* Borg-Warner automatic transmission.
† Laycock de normanville overdrive.

AUTOCAR, 13 November 1964

Rover 3-litre Automatic 2,995 c.c.

ALTHOUGH British craftsmen once led the world in the sphere of top-quality specialist coachwork, taxation and the tempo of modern life have seen to it that only a handful of the old specialists remain in business today. There are, however, a select few manufacturers of production cars who manage to perpetuate on the production line much of the refinement, luxury and attention to detail that were once the exclusive right of the coachbuilders. The Rover company are one of these; and in the 3-litre saloon they have achieved in a quantity-produced car a degree of finish, comfort and silence of which even the one-off craftsmen would have been proud.

We last tested an automatic saloon in the issue of 1 December, 1961, since when the familiar six-cylinder engine has received attention from Harry Weslake, largely on the induction side, raising the output from 115 to 134 b.h.p. at 5,000 r.p.m. A somewhat more sporting Coupé version of the car was introduced at the Earls Court Show of 1962, and it was the combination of this modified engine and new model that we last tested, in the issue of 5 July last year. Performance comparisons between the two cars are not strictly valid, however, since the Coupé was fitted with a manual gearbox. In any case, the engine fitted to the automatic transmission cars has a compression ratio of 8·0

to 1 instead of 8·75, but where refinement, comfort and finish are the main criteria, performance becomes of secondary importance. The only comparisons remaining valid are the prices which are £1,858 3s 4d for the coupé and £1,707 14s 7d for the saloon, both with manual transmission and overdrive and including purchase tax.

The car tested is fitted with the Type DG Borg-Warner automatic transmission, which is available as an alternative to the normal four-speed gearbox (with overdrive as standard) for an extra cost (including P.T.) of £62 4s 7d. It has three speeds and a torque convertor, the road speed for upward and downward changes depending on the load, and the degree of throttle opening. With the selector in "Drive," at full throttle and with the kickdown switch in

PRICES	£	s	d
Four-door Saloon (Automatic)	1,463	10	0
Purchase Tax	306	9	2
Total (in G.B.)	1,769	19	2
Extras (including P.T.)			
Laminated screen	21	16	2
Heated rear window	21	2	11
Lyback fully adjustable front seats	21	15	0

How the Rover 3-litre Automatic compares:

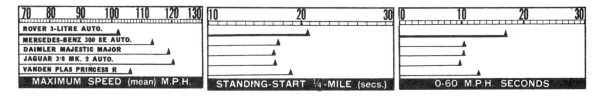

Make · ROVER   Type · 3-litre Saloon Automatic
(Front engine, rear-wheel drive)

Manufacturer : The Rover Co. Ltd., Solihull, Warwickshire

Test Conditions

Weather..............Misty and damp with no wind
Temperature .... 9 deg. C. (48 deg. F.)
Barometer.................................... 30·10 in. Hg.
Dry concrete and tarmac surfaces

Weight

Kerb weight (with oil, water and half-full fuel tank)
33·75cwt (3,780lb-1,714kg)
Front-rear distribution, per cent F. 54; R. 46
Laden as tested........ 36·75 cwt (4,116lb-1,869kg)

Turning Circles

Between kerbs .... L. 38ft 5in.; R. 39ft 5in.
Between walls .... L. 40ft 2in.; R. 41ft 2in.
Turns of steering wheel lock to lock...............3·1

FUEL CONSUMPTION

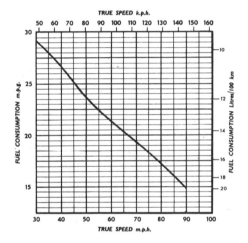

At Steady Speeds in Top:

30 m.p.h.	....	29·2 m.p.g.
40 „	....	26·7 „
50 „	....	23·9 „
60 „	....	21·3 „
70 „	....	19·4 „
80 „	....	17·3 „
90 „	....	14·9 „

Test Distance..........................	1,036 miles
Overall...............................	**15·6 m.p.g.**
	(18·1 litres/100 km.)
Estimated (DIN)	**17·7 m.p.g.**
	(15·9 litres/100 km.)
Normal range	14-20 m.p.g.
	(20·2-14·1 litres/100 km.)
Grade	Premium
	(96-98 octane RM)

OIL CONSUMPTION (SAE 20W)
3,000 m.p.g.

ROVER 3-LITRE AUTO.
MERCEDES-BENZ 300 SE AUTO.
DAIMLER MAJESTIC MAJOR
JAGUAR 3·8 MK. 2 AUTO.
VANDEN PLAS PRINCESS R AUTO.
M.P.G. Overall and Estimated (DIN)

MAXIMUM SPEED AND ACCELERATION TIMES

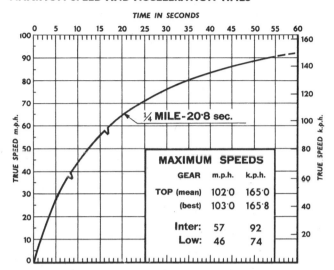

¼ MILE—20·8 sec.

MAXIMUM SPEEDS		
GEAR	m.p.h.	k.p.h.
TOP (mean)	102·0	165·0
(best)	103·0	165·8
Inter:	57	92
Low:	46	74

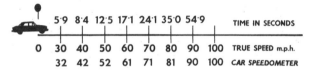

	5·9	8·4	12·5	17·1	24·1	35·0	54·9		TIME IN SECONDS
0	30	40	50	60	70	80	90	100	TRUE SPEED m.p.h.
	32	42	52	61	71	81	90	100	CAR SPEEDOMETER

Speed range, gear ratios and time in seconds

m.p.h.	Top (3·90-9·36)	Intermediate (5·60-13·43)	Low (9·10-21·84)
10—30	—	—	4·4
20—40	11·7	7·3	5·1
30—50	11·7	7·9	—
40—60	12·0	—	—
50—70	13·2	—	—
60—80	17·9	—	—
70—90	30·6	—	—

BRAKES	Pedal Load	Retardation	Equiv. distance
(from 30 m.p.h.	25lb	0·30g	100ft
in neutral)	50lb	0·65g	46ft
	75lb	0·80g	37·6ft
	80lb	0·95g	31·7ft
Hand brake		0·29g	104ft

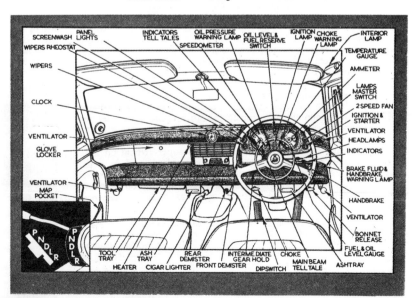

Wide door openings, plenty of leg room front and back, fully reclining front seats, hide upholstery . . . these are among the features of the comfortable interior

Rover 3-litre Automatic . . .

use, these occur from low to intermediate at 28 m.p.h. and upwards from intermediate to top at 57 m.p.h. Kickdown changes from top to intermediate can be made below 51 m.p.h., and from intermediate to low below 22 m.p.h.

Without using the kickdown, upward changes are made automatically at progressively lower speeds as the throttle opening (and therefore the load on the transmission) is reduced; they also take place as soon as one releases the throttle pedal. To avoid "hunting" between intermediate and top when hill-climbing in company with other traffic, or on a twisting road, there is an intermediate hold lever on the left of the steering column, beneath the wheel. This keeps the transmission in the middle gear to a maximum change-up point of 47 m.p.h., at the same time, permitting changes into and out of low, should the load demand it. It does not, however, give an increase in engine braking.

Finally, there is the "L" on the selector which holds the transmission in low, regardless, to nearly 50 m.p.h., (5,500 r.p.m.) when the engine begins to sound unhappy. This position of the selector is useful in extremely hilly country, as it provides engine braking on the overrun.

Though the automatic transmission slows the acceleration down a bit by comparison with the four-speed manual gearbox, the getaway is not sluggish except when the gearbox oil is cold. The transmission is particularly restful in heavy traffic, when the car will creep at well below walking pace. Here are a few comparisons between the performance of this car and of the 3-litre Coupé with manual transmission (Road Test published 5 July, 1963): 0-60 m.p.h., 17·1 sec (15·0 sec); standing ¼-mile, 20·8 sec (19·6 sec); mean maximum speed, 102 m.p.h. (108·7).

In general, gear changes—upward and downward—are smooth enough. Curiously though, on the car under test upward changes into top, particularly, were never quite up to the smoothness of a clean, well-controlled change on a manual box. Perhaps one becomes super-critical on a car whose progress is otherwise so exemplary, and in which silence and smoothness are of such a high standard. Though one's skill at anticipating changes, and catering for them with adjustments of the throttle, increases with experience of

the car, one never quite avoids the slight surge on changing up, or the check when changing down. For silky-smooth chauffeuring the technique is to start with very little throttle, so that top comes in early and smoothly, and then to accelerate reasonably gently to the required speed.

The engine started immediately first time, with or without the choke, in the reasonably warm weather of the test period. There was, however, less chance of its stalling when the selector was moved from "N" to "D" if the choke was used for the initial few seconds of moving off. There is a choke warning lamp which comes on when the engine has reached its working temperature. At all speeds, from tickover to maximum, the engine was soothingly quiet and it is only in contrast to this that we said it began to "sound unhappy" when talking of high revs earlier on.

On the open road one can carry on a conversation in perfectly normal tones right through the speed range. There is almost complete absence of mechanical noise; and, with all windows closed, there is scarcely more than a hiss of air at the front quarter ventilators—even at full speed. Very little sound is transmitted by the suspension from the road wheels to the interior. On motorways the cruising speed is a comfortable, relaxed 90 m.p.h., with the speedometer needle—accurate at this end of the scale—wandering up to the 100 on slight downhills, and occasionally even into the red sector (which begins at 105 m.p.h.) if one does not keep an eye on it. This entirely effortless covering of the miles is one of the car's most endearing features—this, and the ease with which it purrs through traffic.

Though the Rover is a big car, with a kerb weight of nearly 34 cwt, it never seems a handful. This is partly owed

The larger tools are stowed in a compartment to the left of the luggage locker. The spare wheel is carried on a tray beneath the locker floor—and can therefore be removed without disturbing the luggage—and the compartment has its own light

There is considerable "tumble-home" at the level of the door sills, so that the body cannot be damaged against high kerbs

to the excellent view of the road ahead from the driving seat, with reasonably slender screen pillars well back and out of one's line of vision, and the fact that the width is judged very easily. The front corners are exactly where they seem to be, indicated by the practical and sensible little red sidelamp tell-tales. It is also owed to the power steering now standard on all 3-litre models.

Almost all the effort of moving the wheel, which with a big car can be a strain at manoeuvring speeds and in traffic, is removed. Also, it has been possible, because of the power assistance, to raise the steering ratio so that instead of 4·2 turns of the wheel from lock to lock it requires only just over 3. There still remains plenty of feel and at the limit of adhesion one can detect without any doubt the moment that the front wheels start to slide. Directional stability, due to slight and desirable understeer, is first class, the car proceeding arrow-like along a straight road without any conscious help from the driver; it is unaffected by sidewinds.

Driving relatively slowly on twisting roads, there is sometimes quite an appreciable degree of roll, partly because with the very light, high-geared steering one tends to turn the wheel more quickly, and perhaps more acutely, than one really needs to. On the other hand, when taken round a fast, open road corner the car keeps to a very even keel, only an intermittent little rolling "tremor" indicating the strong lateral forces. At all times the Rover feels safe and reassuring, and adhesion in the wet is first class.

The ride in front is very comfortable, helped by good seats which will support one all day without discomfort. The suspension smooths out bigger undulations well, and is affected only by such "unexpecteds" as ramps where new road surfaces are being laid, and by potholes. Over the *pavé* and washboard test surfaces the ride was smooth, and the whole structure gave a feeling of great strength and stiffness.

There is plenty of leg room at the back even when the front seats are fully to the rear end of their slides and the ride and comfort of the seat are completely in keeping with the rest of the car. One is as comfortable in the back as in the front, and as relaxed even after a long day's drive. At 54in, the width is sufficient for three people, though not lavish. Rear doors are good and wide, and even the stiff-limbed have no trouble getting in and out.

Brakes are by Girling, with vacuum-servo assistance, discs at the front and drums at the rear. Their performance is every bit up to stopping this heavy car repeatedly from high speeds. Their feel could not be more reassuring, though the pedal pressure required is slightly heavier than one expects. The handbrake would just about hold the car

on a 1-in-4 gradient facing up or down, but was not man enough for the 1-in-3 either way round. The automatic transmission, as one would expect, moved the car off smoothly on the steeper slope. The handbrake lever is the push-pull type, tucked away but accessible beneath the instrument panel to the right of the steering column, and has a sensibly bright warning light marked "Brake." This tells when one has forgotten to release it and serves as a warning light when the brake fluid level is low.

Interior finish and appointments are excellent, with extensive use of the coachbuilder's traditional materials of leather and mahogany. On the car tested, individual front seats were fitted, though a bench seat is available optionally with automatic transmission cars. These seats have fully reclining backrests, and are adjustable (within a range of nearly 2 in.) vertically for height, as well as having the normal fore-and-aft movement. One would need to be a curious shape indeed if, with all these adjustments, it were not possible to get comfortable and relaxed! Each seat has a separate centre armrest, and the armrests on the doors are adjustable for height without using tools.

Except for the mahogany panel that runs right round the interior, curving neatly from the front doors into the facia, almost everything in front of the driver is finished in matt black leather or paint. This includes the main instrument bezels, so that there are no reflections on the screen by day or night. At first one gets the impression that there are rather too many tumbler switches on the hooded instrument panel, and stalks on the steering column (seven of one and four of the other). These are all logically positioned, however, and so easy to reach that one quickly grows accustomed to them, and one's hand goes straight to the right one at night, which is criterion enough. The switches work in a horizontal plane, and rheostats are incorporated in the panel lighting and wiper motor switches.

There is a two-way switch for the sidelamps, with a separate stalk on the steering column operating the heads— but only when the lights switch is over to the right. With

Overhead inlet, side exhaust . . . the engine is mostly hidden by the large, flat AC aircleaner, though such components as the distributor, coil, dipstick and oil filler are unusually easy to reach

the switch to the left the parking lamps go on—rightside front and rear, without the number plate lighting. There is, however, no safety device to prevent the absent-minded from driving off with only the parking lamps switched on. The longer stalk to the right of the steering column operates the turn indicators and the headlamp flasher.

Wipers sweep a wide area of the screen, and the blades remain in contact with the screen whatever the road speed of the car. There are courtesy lights above each door, coming on automatically when the appropriate door is opened; each can be turned on and off, irrespective of the door, by its own switch. There is a small diameter full-circle horn ring on the steering wheel. Also, very much in the Rover tradition, the fuel reserve switch produces an accurate oil level reading on the fuel gauge. This incidentally, is now operated by a positive switch. On the last car tested one had to hold a spring-loaded switch in the "on" position until the hot-wire fuel gauge reached a steady reading. In our test report we commented on this and it is typical of Rovers that this minor irritation has now been removed.

Further indications of the attention to detail that is apparent throughout the car are the automatic reversing lamps, which come on when the selector lever is put at "R"; and the heater element (an extra) included in the glass of the rear window, which quickly clears condensation. It includes in its switch a warning light, as otherwise it is impossible to tell when the element is turned on. There are childproof safety locks on the rear door handles and the rear view mirror is of the panoramic type, tailored to suit the size and shape of the rear window, so that the view astern is very good.

At both ends of the parcels shelf (which badly needs a non-slip surface to keep parcels from sliding about) there are controls which allow cool air into the car at toe-board level, and there are further cool air inlets in the upper edge of the facia at face level. For cold weather, the fresh-air-heating and demisting system is very powerful, so that with the various controls at one's disposal any required degree of warmth-plus-fresh-air can be achieved quickly.

Headlamp range is ample, both on main and dipped beams, though the softness of the front suspension seems accentuated at night by the dip of the beams under braking and the lift on acceleration. It is perhaps better to set the beams somewhat too low than too high, to avoid annoying approaching traffic when one accelerates, even with the beams dipped.

A minor point, which is of great help in keeping the interior clean and smart, is that there are no door sills to the front compartment—where most of the mud and dirt seems to find its way—so one can sweep such rubbish straight out through the doors.

Quiet, smooth and comfortable, the 3-litre Rover with Borg-Warner automatic transmission as tested is one of the most relaxing cars in traffic that we have yet driven. On the open road it covers the miles in an equally relaxed, long-legged manner. It is beautifully finished, and it gives a lasting impression, however rough the road, of great strength and rigidity.

Specification: Rover 3-litre Automatic

PERFORMANCE DATA
Top gear m.p.h. per 1,000 r.p.m. .... 20·6
Mean piston speed at max. power .... 3,171 ft/min.
Engine revs. at mean max. speed .... 4,951 r.p.m.
B.h.p. per ton laden .... 64·6

▼ *Scale: 0·3in. to 1ft. Cushions uncompressed.*

ENGINE
Cylinders	...	6-in-line
Bore	...	77·8mm (3·06in.)
Stroke	...	105·0mm (4·13in.)
Displacement	...	2,995 c.c. (183 cu in.)
Valve gear	...	Overhead inlet, side exhaust
Compression ratio		8·0-to-1
Carburettor	...	One S.U. H.D.8
Fuel pump	...	S.U. dual inlet electric
Oil filter	...	External full-flow, renewable element
Max. power	...	119 b.h.p. (net) at 4,600 r.p.m.
Max torque	...	161 lb ft at 2,500 r.p.m.

TRANSMISSION
Gearbox	...	Borg-Warner Type DG, with torque-convertor
Gear ratios	...	Top 1·0-2·40; Inter 1·42-3·30; Low 2·30-5·52; Reverse 2·00-4·80
Final drive	...	Hypoid bevel 3·9 to 1

CHASSIS
Construction	...	Integral with steel body

SUSPENSION
Front	...	Independent, wishbones with laminated torsion bars, telescopic dampers, and anti-roll bar
Rear	...	Live axle, half-elliptic leaf-springs, telescopic dampers
Steering	...	Hydrosteer, power-assisted, worm and peg
Wheel dia.	...	17in.

BRAKES
Type	...	Girling, vacuum-servo, discs front drums rear
Dimensions	...	F, 10·75in. dia; R, 11in. dia; 2·25in. wide shoes
Swept area	...	F, 260 sq in.; R, 155 sq in. Total 415 sq in. (232 sq in. per ton laden)

WHEELS
Type	...	Pressed steel, 5 studs, 4·5in. wide rim
Tyres	...	Dunlop RS5 6·70—15in.

EQUIPMENT
Battery	...	12-volt 57-amp. hr.
Headlamps	...	Lucas sealed beam 60-45 watt
Reversing lamp	...	Standard
Electric fuses	...	3
Screen wipers	...	Variable-speed, self-parking
Screen washer	...	Standard, Lucas electric
Interior heater	...	Standard, fresh air with two-speed blower
Safety belts	...	Extra, anchorages provided
Interior trim	...	Hide seats, leather-cloth headlining
Floor covering	...	Carpet
Starting handle	...	Standard
Jack	...	Screw pillar
Jacking points	...	2 each side
Other bodies	...	Coupé

MAINTENANCE
Fuel tank		14 Imp. gallons (inc. 1·5 reserve)
Cooling system		24 pints (inc. heater)
Engine sump	...	11 pints SAE 20W. Change oil every 3,000 miles; change filter element every 6,000 miles
Gearbox	...	15 pints ATF Type A. Change oil every 12,000 miles
Final drive	...	3 pints SAE 90EP. Change oil every 9,000 miles
Grease	...	1 point every 6,000 miles
Tyre pressures	...	F, 24; R, 22 p.s.i. (normal driving) F, 26; R, 30 p.s.i. (full load) F, 30; R, 34 p.s.i. (fast driving with load)

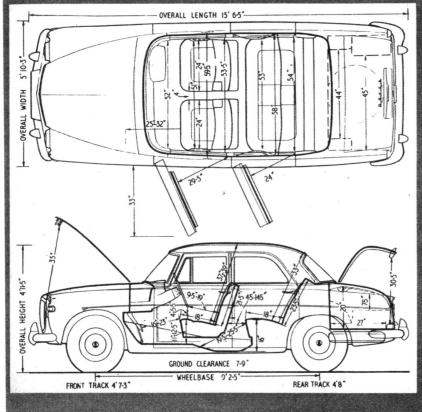

The Rover 3-litre

An unusual view of the Rover 3-litre engine—the air-cleaner has been removed to show the cylinder-head and valve cover.

CONTINUED FROM PAGE **59**

latter occurs it could denote a faulty hydraulic tensioner or lack of oil pressure.

Visual inspection will show any bad oil leaks and these should be regarded with suspicion because the engine is normally a fairly clean unit apart from a little inevitable seepage from the base of the clutch housing; excessive oil at this point, however, suggests a faulty rear-main-bearing seal and the car is best left alone, unless it is worth a replacement engine. Roughness may be due to faulty engine mountings, but the only way to confirm this is by replacing them, as visual inspection does not help.

The cost of a complete re-conditioned engine, less auxiliaries but complete with clutch, is £68, excluding fitting. All major components and assemblies, incidentally, can be replaced under a service exchange scheme.

Transmission

The clutch should normally be smooth, but if judder occurs it can be due to a worn centre bearing in the propeller shaft, and this is a relatively inexpensive item to renew. Be sure that the trouble does, in fact, lie at this point because otherwise clutch replacing may be necessary.

Mk. I and IA models had a long gear lever with a slightly whippy action which, however, is quite satisfactory once you become used to it. Later types have a very good remote control.

The gearbox itself, like most others, produces some noise on bottom and reverse gears, but should be fairly quiet on the upper ratios. Equally, no noticeable sound should come from the rear axle. If it does, make sure that the trouble really is in the axle and not the result of fitting of certain all-weather types of tyre which produce a growl very much like a worn axle.

The 3-litre, incidentally, is sensitive to the tyre equipment and the maker's recommendations are Dunlop C41 or Avon HM New Safety for the Mk. I and Mk. IA models and Dunlop RS5 or Avon Turbospeed for Mk. II models. Radial-ply tyres are not favoured as they produce heavy steering and a hard ride on this car.

IDENTITY PARADE Mk I MODEL

September 1958: 3-litre model first announced.
August 1959: disc front brakes replaced drums in production; heavy-duty starter also fitted.
September 1959: moulded-rubber petrol filler hose replaced by metal tube with rubber connections to eliminate fumes in boot.
March 1960: Girling Mk. II brake servo, and electric screen washer fitted.
June 1960: improved main-bearing oil seal introduced; further improvements to fuel tank breathing to reduce fumes in boot.
September 1960: more powerful heater.
October 1960: introduction of latest 2nd-speed start Borg-Warner automatic transmission; also hand-brake warning light and stainless-steel body mouldings.
December 1960: optional power steering introduced.
May 1961: 5-point engine mounting adopted.

Mk IA MODEL

September 1961: Mk IA model introduced; improvements included brake-fluid level and hand-brake warning light, twin electric fuel pumps (one for reserve), electrically operated intermediate hold on B-W transmission, combined hub-and-wheel-trim plates (of stainless steel), improved bumper mountings, improved distribution of heater air, addition of hinged ventilators to front door windows and removal of former louvres above front and rear windows.

Mk II MODEL

September 1962: Mk II model introduced; new features include engine with Weslake head giving extra 13 b.h.p. net, improved floor mounted gear lever and close-ratio box, lowered suspension (1 in.), new exhaust system, dual fuel pump (instead of two), deletion of brake vacuum reservoir, revised instrument, adoption of Dunlop RS5 tyres, improved front seats.
February 1963: Mk II Coupé introduced with lower roof line, extended windscreen and rear window, swivelling ventilators on all doors, front seats adjustable for height, rake and reach, and power steering as standard.

On the road

The steering should give accurate control with slight understeer tendencies and, provided that suitable tyres are fitted, any troubles in handling are likely to be due to unbalanced wheels or to worn steering or suspension joints (which can also cause a front-end clank). Be careful of front suspension irregularities on early cars, however, as these could be expensive to repair.

On cars with power steering, a slight click may be noticeable if the wheel is waggled with the car stationary. This is quite normal and no cause for worry. Similarly, a slight groan or sigh may be heard when the steering is moved over on to full lock, but this again is functional and not harmful; it is merely the blow-off valve working. Owners of power-steered cars should be careful not to run the engine with the steering pressed hard against a kerb on full lock as this can cause internal damage,

Spares

The spares position on 3-litre models is excellent and appropriate literature is available, including a workshop manual at 30s.

Previous Spot checks

Vauxhall Victor I	March 14 1964
Ford Consul Mk. II	March 21
Austin A30/35	March 28
Standard 8/10	April 4
Renault Dauphine	April 11
Morris Minor	April 18
MG TD/TF	April 25
Hillman Minx Series III . . .	May 2
B.M.C. 1½-litre "Farinas" . . .	May 9
Standard Vanguard III	May 16
Ford 100E	May 23
Triumph TR2/TR3	May 30
Austin A40	June 6
Jaguar 2.4/3.4	June 13
Vauxhall Velox/Cresta	June 20
Skoda Octavia	June 27
Triumph Herald	July 11
B.M.C. Sixes	July 25
B.M.C. Minis	August 8
VW 1200	August 15
Sprite I and II	September 5
Rover P4	September 19
Ford Cortinas	October 3
Wolseley 1500 and Riley 1.5 ,	October 17
Vauxhall Victor FB	November 7
Citroen DS/ID/DW and Safari .	November 21
Volvo B16 and B18	December 5
Fiat 600 and 600D	December 19
Hillman Husky	January 9 1965
Saab	January 23
The Big Healeys	February 6
Ford Anglia 105E/123E . . .	February 13
Simca 1000	February 27
Renault 4L	March 27
XK Jaguars	April 3
Ford Capri and Classic . . .	April 17
Triumph Spitfire	May 1
Armstrong Siddeley Sapphires .	May 15
Ford E93 variants	May 29
Peugeot 403	June 12
B.M.C. 1100s	June 26
Hillman Imp	July 10

Autocar ROAD TEST
NUMBER 2078

Rover 3-Litre Coupé Mk III 2,995 c.c.

AT A GLANCE: Exceptionally quiet car offering armchair comfort for four. Fully adjustable seats give excellent driving position. Controls very light, including the high-geared power-assisted steering. Too much roll on corners, and brakes overheated during fade test. Many gadgets and refinements for the enthusiast owner. A fast car providing really relaxed travel.

MANUFACTURER

The Rover Co. Ltd., Solihull, Warwickshire

PRICES

Basic	.. ..	£1,600 0s 0d
Purchase Tax	.. ..	£334 17s 11d
Total (in G.B.)	..	£1,934 17s 11d

EXTRAS (INC. P.T.)

Heated rear window	..	£28 7s 11d
Passenger headrest	..	£12 1s 8d
Twin-speaker Radiomobile radio	.. .. ..	£43 1s 11d
Front safety belts (each)	..	£5 0s 0d

PERFORMANCE SUMMARY

Mean maximum speed	..	107 m.p.h.
Standing start ¼-mile		19.6 sec
0-60 m.p.h.	.. ..	15.3 sec
30-70 m.p.h. (through gears)		15.4 sec
Overall fuel consumption		18.2 m.p.g.
Miles per tankful	.. ..	255

AS a true definition, a coupé is a closed two-seater; in the Rover version it is interpreted as a lowered roofline variation of the 3-litre saloon, with a more flowing look to the exterior and with a number of adaptations for the enthusiast owner in the interior and fittings.

At last year's London Show the latest Mark III versions of both saloon and Coupé were announced. No significant mechanical improvements have been made since their introduction three years ago, and the 3-litre 6-cylinder engine still develops the same maximum power of 121 b.h.p. at 4,800 r.p.m. A small increase in weight, making the new Coupé ¾cwt heavier, has had no measureable effect on the acceleration figures, and the performance through the gears is within a second of the previous car's times right up to 80 m.p.h.

Except for the newly announced 2000 TC, for which a maximum of 112 m.p.h. is claimed, the Coupé is the fastest of the Rover range. In favourable conditions it can exceed 110 m.p.h., although the high gearing of overdrive top makes it susceptible to wind, and the mean for two-way runs worked out at 107 m.p.h. The term "cruising speed" has little meaning in the 3-litre, as the car effortlessly sustains any speed which the driver chooses, right up to the maximum, with only small increases in the low level of wind and mechanical noise; the quietness and ease of the Rover's fast cruising is one of its most impressive features.

Mechanical refinement extends even to the action of the starter motor, which is quiet enough for the occupants not to notice its action. It is usually necessary to operate the rich mixture control for the first start of the day, but if its T-handle is inadvertently left out, a bright amber warning lamp ahead of the driver lights up when a predetermined engine temperature is reached.

Automatic transmission remains an option for both the saloon and the Coupé, and the basic transmission is a 4-speed gearbox, with the standard overdrive working on top gear. The car was tested in this form, and nearly all who drove it criticized the out-of-character whine and slight harshness in bottom gear, sufficient to encourage an early change up to the quieter second.

The remote-control gear lever has a fairly long travel and the lever action is light and positive, but some drivers did not like the "feel" of the gear lever knob with its reverse stop button on the top. The button has to be depressed only a little way to allow the lever to move left into the reverse gate. There is no synchromesh for first gear, but on the three upper ratios it is effective,

AUTOCAR, 6 May 1966

Autocar Road Test 2078

MAKE: **ROVER**

TYPE: **3-litre Coupé Mk III**

TEST CONDITIONS
Weather dry, cloudy-bright with 5 m.p.h. wind
Temperature .. .. 11 deg. C. (52 deg. F.)
Barometer .. .. .. 30·5in.Hg.
Surfaces.. .. .. Dry concrete and asphalt

WEIGHT
Kerb weight (with oil, water and half-full fuel tank):
34·25 cwt (3,836lb-1,822kg)
Front-rear distribution, per cent F, 53·3; R, 46·7
Laden as tested 37·25 cwt (4,172lb-1,974kg)

TURNING CIRCLES
Between kerbs .. L, 38ft 8in.; R, 39ft 0in.
Between walls .. L, 40ft. 6in.; R, 40ft 10in.
Steering wheel turns lock to lock .. .. 3·25

PERFORMANCE DATA
Overdrive top gear m.p.h. per 1,000 r.p.m. 23·8
Top gear m.p.h. per 1,000 r.p.m. .. .. 18·7
Mean piston speed at max. power 3,300ft/min
Engine revs at mean max. speed (o.d.) 4,600 r.p.m.
B.h.p. per ton laden .. .. 61·5

OIL CONSUMPTION
Miles per pint (SAE 20) 500

FUEL CONSUMPTION
At constant speeds in overdrive (direct top in brackets)
30 m.p.h. .. .. .. 31·0 (28·0) m.p.g.
40 m.p.h. .. .. .. 32·0 (26·5) m.p.g.
50 m.p.h. .. .. .. 29·0 (23·8) m.p.g.
60 m.p.h. .. .. .. 25·2 (21·3) m.p.g.
70 m.p.h. .. .. .. 22·0 (17·9) m.p.g.
80 m.p.h. .. .. .. 19·2 (16·0) m.p.g.
90 m.p.h. .. .. .. 16·7 (13·7) m.p.g.
Overall m.p.g. 18·2 (15·6 litres/100km.)
Normal range m.p.g. 16-23 (17·7-12·3 litres/100 km)
Test distance (corrected) .. .. 1,666 miles
Estimated (DIN) m.p.g. 20·0 (14·1 litres/100km.)
Grade .. .. .. Premium (96·2-98·6 RM)

m.p.h.	O.D. Top	Top	Third	Second	First
	3·35	4·3	5·48	8·11	14·52
10—30	—	9·1	7·3	5·0	—
20—40	11·9	9·0	6·4	4·9	—
30—50	12·5	9·3	7·3	5·7	—
40—60	13·7	9·8	8·8	—	—
50—70	16·1	10·8	9·0	—	—
60—80	18·8	13·1	—	—	—
70—90	23·9	19·4	—	—	—

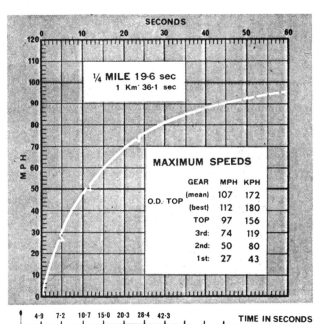

¼ MILE 19·6 sec
1 Km 36·1 sec

MAXIMUM SPEEDS
GEAR		MPH	KPH
O.D. TOP	(mean)	107	172
	(best)	112	180
TOP		97	156
3rd:		74	119
2nd:		50	80
1st:		27	43

TIME IN SECONDS

TRUE SPEED MPH
INDICATED MPH

BRAKES
	Pedal load	Retardation	Equiv. distance
(from 30 m.p.h. in neutral)	25lb	0·39g	77ft
	50lb	0·75g	40ft
	75lb	1·0g	30·1ft
Handbrake		0·42g	72ft

CLUTCH Pedal load and travel—35lb and 5in.

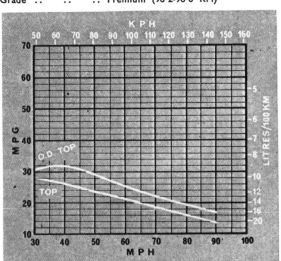

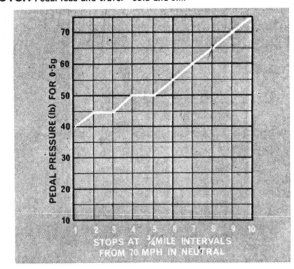

STOPS AT ¼ MILE INTERVALS FROM 70 MPH IN NEUTRAL

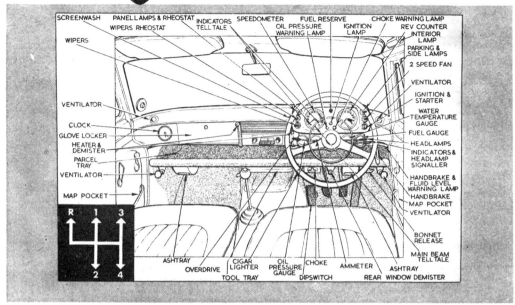

Rover 3-litre...

allowing quiet gear changes no matter how rapidly the lever is moved.

An inhibitor prevents engagement of overdrive on a trailing throttle, but this becomes a nuisance when the driver wants to slip into o.d. top at fairly low speeds, and is even more inconvenient when it prevents the overdrive from disengaging until the throttle is opened quite a long way. Although overdrive provides such effortless cruising (95 m.p.h. at only 4,000 r.p.m.) it does not reduce acceleration as much as in some cars, so there is less need than usual to switch in and out of overdrive. The control switch is mounted on the left side of the steering column, and can just be reached without taking one's hand from the wheel.

In previous tests of the 3-litre we have commented on engine vibration at high revs, and in this respect the latest Coupé was much better than earlier cars. Although the Rover is given a sporting flavour and fitted with a rev counter, its engine is far from being high-revving. A yellow warning sector changes to red at 5,200 r.p.m. on the rev counter, and is best heeded for the most efficient through-the-gears acceleration. For all ordinary driving it seems to suit the car's dignity much better, and costs little in performance, to change gear early, often as low as 3,000 r.p.m.

Part of the relaxed and effortless feeling that goes with the car undoubtedly is given by the lightness of all the controls, particularly the steering. Hydrosteer power assistance is standard on both saloon and coupé, and the mechanism is high-geared with a varying ratio that increases the effectiveness of small movements of the wheel towards full lock; only $3\frac{1}{4}$ turns are needed between the stops. Such low effort, high-geared steering takes a little while to get used

to, particularly when driving on slippery roads, as there is no indication of just how hard one is cornering. Used intelligently, it is easy and satisfying to weave the car along winding lanes with so little muscular effort. Response about the central position is less definite. Nose-heavy weight distribution contributes to excellent straight-line stability at speed and freedom from side-wind effects.

Cornered fast, the 3-litre goes round without fuss and with the predictable behaviour of a pronounced understeerer. Although not too noticeable from within, the amount of heeling over on corners is very obvious to bystanders. The Rover suspension is designed mainly for comfort, and certainly there is excellent insulation from all the smaller irregularities of

ordinary roads; all thumps and resonances seem to be effectively absorbed in the rubber suspension mountings. Just occasionally, sharp humps and dips in the surface catch the suspension out and provoke lively vertical movement of the whole car, taking the edge off an otherwise first-class ride. On *pavé* the car tended to buck about at low speeds, smoothing out to an exceptionally stable ride at about 55 m.p.h.

Hand-in-hand with comfortable springing go improved seats, on the lines of those in the 2000. They are, if anything, slightly firmer than before, but better shaped, giving good support in the small of the back and holding occupants firmly in place on corners. A side lever controls the ample range of fore and aft adjust-

Sound damping materials are used on the underside of the bonnet and on the bulkhead to further reduce the already low level of engine noise. Though no space is wasted, access under the bonnet is good

All four doors open wide, and are held by strong keeps. A single interior lamp above each door is turned on by opening the respective door or by its attached switch. A full width panels shelf, locking facia compartment, and front door pockets give ample space for oddments

ment, and there is a small, low-geared winding handle under each front cushion for raising or lowering the whole seat vertically. A third adjustment is the Bache friction lock for back-rest angle. The forward spring-loading of the backrest is too weak, and it is sometimes necessary to pull the backrest up again from the reclining position. The whole arrangement allows each driver to select his ideal seating position.

The steering column is not adjustable, but an unusual feature is that the angle of the drop down centre armrest between the front seats can be set in any of a number of positions, controlled by a small lever at the side. The armrest is mounted on the driver's squab, so that it remains in place if the passenger decides to recline. All four doors have adjustable side armrests.

A further refinement for the Mark III is the option of headrests for any of the four seats, and one was fitted to the front passenger seat of the test car. It adjusts both to and fro as well as vertically, but most passengers preferred not to use it. It includes a reading lamp, with a separate on-off switch, for the passenger behind.

In the front doors, the swivelling quarter lights are parallelogram shape, instead of triangular, and there are opening vents also in the rear doors. At the expense of some wind whistle when they are opened, they help to ensure a through-flow of air in the car. Because of the high scuttle line, most drivers like to set the seat high for best visibility, and then find that the roofline of the Coupé has been brought down to give only a small clearance between head and roof lining. However, the good suspension comes to the rescue and even when Continental main road humps were taken fast, our heads did not touch the roof.

Since our last 3-litre Rover test we

have introduced brake fade tests and the Girling mixed-disc and drum servo-assisted brakes of the Coupé did not like the routine at all. Pedal loads increased steadily, but even though—by the 10th stop—clouds of smoke from the linings showed that the brakes had had enough of arresting 35 cwt from 70 m.p.h., they were still functioning, but with reduced efficiency. Given more normal road use, they are responsive to light pressures, though with rather more pedal travel than is usual, and are capable of a 1g stop in response to a firm 100lb shove on the pedal. The handbrake has a pull-out lever under the facia, and provides just enough leverage to hold on 1 in 4. Near it is a com-

bined warning lamp for low brake fluid level or forgotten handbrake.

As well as the improved seating, a lot of rearranging and minor improvements to the interior layout have been made. The clock is now recessed in the extreme left of the facia panel, a long way from the driver, but still visible, and the clock itself has its own tiny battery, charged from the car battery. The tool tray is relocated centrally below the full width parcels ▶

Automatic interior lamps are provided in both the engine compartment and the luggage boot. The spare wheel is carried on a wind-down tray beneath the boot floor, and the battery is in the covered box on the right

Full length side rubbing strip, ending in three chrome squares, identifies the Mark III model. All doors can be locked from within, and a ratchet device prevents the key from being turned the wrong way, whether locking or unlocking either of the front doors

		MAXIMUM SPEED (mean) M.P.H.	STANDING-START ¼-MILE (secs.)	0-60 M.P.H. SECONDS	M.P.G. Overall
TOTAL Approx. PRICE	£1,935	Rover 3-litre coupé	Rover 3-litre coupé	Rover 3-litre coupé	Rover 3-litre coupé
	£1,572	Humber Super Snipe	Humber Super Snipe	Humber Super Snipe	Humber Super Snipe
	£1,605	Jaguar 3·8 Mark 2	Jaguar 3·8 Mark 2	Jaguar 3·8 Mark 2	Jaguar 3·8 Mark 2
	£2,355	Mercedes-Benz 230 automatic	Mercedes-Benz 230 automatic	Mercedes-Benz 230 automatic	Mercedes-Benz 230 automatic
	£1,180	Wolseley 6/110 automatic	Wolseley 6/110 automatic	Wolseley 6/110 automatic	Wolseley 6/110 automatic

HOW THE ROVER 3-LITRE COUPÉ Mk III COMPARES:

Rover 3-litre...

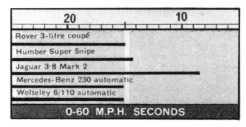

A two-speed heater control, and the front-rear speaker balance control for the radio, are mounted on the propeller shaft tunnel

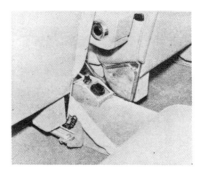

When the rear centre armrest is lowered, a picnic tray including recesses for two cups, can be dropped down to the horizontal. A separate cigarette lighter and ashtray are recessed between the rear seats

shelf, and pulls forward on slides as a picnic or map table.

In the rear compartment, the main change is the tailoring of the individual seats, again on the Rover 2000 pattern, and inclusion of a drop down picnic tray with recesses for two cups or glasses, concealed behind the centre armrest. There is also an extra 2½ in. legroom in the rear compartment as a result of improved shaping of the front seat backrests.

On the Mark III two separate wiper switches are used. The lower one is an on-off switch in the same place as before, and above it is a rheostat control for wiper speed. In heavy rain we timed 66 sweeps per minute on the maximum setting, against 54 on the slow speed. The switch which used to give the oil level indication on the fuel gauge has been dropped, and its place is taken by the changeover switch for the 1½-gallon fuel reserve.

Not only did we obtain almost precisely the same performance as with the Coupé we tested in 1963, but also the identical oil consumption figure of 500 miles to the pint. However, the m.p.g. figure has increased to 18.2, a good consumption for a big car.

The fresh air heater, with scarcely audible two-speed fan, now has outlets to the back with an individual two-speed control. There is sufficient air-flow to, and warmth for, the rear compartment. A feature of the coupé is the positioning of two large main instruments in the binnacle ahead of the driver, with separate instruments beneath for oil pressure, water temperature, amps and fuel level. Drivers would appreciate a better rear mirror than the small diminishing one fitted.

The main attraction of the Rover Coupé is its ability to travel far and fast in a quiet and relaxed manner.

The car has been developed steadily over eight years and in this latest model, the accent has been on passenger comfort and lavish standard equipment.

SPECIFICATION : ROVER 3-LITRE COUPÉ Mk III FRONT ENGINE, REAR-WHEEL DRIVE

ENGINE
Cylinders .. .. 6, in line
Cooling system .. Water; pump, fan and thermostat
Bore 77.8mm (3.06in.)
Stroke 105mm (4.13in.)
Displacement .. 2,995 c.c. (183 cu. in.)
Valve gear .. .. Overhead inlet, inclined side exhaust
Compression ratio 8.75-to-1; optional 8-to-1 (certain exports)
Carburettor .. One S.U. HD8
Fuel pump .. Two S.U., rear mounted
Oil filter .. .. AC Delco full flow
Max. power .. 121 b.h.p. (net) at 4,800 r.p.m.
Max. torque .. 160 lb ft (net) at 2,650 r.p.m.

TRANSMISSION
Clutch .. .. Borg and Beck, 10in. dia.
Gearbox 4-speed
Synchromesh on three upper ratios; overdrive standard.
Gear ratios .. Top 1; OD Top 0.78; Third 1.27; Second 1.89; First 3.37; Reverse 2.97
Final drive .. Spiral bevel 4.3 to 1

CHASSIS AND BODY
Construction .. Welded steel subframe carring engine, transmission, front suspension and steering, steel body integral with chassis

SUSPENSION
Front .. .. Independent, laminated torsion bars, anti-roll bar, and telescopic dampers
Rear .. .. Live axle, semi-elliptic progressive rate leaf springs, telescopic dampers

STEERING
Worm and peg .. With Hydrosteer power assistance
Wheel dia. .. 17in.

BRAKES
Make and type .. Girling, disc front, drum rear
Servo .. .. Girling AHV 689 vacuum-type
Dimensions .. F, 10.75in. dia.; R, 11in. dia. 2.25in. wide shoes
Swept area .. F, 260 sq in.; R, 154.4 sq in.
Total .. .. 414.4 sq. in. (222 sq in.) (per ton laden)

WHEELS
Type .. .. Pressed steel disc, 5 studs, 5in. wide rim
Tyres .. .. Dunlop RS5 tubed.
Size .. .. 6.70—15in.

EQUIPMENT
Battery .. .. 12-volt 57-amp hr.
Generator .. Lucas C.42 30-amp.
Headlamps .. Lucas F700 sealed 45/75 watt

Reversing lamp .. Standard
Electric fuses .. 11
Screen wipers .. Variable speed, self-parking
Screen washer .. Lucas electric, standard
Interior heater .. Fresh-air blending, standard
Safety belts .. Extra; anchorages provided
Interior trim .. Leather seats, p.v.c. headlining
Floor covering .. Pile carpet with felt underlay
Starting handle .. Standard
Jack .. .. Mechanical Bevelift
Jacking points .. Two each side under sills, between wheels
Other bodies .. Saloon

MAINTENANCE
Fuel tank .. .. 14 Imp gallons (1.5 gal. reserve) (64 litres)
Cooling system .. 26 pints (including heater) (14.8 litres)
Engine sump .. 10 pints (5.5 litres) SAE 20. Change oil every 5,000 miles; change filter element every 5,000 miles
Gearbox and overdrive .. 3 and 1.5 pints SAE 90EP and 20W. Change oil every 10,000 miles
Final drive .. 3 pints SAE 90EP. Change oil every 10,000 miles
Grease .. .. 1 point every 5,000 miles
Tyre pressures .. F, 26; R, 26 p.s.i. (normal driving) F, 30; R, 30 p.s.i. (fast driving) F, 30; R, 34 p.s.i. (full load)

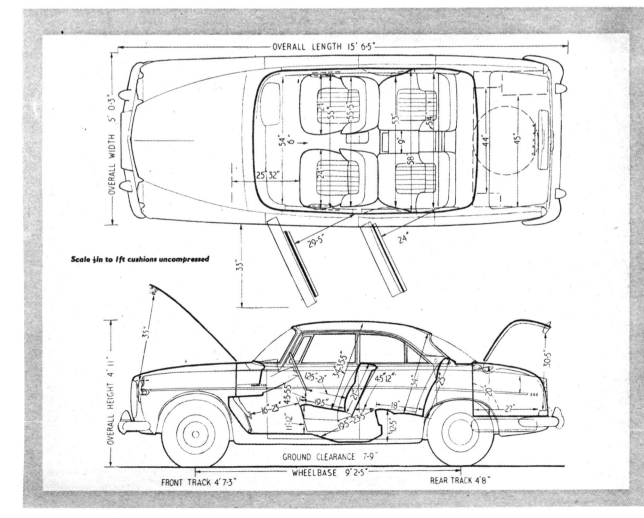

Scale ¼in to 1ft cushions uncompressed

FOR OLDER MEN

Comfort and luxury personified in the 3-litre Rover Mk. III Coupe

OLD age is a miserable business, as the late Somerset Maugham so graphically explained. Sight and hearing are impaired, the palate wearies, you tire quickly and are beset by ailments. You continue to look at women but they do not look at you. Approaching this unhappy state reactions slow and you tend to drive slowly along in the middle of the road, obstructing others—although I note that this is also a habit of many drivers but half my age. . . .

These thoughts were brought on when, going to Rover's London depot to collect for test a 2000TC, I was given instead a 3-litre Mk. III.

When the enthusiastically-announced Rover 2000 was a new car, MOTOR SPORT published a full road-test report on it and we later added further to our initial impressions of this loudly-acclaimed newcomer. But that was a long time ago, November 1963 and January 1964, respectively, and as a considerable amount of development work has since been done by the Solihull engineers, I thought it would be a good idea to re-assess the Rover 2000, in its latest, faster TC form.

Alas, the car I was to have tried was involved in an accident and has not, to date, been repaired—what a lot of Press cars become unavailable at the last moment from this cause these days! We were to have had a reconciliation with Alfa Romeo by driving a Giulia Veloce but this, also, was crunched by a lorry or something just before I saw it. Anyway, that is how I came to be driving about in a massive 3-litre Rover, a car which in appearance seems to have just happened, for surely it cannot have been " styled " ?

Within, though, it is mighty comfortable and very fully equipped in a notably individualistic style. The leather-upholstered seats are particularly restful, the gears can be changed quite pleasantly by a central lever, reverse safeguarded by a press-button in the lever-knob. Bottom gear whines, the others are quiet. This 4-speed transmission is supplemented by overdrive controlled by a l.h. steering-column stalk, but this is not effective on a trailing throttle, nor is it possible to get overdrive to disengage at small throttle openings. This is mildly inconvenient and I prefer positive selection, if one must have o/d at all.

Every comfort has been built into this big Rover. The front seat squabs recline after a Bache friction-lock has been released, fore-and-aft adjustment is controlled by a side lever, and a rather protuberant winding handle at the front of each seat enables its cushion to be wound up or down. If the passenger decides the old man drives reasonably and wishes to recline, the driver's central arm-rest is unfolded, remaining in place as her seat-squab is lowered; having its own range of adjustment. The four side arm-rests are similarly adjustable. Head-rests can also be provided for any of the four seats; they incorporate reading lamps for those behind if fitted to the front seats.

The speedometer and tachometer are set high before the driver in a separate nacelle, and are flanked by vertical batteries of flick-switches, one for putting the wipers into action, another for controlling their speed, others for 2-speed heater fan and side/parking lamps, while there is rheostat instrument lighting control and, particularly commendable, a fuel-reserve switch—would that all cars had one.

Another individual feature of the 3-litre Rover is that the subsidiary instruments are set in separate nacelles, as it were, below the main panel—a Lucas ammeter and Jaeger oil-pressure gauge, fuel gauge and thermometer. This leaves the facia, which

like the window cappings, is of African cherry wood, clear of dials except for an electric clock, angled at the extreme left, this running off its own battery, charged from the main battery. There is a lockable wooden-lidded cubby-hole, the radio, if fitted, occupies the centre of the facia, and beneath it there is a deep, full-width parcels' shelf, supplemented by stiff-topped door pockets.

Ventilation is looked after by aircraft-type thumb-adjusted flap-valves, brought in by separate knobs, at the facia-sill extremes, openable parallelogram-shaped front and back quarter-lights and very neat, clearly-labelled heater/demister vertical quadrant levers, one each side of the radio panel. The rear-window can be electrically demisted from a knob under the facia, the front-seat passenger has a big under-facia covered ash-tray, and clear, labelled warning lamps for convenient pull-out handbrake on/low brake fluid level and choke in use, are additional Rover refinements. The dip-switch is a proper treadle, a cigar lighter is fitted, and a rather small-diameter horn-ring circles the steering wheel. Courtesy action of individual roof lamps (with their own switches) as a door is opened, thick carpets with underfelt, counter-balanced bonnet and boot-lid with automatic illumination of the compartments they normally cover, front/rear radio-speaker balance and 2-speed heater control on the propeller-shaft tunnel in reach of all occupants, a tool-tray which draws out from under the facia to form a shelf, and a tray with two cup-holders in the rear-seat folding centre arm-rest, add to the comfort and convenience of Rover owners.

In a country in which speed is officially discouraged I think there is quite a lot to be said for motoring in quiet and comfort. The 3-litre Rover is extremely comfortable, in its own characteristic style, while its degree of hush must be close to that of the World's most expensive luxury cars—yet it costs only just over £2,000.

There is a saloon version for bulky people or people who crave a bulkier car, but the low-roofed coupé has adequate room in its rear compartment, with separate-type seatings, for two people, and another on the arm-rest, and there is an enormous boot with the spare wheel in a wind-down container under its floor.

It was when I came to go quickly in the 3-litre Rover that my enthusiasm diminished. I have never liked Hydrosteer power-assisted steering and while that on the car from Solihull was better than that of the only 4-litre R-type Vanden Plas I have driven, it was far from perfect. Visibility to the near-side was restricted, the servo-assisted Girling disc/drum brakes were spongy and not very reassuring, and the degree of roll on corners, even before the 6.70 × 15 Dunlop RS5s protested, was not to my liking. Maybe I really am senile, for several of my friends whom I regard as discerning drivers love their 3-litre Rovers, or profess to. To me, however, this big Rover seems to be an inexpensive luxury car for the older motorist. . . .

The test car had a tendency to engine stalling, even when warm, at disconcerting moments, and its diminishing rear-view mirror was scarcely a safety factor. By judicious use of the rather odd overdrive I obtained 19.8 m.p.g. of premium petrol, and after 670 miles the 121-b.h.p. 77.8 × 105 mm. (2,995 c.c.) 6-cylinder engine would have liked about a quart of oil. Incidentally, there is more individuality in the power unit, where inlet valves set above side-by-side exhaust valves prevail. . . .

The side rubbing strips along the body sides end, amusingly,

CONTINUED ON PAGE 81

JOHN BOLSTER describes and tests

THE NEW ROVER 3.5 V8

OVER many years, the Rover Company built up a reputation for producing very refined cars of the highest class. On the Continent the six-cylinder Rover was habitually regarded as a smaller Rolls-Royce, and no car was better made and finished. Recently the old firm has successfully entered a different market with the 2000 and 2000 TC models. Nevertheless, there are those who find these four-cylinder cars lacking in the more gentle virtues, and for them the announcement of the new 3.5 Litre will come as a most welcome surprise.

Basically the body structure stems from the well-known 3 Litre 6-cylinder Rover, a car that gained in speed, silence and road-holding with every year of production. It is sensible to retain such a well-developed chassis and to endow it with an ultra-modern engine. The unit chosen is an over-square light-alloy V8, distantly related to an American forbear but now very British with its twin SU carburetters. With a capacity of 3528 cc, the eight-cylinder Rover engine develops a gross output of 184 bhp at 5200 rpm, or 160.5 bhp as installed. Not only is the V8 more powerful than its predecessor, but it is much lighter, the weight saving being 200 lb. It is mounted in unit with a torque converter and a 3-speed automatic gearbox, with a short central selector lever mounted on the console. This moves in a quadrant on which the various positions are indicated, with faint illumination at night to make selection easy. D2 gives only the upper two gears for smooth town driving or slippery surfaces, but D1 gives all three speeds for maximum performance. There is an L position for retaining a low gear and in addition to the ordinary neutral there is a parking lock. In front the suspension is by wishbones and laminated torsion bars, Hydrosteer power-assisted steering being standard. At the rear the rigid axle is on semi-elliptic springs with progressive rate characteristics. There are disc front and drum rear brakes, with a vacuum servo.

It is easy to distinguish the V8 from the "six", for there are many styling differences. These include full-length body side mouldings with repeater flasher lamps, a pointed coach line underneath, and a deeper front lower body panel and wings. The radiator grille is also new and so are the wheels. The interior is beautifully furnished and the fairly high seats are extremely comfortable.

When I first drove the new Rover, I was absolutely astonished at its silence. This is a really quiet car, whether the engine is idling or pushing the vehicle along at 90 mph. Driving through London with the lever at D2, I greatly appreciated the silence and smoothness of the Rover. Other cars sounded remarkably noisy and the radio could be enjoyed irrespective of the speed. By changing into D1, I altered the character of the car completely. It then felt really lively, accelerating briskly past slower cars and changing into top just below 70 mph. Some engines simply do not suit automatic gearboxes but this one does, and it makes light of the considerable weight which is a penalty of such luxury.

The Rover is a heavy car but it is light to handle, the power-assisted steering being impossible to fault. It has greater cornering power than its six-cylinder predecessor and its rear axle is better behaved. The car understeers initially, but less as the driver becomes confident and makes use of the good roadholding. One is reminded of the dear old Rover 90, in which one sat high up and really threw the machine about, in spite of its dignified appearance. The brakes have no tendency to fade during hard driving, remaining smooth and powerful at all times. A speed of 115 mph is claimed by the makers. This I was able to attain under favourable conditions, but I was satisfied to time the car at 108 mph both ways. Incidentally, there is a red mark on the speedometer dial between 115 and 120, but nothing untoward took place when I invaded this area. The car feels as though it is scarcely moving at a genuine 90 mph, the effective ventilation allowing the windows to remain closed.

The high seating position gives a good all round view, in spite of the unfashionably shallow windows. Actually, the appearance is pleasing, the Rover having great dignity, in spite of its raffish new wheels. Nevertheless, quite a few casual passers-by were critical of these wheels, and I think the makers would be wise to offer an alternative type to their more conservative customers. All the occupants travel in great comfort and the quality of the upholstery and trim gives a great sense of well-being. The cushions have evidently been chosen to match the springing of the car and as a result I was able to cover some long journeys with no sensation of fatigue. Even the way in which the doors close is satisfying. Except when the engine is warm, it is necessary to use the cold-start knob. The engine starts easily but can be a bit tricky and inclined to stall thereafter, though I soon became used to this. To endow a substantial car with a lively performance must entail an appreciable consumption of 100 octane fuel. Continuous high speeds will result in a petrol consumption of 16 mpg or so, but more normal driving is likely to improve this figure by at least 2 mpg.

The new 3.5 Litre Rover is a phenomenally quiet car of great refinement. It is a worthy successor to a long line of Rover "sixes" and adds a useful turn of speed to their many virtues.

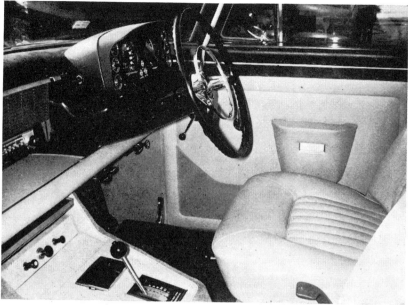

MAX. SPEED 108 M.P.H.

¼ MILE

ROVER 3·5

M.P.H. / SECONDS

SPECIFICATION AND PERFORMANCE DATA

Car Tested: Rover 3.5 Litre 4-door saloon, price £1999 3s 4d including PT.

Engine: Eight cylinders, 88.9 mm x 71.12 mm (3528 cc). Pushrod-operated overhead-valves. Compression ratio 10.5 to 1. 184 bph (gross) or 160.5 bhp (net) at 5200 rpm. Twin SU carburetters. Lucas coil and distributor.

Transmission: Hydraulic torque converter and 3-speed automatic gearbox, ratios 1.0, 1.45 and 2.39 to 1. Open propeller shaft. Hypoid rear axle, ratio 3.54 to 1.

Chassis: Combined steel body and chassis. Independent front suspension by wishbones and laminated torsion bars. Hydrosteer power-assisted steering. Rigid rear axle on semi-elliptic springs. Telescopic dampers all round. Disc front and drum rear brakes with vacuum servo. Pressed-steel chromium-plated wheels with exposed nuts, fitted 6.70-15 ins tyres.

Equipment: 12-volt lighting and starting. Speedometer. Ammeter. Fuel gauge. Water temperature gauge. Clock. Heating, demisting and ventilation system. Variable speed windscreen wipers and washers. Flashing direction indicators. Heated rear window (extra). Radio (extra). Reserve petrol control.

Performance: Maximum speed: 108 mph. Standing quarter-mile: 18 secs. Acceleration: 0-30 mph, 4 secs; 0-50 mph, 8.8 secs; 0-60 mph, 12.4 secs; 0-70 mph, 18.4 secs.

Fuel Consumption: 16 to 18 mpg.

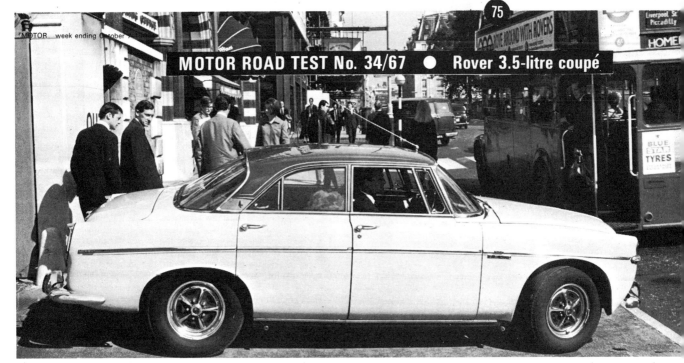

MOTOR week ending October 7

The "alloy" wheels which are a feature of the new car are made of pressed steel, chromed and painted.

Power with pomp

' . . . lifted into the high performance class by its new engine . . . considerable improvement in handling . . . . '

WHEN you add two cylinders, 40 b.h.p. and 50 lb.ft of torque to the engine of a car and lop 200 lb. off its weight, you can expect it to go quicker, and this the new Rover 3.5-litre certainly does. Compared with the 3-litre automatic which we tested in 1966, the new V-8 (automatic transmission as standard) has a top speed of over 110 m.p.h. instead of 101.2 m.p.h., and even with the gearbox set to its "leisurely" D2 mode, will accelerate from rest to 60 m.p.h. in 14.1 seconds against the 17 of the older car. The comparison is not quite exact because the earlier test car was a saloon and this one the coupé, and the figures show how the big Rover has been lifted into the high performance class by its new light-alloy 160.5 b.h.p. V-8 engine. As explained elsewhere in this issue, the V-8 has been developed by Rover from the famous General Motors power unit which has also been the progenitor of the Repco-Brabham Grand Prix engine. So many who regard this Rover—with its wood-panelled interior and four thick, leather armchairs—as being the finest London club on wheels, will now have to accept it as being the fastest as well.

But high performance is of little use to prospective buyers of this sort of car unless it is achieved with dignity and restraint. Here again, the new engine and transmission score for in general they are as quiet and smooth as those of the best American cars. And the Rover is so well insulated from all sources of noise that a Jeeves-like calm nearly always prevails; even when the engine is at its most discreetly agitated it emits nothing more than a purposeful hum.

Two other benefits accrue from the V-8 installation. The first is

an unchanged overall fuel consumption, despite the great increase in performance, and the second is the considerable improvement in handling brought about by the 200 lb. weight reduction, most of it at the front. Roll, understeer and tyre squeal have all been reduced.

The new engine has inflated the price by only £65 to £2,097 at which the car is excellent value for money. Only in such matters as the ride on rough surfaces and a certain imprecision of the handling when pressed hard, does the basic chassis design show its age.

Performance and economy

One excellent American design feature has unfortunately been left out by Rover in their Anglicizing work on the GM unit: the reliable, foolproof automatic choke which is usually to be found on a big U.S. V-8. Instead, there is the traditional Rover T-handle under the facia which must be pulled out for Cold Start. So long as the engine fires immediately, everything works well: it runs and pulls smoothly when the transmission is put into drive, making a faint, dry rattle until the alloy block reaches its working temperature—a warning light on the facia glows after a minute or two when the choke should be returned. However, on several occasions our test car refused to start at once, and thereafter required several minutes of churning and juggling with throttle and choke before it would, and even then tended to stall when put into gear.

These occasional fits of temperament conquered, a gentle pressure on the accelerator pedal sends the car wafting effortlessly forward into the seventies and beyond. Most of the time the engine merely whispers the car along with the proverbial turbine-like smoothness characteristic of good V-8s; at around 4,500 r.p.m., which is as much as the automatic transmission normally allows it, the note rises to an unobtrusive hum, while if Lockup is selected to hold revs to the 5,200 r.p.m. which is red-lined on the tachometer, the hum becomes a trifle insistent but never loud.

Continued on the next page

PRICE: £1,705 plus £392 10s tax equals £2,097 10s. Radio £42 1s 3d extra with tax, heated rear window £28 17s 8d extra with tax, total as tested £2,168 8s 11d.

Rover 3.5-litre coupé
continued

Just how quick this car has become with its new engine can be seen by comparing the acceleration figures of the V-8 (coupé) with those of the 3-litre (saloon):

	V-8 coupé	3-litre saloon
	(manual auto)	(manual auto)
0– 30 m.p.h.	3.8 sec.	5.6 sec.
0– 40 m.p.h.	5.5	8.1
0– 50 m.p.h.	7.8	11.4
0– 60 m.p.h.	10.7	15.8
0– 70 m.p.h.	14.6	21.4
0– 80 m.p.h.	19.7	29.4
0– 90 m.p.h.	27.3	45.2
0–100 m.p.h.	39.3	
Standing ¼-mile	18.4	20.8

In both cases these are the best figures, obtained by using Lockup to hold the engine to maximum revs in each gear. The 0-60 m.p.h. acceleration time has been reduced by over five seconds, while the 0-90 m.p.h. time is down by no less than 17.9 s. At the time our mean lap speed of 110 m.p.h. was recorded on the banked track at MIRA, the direction of the wind was such as to build up maximum speed just before one banked turn rather than on one of the straights, so the best quarter-mile (obtained from the times achieved on these straights) was the same as the overall maximum. Nevertheless, the car was being slowed by the bankings so there is perhaps justification for Rover's claim of a 115 m.p.h. maximum in neutral conditions, especially as our road test car was a low mileage example.

To satisfy its 10.5:1 compression ratio, 100 octane fuel is necessary but the Rover offsets this to a large extent by allowing owners the option of having their cake and eating it, for the overall fuel consumption of 17.2 m.p.g. is virtually identical to that of the 3-litre. Most cars will be driven in a more stately fashion than is the custom of our test staff, and should have no trouble in attaining around 19 m.p.g., which with a fuel tank capacity (including reserve) of 15½ gallons gives a range of nearly 300 miles.

Transmission

The Borg-Warner 35 automatic gearbox offers the driver three kinds of travel. In D2, only the Intermediate and High gears are used to give progress which is smooth and deceptively leisurely— the quoted 0-60 m.p.h. time of 14.1 seconds is quick enough to keep the car well ahead of most others. Upward and downward changes are only noticeable if you happen to be looking for them, except perhaps for the full-throttle upward change from Intermediate to High which occurs at 70 m.p.h. and 4,500 r.p.m. and is a little more obvious. A certain amount of dignity can be sacrificed for alacrity by selecting D1, in which Low gear is used as well as Intermediate and High during full-throttle take-offs or when kicking down below about 40 m.p.h. With a change from Low to Intermediate at just over 40, this improves the 0-60 m.p.h. time to a respectable 11.7 seconds with the penalty of an occasional violent thump when kicking down into Low, or when Low engages automatically as the car slows down. Full performance—which means knocking another second off the 0-60 m.p.h. time—can be extracted by using Lockup to hold the engine to its red-lined 5,200 r.p.m. maximum in Low and Intermediate (equivalent to 49 and 80 m.p.h.), a procedure which is only likely to be adopted when the excellence of Father's car is being demonstrated to a girl-friend!

Inheritance of both the final drive and the gearbox ratios of the previous car means that the 3.5-litre is set up to attain maximum speed at maximum engine revs. As the Rover engineers insist that these revs should not be exceeded, they have taken the unusual step of red-lining the speedometer (which was 3½ m.p.h. fast at 100 m.p.h.) at the theoretical maximum speed of 115 m.p.h.— and this, of course, is in addition to the red line on the tachometer. Something more of an overdrive ratio for top gear might be expected (at least for export users) of a car of this kind, but in fact the chosen

Performance

Conditions

Weather: Warm and dry.
Temperature 58°–61°F. Barometer 29.60 in. Hg.
Surface: Dry concrete and tarmacadam.
Fuel: Super Premium 101 octane (R.M.), 5 star rating.

Maximum speeds

	m.p.h.
Mean lap banked circuit	110.0
Best one-way ¼-mile	110.0
Intermediate } at 4,500 r.p.m.	70.0
Low	42.0

"Maximile" speed: (Timed quarter mile after 1 mile accelerating from rest)
Mean 107.0
Best 108.3

Acceleration times

m.p.h.	D2 sec.	D1 sec.	Manual Control sec.
0-30	5.4	3.9	3.8
0-40	8.1	5.6	5.5
0-50	11.1	8.4	7.8
0-60	14.1	11.7	10.7
0-70	18.2	15.6	14.6
0-80	24.3	21.6	19.7
0-90	32.3	29.8	27.3
0-100	44.3	41.8	39.3
Standing quarter mile	20.5	18.8	18.4

	Kickdown D2		Kickdown D1
m.p.h.	sec.		sec.
10-30	3.8		2.9

20-40	4.9	3.2
30-50	5.7	4.5
40-60	6.0	6.1
50-70	7.1	7.2
60-80	10.2	9.9
70-90	14.1	14.2
80-100	20.0	20.2

Brakes

Pedal pressure, deceleration and equivalent stopping distance from 30 m.p.h.

lb.	g	ft.
25	0.40	75
55	0.98	31
Handbrake	0.43•	70

Fade test

20 stops at ½g deceleration at 1 min. intervals from a speed midway between 30 m.p.h. and maximum speed (=70.0 m.p.h.).

	MAXIMUM SPEED	ACCELERATION
	75 80 85 90 95 100 105 110 115 120 125 130 135	24 22 20
Rover 3.5-litre coupe £2,097	m.p.h.	seconds
Vauxhall Viscount £1,397		
Vanden Plas Princess R £2,030		
Jaguar 420 £2,064		
Rambler Ambassador £2,295		
Mercedes 250S £2,724		

The large leather armchairs at the front have a wide range of fore-and-aft adjustment. The armrests on the doors are adjustable for height.

The front seats are unusual in having a wind-up adjustment for height.

Above: In the coupé version of the car, rear seat head and legroom is rather cramped.

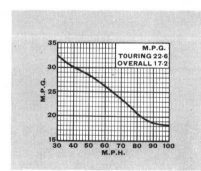

A second picnic tray at the rear folds down from above the armrest.

	lb.
Pedal force at beginning	23
Pedal force at 10th stop	23
Pedal force at 20th stop	27

Speedometer

Indicated	10	20	30	40	50
True	11	21	31	40½	50
Indicated	60	70	80	90	100
True	58½	67½	77½	86½	96½
Distance recorder					accurate

Steering

Turning circle between kerbs: ft.
Left 37½
Right 38
Turns of steering wheel from lock to lock . . 2.7
Steering wheel deflection for 50 ft. diameter circle . . . . 1.0 turns

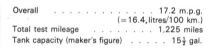

Fuel consumption

Touring (consumption midway between 30 m.p.h. and maximum less 5% allowance for acceleration) 22.6 m.p.g.

Overall . . . . 17.2 m.p.g.
(= 16.4 litres/100 km.)
Total test mileage . . . . 1,225 miles
Tank capacity (maker's figure) . . . . . 15½ gal.

Weight

Kerb weight (unladen with fuel for approximately 50 miles) . . . . 31.4 cwt.
Front/rear distribution 51.5/48.5
Weight laden as tested . . . . 35.1 cwt.

Parkability

Gap needed to clear a 6 ft. wide obstruction parked in front:

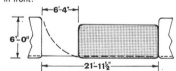

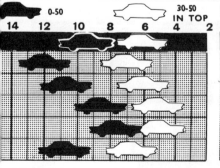

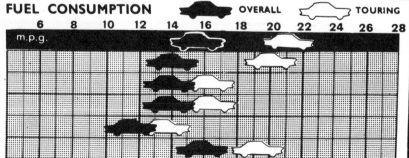

From the rear, only a discreet "3.5-litre" motif distinguishes the V-8 car from the old 3-litre.

Under the slide-out picnic tray at the front is a nest of tools.

The choke, fuel reserve and air vent knobs shown in this picture are all out of reach to a driver wearing a seatbelt, as is the handbrake.

Safety Check List

Steering assembly

Steering box position	Well forward
Steering column collapsible	No
Steering wheel boss padded	No
Steering wheel dished	No

Instrument panel

Projecting switches	Yes
Sharp cowls	Yes
Padding	Above and below facia

Windscreen and visibility

Screen type	Toughened (laminated optional)
Pillars padded	No
Standard driving mirrors	Interior
Interior mirror framed	No
Interior mirror collapsible	No
Sun visors	Crushable

Seats and harness

Attachment to floor	Via slides
Do they tip forward?	Yes
Head rest attachment points	Yes
Back of front seats	Padded
Safety harness	3-point
Harness anchors at back	Yes

Doors

Projecting handles	Yes
Anti-burst latches	No
Child-proof locks	No

Rover 3.5-litre coupé
continued

arrangement pays off, for in addition to providing the excellent acceleration already discussed, it is quite possible to cruise at well over 100 m.p.h. with the radio comfortably audible and the engine sounding quite unstrained.

Handling and brakes

Like almost all power steering systems (with a few shining exceptions) the Hydrosteer variable ratio unit fitted to the Rover gives little feel of the road; instead there is a slight "frictional" resistance at the wheel which remains constant regardless of cornering or parking forces. It is perhaps this characteristic which led to a slight divergence of opinion among our test staff: one group felt that the car handled well, but the other was a little less enthusiastic.

Under virtually all driving conditions the feelings of the No. 1 group are fully substantiated—the Rover does handle well. The lightness and apparent precision of the steering make it easy to weave through traffic and manoeuvre in confined spaces, and if the boy racer's imaginary helmet is substituted for the chauffeur's cap, the car can be hurled into corners with considerable abandon. Roll, understeer and tyre squeal are less than in the old 3-litre and many other cars of the same size, so the 3.5 can be pressed quite hard through the twists and turns of "back doubles" without undue discomfort or much noise from the Dunlop RS5 tyres. This improvement in agility is the result of an engine that is some 200 lb. lighter than before, together with harder damper settings and the same spring stiffness—ride height is maintained unaltered at the front by turning the torsion bars in their mountings.

Both traction and adhesion are good in the wet. Wheelspin is rarely provoked, however hard you stamp on the accelerator (when in D1), and it is possible to get tyre squeal on quite wet surfaces during cornering, showing that the treads are doing a good job of clamping on to the road from which they have first squeegeed the water.

Understeer, however, remains aplenty, although there is enough power to bring the tail round a little on the slower corners. Hard cornering involves large, coarse movements of the steering wheel because although this variable ratio system gives 2.7 turns for a fairish lock, it is at its lowest geared near the straight-ahead position. Near full lock it speeds up to reduce wheel winding in low-speed and parking manoeuvres.

The minor misgivings of our No. 2 group were to some extent confirmed when the car was hustled fast along winding country roads: a certain difficult-to-define imprecision in the steering then made itself apparent, and this tended to induce a slight feeling of insecurity. It is only fair to add that very few examples of the 3.5-litre are likely to be driven in this way—we passed quite a few sedately conducted examples of the older 3-litre models when doing so. However, the same feeling of insecurity was associated with travelling at more than 100 m.p.h. on certain types of surface in a straight line, which is rather less forgiveable.

The good 0.98g maximum deceleration was achieved with a

The 8.7 cu. ft. capacity of the boot is not outstanding for a large car, but its shape did not suit our angular boxes, and there was room for some soft luggage.

14" X 11" X 5"

21" X 15" X 7"

24" X 18" X 8"

Specification

Engine

Cylinders	. . . .	8 in vee formation
Bore and stroke	. . . . . .	88.9 mm. x 71.12 mm.
Cubic capacity	. . . .	3,528 c.c.
Valves	. . . .	pushrod o.h.v.
Compression ratio	. . . . .	10.5:1
Carburetters	. . . . . .	2 SU HS6
Fuel pump	. . . . . .	AC-Delco mechanical
Oil filter	. . . .	Full flow
Max. power (net)	. . .	160.5 b.h.p. at 5,200 r.p.m.
Max. torque (net)	. . . .	210 lb. ft. at 2,600 r.p.m.

Transmission

Clutch	. . . . . .	Borg-Warner torque converter
High gear	. . . .	1.00–2.10
Intermediate	. . . . . .	1.45–3.20
Low	. . . .	2.39–5.02
Reverse	. . . .	2.09
Final drive	. . . . .	Hypoid bevel, 3.54:1
M.p.h. at 1,000 r.p.m. in:—		
High	. . . .	22.4
Intermediate	. . . . . .	15.4
Low	. . . .	9.4

Chassis

Construction	. . . .	Unitary

Brakes

Type	. . . . .	Girling discs/drums with Lockheed vacuum servo
Dimensions	. . . .	Discs 10¾ in. dia.; drums 11 in. dia.
Friction areas:		
Front	. . .	27.12 sq. in. of lining operating on

260 sq. in. swept area of disc

Rear	. . . .	74.8 sq. in. of lining operating on 154.8 sq. in. swept area of drum

Suspension and steering

Front	. . . .	Independent by unequal length wishbones, laminated torsion bars and an anti-roll bar
Rear	. . . .	Live axle on semi-elliptic leaf springs
Shock absorbers:		
Front	. . . .	Woodhead-Monroe telescopic
Rear	. . . .	
Steering gear	.	Hydrosteer power-assisted worm and peg variable ratio
Tyres	. . .	6.70–15
Rim size	. . .	5J

Coachwork and equipment

Starting handle	. . . .	No
Jack	. . . . .	Screw pillar
Jacking points	. . .	Two each side under sills
Battery	. . . . .	12-volt negative earth, 57 amp. hrs. capacity
Number of electrical fuses		12
Indicators	. . . . .	Self-cancelling flashers
Screen wipers	. . . .	Variable speed electric
Screen washers	. . . .	Electric
Sun visors	. . . .	2
Locks:		
With ignition key	. .	Doors
With other key	. .	Boot
Interior heater	. . . .	Fresh air front; recirculating rear
Extras	. . . .	Heated rear window, lami-

		nated screen, headrests
Upholstery	. . . . .	Hide
Floot covering	. . . .	Carpet
Alternative body styles	.	Saloon

Maintenance

Sump	. . . . .	10 pints SAE 10W-30
Gearbox	. . . . .	14½ points SAE AQ/ATF Type A
Rear axle	. . . . .	3 pints SAE 90 EP
Steering gear	. . . .	Castrol TQ, Duckhams Holmatic ATF, Esso automatic trans. fluid
Cooling system	. . .	16 pints (3 drain taps)
Chassis lubrication	. . .	None
Minimum service interval	.	5,000 miles
Ignition timing	. . . .	6° b.t.d.c.
Contact breaker gap	. .	0.014-0.016 in.
Sparking plug gap	. . .	0.025 in.
Sparking plug type	. . .	Champion L87Y or AC 43FS
Tappet clearances	. .	Not applicable—hydraulic tappets
Valve timing:		
Inlet opens	. . . .	30° b.t.d.c.
Inlet closes	. . . .	75° a.b.d.c.
Exhaust opens	. . .	68° b.b.d.c.
Exhaust closes	. . .	37° a.t.d.c.
Front wheel toe-in	. .	0 ± 1/16 in.
Camber angle	. . . .	2°
Castor angle	. . . .	1°
King pin inclination	. .	4.5°
Tyre pressures:		
Front	. . . . . .	26 lb./sq. in.
Rear	. . . . . .	26 lb./sq. in.

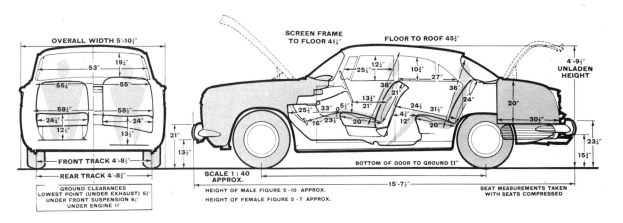

OVERALL WIDTH 5'-10½"
SCREEN FRAME TO FLOOR 41½"
FLOOR TO ROOF 45½"
4'-9½" UNLADEN HEIGHT
FRONT TRACK 4'-8½"
REAR TRACK 4'-8½"
GROUND CLEARANCES
LOWEST POINT (UNDER EXHAUST) 5¼"
UNDER FRONT SUSPENSION 6¼"
UNDER ENGINE 11"
SCALE 1 : 40 APPROX.
HEIGHT OF MALE FIGURE 5-10 APPROX.
HEIGHT OF FEMALE FIGURE 5-7 APPROX.
BOTTOM OF DOOR TO GROUND 11"
15'-7½"
SEAT MEASUREMENTS TAKEN WITH SEATS COMPRESSED

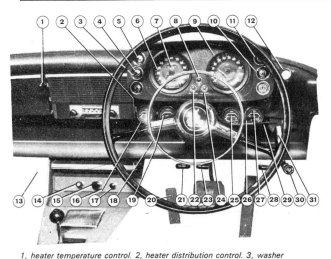

1, heater temperature control. 2, heater distribution control. 3, washer button. 4, wiper speed rheostat. 5, panel lights rheostat. 6, speedometer. 7, trip mileometer. 8, ignition warning light. 9, rev-counter. 10, heater fan switch. 11, lights switch. 12, fresh air vent. 13, picnic tray catch. 14, rear window heater switch. 15, cigar lighter. 16, oil pressure gauge. 17, foglamp switch. 18, horn ring. 19, ammeter. 20, dipswitch. 21, choke. 22, oil pressure warning light. 23, fuel reserve. 24, choke warning light. 25, water temperature gauge. 26, headlamp stalk. 27, fuel gauge. 28, bonnet catch. 29, indicator stalk. 30, air vent control. 31, handbrake.

pedal pressure of only 55 lb. This could be a little low for the emergency jab of the less sensitive driver. Although free of fade, the brakes were a little unprogressive, and on our test car pulled to the right occasionally on light applications. Moderately hard applications from a high speed—say 0.6g from 80 m.p.h.—tended to make the car weave slightly from side to side if the surface was in any way bumpy. A strong pull on the unpromising-looking umbrella-type handbrake, on the other hand, produced an excellent 0.43g stop.

Comfort and controls

Although firmly sprung, the Rover 3.5 rides reasonably well, with none of the car sickness inducing up-and-down wallow that sometimes characterizes large saloons. Sharp surface discontinuities, however, tend to cause harsh, rapid movements of the body, while any attempt to drive fast along generally bumpy roads results in a good deal of movement.

Front passengers are to some extent protected against any deficiencies in the ride by the sheer opulence and luxury of the seats. Although regarded by some as being ostentatiously thick— the apparent thickness of the backrests is actually due to the padding over the frames—most people found them comfortable, providing good lumbar, thigh and lateral support. In addition to

Continued on the next page

Rover 3.5-litre coupé
continued

Insurance

AOA group rating 5
Lloyd's 5

the excellent range of fore-and-aft adjustment, the backrests have friction-lock infinitely-variable adjustment for rake, and the whole seat can be raised and lowered by turning a handle at the front. However, some drivers found the thick bolstered edges anatomically imperfect and complained of a tendency to slide down the slippery leather into an uncomfortable slumped position, suggesting a need for either a shade more lumbar support, or the means of adjusting such support. Although the rear seats looked just as good, the lack of head and legroom in our coupé test car made them uncomfortable on a long journey for tall people.

Steering wheel, pedals and transmission selector lever are all well located in relation to each other, but some taller drivers found nowhere comfortable for the left leg: if it were stretched out the foot got nipped under the brake pedal; rested on the dipswitch (which on first encounter seems like a spring-loaded footrest) the ankle began to ache. Minor controls such as the horn ring and headlamp and flasher stalks are easy to reach quickly, but few of our staff liked the arrangement of the switches in the nacelle behind the steering wheel. Apart from the fact that they work in a horizontal plane, which makes familiarization difficult, there seem to be too many of them: two, for example, are needed to operate the variable speed wipers. A much graver defect of the minor controls, however, is the fact that so many of them are out of reach to a driver wearing a normal seatbelt: handbrake, choke, fuel reserve tap, lower air vent control, heater controls and radio all come into this category. This situation would be a little eased by the use of inertia reel belts in place of normal ones, but even

then the heater temperature control is a long stretch from the driver's seat.

Despite the high-waisted and rather old-fashioned—though handsome—body design, all-round visibility is good, while the bonnet is shaped for easy aiming through small gaps and the boot is just visible to a tall driver. A design feature well worth preserving is the use of plastic tell-tales on the front wings, visible to the driver, which glow when the sidelights are switched on. Similarly excellent were the headlamps which gave a tremendous blaze of light and are well up to the performance of the car. On the new model fog- and spotlights are supplied as standard and are permanently recessed into the front of the car under the headlamps.

Elaborate heating and ventilation facilities are provided. In addition to a normal heater with the usual temperature and air distribution controls, there are upper fresh air vents controlled by butterflies and lower ones controlled by pull-out knobs. At the back there is an independently controlled underseat heater which in summer can be used to circulate cool air in the rear of the car when the heater water tap at the rear of the engine is turned off.

So long as all the windows remain closed, the noise level in the car is exceptionally low. To go with the quietness of the engine, there is little transmission noise and little wind noise, even at more than 100 m.p.h.; generally there is also little road noise, but certain surfaces catch the insulation arrangements out.

Fittings and furniture

Probably the Rover design staff responsible for the equipping of such cars as the 3.5-litre consider its fitments to be the bare minimum appropriate to a gentleman's motor carriage. This splendid, old-world attitude means more luxury than most of the opposition even attempt. In coupé form, the combined fuel gauge, temperature gauge and ammeter which flanks the speedometer is replaced by a rev-counter, and a separate fuel gauge, thermometer and ammeter—plus an oil pressure gauge—are mounted beneath the instrument nacelle. But these are the bare necessities of life: what distinguishes the Rover from its competitors is the number of undeniably practical items which afford almost childish pleasure every time they are used. These include a slide-out picnic tray at the front with a nest of tools underneath it; another picnic tray at the rear which folds out above the armrest and has cut-outs for cups or glasses (anyone for champagne?); armrests on the doors which are adjustable for height, and ashtrays front and rear with cigar lighters beside them which are illuminated with the sidelights.

Servicing and accessibility

The new V-8 fits quite comfortably into the engine compartment of the old six, and its numerous auxiliaries such as brake servo and steering pump reservoir are scattered around it rather than above it as is often the case with American V-8s. All the usual service points—oil filler cap, distributor, dipstick, carburetters etc.—are therefore quite easy to get at. Another good feature of the engine compartment is the way the electrics are arranged, with a fuse for everything and all the fuses clearly marked. Servicing is required every 5,000 miles at which the main job is a change of engine oil; little chassis lubrication is needed. The jack was very easy to use, if a little slow in action. **M**

1, radiator filler cap. 2, brake servo. 3, washer bottle. 4, oil filler cap. 5, brake fluid reservoir. 6, automatic transmission dipstick. 7, air cleaner. 8, dipstick. 9, power steering reservoir.

Maintenance summary

Engine. Every 5,000 miles—Change oil and oil filter, check carburetter slow-running, clean and check plugs. Every 10,000 miles—Replace plugs, lubricate and adjust distributor, check fan and power steering pump belts. Every 20,000 miles—Replace air cleaner elements, fuel filter and breather filter, clean flame traps.

Transmission. Every 5,000 miles—

Check gearbox and back axle oil levels.

Steering, suspension and brakes. Every 5,000 miles—Check power steering fluid reservoir and brake fluid reservoir, and front pad thickness. Every 20,000 miles—check rubber boots on steering joints, check toe-in, check front hubs for leakage.

MAKE: Rover. MODEL: 3.5-litre V-8 coupé. MAKERS: The Rover Co. Ltd., Solihull, Warwickshire.

TWO ROVERS

Continued from page 35

Earlier 3-litres developed uncomfortable choppiness when irregular surfaces caught the suspension off balance.

Stopping is completely taken care of by 10.8-inch Girling discs at the front and drum-type brakes behind. Power-assisted, too.

It is very difficult to lock the wheels, even with the clumsiest diving foot—yet light pressures wash off speed very rapidly.

Fade is non-existent: I've had the disc pads smoking without noticeably losing stopping power.

Equipment, Comfort

So far as equipment and finish goes, the 3-litre hasn't changed at all since it first was announced three years ago.

Everything that goes for safe, comfortable motoring is standard equipment: heater-demister, reversing lights, windscreen-washers, adjustable centre and door armrests for both bench seats, four door-operated courtesy lights, coat hooks, assist straps—even a device for checking engine oil level on the fuel gauge.

All-round vision is good. Instrument cluster, set in a neat binnacle, lacks only an oil-pressure gauge.

The whole business is rounded off by pile carpets, solid leather upholstery and polished wood on dash and door sills.

Driving position is good—and the intermediate gear hold for the auto, previously set way down in the middle of the parcels shelf, has been moved to a much handier steering-column position.

The overdrive switch on the manual version is an equally handy fingertip stalk on the steering column.

The Laycock overdrive unit—suitably modified by Rover—switches in and out with barely a ripple felt in the smooth power flow through the transmission. It works on top gear only and is purely a means of reducing engine revs when cruising far and fast.

The Borg Warner is controlled by a steering-column quadrant with the usual PNDLR legend; a light, fairly quick stick shift controls the four-speed standard gearbox. Good—but still not as good a linkage as you'd expect from the Rover. Synchro on the top three ratios only.

A big feature of the engine is its seven-bearing crankshaft—sixes normally have only four. The unit is almost vibrationless, and its bottom end should last far longer than most. Peak revs of 4750 aren't unduly high.

If you want permanence, performance and comfort in a motor car—and can pay the best part of £3000 for it—there's more for your money in a 3-litre.

For the convenience of the automatic you inevitably pay in performance and fuel economy; on the other hand, if you fancy yourself as a driver, the manual will give you all the fun you want.

FOOTNOTE: Checking back on the 1959 test, I was surprised to find the earlier automatic seemed to accelerate faster. Explanation: my fifth-wheel speedo was playing up at the time, though I didn't discover it till later.

● ● ●

ROVER 3-LITRE
— THAT VIKING TENACITY

Continued from page 52

Suspension helped enhance the impression that for all its apparent and traditional dignity, the Rover 3-litre was a very active car indeed.

At the front, the big wheels are suspended on long, firm torsion bars. Springing at the back is by long, longitudinal leaf springs gaitered and packed with graphite grease.

On rough roads, the springs and shockers took all the harshness out of driving, and on better terrain they held the big body down like strong, taut chains.

It was almost impossible to bottom the Rover springs and even really hairy cornering would produce no more than a really mild roll.

At times, the sweet silence of the car is almost uncanny. It is no exaggeration to say that at high speed on a good road, all the travellers inside the 3-litre can hear is the ticking of the exceptionally loud electric clock on the dashboard.

Wind roar is virtually non-existant, you just don't hear road surface noises or thumps from the suspension and there isn't a squeak or rattle in the beautifully assembled body.

Good design, careful workmanship and heaps and heaps of rubber and other insulating materials are the secret of the Rover's lack of noise.

Even without driving the car, you expect it to travel something like a huge, super-deluxe glider.

On first stepping into the car, the critic is confronted with a lavish arrangement of deep pile carpet, thick, leather covered armchairs, slab upon slab of polished wood and roll upon roll of safety padding.

There is a soft luxurious feel about everything, from the steering wheel to the drawer of tools (including spare tubes of paint to match the particular model's color), firmly clipped in foam rubber under the parcels' tray.

The instruments are comprehensive and the minor controls are neat toggle switches. They work just about everything including a gauge that shows not only how much petrol you have, but also the level of oil in the sump.

A first class heater and demister is standard equipment and also two separate fresh air ventilation systems.

There are even neat touches in such oft-neglected parts as the boot. The luggage compartment is completely lined in vinyl—even the jack and other large tools which do not fit in the under-dashboard tray are covered by a sturdy vinyl flap.

The spare wheel is sensibly housed in a separate compartment below the boot, whence it is wound down with the crank handle—yes, bless them, Rovers have a crank handle.

Fully-imported, the body is impeccably finished and looks likely to withstand the harsh Australian conditions.

As a distinctive, dignified carriage with a timeless air of desirability and extremely good road manners, the Rover has few peers today and is unlikely to have many for a long time—not until Rover builds its successor. #

CONTINUED FROM PAGE 72

in three chromium squares to signify Mk. III, reminder that eight years' steady development have gone into the car, which is available with automatic transmission if required. Rover engineering has been on the up-and-up since 1933 and the modern bodies are very conscientiously undersealed and sound-damped.

If top speed is of interest, this Rover will do 107 m.p.h. and for a car which is in the top-bracket comfort-category the all-up price of £2,028, as tested, I regard as commendably moderate. Moreover, on the service side, Rover do things rather nicely with their spacious London Depot in Seagrave Road (just past the historic Rolls-Royce Lille Hall), where gold-braided attendants are on duty day and night.

But dash it, I *had* intended to test the Rover 2000TC and still await it with interest, and, I hope, a steady hand.—W. B.

A WEEK OF LUXURY

Making the acquaintance of the new

3½-litre V8 Rover Saloon

"*. . . Penetrated into deepest Sussex . . . .*" *The Rover with some of the locomotives of the famous Bluebell Line railway.*

IT HAS been common knowledge for some time that the Rover Company was introducing a V8 engine for their former 3-litre model. This car was released at the Earls Court Motor Show, and, as we announced last month, Great Aunt Rover has certainly lifted her skirts up; she has also changed her elastic-sided boots for running shoes. (See picture of new Rover wheel.) Through the enterprise of Rover's Managing Director, Mr. Martin-Hurst, the design rights of the former Buick Special/Oldsmobile F.85 light alloy V8 engine were obtained. Rover's found it impractical to die-cast the components of this engine and consequently made it by sand-casting and using pressed-in dry cylinder liners. In America they contrived to cast the cylinder liners directly into the block. This new engine has been installed into what is virtually the old 3-litre coupé and saloon Rover with certain modifications in an endeavour to bring it up to date and more in keeping with the new and sophisticated power unit.

Having missed the Rover pre-view day I was able to make acquaintance with the more sporting " Great Aunt " in the week preceding the Earls Court Motor Show. Arriving at Rover's Seagrave Road depot, where staunch Rover clients down the decades have waited for their newly-serviced Rovers in a spacious waiting room, their inquiries dealt with by uniformed commissionaires, very much in the top bracket manner, I was able to transfer from a London taxi to a Rover V8 saloon. Driving it out of London in a rainstorm down the M4 I found it difficult to keep down to Castle cruising speed, in spite of the congested traffic on this two-lane motorway on which crawling private cars were forcing commercial vehicles to take repeatedly to the outer lane. First impressions of the Rover were that it is remarkably smooth and quiet, and this was later confirmed. The new engine is indeed so quiet that the creaking of the seats and, on the test car, a most irritating hunting noise from the speedometer drive, spoilt the otherwise quiet running of the car. At idling speed, the engine is quite inaudible, so that the noise of the windscreen wipers is a distinct disadvantage. After a day of local journeys, I penetrated into deepest Sussex to inspect a pre-war Opel P4 Cabriolet which was looking for a new home in this fine car, and on the Sunday before the Motor Show, I drove the Rover on a cross-country route to Silverstone for the Guild of Motoring Writers test day. Although my driving permit had failed to arrive from the office, I was able to enjoy hot steak and kidney pudding in a heated marquee generously provided by B.M.C. Their's was certainly the most popular luncheon party of the day and if their cars do as well, they have nothing whatever to fear from their rivals in the industry! On this cross-country journey the Rover proved extremely easy to drive and outstandingly comfortable, but on bad surfaces and round sharp bends on deserted roads I was conscious that the road-holding and ride have not changed appreciably since I road-tested the 3-litre 6-cylinder coupé some time ago. The ride can be distinctly lively and the big 15-in.

Dunlop RS5 tyres tend to be deflected by road undulations at the expense of completely accurate steering. The Hydrosteer power steering itself is light and direct and I have no complaints about it except when one is driving the car hard rather more positive control would be appreciated.

There is no need to deal in detail with the Rover control arrangements as these are not greatly changed from previous models. There is the familiar nacelle before the driver with a series of rather fumbly flick switches each side of the instruments for controlling the minor services. Of these it is necessary to make three actions to bring all the lights into operation, the headlamps being selected by a right-hand stalk below the turn indicators/flashers' control after the sidelamps have been switched on by means of one of the flick switches, and dipping is then a matter of operating the foot control. In similar vein, the wipers have two switches, one to switch them on and the other controlling their two-speed action, while the screen-washers are operated by a button round the left side of the nacelle. The rheostat instrument lighting is controlled by one of the flick switches, which does not give a very precise action. All this, however, is of little moment if the Rover is driven as most Rover owners are likely to drive it. During the test, however, the switch controlling the instrument lighting got extremely hot and also heated up the nacelle adjacent to it, so that something within was obviously " shorting."

Following the Silverstone Sunday the Rover was used mainly for motoring up to London and for a considerable amount of commuting in town. On such journeys it is an extremely restful car, the high seating position, the driver's seat controlled for height by a small crank handle, giving good visibility for traffic motoring.

Not only does the good torque of the new engine, which reached its maximum at 2,600 r.p.m., make for good acceleration, in traffic, but the Borg-Warner type 35 fully automatic transmission, with torque convertor and 3-speed epicyclic gearbox function smoothly and easily, the central gear-lever, very well located, providing for " Hold " in the lower speeds when this is required for extra efficient acceleration. Rovers are insistent that the engine should not exceed 5,200 r.p.m., so that the speedometer of the saloon is marked at a maximum of 47 and 77 m.p.h., for observing should the " Hold " control be in operation. In addition, one has the usual D.1 and D.2 settings, the D.2 position cutting out wheel-spin when starting on slippery roads. The Girling disc/drum brakes with Lockheed vacuum servo are extremely smooth and powerful, perhaps slightly insensitive if casually operated, but otherwise some of the best brakes I have come across on a car of this size and weight.

In typically Rover manner the car is splendid equipped, with rear window de-misting, a parcels' shelf which slides out from under the facia and which, below that, has the traditional tool tray, a lockable cubby-hole, and between the seats a heater control and separate control for the rear speaker of the radio within long reach of the rear-seat passengers. I was, however, rather disappointed to find that neither the lockable cubby-hole nor the parcels' shelf would accommodate a Rolleiflex camera. It need hardly be added that the spacious leather upholstered seats with individual arm-rests, the back one incorporating a second picnic tray, and the quality finish of the entire car are fully in keeping with Rover's idea of how the luxury market should be catered for. It is inevitable that this car will be compared with the Jaguar 420. While this has independent rear suspension and disc brakes all round, and is probably a faster vehicle, there is little doubt that its considerably more powerful twin-cam 6-cylinder engine is both faster and noisier, at any rate towards peak speed, than Rover's new V8. There is an irresistible smoothness of running, and fascination about eight cylinders, as Ford proved to the Plebs many, many years ago. The Rover is considerably less powerful than the equivalent Jaguar model but smoother and quieter, and it is on these grounds that it will appeal to the Rover clientele and should therefore continue the life of the former 3-litre model for a considerable time to come. Whether everyone will like the new wheels, which are not, as they first appear, of magnesium alloy, but are a rather clever form of pressed-steel wheel, is open to debate.

The test car continued to serve me faithfully during the harassing days just before the Motor Show, with no troubles apart from the aforementioned short circuit in the rheostat lighting switch and a heater-fan which ceased to operate and left me with cold feet while driving to London on Earls Court Press Day, and breakage of the exhaust tail-pipe bracket. The new engine has considerably increased the performance of the car, so that a top speed of around 110 m.p.h. and a standing-start ¼-mile accomplished in under 18½ seconds has completely dispelled the staid aspect of the biggest car from the Rover factory. All the details are nicely contrived and the engine installation with its twin S.U. carburetters feeding into a water-heated manifold is in keeping with the demeanour of the car. With a compression ratio of 10½ to 1, the best quality petrol is required. On long runs I got rather better than 20 m.p.g. and the overall consumption worked out at 18.4 m.p.g. After 600 miles ½-a-pint of oil would have restored the level on the sump dipstick—there is also a transmission dipstick—which is fairly easy to withdraw but difficult to read, as it is much the same hue as the oil.

Aircraft-type fresh-air vents on each side of the facia functioned effectively and the heater controls are simple to use. The gearbox has a separate oil radiator below the main water radiator.

There are other typically Rover aspects of this fine car. For instance, there is a petrol-reserve toggle under the parcels' shelf alongside the mixture-enrichener toggle. This is a useful item, although the engine sometimes dies out entirely before it can be operated and some delay ensues before it will prime—however, the petrol gauge is reasonably accurate and sufficiently pessimistic for an observant driver to obviate this occurrence. (Range, before using reserve supply, approx. 230 miles.) Cold starting calls for mixture-enrichment but this control can be left out until the " choke " warning light comes on. The side-lamp tell-tales found on the Rover 2000 feature on the V8 and the boot lid shuts with the same precision under gentle persuasion. On the V8 the bonnet is self-supporting. A small horn-ring, to obviate blanking the Jaeger speedometer and matching general-services dial, operates the horn and the r.h. " umbrella-handle " hand-brake pulls out from above the parcels' shelf, and has a bright warning light. There is a well-placed quick-action fuel filler on the n/s, but it does not lock, as on the Rover 2000.

The rheostat' instrument lighting works in conjunction with the L., D.1, D.2, N., R., P. gear-gate and the Kienzle clock on the far left of the facia, and can be switched off completely. The interior décor is a fine combination of leather (but what a horrid sick shade on the test car!), African cherrywood and black crash padding, with such luxuries as ash-trays front and rear, with lighter on the console, which it shares with the rear window heater and fog-lamp switches, roof-" pulls," a rest for the driver's left foot, adjustable door arm-rests with pocket, front-door pockets, 4-door courtesy interior lighting, etc. Some of the minor controls would be out of reach of seat-harness wearers and there are only single, but effective, Lucas headlamps, and with inbuilt Lucas fog-lamps below. Instrumentation (in the r.h. dial) includes an ammeter and an oil gauge. The spare wheel is in a wind-down tray (which has an ingenious wire-locking device) below the luggage boot.

Qualifying earlier remarks, although the power-assisted Hydrosteer variable-ratio steering feels unduly light at times, and the suspension is too lively over bad surfaces and develops considerable roll angles,

" . . . On a cross country route to Silverstone . . . ." A picture showing the chunky build of the four-door Rover V8 saloon.

the general handling *has* been improved, and on longer acquaintance with the V8 Rover I found it could be hurried along, even on wet roads, without anxiety, and certainly with very little driver-effort. I would describe it as similar to a Rolls-Royce Silver Cloud to drive—out-dated, but highly satisfying. (The three snags that arose, in 560 miles, might also typify what could be expected from a very high-mileage used Silver Cloud?) There were rather too many extraneous noises, such as upholstery creaking, that speedometer drive chuntering, those noisy wipers and, towards the end, a rattle from the twin exhaust tail-pipes, whose bracket, as I have said, had broken, to enable full enjoyment of the very quiet engine to be obtained. But the high, comfortable seating, with friction-adjustable back rests, as on Rover 2000s, the rear seats separate " arm-chairs," the great dignity of the 3½-litre Rover V8, and its very good acceleration with no sense of any effort from the new 160-h.p. power unit, make this a highly-desirable car for the aged or the more lazy driver. For me it certainly eased the trying days preceding the Motor Show, with its silent travel and effortless traffic negotiation, and at just under £2,000 in saloon form I would regard it as a very good purchase. (Price with extras as tested is £2,069 4s. 3d.)—W. B.

A new pressed-steel wheel fitted to the 3½-litre Rover V8.

THE long-awaited Rover version of the aluminium GM V8 motor from which the now-famous Repco-Brabham three-litre F1 racing engine was originally developed, has been announced.

It is a 3.5-litre (3,528.5 cc.) ohv oversquare unit developing 160.5 bhp at 5,200 rpm installed. Gross output is 184 bhp and the torque is 210 lb. ft. at 2,600 rpm installed or 226 lb. ft. at 3,000 rpm gross.

Initially the lightweight engine with cast-iron liners and 10.5:1 compression will go into a revamped version of the Rover P.3 (Three Litre). It turns the stately-looking limousine into a 115 mph car with a 0-60 mph acceleration figure of 12.1 secs. The new engine is 200 lb. lighter and 30 percent more powerful that the steel six it replaces.

The unit will be coupled to a three-speed Borg Warner type 35 gearbox. There are no plans as yet for a conventional gearbox.

The new unit has taken three years to bring into production. With its twin H.S.6, S.U. carburettors — one for each bank — the engine is way understressed and has obviously been developed for long, trouble-free life.

But even in its present form of development installed in the award-winning Rover 2000 it could be a real winner.

Winner

The present series will be produced in both saloon and coupe versions. The body will be distinguishable by new type road wheels, full-length body side mouldings with "repeater" flasher lamps and a painted coach line underneath. There's a matt black-painted body sill, stainless steel mouldings and a deeper front lower body panel and wings with depressions for fog lamps in the front wings, new radiator grille with a slimmer spine and a Rover motif in gold. A gold-plated (gilt) "3.5-litre" motif is on the boot lid.

Internally, the most noticeable feature is the new console unit which houses the automatic gear lever, ash tray, trinket tray, leather-trimmed switch panel with cigar lighter, fog lamp switch and provision for extra switchgear.

The many small touches that made the normal Three Litre worth owning are retained, fortunately.

They include front seat armrests which are adjustable for height and rake, front and rear courtesy lights, a picnic tray for rear seat passengers, and a combined picnic/tool tray for front passengers.

Among the extras offered is an electrically heated rear window, front and rear headrests, the front headrests incorporating reading lights for rear seat passengers.

The new type road wheels are similar looking to those fitted on Rover 2000 TCs destined for the American market.

They are a gaudy pressed steel type plated and painted to look like the sporty alloy wheels currently popular on some American cars. While they might look smart on these Americans they don't really fit the sedate Rover picture.

Radial ply tyres aren't offered as an option despite the V8's high speed potential. The conventional brands offered—Dunlop RS5 and Avon Turbo-

The suburbanite's Repco-Brabham? Not quite, reports Harold Dvoretsky from London after test drive, but this similarly-based V8 has possibilities . . .

USUAL Rover luxury shows up in new V8 3.5-litre interior, but centre console selector for Borg Warner box is new.

RIGHT: Alloy V8 in new 3.5-litre car develops modest 160 bhp. Like Repco-Brabham racing engine, Buick-derived.

BELOW RIGHT: Externally, new car looks much like old 3-litre. Later version may use Rover 2000 body shell.

Manufacturer: Rover Co. Ltd., Solihull, England.

Price: See text.

SPECIFICATIONS

ENGINE

Water cooled, 8 cylinders in Vee formation. Cast alloy block, five main bearings.

Bore x stroke	88.9 x 71.12 mm.
Capacity	3,528 cc.; 215 cu. in.
Compression	10.5 to 1
Carburettor	Twin HS6 SU
Fuel pump	Mechanical
Fuel tank	15.5 gallons
Fuel recommended	Super
Valve gear	p'rod ohv
Max. power (gross)	184 bhp at 5,200 rpm
Max. torque	226 lb. ft. at 3,000 rpm
Electrical system	12v.

TRANSMISSION

Three speed torque convertor automatic.

Gear	Ratio
Rev.	2.09
Low	2.39
Inter.	1.45
Direct	1.00
Final drive ratio	3.54 to 1

CHASSIS

Wheelbase	9ft. 2½in.
Track front	4ft. 7½in.
Track rear	4ft. 8in.
Length	15ft. 6½in.
Width	5ft. 10½in.
Height	5ft. 1in.
Clearance	6½in.
Kerb weight	1 ton 11 cwt. 26 lbs.
lb/bhp	19 lb.

SUSPENSION

Front: Independent wishbones and laminated torsion bar. Telescopic shock absorbers.

Rear: Rigid axle by semi elliptics and telescopic shock absorbers.

Brakes: Disc/drum, servo assisted; 260 sq. in. of swept area.

Steering ..... Worm and peg, power assisted

Turns lock to lock	2½
Turning circle	40ft.

Wheels: Steel disc with 6.70 by 15 cross ply tyres.

PERFORMANCE

(maker's figures)

Top speed	115 mph.
Standing quarter mile	18.6 sec.

Acceleration

Zero to	seconds
30 mph	4.26
40 mph	6.17
50 mph	9.01
60 mph	12.14
70 mph	16.17
80 mph	22.73
90 mph	31.02
100 mph	39.15

Consumption: 17.6 mpg in normal country and suburban use.

speed—are well up to the car's capabilities, nonetheless.

One cannot believe that Rover intend this present body (introduced in 1959 originally) to last much longer in production. But they are probably aiming at reducing any bugs that may turn up in the engine and attending to the installation (if the rumor is true) in the 2000. Once this has been accomplished a new, sleeker body can be expected.

With the Humber Hawk and Snipe series now out of production the Rover has a unique place in this semi-limousine price range.

Rover have also managed to keep the price of the V8 down. The new versions, compared with the old P.3 automatic 6-cylinder Rovers, are only **£54 stg** basic extra. Saloon is now **£1625 stg.** basic and coupe **£1705 stg.**

Livelier

A 75 mile drive around the Cotswolds before release showed the new Rover, as expected, to be much livelier than the old 3-litre. At lower speeds there's the unmistakable sound of a vee beneath the bonnet but happily as the revs increase, this disappears. The strangely curved cooling fan aimed at being the best compromise for least noise with greatest efficiency seems to work well. There were no flat spots in performance and the modified 35 Borg-Warner automatic worked very smoothly indeed.

The lighter power unit has made the car far better balanced than before though the only mods to suspension are stronger shock absorbers. Corners can be taken with much more verve without the car losing any of its semi-stately limousine type charm.

Technically, the new unit is virtually a direct copy with certain modifications from the original GM mainly concerned with the thin steel liners and slight alterations to the crankcase. Rover engineers, incidentally, are full of praise for Phil Irving, the man mainly responsible for turning out the original Repco-Brabham engine from the same design.

More power

In fact, it now transpires that there was quite a reasonable amount of information exchange between Rover and Repco during the development of both engines. (Irving is said to have solved the bearing problems, among other things.)

Rovers are fairly emphatic that bore widening might impose too many problems if the engine had to be "stretched" but that engine size could be increased by other means. There is no problem in increasing output.

One can assume by this that Repco development with Lucas fuel injection and head design could be down-graded to suit everyday use.

No doubt Sir Donald Stokes, boss-man of the mighty new combine of Leyland-Standard-Triumph under which the Rover banner now flies, has been thinking ahead so far as Australia and South-East Asia are concerned.

I can't help wondering whether he has already foreseen the possibility of using Repco's resources to produce a V8 in Australia as a natural start for increasing local content for either Rover or Triumph 2000 models.

Is it possible? As I say, one can't help thinking. . . . •

rover GOES V8

ROVER and the
East African Safari

ROVER 3-LITRE SALOON
WINS BIG CAR CLASS

Drivers: Mr. A. E. Bengry and Mr. G. E. Goby

(subject to official confirmation)

Only 7 cars finished—the Rover the only car over 2½-litres

The world's hardest rally, the East African Safari—this year tougher than ever!   Mud, rain and rocks retired all but 7 of the 84 starters. Not only was Mr. Bengry's Rover the only finisher in the over 2,500 c.c. class (without any mechanical trouble whatsoever!), but he had the distinction of being the only U.K. driver to finish.   This particular car, a perfectly standard 3-Litre saloon with extras available to all Rover owners, competed successfully in last year's Liège-Sofia-Liège and R.A.C. Rallies—a hard life even for

ONE OF THE WORLD'S BEST ENGINEERED CARS

The Rover Company Limited · Solihull · Warwickshire · London offices and showrooms : Devonshire House · Piccadilly Makers of fine cars and the world-famous Land-Rover.

GROUP TEST

'Motor's' test team go driving in convoy to try competitive cars under identical conditions

● **Mercedes 220** ● **BMW 2000 TI Lux** ● **Jaguar 420** ● **NSU Ro80** ● **Rover 3½-litre**

The cars

Mercedes 220 £2,297
Integral steel body; all independent suspension (coil and wishbone front, semi-trailing arms rear); worm and sector steering; servo-assisted all-disc brakes; 2.2-litre s.o.h.c. four-cylinder engine; four-speed manual gearbox; Continental radial tyres. Also available: 2½-litre engine, four-speed automatic gearbox.

BMW 2000 TI Lux £1,999 (1968 type)
Integral steel body; all independent suspension (MacPherson struts front, semi-trailing arms rear); worm and roller steering; servo-assisted disc/drum brakes; 1,990 c.c. s.o.h.c. four-cylinder engine; four speed manual gearbox; Firestone Phoenix radial ply tyres. Also available: automatic transmission, 1.8-litre engine, coupé body.

Jaguar 420 £2,282*
Integral steel body; all independent suspension (coil and wishbone front, lower links and drive shafts rear); Adwest Varamatic power-assisted steering; servo assisted all-disc brakes; 4.2-litre d.o.h.c. 6-cylinder engine; four-speed manual gearbox with overdrive; Dunlop SP41HR tyres.

Also available: three-speed Borg-Warner automatic transmission.
* Price as for mechanically identical Daimler Sovereign which remains in production.

NSU Ro80 £2,232
Integral steel body; all independent suspension (MacPherson struts front, semi-trailing arms rear); ZF power-assisted rack and pinion steering; servo-assisted all-disc brakes; twin-rotor Wankel engine with 1,990 c.c. equivalent capacity; three-speed semi-automatic gearbox; Michelin XAS tyres.

Rover 3½-litre £2,174
Integral steel body; coil and wishbone front suspension, live rear axle; Hydrosteer power-assisted worm and peg steering; servo-assisted disc/drum brakes; 3.5-litre V-8 engine; three-speed automatic transmission; Dunlop RS5 tyres. Also available: coupé body.

Other possibilities: Lancia Flavia Injection £2,076; Citroën DS21 £2,077.

No. 8 : £2,000 + luxury saloons

AT THE £2,000 price level, a British buyer in search of a comfortable saloon can choose between one or two large-engined home-produced cars or from a group of Continental vehicles which, because of import duty, freight charges and internal tax policies, have much smaller power units. As a result the engine capacity of the cars in this group varies from the 1,990 c.c. of the BMW (and NSU Ro80) to the 4,235 c.c. of the Jaguar 420 (as tested this is virtually the same as the Daimler Sovereign which continues in production). Despite this, differences in practical performance were relatively small as we found out during our period of give-and-take motoring, which included a fair amount of motorway running—this time we used a day's driving on the quiet roads of Northumberland to explore handling characteristics, but drove up and

Continued on the next page

Group test No. 8

continued

back almost entirely on motorways and dual carriageways.

Even academically, performance differences as defined by such figures as maximum speeds and standing-start acceleration times are much less than might be expected, the BMW, for example, being very nearly as quick as the Jaguar even though its engine is less than half the size. Similarly, differences in interior space are moderate—or if anything biased in favour of the more compact and more recently designed Germans. And in the sense of having comfortable seats, lavishly trimmed interiors (though in widely varying styles) and such trimmings as cigar lighters and rev-counters all the cars could be described as luxurious.

The main differences, however, we found to be those of character, for which our test proved to be a most useful voyage of rediscovery; some reputations were amply confirmed, but there were surprises. Driving the NSU Ro80 for the first time since our Italian test earlier this year we again find it difficult to express the depth of our admiration for a car which scores in so many ways over all others. First and foremost it is an honest, integrated design, essentially free of styling gimmicks which means that the bodyshell has plenty of room inside as well as good aerodynamics; next it has immaculate roadholding and handling and finally there is the utterly smooth and unstrained Wankel engine. But the new Mercedes, we felt, runs it a close second in some respects, particularly handling. The BMW also has very good handling and roadholding, but is notable for the tremendous performance provided by its 2-litre 120 b.h.p. engine. Judged by such high standards, the two British cars emerged less favourably, although we were surprised by the agility of the Rover and its predictable handling on smooth roads—it could not cope very well with bumpy surfaces—and reminded of its general quietness and refinement. We were equally surprised—in view of its sporting and racing ancestry—to find that although the Jaguar was not much affected by bumps, its feel-less power steering gave rather uncomfortable handling and some drivers felt that adhesion was relatively easily lost at the rear. But it, too, was a very quiet car with the most comfortable ride.

Performance charts are based on figures recorded for previous solo test cars. Those for the Jaguar 420 are taken from the test of the mechanically identical Daimler Sovereign.

Halt on a hill: "Motor" testers take a breather.

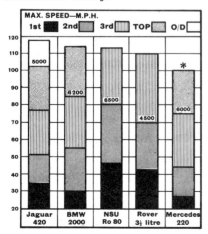

MAX. SPEED—M.P.H.

1st   2nd   3rd   TOP   O/D

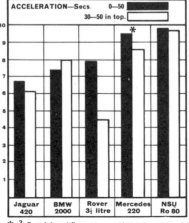

ACCELERATION—Secs.   0—50   30—50 in top.

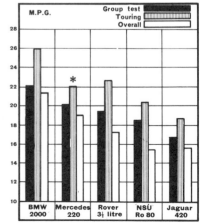

M.P.G.   Group test   Touring   Overall

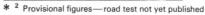

* 2 Provisional figures—road test not yet published

Performance

Of all the engines in the group the most impressive was the Wankel unit of the NSU Ro80 which sounded and felt just as unfussed at its red-line maximum of 6,500 r.p.m. as at 3,000; indeed although the pitch of the engine note rises still further it sounds equally calm at 8,000 r.p.m.—we hasten to add that the very smoothness of the twin-rotor unit tempted us to use such high speeds experimentally but only once, and briefly. The penalty of such an indulgence, be it noted, is not a bent valve or worse, but simply increased oil consumption and accelerated rotor tip wear. If the Wankel and Rover V-8 were compared for smoothness on a test bed we suspect that the V-8 might turn out the loser by a small margin but, as installed its extreme quietness entitles it to be considered at least the equal if not the superior of the epitrochoidal device.

Almost as quiet and smooth was the Jaguar engine, but—unusually, for this make—the example fitted to our test car became rough above about 4,500 r.p.m., and, by the high standards set by Rover and NSU, noisy as well in all gears except overdrive top when the sound became camouflaged in the general humming of high speed. In comparison, the four-cylinder engined Mercedes and BMW were not in the same league for smoothness and quietness, but by absolute standards they were still good, the Mercedes being a little better than the BMW which transmitted some vibration to the steering column and accelerator pedal.

With the double advantages of a good many litres and a torque converter the Rover has easily the best flexibility and will surge smoothly away at any speed. The even greater capacity of the Jaguar does not quite compensate for the lack of a torque converter but it, too, will pull very powerfully and smoothly from low speeds in top gear. Next best is the Mercedes which performs very well for its engine size—though naturally its

efforts cannot compete with the bigger-engined or torque-converted British rivals —but the BMW has rather less pull at low revs., presumably sacrificed for the very high power output. Although the NSU had the poorest top-gear acceleration at low speeds, the smoothness and lack of hesitation or snatch made up for this to some extent.

Despite some differences in the figures, there was very little to choose for performance on the road between the Jaguar and the BMW: both cars are very quick in acceleration and will cruise comfortably at speeds well above 100 m.p.h. The top speed and acceleration from a standstill of the Rover V-8 is nearly as good, and achieved so unobtrusively that the driver often thinks that the car is slower than it actually is. In fact it was never in any danger of being left behind. Possibly the slowest car on acceleration was the Ro80, but it amply made up for this by being very fast round corners and having as high a top speed as any.

Continued on the next page

Group test No. 8
continued

Dicing in the dust, with the Jaguar just about to break away its tail.

The BMW 2000TI is almost as fast as the Jaguar.

This ground-level shot accentuates the down-sweeping aerodynamic line of the NSU Ro80

The 220, a brilliant newcomer to the Mercedes range, corners with very little roll.

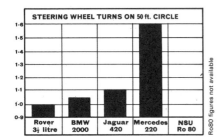

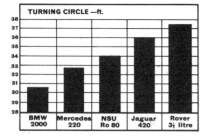

Economy

For all the five cars the overall "circuit" fuel consumption was better than the overall consumption recorded on our previous road tests and in all cases the values obtained were acceptable, the 22.1 m.p.g. of the BMW being particularly good in view of its high performance and the hard driving of our group test. Even the 16.8 m.p.g. attained by the Jaguar—the thirstiest car—represented a highly commendable disregard of its weight and engine size. The 18.4 m.p.g. of the Ro80 is a reasonable figure for a 2-litre car with a torque converter and much better than the 15.3 m.p.g. recorded with our original road test car, which was running with over-rich carburation. And a further small improvement might have been achieved had we been able to reduce the idling speed of our group test car from around 1,200 r.p.m. to a more reasonable speed. An important factor in fuel consumption, we found, was continued use of the NSU's universal second gear which is ideally suited to twisty road driving. One staff member took the car on a long journey after the group test and attained 22.4 m.p.g. with fast but more normal driving, but a heavy load of two adults, two children, a largish dog and a lot of luggage.

Transmission

A buyer with around £2,000 in his pocket can afford to decide exactly how he changes gear—or indeed whether he changes gear at all—and the cars in our group include a wide selection of possible alternatives. Three of them, the Mercedes, BMW and Jaguar, were fitted with the conventional four-on-the-floor arrangement—plus overdrive for the Jaguar (with automatic transmission available as an option in all cases), but the NSU is only available with its "comingthing" semi-automatic transmission, while the fully automatic gearbox of the Rover is also a standard fitting and works so smoothly and quietly that it makes the car effectively gearless.

Most of our drivers liked the long, slicing action of the BMW box best of all the manual changes, preferring it to the Jaguar change and the precise but slightly notchy feel of the Mercedes. Once again the BMW clutch was a bit "up in the air" though very much better than on previous BMWs; the clutches of the other two cars elicited little comment from our drivers, and were smooth and progressive in action. Feelings were a little mixed about the gearchange of the Ro80. After a little practice—mainly in releasing the touch-sensitive gearlever knob which controls the clutch—our drivers found it easy to achieve smooth changes and obtained great satisfaction from doing so. But during car park manoeuvring the change was notchy and obstructive, particularly into reverse, although this may have been faulty due to the unnaturally high engine idling speed. The small lever-and-release-button arrangement governing the Borg-Warner box of the Rover worked well and allowed the easy selection of L to hold a gear for a corner: this was rarely necessary to obtain more power but was sometimes useful to prevent a change in mid-bend. Only the Jaguar and the NSU made any significant transmission noise, the Jaguar's being a powerful whine in all the indirects while our test NSU suffered from a very loud overrun howl which we have not previously met on this model.

Perfectly chosen ratios, a good torque converter and the wide rev-range of the Wankel engine made the NSU probably the best geared of all the cars. Its second gear, in particular, was astonishingly versatile, with a 0-80 m.p.h. speed range which made it suitable for almost all requirements—especially English country lanes—except rapid or steep hill starts and motorway running. The BMW also had well-chosen ratios, nearly 85 m.p.h. being attained in third, for example, giving the car an excellent high speed overtaking capability. Although the Jaguar was almost 10 m.p.h. slower in third, this did not matter very mcuh as there was a good deal of pull in direct top, with overdrive top available for relaxed cruising. As the automatic gearbox of the Rover was set to change up from second at a modest 70 m.p.h. and 4,500 r.p.m., a floored throttle sometimes did not provide the action that the occasion demanded. The bottom and second gear ratios of the Mercedes were, we felt, a trifle low.

Handling and roadholding

If a Superior Being from another planet were to bring with him his own personal wheeled vehicle we could expect it to handle much like the NSU Ro80. Briefly, this car has light and supremely responsive power steering, goes where you point it and has a limit of adhesion which is almost impossible to reach on the open road, although there is a fair amount of roll and at times some tyre squeal. Such antics as deliberately and sharply lifting off when cornering hard leave the car completely unmoved.

Both the Mercedes and the BMW also had extremely good roadholding, but while the Mercedes reached a gentle and controllable final oversteer, the tail of the BMW tended to flick outwards rather sharply—but some thought at a higher limit—when pressed very hard. The BMW was more responsive and had less initial understeer than the Mercedes, but the latter car exhibited remarkably little roll.

A welcome surprise was the amiable way in which the Rover could be trundled quickly along twisty roads and the ease with which it could be put through a series of bends. So long as the surface remained smooth it cornered well with little roll or tyre squeal, but bumps tended to put it off line and converted its strong understeer into a series of lurches. Less pleasant were the discoveries we made about the Jaguar: no one was enthusiastic

Continued on the next page

Vital statistics

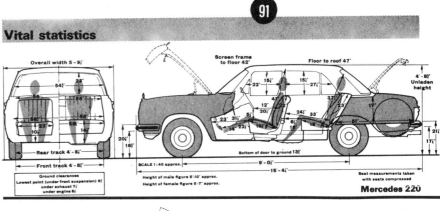

Mercedes 220

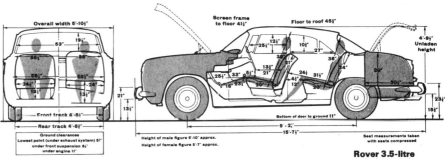

Rover 3.5-litre

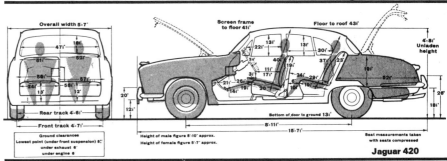

Jaguar 420

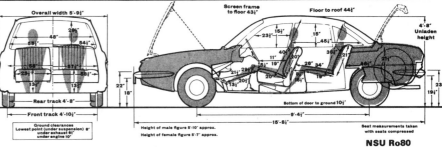

NSU Ro80

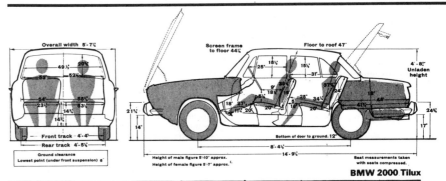

BMW 2000 Tilux

Specifications	Mercedes 220	BMW 2000 TI Lux	Jaguar 420	NSU Ro80	Rover 3½-litre
Cylinders	4	4	6	2 rotors	8
Capacity	2,197 c.c.	1,990 c.c.	4,235 c.c.	1,990 c.c.	3,528 c.c.
Brakes	Discs	Discs/drums	Discs	Discs	Discs/drums
Service intervals	3,000 miles	4,000 miles	3,000 miles	3,000 miles	5,000 miles
Fuel grade	4-star	5-star	4-star	3-star	5-star
Insurance rating	5	Group 6	Group 6	O.A.	Group 5
Tyre size	175-14	175-14	185-15	175-14	6.70-15
Weight (cwt.)	25.8	22.6	32.9	23.5	31.4
mph/1,000 r.p.m. in top	17.6	18.4	23.0	18.8	22.4

about the power steering, the varying ratio of which may be fine for sleepy drivers on Freeways but not well suited to judging how much to wind on when taking a corner. Both the Jaguar, incidentally, and the Rover with a less obtrusive variable ratio to its power steering, felt unpleasantly slack at the wheel on motorways when the steering is most near the straight-ahead position. Such characteristics made it difficult to corner the Jaguar tidily and, in addition, several drivers complained of premature rear-end breakaway.

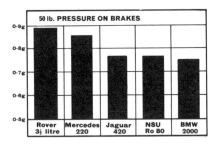

Brakes
On one of the twistier downhill sections the Rover's brakes—perhaps taxed by considerable weight and a lack of overrun braking began to pull and lock up prematurely and were seen to be smoking merrily when the car was stopped for another reason. After a period of running to cool off, however, they functioned properly for the remainder of the test, though were never quite as progressive as they should be. The BMW brakes were heavy, but like the braking systems of all the other cars worked well throughout the test.

Comfort
Unusually, none of our drivers had any complaints about inadequate legroom or a poor range of seat adjustment—everyone managed to find a comfortable driving position. There were few complaints, too, about the seats themselves, except, perhaps, that those of the Jaguar lacked lateral support and provided insufficient lumbar support while to a lesser extent the Rover seats elicited similar criticisms. But the front seats of the three Germans were considered to be well shaped and to have just the right degree of firmness.

Previous group tests
May 18th Fiat 124, Ford Escort 1300 GT, Riley Kestrel, Saab V-4, Vauxhall Brabham Viva.
May 25th Austin Mini Mk. II, Reliant Rebel, Fiat 850, Hillman Imp. Renault 4.
June 1st MGB, MGC, Fiat 124S coupé, Triumph GT6, Triumph TR5, Reliant Scimitar.
June 8th Rover 2000, Triumph 2000, Sunbeam Rapier, Audi 90, Vauxhall Ventora, BMW 1600.
June 15th Austin 1800, Ford Corsair 2000, Ford Cortina GT, Hillman Hunter, Renault 16, Vauxhall Victor.
June 22nd Ford Escort 1100, Vauxhall Viva, Triumph Herald 1200, Volkswagen 1300, NSU 1000C, Austin 1100 Mk. 2.
September 7th Triumph TR5, Lotus Elan S4 coupé; Marcos 1600, Mercedes Benz 280SL, AC 428 Fastback.

The Le Mans-evolved independent rear suspension of the Jaguar gave easily the best ride of the five cars; this was especially apparent on some of the very bumpy and little-used roads over which we travelled during our test. Unfortunately, the excellence of the Jaguar's ride was a little spoilt for us by the tendency for the car to bottom severely with frightening noises on sharp humps when driving fast but this may have been due to partly worn dampers, and few owners are likely to throw their cars around on roads of this sort as we did. Both the NSU and Mercedes had almost as good a ride, but the BMW was harder and suffered from pitch. A sharp bouncing movement on rough roads was a fault of the Rover.

Age of design seems the determining factor for visibility: thin pillars and no quarterlights giving the NSU the least cluttered field of vision, though both the Mercedes and the BMW were also good in this respect, despite their quarterlights. Thicker pillars, quarterlights and higher scuttles put the Jaguar and more particularly the Rover at a disadvantage for visibility, the Rover being noticeably worse than the other cars with a strongly convex mirror that no-one liked.

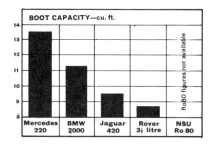

Accommodation
Boot space and accommodation in the rear seats also depends thoroughly on how recently the body has been designed. Thus the NSU has good rear seat legroom and a very large boot, while the even more recently designed Mercedes has an enormous boot—which will take 13.5 cu.ft. of our test boxes—and also has plenty of space at the back. The BMW is similarly dimensioned, though with a slightly smaller boot than the Mercedes. But the old-fashioned body of the Rover has a boot which will only accommodate around 9 cu.ft. of our test boxes, and legroom behind the driver's seat when it is fully back is distinctly cramped. The Jaguar bodyshell was rather better but subject to the same criticisms.

Instruments and switches
All the cars were fitted with well-located, pleasant-to-look-at and easy-to-read instruments, the Jaguar having the most comprehensive set. No rev-counter is fitted to the Mercedes (but change-up points are marked on the speedometer) nor to the Rover, which does not need one.

Although each of the switches in the imposing row on the Jaguar facia is labelled, they are difficult to memorize and find in the dark. Some drivers also found it easy to confuse the indicator and overdrive stalks. A much more ergonomic and successful two-stalk layout was that of the Ro80, the left-hand stalk controlling the headlamps and indicators with the right-hand stalk for wipers, washers and horn. All the minor controls and warning lights are unlabelled, however, and we accidentally reset the trip mileometer in our initial efforts to find the wiper switches. The BMW has two-stalk

controls, though with different functions, and the lights and wiper switches are mounted prominently on the facia. The Mercedes had a single stalk controlling the two-speed wipers, the washers and the headlamp flashers; perhaps the only fault of the arrangement was the location of the light switch immediately behind this stalk, for the heater controls are particularly easy to identify and use on the move. The Rover's switches were easy to reach on a nacelle immediately in front of the driver, but their action was unfamiliar as they worked in a horizontal plane, and the wipers needed two switches, one for on and off and one to select the two speeds. Handbrake and heater controls were a long way away to a driver held in by normal seatbelts—one of the inertia reel type would be essential for this car.

Heating and ventilation
While the rest of England soaked and suffered in the rain, we boiled on our group test on the roads around Hadrian's Wall, so the importance of good ventilation soon became apparent to us. An easy winner was the Mercedes with its easily understood and manipulated controls and tremendous throughput of air via two separately controlled vents at each end of the facia plus a large central one. Next was the NSU, with two vents near the centre of the facia with a common flow control but separate direction controls. An adequate flow could be obtained in the Rover by opening the small butterfly vents at the ends of the facia and the larger, lower ones as well. Surprisingly, the BMW has no fresh air ventilation, though some cool air can be obtained from the screen vents—but this fault has been eliminated from the new model which has a proper fresh air ventilation system. Playing with the Jaguar's numerous heating and ventilation controls failed to relieve the stuffiness—open quarterlights were the only solution and these let in noise as well as air. All the cars had powerful and effective heaters.

Noise
Making allowance for transmission overrun noise which was thought to be non-standard, the NSU had probably the lowest noise level under all conditions: once we had corrected the faulty window sealing on our test car there was very little wind noise at all; tyre noise was limited to a little radial ply thump and the smooth untiring note of the engine effectively made it one of the quietest subjectively, if not in decibels. A close rival, if not the equal of the NSU, was the Rover which seldom emitted more than a gentle sighing, although the engine and transmission were so exceptionally well silenced that modest wind noise and more considerable road noise sometimes became noticeable in contrast. At high speeds in overdrive top the Jaguar was astonishingly quiet except for a little wind noise, but on other occasions the gearbox whine was obtrusive and the engine became rough and quite vocal above about 4,500 r.p.m. Both the Mercedes and BMW were noiser—though still very quiet and refined cars—the BMW having a little more road noise than the Mercedes, and a slightly noiser and more vibratory engine as well. **M**

••••••••••••••••••••••••••••

Next week
Personal choice
Our testers give their strictly personal views on this week's five cars.

Sequel to last week's group test

Personal choice

Out of five Motor testers, four choose this car

IT'S NOT just the Wankel engine that makes the Ro80 an easy first choice. If selection is based on a combination of handling, roadholding, comfort, smoothness and individuality, what else is there in this price range to beat it? Don't be influenced by those scribes who say it rolls and lurches and understeers; this merely betrays that they have not driven it on the road (only at a Silverstone test day) and have therefore never discovered that this Teutonic masterpiece will out-corner practically any sports car, out-smooth a V-8, and out-carry many estates. Add to this the world's best power steering, and striking, if not beautiful, styling—not to mention the ego-boosting influence of its mechanical individuality—and you have one of the world's great cars.

If it doesn't sound too much of a contradiction after such lyrical praise, I thought that the 220 Mercedes ran the Ro80 very close overall, even surpassed it in some departments like ride, solidity, roll-free cornering and trim. But the manual steering and notchy gearchange called for quite hard labour in busy town traffic and the engine, though astonishingly smooth and potent for a modest four, is no match in appeal for the Wankel. Perhaps the six-cylinder 250 option with power steering really is an Ro80 beater—but I don't know for I haven't driven one.

Although the BMW 2000TI lacks the "1970" feel of the NSU and Merc, particularly in respect of ride, it takes second place on my card for being so entertaining to drive; the handling, gearchange and performance are a real inspiration if you enjoy potent, well mannered machinery.

I'm not at one with colleagues who couldn't come to terms with the Jaguar; its performance and ride are superb, and the roadholding, smoothness and gearchange very good. What lets it down is the power steering and its excessively soft, wallowy handling when you're pressing on. Had the vastly superior XJ6, which rides and handles perhaps even better than the Mercedes, been available for this group test, then a Jaguar could well have headed the list. The Rover is not for me:

despite its ultra smooth, quiet engine, lavish appointments and unexpectedly respectable performance and roadholding, it was not the most comfortable car in the group and certainly not the most fun.

Roger Bell

●●●●●●●●●●●●●●●●●●●●●●●●

I THOUGHT we were becoming a class-less society, but I just can't begin to aspire to the cars in some of these groups; I can still enjoy driving them and so consider them purely from a driver's viewpoint, but hardly as a potential owner. A surprising first choice was the Mercedes 220, a really great improvement over its predecessor; it is comfortable and spacious but the big appeal is its controls and the uncanny revability of the four-cylinder engine, which really propels quite a heavy car with a very fair turn of performance. I like the gear lever, thin with a flickswitch precision about its movement if you time it right, and the ratios seem better than before. Road-holding, too, is better even than with the low-pivot swing axle, but still not as good as the fantastic Ro80, which is quite indecently unstickable at ridiculously high cornering speeds. The NSU is a great car for its road behaviour alone, let alone its spaciousness and the Wankel; I like these selective automatics as well particularly when attached to really useful ratios and a very wide rev range; the only drawback to this is that you spend a lot of time torque-converting. I'm not sure why I prefer the Merc, possibly a little more solidity of feel, but something just offsets the Wankel appeal.

I've always been a BMW fan but, having really fallen for the 2002, I find the larger ones clumsy and sloppy by comparison, although they still have the same delightful mechanicals. Didn't like the wind noise on the Tilux either, but it is still a highly entertaining car to drive and well able to keep up with the Ro80 cross country with its better acceleration and good handling if not ultimate grip. I used to like the S-type Jags as well as anything but they have dated surprisingly.

They still have an excellent ride and a high standard of comfort, but the roadholding is just not very good any more, oversteer starting very early. Still a superb engine, though.

Just as it has always been with the 3-litre engine, the Rover is the sort of car you like if that's the sort of car you like: I don't. It is quiet, comfortable on good roads, and really quite quick if you give your mind to it and forget passengers, but as the only live-axled car in the group its performance on bumpy corners was a tribute to independent suspension. But I have to concede that it's still pretty good value as a chairman's barouche.

Michael Bowler

●●●●●●●●●●●●●●●●●●●●●●●●

WHEN it comes to attempting a personal choice, this is one of the most difficult groups yet assembled. They are all extremely good cars and each one is outstanding in several respects, but no single one of them embodies in the same car all the features in which I am interested.

If you want to drive fairly quickly around England (which I usually do) you need a small, quick, light and responsive car. Regretfully, therefore, I am inclined to rule out the Mercedes 220, the Jaguar 420 and the Rover 3.5 litre as being larger than I need. Regretfully, because the Mercedes feels and behaves like a light responsive car and an exceptionally good one at that; because the Jaguar (now out of production but perpetuated as the Daimler Sovereign) has such a superb blend of performance, quietness and ride that I should certainly choose it out of the group for long Continental journeys; and because the Rover was quite the most surprising vehicle of the lot. It still looks like its predecessor, the 3 litre, but it doesn't feel like it. The smoothness and silence of its engine and transmission are remarkable even in this high quality group; it now rolls very little and it goes round smooth corners so quickly, with a minimum of fuss and drama, that it was able to keep station with the convoy very easily. Rough corners it doesn't like so much, and I wish it had instru-

The group test convoy headed (left) by the NSU Ro80, Mercedes 220 and BMW 2000 Tilux. British contenders were the Jaguar 420 (above) and Rover 3½ V-8.

ments, controls and switches like the 2000 or the 3500.

So that leaves the BMW and the NSU at the top of my list and I choose the latter because of its versatility. Its steering, road-holding and handling were approached by some of the other cars but not equalled and this, together with moderate external dimensions and very light controls, made it the fastest car on narrow twisty roads. And because of its ride (in the top three) and effort-less high speed gait it is equally at home cruising along motorways at over 100 m.p.h. There is still scope for someone to make a car with Ro80 road manners, BMW gearbox and fuel economy, Rover refinement, Jaguar per-formance and ride and the Mercedes feeling of solid quality.

Charles Bulmer

● ●

BACK in the late 'forties the big advances in science and technology that had occurred dur-ing the previous 10 years were often held to have resulted from the competitive pressure exerted by the war. Penicillin, the jet engine and radar were the favourite examples quot-ed, though only the last of these could be said to owe both its invention and its development to that event. Fortunately, we now see that technological progress does not depend on the stimulus of wars (major ones at least) for the science of today makes the science of those times look like the phlogistications of an alchemist; the trouble is that not much of it seems to have rubbed off on cars.

For this reason the NSU Ro80 appeals to me greatly as being both scientific and honest in its design—a vehicle worthy of the space age. And when science is tempered with sound judgement it really pays off, for the Ro80 is superior to the other cars—them-selves setting very high standards—in certain important respects, equal and near equal in others. Thus the NSU had the best roadhold-ing and handling of any car in the group (though the Mercedes ran it close) with a ride almost as good as the Jaguar's which was

very good indeed in this respect. In terms of decibels the noise generated by the Ro80's engine and gearbox (neglecting the untypical overrun whine) probably exceeded the gentle sighing emitted by the Rover's propulsive elements by a comfortable margin, but the note of the Wankel is so smooth that, subjec-tively, there can't be much in it. Then there is its body which manages to be roomy, aesthet-ically pleasing and aerodynamically efficient all at the same time. Economy is perhaps its weak point: 18.4 m.p.g. is not outstanding for a 2-litre car, though this may have been partly due to the unnaturally high idling speed of our particular model.

Another cause for thirst is the torque con-verter and the three-speed semi-automatic transmission which I'm not sure that I like despite its all-purpose second gear and NSU don't seem to be as 'convinced of the low-speed torque capabilities of the Wankel engine as they might be—I have happy memories of driving the manual-gear-boxed Mazda 110S, which went very well without a torque converter. Nor is the NSU very fast, especially when compared with the BMW, which has an engine of the same equivalent capacity but has almost the same performance as the Jaguar. But these are minor blemishes: it's still the Ro80 all the way with me.

Tony Curtis

● ●

PERHAPS the most outstanding group we have tried so far with a clear distinction between the more technically advanced 2-litre German cars taxed on to a price par with the larger, luxurious and more traditional British Rover and Jaguar. Unless I lived at one end of the M1 and worked at the other, my choice would come from the German trio and even without the Wankel engine the Ro80 is firm favourite. To throw it round corners with one hand and almost without thought for setting it up is sheer delight; and with such incredible roadholding, who wants handling? You just never seem to reach the limit. Add the effort-

less smoothness of the rotary engine with its almost constant noise level and a seemingly limitless intermediate gear range and you have a car which feels just right in any conditions. Poor window sealing, a rather noisy transmission and some clonking bet-ween gears at rest were irritating but perhaps not typical.

Almost as appealing and difficult to sepa-rate were the Merc and BMW, in that order. The new 220 unit is so smooth that you would hardly guess it was no longer a six. And the new semi-trailing rear end gives a good well insulated ride with exceptionally flat and fast cornering, even if you do have to work a little harder than in the NSU. Perhaps it was tyres but the BMW seemed to break away at the back a little earlier and the engine, though still smooth and extremely lively for a 2-litre, was less flexible low down and a bit more thrummy near the top.

Though not quite my cup of tea, I was pleasantly surprised by the Rover V-8. Big Rovers on mountain roads used to be as manageable as 2 cwt. of cement in a 1 cwt. sack. Now with less weight up front and stiffer suspension, the 3½-litre is quite chuck-able on smooth roads with very little roll, and the onset of the eventual understeer delayed to a limit inconceivable with the 3 litre. The engine is uncannily quiet, showing up wind and tyre noise, and the transmission is about the best mannered automatic I can recall, even though the high intermediate ratio takes some of the punch out of kick-downs.

That I was least happy in the Jaguar is more a tribute to the others than a con-demnation of the sumptuous 420, which is obviously not really at its best on this kind of trip. Steering completely effortless in town is too undergeared and vague to cope with the two-bite technique often called for on tight turns by the generally low levels of adhesion. And the soft suspension swallows irregulari-ties in its path but lacks damping, spending much of its time on the bump stops or the front cross-member over the switchback stuff.

Jim Tosen

M

AUTOCAR 11 June 1970

SED CAR TEST

No. 304
1967 ROVER 3.5-LITRE

PRICES

Car for sale at Nottingham at	£1,475
Typical trade advertised price for same age and model in average condition	£1,500
Total cost of car when new including tax	£2,009
Depreciation over 3 years	£534
Annual depreciation as proportion of cost new	8.5 per cent

DATA

Date first registered	6 April 1967
Number of owners	1
Tax expired	31 May 1970
M.o.T. expires	8 April 1971
Fuel consumption	19-22 m.p.g.
Oil consumption	300 m.p.p.
Mileometer reading	2,512*

*New instrument fitted at 25,346

PERFORMANCE CHECK

(Figures in brackets are those of the original Road Test, published 28 September 1967)

0 to	30 mph	4.5 sec	(4.8)
0 to	40 mph	6.4 sec	(6.6)
0 to	50 mph	8.9 sec	(8.9)
0 to	60 mph	12.2 sec	(12.4)
0 to	70 mph	16.5 sec	(16.3)
0 to	80 mph	23.3 sec	(21.8)
0 to	90 mph	32.5 sec	(31.5)
0 to	100 mph	47.1 sec	(45.0)
Standing ¼-mile		18.4 sec	(18.3)

In top gear:

20 to	40 mph	6.1 sec	(6.8)
30 to	50 mph	7.3 sec	(7.6)
40 to	60 mph	8.9 sec	(8.5)
50 to	70 mph	10.2 sec	(9.6)
60 to	80 mph	11.5 sec	(11.8)
70 to	90 mph	15.5 sec	(15.5)
80 to	100 mph	24.1 sec	(19.8)
Standing Km		34.2 sec	(34.1)

TYRES

Size: 6.70—15in. Avon Turbospeed on all wheels. Approx. cost per replacement cover £11 15s. Depth of original tread 8½mm; remaining tread depth, 7mm front and spare; 6mm rear.

TOOLS

Only one item missing from fitting tray in console; all other tools and handbook complete and little used.

CAR FOR SALE AT:

NCV of Nottingham Ltd., Bulwell Forest Works, Bulwell, Nottingham. Tel: Nottingham 272915.

AT one time the big quality cars for sale secondhand used to be called a "drug on the market", unsaleable except at absurdly low prices. There were not many used cars which could still command more than £1,000 after a couple of years. But times have changed rapidly in this as in other aspects of values, and whereas £775 was the price asked for a 3½-year-old Rover 3-litre tested in this series in 1966, its successor today is valued at £1,475.

However, to give the full picture it has to be pointed out that this figure buys the later model with vee-8 3,528 c.c. Buick-designed engine, Borg-Warner automatic transmission and the other improvements described overleaf. The car is also younger by six months, has covered about 10,000 miles less, and is in even better condition, so perhaps the relative gap in values is not quite as great as may at first appear.

Only the third to be built, this example of the 3.5-litre has a special history since it has been a chauffeur-driven staff car with the Rover Company at Solihull until February this year, and this undoubtedly accounts for its outstanding condition. It has also been brought up to the current specification by addition of automatic mixture enrichment for cold starting instead of the manual control originally fitted. The engine starts immediately whether hot or cold, has the same slight tremor and unevenness which we remember with the original test car, and is extremely smooth and quiet at all speeds.

Every indication is that the engine is in absolutely peak condition, and we were again reminded of the remarkable economy of the unit, with 20 mpg or more readily available while cruising at about 90 mph. In spite of testing on a rather more windy day than we had for the original Road Test in 1967, the Rover still reached 100 mph in 47 sec (only 2 sec longer). A slight oil leak is noticed from the front of the engine.

The automatic transmission has also been updated, and in place of the original D2, D1 and L selector is the more modern and improved D, 2, 1 layout. The lever can be pulled straight back from D to 2, to hold intermediate; the safety button has to be pressed to bring the lever right back to position 1 which holds low ratio. The big advance over the earlier layout is that there

USED CAR TEST . . .

In all respects, particularly appearance inside and out, this is one of the best used cars we have ever reported on in this series. It has, incidentally, the bench rear seat which was a listed alternative to the shaped twin rear seats fitted as standard

is no unwanted locking up of first gear. Maximum speeds in the three gears are 47, 77 and 108mph.

Power-assisted steering was standard, and little effort is needed at the wheel even at manoeuvring speeds, but control is rather vague and woolly with a feeling of looseness about the front end of the car. Directional stability is not quite up to the standard of the 3-litre, with its appreciably greater nose weight, but the 3.5 behaves well as a motorway car, and is little affected by side winds. The suspension is still well damped and taut; there is some tremor over certain surfaces but no float on undulations. With the windows open there is quite a lot of tyre roar, but the usual exceptional Rover quietness is regained with the windows closed, marred only by slight wind whistle around the quarter vents.

Firm pedal load is needed for the brakes but response is good; the brakes are disc at the front, with drums at rear and Lockheed servo. The pull-out handbrake on the right, below the facia, is also very effective.

Bodywork condition is described in the appropriate section below, from which it will be seen that the 3.5 is still in practically new condition. A slight tremor at about 70-80 mph suggests that the wheels are out of balance, but apart from this and the small oil leak mentioned earlier, the car earns a completely clean bill of fitness on all mechanical and driving aspects. Over the years we have had a number of outstandingly well-preserved cars in this series, but this is undoubtedly among the best of them. □

Condition Summary

Bodywork

Close examination reveals that the entire finish has at some time been resprayed, in black, but the work has been very expertly done and does not·appear to be recent. It is certainly not the ''quick squirt'' to smarten up for sale, which many used car buyers are rightly cautious of, and it may explain the colour change from white to black, noted in the log book. The coachwork now is as near faultless as one may ever hope to find in a used car. Similarly the chromium plate and stainless steel brightwork are practically as new. Inside the car, the slight creasing of the maroon leather seats and mild fading of the matching carpets show that the car is not new, but elsewhere—door trim, beige roof lining and polished wood facia and window fillets—the interior is unmarked. Condition is also exceptionally good underneath, because not only has the standard rubberized coating kept rust at bay, but the underneath is also surprisingly clean. Only on the exhaust, where it passes over the back axle, is there any appreciable corrosion, and even here it is still nowhere near due for replacement. Confirming the fairly certain conclusion that this has been a chauffeur-driven car for most of its life, the left passenger door at the front is stiff from lack of use.

Equipment

Last time we had a used car for test from NCV of Nottingham we were challenged to find anything wrong with it, but were able to point out some trivial fault. They obviously take pride in handing out a near perfect car, but we were amused again to come across a detail that had been overlooked—one of the indicator repeaters not working; but everything else is in excellent

order. The speedometer is optimistic, reading 108 at true 100 mph.

Accessories

Basic equipment includes twin fog lamps, efficient fresh air heater, electric washers and variable speed wipers. Twin wing mirrors have been added, but they are rather ugly and wind pressure tends to move them back against their springs at speed. A roof-mounted aerial remains with the car, but the radio has been removed neatly and the centre glove locker lid has been refitted. Clumsy Irvin safety belts are fitted in the front.

About the 3.5

Rover's P5 3-litre saloon was introduced as a new model in September 1958—only the engine bearing any relationship with former Rover products. Overdrive or Borg-Warner automatic transmission were available, and the seven-bearing six-cylinder 3-litre engine with overhead inlet and side exhaust valves developed 115 bhp. Disc brakes replaced the original drums in 1959, and in 1961 the lowered roofline Coupé model was added to the range. Revised cylinder head and induction raised power output to 134 bhp (gross) at 5,000 rpm, and the range became the

3-Litre Mk II, in July 1962. Even more luxuriously trimmed versions of the saloon and Coupé were introduced as the Mark III range in October 1965, identified by a bright strip on each side ending in three square blobs at the rear.

As a big innovation in 1967, the car was given the vee-8 3,528 c.c. engine of all-aluminium construction originally developed for the Buick Special compact, but adapted and built by Rover. With compression of 10.5 to 1, the engine produces 160.5 bhp at 5,200 rpm, and on Road Test gave a top speed of 108 mph (mean). Borg-Warner 35 automatic transmission was standard and even today there is still no manual transmission model. Larger capacity brake servo and special brake pads were developed for the car, while Rostyle wheels and yet another version of the side flash (incorporating two indicator repeaters on each side), plus a 3.5 litre motif on the boot lid, identify the vee-8 version.

Production started at chassis no 84000001, so this car was only the third to be built. Although the introduction was not until 28 September 1967, a small batch was made in April that year, including this used example and our original Road Test car which we took to Sweden for the rule of the road changeover on 3 September 1967.

Classic choice

Rover 3.5

Saloon and Coupe

IF you were glued to the television screen during the recent General Election you may well have witnessed the comings and goings from Buckingham Palace. It must be a peculiarly British state of affairs that our past and present Prime Ministers were conveyed to those august portals in a discreetly luxurious car that ceased production no less than *six years* ago.

The vehicle in question is, of course, the Rover 3½ litre, a car whose roots were well and truly planted in the 'fifties and represents the last vehicle to be produced by the traditional Solihull formula of conservative styling, luxurious leather and wood interior that is a world away from the latest, popular and stylish SD1.

First announced as a 3 litre in 1958 the model received its V8 engine in 1967. Therefore although this article concentrates on the points to look for when buying a 3½ litre many of the checks also apply to the earlier engined version. Not surprisingly, body problems are identical.

To pinpoint the model's shortcoming I went to talk to Richard Stenning, who is technical adviser to the Rover Sports Register and well steeped in Solihull lore. But first a spot of history. The 3 litre was first announced in September 1958 and was significant because it was the first Rover to have a monocoque bodyshell and was called the P5. The styling was carried out by a youthful David Bache being his first commission for the company. (He was later responsible for styling the Rover 2000 and the present SD1 shape). The six cylinder 3 litre engine was developed from the 90 and used the well proven F head layout with overhead inlet side exhaust valve configuration. Although it was externally similar it had a stronger seven bearing crankshaft and roller tappets. The engine, in fact was later to appear in a short stroke 2·6 litre form in the 100 of 1960 and it is still soldiering on in final form (just!) in the Land Rover.

The car was available with a manual or Borg Warner DG automatic gearbox and was the first Rover to be so equipped. As a result the company's slightly complicated home brewed semi automatic, the 105R was dropped.

Front suspension was also a departure from previous practice with laminated torsion bars providing the suspension medium. These were, in effect, leaf springs designed to twist rather than to bend. The suspension and engine and gearbox unit were all mounted on a sturdy box section subframe which terminated beneath the front seats. By contrast the manual gearbox and rear axle were both variations on the P4 theme.

The first change to the specification came in 1960 with disc brakes introduced on the front wheels, trailing shoe drums (like the 90 and 105) had been originally listed. October of the same year saw an optional power steering box introduced, while in July 1961 the Mark 1A appeared, being identified by quarter lit windows and wheel discs destined to appear on the P4 110 of the following year. In July of 1962, the P5 benefited from the Weslake designed cylinder head (also shared with the 110) and being designated the Mk 2. A coupe version was introduced at the same time being only available with power steering it being standardised on the saloon in August 1964. The Mark 3 of

September 1965 had improved seating though the most significant change was the option of the Borg Warner type 35 box in place of the DG unit from the same suppliers.

In 1967 came the major engine change with the lighter all alloy ex-Buick V8 being fitted, the first Rover to be so equipped, the distinctive Ro-style wheels being the most obvious identifying feature. It was designated P5B. The aforementioned type 35 automatic gearbox was standardised and equipped with a floor mounted gear change. A few minor alterations were made during the model's final six years of production. Thinner seat squabs were introduced and built in fog lamps came in September 1968. In all a mere 18,536 saloons and low roof line coupes were built in V8 form, compared with 48,548 three litres. And just to complicate things on the larger engined car, it was originally known as the 3·5 but with the introduction of the V8 version of the 2000 in 1968 it became known as the 3½ litre even if the car's badges perpetuated the original name. The newly introduced model was then dubbed the Three Thousand Five.

So if you're faced with the purchase of one of these cars just what snags are you likely to experience? We'll start with the bodywork because this model really is vulnerable to rusting (far more so than the P4 range which boasted aluminium doors, bonnet and boot lid until 1963 and a separate chassis) and once corrosion really has got a hold there's very little that can be done to halt its advance.

Bodywork

Beginning at the front of the car, first examine the tops of the wings around the side lights. These can rust, as can the lights themselves (and they're expensive to replace). Also rot can manifest itself from the side light in a line down to the front wheel arch along a spot welded seam. Also the bottom of the front wing adjacent to the door is a suspect area. Inside the front wheel arch, the inner wing panel (which gets more than its fair share of stones and mud) will often rot away. You can tell whether this has happened by examining the state of the front carpeting for dampness. On the Coupe, the offside of the scuttle above the wing is one of the more unlikely areas for rusting. Get down on your hands and knees and look for rust on the outer and inner sills together with the jacking points. The bottom of the doors also rust and when you open the rear ones check the shut face and the area of wing adjoining it. This part of the wing is double skinned, the metal being separated by absorbent rubber, so once water has made its presence felt, it tends to stay there. The rear wing inner panel can suffer in a similar way to the front and if this is the case, you may be able to see the red lenses of the rear light cluster if you look towards the back of the car through the wheel arch. Any corrosion may also break through to the boot so examine that together with the lower edge of the boot lid and the panel below it. Finish off the inspection with an examination of the top of the rear wing for tell tail signs of bubbles in the paintwork showing that all is not well below the surface.

CONTINUED ON PAGE 100

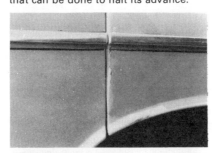

Anti-clockwise from left, aft of the rear door is a rust point; rusting below offside of windscreen is an unusual area to find rust, but not on this model; the area around those sidelights is a point to watch.

USED CAR

No. 353
1970 ROVER
3½-Litre Coupé

PRICES

Car sold at Ruislip at	£1,800
Typical trade value for same age and model in average condition	£1,460
Total cost of car when new including tax	£2,320
Depreciation over 2 years	£860
Annual depreciation as proportion of cost new	18½ per cent

DATA

Date first registered	23 January 1970
Number of owners	1
Tax expires	31 May 1972
MoT	Not yet needed
Fuel consumption	14-20 mpg
Oil consumption	280 mpp
Mileometer reading	27,927

PERFORMANCE CHECK

(Figures in brackets are those of the Road Test of the saloon model, published 28 September, 1967)

0 to 30 mph	**4.2** sec (4.8)
0 to 40 mph	**6.3** sec (6.6)
0 to 50 mph	**8.6** sec (8.9)
0 to 60 mph	**11.9** sec (12.4)
0 to 70 mph	**15.8** sec (16.3)
0 to 80 mph	**21.5** sec (21.8)
0 to 90 mph	**29.6** sec (31.5)
0 to 100 mph	**43.8** sec (45.0)
In top gear:	
10 to 30 mph	— sec (—)
20 to 40 mph	— sec (—)
30 to 50 mph	— sec (—)
40 to 60 mph	**9.2** sec (8.5)
50 to 70 mph	**10.0** sec (9.6)
60 to 80 mph	**11.3** sec (11.8)
70 to 90 mph	**14.8** sec (15.5)
80 to 100 mph	**18.9** sec (19.8)
Standing ¼ mile	**18.0** sec (18.3)
Standing Km	**33.9** sec (34.1)

TYRES

Size: Avon Radial 185HR15 on road, Dunlop SP on spare.
Approx. cost per replacement cover £12.
Depth of original tread 7mm; remaining tread depth 7mm (fronts), 6mm right rear, 5mm left rear, 2mm on spare.

TOOLS

Wheelbrace and jack in boot. Fitted tray of hand tools in centre console.

CAR FOR SALE AT:

Ruislip Motors Ltd., West End Road, Ruislip, Middlesex. Tel: 01-845 2288/9.

IN these days of ever-increasing standardization, it is refreshing to come across any car which is noticeably different from the rest. While only in some respects technical innovators, Rover have always produced cars of character, and in no case more so than in the biggest model in the saloon car range. The 3½-litre, particularly in this coupé form, is a completely individual design; you either like it very much or have no interest in it.

This particular example, a two-year old car which shows relatively few miles on its mileometer and has only one owner listed in its log book, gave the impression of being a car that has seldom been driven near its full extent. Ruislip Motors explained to us that they had not had time to give it a full service before handing it over for this test, and from the way it behaved at first we were somewhat disappointed. The car tended to stall when ticking over in Drive, there was an obvious rough patch on at least one of the disc brakes which produced a rhythmic vibration at low speed, and when we first gave it its head before

performance testing began, it emitted considerable oil smoke on over-run and not a little. with power on. Happily all of these symptoms of a too-sedentary life disappeared with a little brisk (but not unkind) use.

The vee-8 aluminium engine is quiet and very smooth. Full application of the rather heavy throttle still gives good performance, as the figures show. The Borg-Warner Type 35 automatic transmission is up to standard, giving quite smooth changes up on full throttle, but not so smooth on a light throttle, coupled with the customary reluctance to kick-down quickly when required; it also has an alarming habit, which we met on the Road Test saloon 3½, of making a very noticeable "bonk" while changing down as one coasts to a halt at traffic lights; this became worse during the short test period.

The car is at its best in town, where it rolls along most pleasingly quietly. In such environments this luxurious Rover is something not that far removed from driving a favourite club armchair. It is the sort of car which Britain can produce better than any other country. The large, firm, yet well-shaped seats with their adjustable armrests in front are very comfortable, even if a 6ft driver is encouraged to recline the seat back somewhat in order to give his head reasonable clearance from the roof. You sit very high in this Rover whatever the adjustment of the seat, and of course vertical adjustment by winding handle at the front of the seat is provided as well.

The power steering is light and virtually devoid of feel; the vendors assured us that the constant slight pull to the left would be rectified before sale. Roll is reasonably well controlled and in spite of the car's bulk it can be hustled along, should the fancy take you, with surprising aplomb. Some attention to wheel balance would eliminate the slight vibration felt at speed. The lock is not generous, which must be remembered when parking. Ride is quite good.

Curiously upthrust, the instrument binnacle with its lower encrustation of lesser binnacles for the minor instruments is another point of individuality which one notices immediately on getting into the driving seat. The Rover is one of the few cars where it is sensible not to put your ignition key on even an average-size key fob, as this hangs down and hides the view of the fuel gauge. Headlamps give an excellent amount and range of illumination.

In addition to the untypical initial slow-speed braking vibration which disappeared after a while, there was also a tendency for the brakes to rumble during any repeated long stop from high speed, such as one finds oneself making while driving along a fast dual carriageway with frequent roundabouts.

Condition summary

Bodywork

Paintwork is in excellent condition and we found no suggestions of either accident damage or misuse — no paint chips at the front, no obvious corrosion anywhere. It was that much more surprising to hear the bonnet hinges creak loudly and to find that three of the four jacking point bungs were missing. Underneath the only obvious point needing minor attention was the gaiter on one rear spring which needed re-fixing. A new exhaust has recently been fitted. The only slight oil leaks were one from the differential and another from the timing case by the water pump; otherwise this was a most clean engine. There was also a small leak from the top water hose. One wheel centre badge was missing. Two stains, one an ink one, mar the upholstery's good preservation, and some scratches and obvious attempts to touch up small blemishes can be seen on some of the handsome door wood cappings. The left-hand back door lock needed a heavy push to make it secure, suggesting the need for a drop of oil.

Equipment

All lamps work as they should, though the winkers do not always self cancel. We wondered whether the very small wiper blade size was right. The ones fitted left very large areas of screen uncleared; during the test the driver's one broke its arm. Only 4 mph optimistic at 100 mph, the speedometer needle is delightfully steady, but the fuel gauge shows only $\frac{7}{8}$ full when the tank has been brimmed. The $3\frac{1}{2}$ is in one small respect more sensibly equipped than its smaller brother the 2000; the convex interior mirror is unlike the 2000 one — not too small or so heavily convex, ensuring that one is not given such an unnecessarily diminished image. This car also has good wing mirrors.

Accessories

It was nice to find a compass left on the car, although as usual one regrets that no one seems to make such a useful accessory that looks better than a rather vulgar cheap toy, its design out of place on such a car. The radio had been removed from the car, but not the roof aerial, which was, however, loose, as was the washer nozzle in front of the driver. Everything else that most discerning drivers would demand of a properly equipped car is standard and in good order.

About the Rover $3\frac{1}{2}$ coupé

The coupé version with its strikingly swept-down roofline first appeared in 6-cyl 3-litre form two years after the P5 saloon was announced in September 1960.

With the introduction of the originally Buick-based, then Rover-developed, $3\frac{1}{2}$ litre aluminium alloy vee-8 power unit, the car took on a new lease of life in September 1967. The engine appeared in the big saloon and Coupé before the smaller 2000 body. No manual gearbox was then available to take the greatly increased torque of that lively yet very refined engine, so automatic transmission became the only form of gearbox available on this model. The car remains in production today, having laminated torsion-bar double wishbone front suspension with power assisted worm-and-peg steering and a half-elliptic leaf-sprung live axle at the rear. □

The Rover is finished in the attractive shade of dark maroon which suits it very well, and the paintwork is in very good condition, free from any chips or minor blemishes. The chromium brightwork also shows no rust pockets or scratches. The engine (above) is pleasantly clean, confirming that the car has been cared for and kept well serviced. There are no oil leaks from the engine, but a small water leak from the top water hose was noticed. There are one or two small blemishes inside the car, and reasonable signs of use, including general staining of the grey floor carpets. Rovers are somewhat prone to this. The leather seat upholstery is unmarked and the seats themselves extremely comfortable. A pull-out tray in the centre of the console opens to reveal a fine tray of fitted tools. Below: Apart from some marks on the rubber floor mat, the boot interior is also pleasantly clean

You would not expect it from a look at the shape of the car, but owing to the tendency one develops towards slouching, there is enough space for a tall adult in the back, both in headroom and kneeroom, even when the person in front is also tall and has set the seat-back reclined sufficiently to give himself enough headroom. The only unwelcome intrusions upon one in the back are, physically, the awkwardly placed seat-belt reels which are set noticeably towards the centre of each footwell, and, visually, the side pillars which blinker one somewhat.

In spite of these — in the main — minor criticisms there is much to recommend this model to the sort of buyer who wants a solidly built car, distinguished as something that stands out in that peculiarly contradictory English way, by not being conspicuous.

CONTINUED FROM PAGE 97

Engine, gearbox and transmission

The six cylinder 3 litre engine is a hard-working unit and will go on practically indefinitely, the main symptom of excessive wear being an inexhaustible demand for oil. When new these engines were never particularly economical in that direction, consuming lubricant at a rate of 400 to 500 miles to the pint. An engine in average condition should use about a pint of oil every 250 miles but anything below that tends to be something of an annoyance. If you want to check the oil consumption, let the engine tick over for a minute or so and then blib the throttle. Clouds of blue smoke will tell you too much of the stuff is finding its way into the combustion chambers, probably via the inlet valve guides.

Similarly the V8 is an extremely reliable power unit but like any engine it does have its shortcomings. Top end noise is likely to be caused by excessive wear of the rockers and rocker shafts. Also if the car has been standing for any length of time, the hydraulic tappets may sound somewhat on the noisy side and you'll have to give the oil a chance of circulating. Be particularly suspicious of a mis-fire which is often difficult to detect on an eight cylinder engine. The thing is that it isn't such a minor problem as might first appear because it can be caused by the block warping and compression thus being lost, a tiresome and expensive problem to sort out. Then the distributor can give trouble. From 1967 until 1972 the base plate was mounted on an offset pivot and if undue wear occurs it can affect the dwell angle and starting problems can ensue. However, in the autumn of 1972 a concentric base was introduced and the problem resolved.

On the 3 litre the gearbox is a sturdy enough unit but the front bearing in the layshaft can wear, a shortcoming also found, naturally enough, in the P4 range. Otherwise the box was a strong and robust component. However, on the 3½ litre a Borg Warner type 35 box was fitted and there might be problems with this rather lightweight unit. Remember that V8 engine produces 160 bhp. You may experience problems with the floor change shift for this can become sloppy through the nylon bushes wearing. The rear axle, common to both cars, dating back in design to the early 'thirties' is exceptionally strong and reliable. It is important to keep the oil breather clear as if it becomes blocked, pressure can build up in the axle casing.

Steering, suspension and brakes

The problem area in the steering department on these cars centres on the power steering unit that was standardised in 1964. This can, unfortunately, develop leaks, usually from the rocker shaft. It is a major exercise to remove the box and a new replacement is £356 plus VAT or £126 plus VAT exchange. An annoying side effect of the box leaking is the fact that the fluid tends to drip onto the front suspension rubber which isn't a particularly good idea. A minor problem is that the steering wheel tends to crack around the edge, a state of affairs somewhat disguised by the horn ring.

Compared with the P4, the independent front suspension on the P5 and 5B is extremely long lasting. The swivel pins are sealed and tend to have a long working life but are expensive to replace when the time comes. Suspension at the rear of the car is by half elliptic springs and these are inclined to settle with age rather than break. The trouble is that a new pair costs around £200. A rather unlikely check point on these units are the rubber rear spring shackles. They do perish and when the car is jacked up on the body they can be subjected to undue strain.

The brakes are discs at the front and drums at the rear and any problems will probably be associated with the former. Scored discs are obviously a point to check and these units are fairly prone to seized wheel cylinders, particularly if the vehicle has been stored for any length of time. The pistons themselves are chrome plated and rust can break through.

Interior

This is a major plus. The cars are extremely well finished and trimmed with leather. They are essentially four seaters, the rear ones being separated with a substantial arm rest. Sound deadening contributed to produce a particularly quiet car. The wooden door fillets are a pleasant feature and the floor is well carpeted. Avoid an example that requires major attention to the seats. Trimming is an expensive business these days.

Spares

Fortunately the spares situation is in a fairly healthy state at least at present. Most mechanical and body parts are still available, many at specially reduced prices. Some items are expensive. The front bumper for instance costs over £100. But if you are thinking of opting for a V8 then this is a major plus. It remains to be seen, however, how long this state of affairs lasts.

The club that caters for both the 3 litre and 3½ litre is the Rover Sports Register, the membership secretary being Adrian Mitchell, 42 Cecil Road, Ilford, Essex.

How much?

Now just how much would you expect to pay for either a 3 litre of 3½? Let's take the older model first. At the present time these really are worth next to nothing, particularly as they are prone to body rot, so anything up to £100 should secure a good one. The V8 is rather a different kettle of fish. Prices seem to start around £600 while £1600 is the going rate for one in particularly good condition. And although they're half a litre larger than the older version they're slightly more economical (19·2 mpg, as opposed to 18·2 mpg, according to Autocar). They're also marginally faster with a maximum speed of 108 mph.

Comfort, reliability and good spares availability (that V8 should remain in production for years) make a 3½ Rover a particularly attractive proposition. But don't forget that body rot!●

Clockwise from above, Great Auntie has a stately presence — hence her use on State Occasions!; in the back sculptured leather armchairs and all mod-cons; the pull-out tool tray was a feature; the engine is still used today in SD1, so spares should be available for some time.

a new ROVER

This — the Rover 3 litre — is an entirely new car. It is longer, lower, wider, yet it handles with a quite delightful delicacy. Comfort and visibility are outstanding, and the performance exceeds that of any other Rover.

PART 2

. . . and the 60, 75, 90 and 105 are all improved

These four famous Rovers are now improved both in appearance and in technical specification. Prices: 2 litre 60: £1349.17.0 (inc. p. tax); 75: £1478.17.0 (inc. p. tax); 90: £1538.17.0 (inc. p. tax); 105: £1628.17.0 (inc. p. tax)

THE ROVER COMPANY LIMITED, SOLIHULL, WARWICKSHIRE AND DEVONSHIRE HOUSE, LONDON, W.1.

WHAT LOOKS RIGHT is right! The Rover is indeed lovely to look at and the Italian influence in its design is immediately apparent.

promise between the separate-chassis and unitary principles; the main hull being compositely built, and having attached to it, with rubber abutments, a sub-frame carrying the engine and front suspension units. This allows of a lower floor than would normally be possible with the conventional type of chassis frame, and gives many of the advantages of the chassis frame in respect of an accident to the front of the car, in that engine, suspension and steering relationship are controlled by the sub-frame, which is easily replaceable. When I first inspected this lay-out, and before having driven the 3-litre, I was a little dubious, suspecting a lack of stiffness at the junctions between the two elements. In practice, however, the car gives a feeling of tremendous tautness, with less suggestion of flex in

As the proud and enthusiastic owner of one of the first 3-litre Rovers to go into circulation on the roads of Britain, I am glad to say that the makers of the car have been able to give even me a real surprise, and a new thrill. I had previously owned a series of four Rover "105s", and I honestly could not see how, at or anywhere near its price, the makers could improve on this car in anything other than minor details.

Well, they have certainly done it. Rover fans all over the world, their appetites whetted by rumours of a new model in the offing, had a long wait for the 3-litre's public debut last September; and many of them are having another long wait for the fulfilment of eagerly-placed orders. If ever a car were worth waiting for, this is it. With the special opportunities which I have for sampling current cars of every type and nationality, I can say with absolute sincerity that there is nothing to touch the 3-litre Rover in the under-£1700 bracket (tax included) today.

One might sum it up as an upper-class automobile at a middle-class price. It is fast, with a higher maximum speed than the great majority of family motorists would ever wish to use. It is economical on fuel (relative to its weight and carrying capacity) and has the special merit that its "thirst-curve" does not make a startling upswing when the full performance potential is used. Driven as a "racing car" the consumption is 19/20 m.p.g., and at considerably lower speeds, making full use of the overdrive, and cruising around 70 m.p.h., I have done a test run giving figures of 24/25 m.p.g. It is handsome—if you like the kind of sober good-looks which are essentially British, and no poor imitation of a foreign theme. It is luxurious to a degree that is outside the experience of many people who pay more for their transport. All the qualities—plus others that I shall put down as they come into my head—add up to a pervasive charm that is as hard to describe as it is irresistible.

As the final "credit" in the ledger, I would add this: The Rover Company, not content with a specification that it bristling with good and ingenious points, take pains to eliminate the bad ones. To do so sounds obvious enough, but how many manufacturerers mar basically sound designs by such little idiocies as obscuring an important instrument behind a wheel

THE FINEST ROVER OF ALL
Raymond Mays views the latest disc-braked car from Solihull

spoke, carpeting a floor in such a way that it cannot easily be swept out, or positioning a window-winder so that it barks the knuckles?

With frequent commitments at faraway Continental destinations, usually in connection with the B.R.M. racing programme, my prime requirement in a car is that it shall be fast in the broadest sense, (not merely capable, that is to say, of spectacular but brief speed bursts), safe, and reliable at any speed within its scope, and comfortable and quiet enough to enable driver and passengers to cover distances of seven or eight hundred miles in one day without having to take the next day off for rest and recuperation. Demonstrably, the 3-litre meets these needs, in a manner which I find constantly reminding me, as one who has owned many modern Bentleys, of these first cousins to "The Best Car in the World."

In matters of steering and general roadability, advanced technical terminology does not come easily to me, but I do know that this 3-litre, with its widened track, laminated torsion-bar front springing, and ingenious bonded-rubber substitute for normal shackles at the rear end of the rear semi-elliptics, holds the road in an exemplary way. In my opinion the steering of the car is exceptionally light for a car of its weight. The impression one gains, in spite of the retention of a live back axle, and the usual penalty this entails in terms of unsprung weight, is that the road wheels follow the slightest surface irregularity as though pinned down by a weight far in excess of the Rover's ton and a half (dry).

This characteristic of the suspension would account for many of the virtues that the car does in fact possess: e.g. tenacious braking (more of that anon), the ability to maintain high cornering speeds almost regardless of surface roughness, and a sense of isolation of the hull and its occupants from nether shocks and shake-ups. The car's structure is a com-

the frame than most rivals based on a fully-fashioned chassis. In-built rigidity is important, of course, not merely from the handling point of view, but also as insurance against the development of body creaks and rattles in hard service; and here the 3-litre easily maintains the makers' tradition of lasting silence.

One would have to be unlucky in one's encounters to become involved in misadventures with the 3-litre Rover, but it is nevertheless reassuring that the car's wings are detachable units, and thus relatively inexpensive to repair in the event of shunts. This 3-litre is quite one of the most docile and gentle cars to handle that I have ever driven, and its capabilities can be fully enjoyed by a driver who does not wish to extend the car.

The Rover Company paid me the compliment of equipping my car with the braking system which is now standard on the 3-litre, consisting of discs at the front and drums at the back, both by Girling. For these no praise is too high, and it is impossible to conceive that "discs-all-round" treatment could bring any improvement. For my own interest, and because the makers wanted an independent opinion based on the hardest usage, I have repeatedly made "crash" stops from an indicated 100 m.p.h. Under this punishment the brakes have never squealed, locked, developed fade, or pulled a hairsbreadth out of a straight line. Pedal pressures are extremely light too. With 10,000 miles now on the clock, the front brake pads have plenty of life left, and even at the speeds at which the car was driven it appears from measurement that the pads would have lasted for 20,000 miles.

I have not had an opportunity to time the car for maximum speed, but the speedometer needle has often been round to the point on the dial that would signify 105 m.p.h. (100 is the highest actual calibration); and, it being Rovers' policy to shun excessive "flatter", I consider it probable that a genuine century has been topped. This, of course, would not be an unreasonable assumption, with 115 b.h.p (gross) harnessed to a car of moderate height and what appears a quite good aerodynamic shape.

Like most owners, and prospective owners of Rovers, however, I am not so much concerned with flat-out maximum so long as I can cruise effortlessly and tirelessly at speeds in the 85 to 95 m.p.h. region. Crossing France *en route* for this year's Geneva Motor Show, and sharing the driving with my manager, Henry Coy, we did better than that, keeping the needle between "90" and "100" for much of the journey. Our best one hour average was 76 m.p.h., between Rheims and Troyes, and I have quite often put 60 miles into the hour on Continental journeys.

On a more recent journey to Monte Carlo, in connection with the Grand Prix there, the Rover put up some really staggering performances. Before leaving Bourne I fitted a set of experimental type India tyres, and I set off with the intention of really thrashing the 3-litre and the tyres, to see what would happen.

My usual route from London to Lausanne, just short of 600 miles, was done in the first day, at a very high average speed. During this run I came across two different makes of car, both considerably faster in maximum speed than the Rover, but on the hilly, twisty sections of the road running towards Dijon I was able to overtake and leave these cars purely through the amazing road-holding qualities of the Rover around corners with a bumpy surface. From Lausanne to Beaulieu-sur-Mer, our headquarters for the Monaco Grand Prix, I travelled by Grenoble over the Route Napoleon to Digne, and over the Alpes Maritimes to the Mediterranean coast. Here again my average speed was extremely high but, as always on this Rover, my journey's end was reached with no fatigue, and no backache whatsoever, owing chiefly to the perfect padding of the driving seat, and the way in which the steering wheel, and for that matter all the controls, virtually fall into one's hands.

At Monte Carlo the car was used merely for backwards and forwards journeys to the circuit and the garage, plus a few runs into the lower and higher Corniche, where again I was able to test the 3-litre's cornering abilities and the brakes.

My return journey is worthy of a little more detail. As I was travelling alone there was nothing to interfere with my determination to make this a real test run. I left Beaulieu at 6.45 a.m., and other than stops for petrol, my first port of call, for a really fantastic luncheon, was at the Pyramid Restaurant, Vienne. After leaving Vienne I had one short break for an orange juice and cassis at Chatillon, and again, other than petrol stops, I drove straight through to my night's destination at Rheims. With detours, of which there were several, the mileage was 612, and this I covered in a running time of 10 hours 10 minutes. From Rheims I set off the following morning to catch the Townsend Ferry at Calais, and, with the detour after St. Quentin, the mileage of 178 was covered in exactly 2 hours 41 minutes. During this spell, on the very fast roads north

GIRLING DISC BRAKES are fitted on the front and proved to be utterly reliable for repeated crash stops made by Mays. Life of the brake pads would appear to be in the region of 20,000 miles.

of Rheims, I covered one stretch of 40 miles in exactly 30 minutes, another 50 miles was covered in 39 minutes, and for several kilos. on end the speedometer was consistently reading past the 100 m.p.h. mark. I realise that it is most unlikely that anyone except an experienced driver of high-speed machinery would attempt these speeds with safety, but I can with truth say that I observed all the danger spots and speed limits with real care.

On the 3-litre, Rovers give an option between automatic transmission or a normal synchromesh gearbox with Laycock Overdrive. My car has the latter, which is particularly suited to the good pulling power of the enlarged engine (torque for the 3-litre is quoted as 164 lb. ft. at 1,500 r.p.m., compared with 138 lb. ft. at 1,750 for the smaller unit). Although no longer the height of fashion the long-stroke engine—77.8 by 105 mm. in this case—deserves full credit for lusty pulling, witness the fact that I have formed the habit of flicking into overdrive at speeds as low as 50 m.p.h., except when maximum acceleration is needed.

The Rover version of the Laycock system has two features which appeal to me; one is a kick-down switch for getting back into normal top in a hurry without moving a hand from the wheel rim; the other is a throttle switch (nothing new, of course), as a safeguard against manual down-shifts out of overdrive whilst on the over-run, with consequent snatch.

To revert for a moment to engine performance: one must pay tribute to the Rover's absolute lack of vibration, regardless of speed or load. Mention of this characteristic recalls that the new unit, although sharing such features as overhead inlet and side exhaust valves with Rovers' smaller sixes, is virtually a brand new design, examplified by its use of a seven-bearing crankshaft and roller tappets.

On every score except one very minor one—a badly placed windscreen washer pedal—all the controls and interior appointments are excellently thought out and executed. The central gear lever is

placed exactly where the hand drops on to it naturally. The relative positions of the gear lever and the long-stemmed overdrive switch (the latter projects from the left-hand side of the steering column cowl) are perfect for "playing tunes" on these inter-related controls. The lever-type switches for the head lamps and the flashers (on the right of the column), have a beautifully delicate and responsive touch, and are of different lengths to avoid any possibility of muffed fingering.

The heating and ventilating arrangements are thorough in the extreme. Breaking away from normal practice of today, the driving compartment side windows do not have a pivoting triangular pane; instead, all four winding windows are topped by horizontal louvres, and these, for my money, have distinct advantages, both as regards rain exclusion, and *genuine* no-draught ventilation. Independently controlled by driver and front-seat passenger are two separate vents in the corners of the sponge rubber anti-crash roll that sweeps right round the top of the dash; and these ventilators can be regulated to direct cool, fresh air either into your face or over your head, the latter stream circulating throughout the whole of the interior of the car, thus keeping the atmosphere round the face fresh, even when the interior heaters are working. Another neat feature is the combining of two functions in the main heater control lever; moved vertically in its slot it takes care of the hot/cold transition; whilst the system's booster is brought into action by simply pulling the same lever towards you. Under the facia panel there is a full-width tray for personal oddments, and, below it, two additional cold-air vents with "pull-out and twist" regulators, that enable cooling blasts to be directed at the feet of the driver and his companion.

Since I owned my first Rover, a "14", back in war-time days, the Solihull firm has produced many fine cars. But they are going to have to do some hard thinking before they build one to beat this superb 3-litre.

The  3-litre in detail

Of now traditional Rover design, the 3-litre engine has overhead inlet and side exhaust valves. There are 7 copper-lead crankshaft bearings. The cylinder block is cast integrally with the crankcase; the cylinder head is of aluminium alloy. The camshaft is driven by a double roller chain and has an hydraulically-operated automatic tensioner.

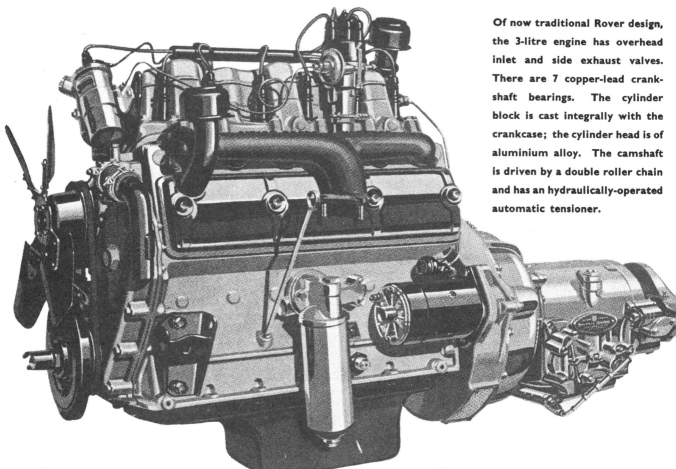

Engine, clutch, gearbox, front suspension and steering components are all mounted on a welded steel chassis unit, the whole assembly being secured to the unitary-construction body by six rubber mountings which provide insulation against noise and vibration. Front springs are laminated torsion bars. Hydraulic telescopic dampers are employed at front and rear. The engine's valve gear employs roller-type cam-followers.

The Rover 3-litre Saloon

THE name of Rover has for many years been synonymous with thoughtful design and quality workmanship in what might be called the "upper-middle" price range.

One expects a Rover to reach a high standard in all matters having a bearing on refinement of operation, ease of servicing and long life. One expects a Rover to hold a particularly strong appeal for many mature, experienced motorists who take a pride in their driving and in the cars that they drive.

The Rover 3-litre, which we recently had on test for five days, has all the expected Rover attributes in generous measure—and, in slightly favourable conditions, it will attain a speed of 100 m.p.h.

Beneath its deliberately rather conservatively-styled body, the Rover 3-litre has many ultra-modern mechanical features. Studying this car's design, one comes to the conclusion that it has been conceived by a firm which is eagerly progressive at heart (as, indeed, has been proved by Rover's experimental gas-turbine cars) but which firmly resists the temptation to offer anything to the public until it is fully satisfied that, in addition to providing advantages of performance, the innovation will endorse—or, preferably, enhance—the marque's name for long, trouble-free service.

An example of this is found in the structure of the vehicle, which is a combination of chassis and chassisless construction. There is a half-chassis at the front to carry the engine and the front suspension system. By means of six rubber mountings, this is attached to an all-steel unitary-construction body hull to which box reinforcements are welded to carry the rear suspension system. Quite extraordinary precautions are taken to guard against rust attacking the body, and lavish use of sound-deadening materials insulates the vehicle's occupants from road-excited noise.

Thus does Rover seek to offer "the best of both worlds" : the weight-saving (and therefore performance advantage) of unitary-construction together with the benefits more commonly associated with the use of a separate chassis.

A similar process of reasoning results in : an engine with overhead inlet and side exhaust valves; the use of roller cam - followers, permitting valve openings and "dwell" that ensure improved breathing without disadvantage; the employment in the front suspension of laminated torsion-bar springs which, like leaf springs but unlike coil or solid torsion-bar ones, possess inherent self-damping effect.

Throughout the car there is a wealth of evidence of the manufacturer's determination to please the more fastidious type of motorist and to ensure that he shall be troubled by an absolute minimum of maintenance. By means of rubber in some places and sealed-in lubricant in others, grease nipples are avoided and chassis lubrication, in the accepted sense, is virtually eliminated. The recommendation regarding the lubrication of the

continued on page 107

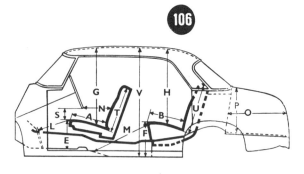

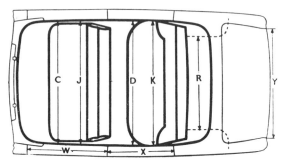

INTERIOR DIMENSIONS

		Inches
A	Front to rear of front cushion	18½
B	Front to rear of rear cushion	18
C	Width of body at front of front seat	59
D	Width of body at front of rear seat	59
E	Top of front cushion to floor	12
F	Top of rear cushion to floor	16
G	Headroom—Front seat	36½
H	Headroom—Rear seat	34
J	Width of body at rear of front seat	59
K	Width of body at rear of rear seat	59
L	Front cushion to accelerator pedal	19½
M	Rear cushion to foot rest	24
N	Front squab to steering wheel	13½
O	Locker depth	30
P	Locker height	19½
R	Locker width	43
S	Top of front cushion to steering wheel	5¼
T	Front squab height	22
U	Rear squab height	23
V	Height of interior of body	49¾
W	Width of front door at waist	36
X	Width of rear door at waist	30
Y	Minimum external width of boot opening	48½

The **off-side front suspension** system, as seen from above. All ball joints are sealed to retain their lubricant and to prevent the entry of dust and water; the links are rubber-bushed and require no lubrication.

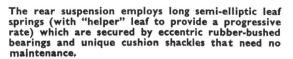

The rear suspension employs long semi-elliptic leaf springs (with "helper" leaf to provide a progressive rate) which are secured by eccentric rubber-bushed bearings and unique cushion shackles that need no maintenance.

Pistons are of inverted V-shape to accommodate the contours of the combustion chamber. Generous provision is made for cooling. The advantageous positioning of spark plugs and the arrangement of overhead inlet and side exhaust valves are evident in this drawing.

continued from page 105

front suspension system, for example, is that it be "checked at 12,000-mile intervals".

Driving the Rover 3-litre, one is immediately impressed by the silence of travel, by the power and smoothness of the engine, and by the obvious care with which the positioning of the controls and instruments has been planned.

As will be seen in the performance panel at the end of this report, we found reasonable maximum speeds in the indirect ratios to be 74 m.p.h. (3rd), 50 m.p.h. (2nd) and 30 m.p.h. (1st)—these correspond with approximately 4,900 crankshaft r.p.m. and the power unit is completely smooth at this speed. There is no doubt that, if expense can be ignored, the ideal is to have a crankshaft supported by a main bearing between each cylinder. The Rover 3-litre has this; the counterbalanced crankshaft of its 6-cylinder engine runs in 7 copper-lead tin-plated bearings, and it is fitted with a harmonic vibration damper.

The gear ratios suit the car excellently. It is entirely feasible to travel at 12-15 m.p.h. in top gear and, if desired, to pull away smoothly from this speed without employing a lower ratio. Provided that the clutch is operated with reasonable delicacy, starts from rest are easily made in 2nd gear, and 1st gear may be regarded as an emergency ratio for use only when starting on an appreciable adverse gradient. There is, in fact, a temptation to do this, for 1st gear is not particularly quiet; 2nd gear, however, is quieter than average, and 3rd gear very noticeably so. Top gear (direct drive) is, of course, silent.

The ratios that are provided by the gearbox are shown in the data panel. The spiral-bevel rear-axle drive provides a reduction of 3.9 to 1, producing overall values of : 1st 13.166, 2nd 7.968, 3rd 5.368 and top 3.9 to 1. The outstanding flexibility of the engine and the good spacing of the ratios provide a generous "overlap" of performance, resulting in the car being uncommonly versatile and in the driver being able to follow almost any procedure that appeals to his mood. Apart from the more obvious techniques, he may if he wishes start in 1st and change straight to top at about 20 m.p.h.; or he may start in 2nd and, again ignoring 3rd, change to top at any speed up to 50 m.p.h.; or he may engage 3rd at little more than a fast walking pace.

A variable ratio is provided by the recirculating-ball worm-and-nut steering gear. When travelling straight ahead the ratio is 17.6 to 1; this gradually increases as the steering wheel is turned, until at full lock it becomes 26.9 to 1. Here, again, one sees the Rover attitude of mind regarding the art of compromise, the objective in this particular instance being to obtain the advantages of quick steering response when travelling fast without the usual attendant drawback of considerable effort being required for parking manoeuvres. The system works well in practice; it is, in our opinion, second only to a first-rate power-steering system—and it is, of course, mechanically far more simple than the latter.

The variable ratio "averages out" at 4½ turns of the steering wheel being required to move the front wheels

A view of the driving controls and instruments. The accelerator-like pedal to the left of the clutch pedal actuates the dip-switch of the headlights and it also acts as a foot-rest.

The engine compartment is well filled by the 6-cylinder 3-litre engine. All components requiring regular attention are readily accessible; particularly evident in this photograph is the high-mounted ignition distributor.

from one extreme lock to the other. There is quite strong self-centering action; the driver never finds it necessary to "unwind" the steering wheel after negotiating a sharp corner.

Good as it is in other respects, the most praiseworthy feature of the Rover's steering is found when the car is being cruised at about 90 m.p.h. The manner in which the vehicle holds to a straight course when being cruised fast is altogether delightful and contributes towards the notable ease with which long journeys are made at high average speeds.

Roadholding is good for this style of car, particularly if the driver uses the accelerator pedal correctly as he travels round fast corners. There is quite marked understeer (a characteristic allied to the car's ability to maintain a straight course at high speed), and excessive exhuberance when cornering can result in audible protest from the front tyres.

It is fair to say that there is very little body roll and no tyre noise when the car is appropriately driven. In this connection it should be remembered that the Rover 3-litre is not a "sports saloon". It is a quality family-car

continued

equipped with a powerful, quiet, docile engine. Rapid acceleration and outstandingly restful high-speed cruising, rather than ultra-rapid cornering, enable it to achieve the high average speeds of which it is capable.

Wind-roar when travelling fast is very much below average, and an excellent ventilation system (entirely independent of the heater which is also a standard fitting) permits the windows to be kept shut and air to be fed into the car's interior via four separate channels, two at head-level and two at leg-level.

A high standard of riding comfort is provided on all surfaces, including untarred, corrugated roads, and in this matter the suspension system is aided by superbly comfortable seats.

The brakes are powerful and show no sign whatsoever of fade during even considerably faster-than-usual motoring. Pedal pressure is light; there is a vacuum-servo. Hard braking from speeds above 85 m.p.h. in the

The spare wheel is carried beneath the floor of the boot; removal of a rubber plug under the floor-covering provides access to the valve of the spare wheel's tyre. The battery is housed in a container on the right-hand side of the boot.

test car did occasionally result in some judder which, although never sufficiently pronounced to make such braking hazardous, was definitely un-Rover-like.

The range of standard equipment and the quality of internal and external finish are fully in harmony with the car's price of some £1,700. On closely inspecting his acquisition, the buyer of a Rover 3-litre will find a multiplicity of pleasing details that reflect thoughtful design. In contrast to these, he may note that, when in the "on" position, the hand-brake lever hinders operation of the off-side front window-winder, and he may feel that exterior appearance would be further enhanced if the end of the exhaust pipe were equipped with a chromium-plated surround. Also, if his fingers are not slender, he may find it difficult to operate the safety catch of the bonnet.

In summary, the Rover 3-litre provides elegant, fast, effortless, luxurious and trouble-free motoring. Many South Africans who appreciate the meaning of quality motoring—with all its aspects and connotations—will undoubtedly find this Rover a most desirable possession.

SPECIFICATION AND PERFORMANCE

BRIEF SPECIFICATION

Make ... ... ROVER
Model 3-litre
Style of Engine Straight 6-cylinder. Water-cooled. Overhead inlet and inclined side exhaust valves; single camshaft, roller cam-followers. 7-bearing crankshaft.
Bore 3·063 ins. (77·8 mm.)
Stroke ... 4·134 ins. (105 mm.)
Cubic Capacity 183 cu. ins. (2,995 c.c.).
Maximum Horse-Power Approximately 115 gross b.h.p. at 4,500 r.p.m. (Compression ratio 7·5 to 1).
Brakes Hydraulic. Servo-assisted (vacuum). Trailing shoes at front; leading and trailing shoes at rear.
Front Suspension Independent. Laminated (5-leaf, square-section) torsion bars. Anti-roll torsion bar.
Rear Suspension Semi-elliptic leaf springs with "helper" leaf to provide progressive rate.

Transmission System Clutch and four manually-engaged forward gears. Synchromesh on 2nd, 3rd and top gears.
Gear Ratios ...
1st 3·376 to 1
2nd 2·043 to 1
3rd 1·377 to 1
Top Direct
Rev. 2·968
Final Drive Ratio ... 3·9 to 1
Overall Length ... 15 ft. 6½ ins.
Overall Width ... 5 ft. 10 ins.
Overall Height ... 5 ft. 0½ in.
Ground Clearance 8 ins. (7·10-15 tyres).
Turning Circle ... 38 ft. 6 ins.
Dry Weight ... 3,350 lbs. approx.
Price ... £1,698 at Coast Ports

PERFORMANCE

Acceleration 0-30 m.p.h. 4·5 secs.
0-40 m.p.h. 7·2 secs.
0-50 m.p.h. 9·4 secs. (2nd gear)

0-50 m.p.h. 11·7 secs. (3rd gear)
0-60 m.p.h. 16·1 secs.
0-70 m.p.h. 22·7 secs.
0-80 m.p.h. 32·6 secs.
In top gear from a steady 20 m.p.h. to 40 m.p.h. ... ... 8·6 secs.
In top gear from a steady 30 m.p.h. to 50 m.p.h. ... ... 9·8 secs.
In top gear from a steady 40 m.p.h. to 60 m.p.h. ... ... 10·9 secs.
In top gear from a steady 50 m.p.h. to 70 m.p.h. ... ... 13·1 secs.
In top gear from a steady 60 m.p.h. to 80 m.p.h. ... ... 20·2 secs.
Maximum Speed ... 97·8 m.p.h.
Reasonable Maximum Speed in 3rd Gear ... ... 74 m.p.h.
Reasonable Maximum Speed in 2nd Gear ... ... 50 m.p.h.
Reasonable Maximum Speed in 1st Gear ... ... 30 m.p.h.
Fuel Consumption ... 24·4 m.p.g.
Test Conditions Sea level. Moderate wind. Dry road. 90-octane fuel.

IT HAS BEEN over seven years since we have had a Rover to test, and fond memories of that earlier car prompted us to make a special effort to get our hands on the completely redesigned 3-liter, or P-5, model.

Our first ride in the 3-liter was a memorable event, for it involved a very close race against time to catch a plane at the London airport. Our driver left the hotel at a modest pace, but when fully aware of the emergency, we really flew. The car felt very lively and we did catch the plane. However, for our first drive and this road test, it was necessary to go to New York City as there were no 3-liters on the West Coast at the time. Frankly, this unusual procedure (for us) brought a few headaches, for finding a suitable stretch of road in that area is all but impossible. Ultimately we found a likely spot somewhere in the middle of Long Island and we managed to lay out a ¼-mile strip without being asked any embarrassing questions by uniformed persons. Speeds above 80 mph were absolutely out of the question in this locale and we made no attempt to get even one top speed run; in fact, it took quite a while (because of traffic) to get a timed run at a steady 80 mph, as required for the speedometer calibration. However, the British Press says this is a genuine 100 mph car and we see no reason to doubt it, provided the 3.9 axle is used.

First impressions of a car sometimes prove wrong, but the Rover never seems to lose its charm. This one had the optional Borg-Warner automatic transmission and in driving out from the firm's new Eastern headquarters in Long Island City, we admitted (grudgingly) that the automatic had its charms—at least in heavy traffic. In fact, the one outstanding virtue of this car is its silky-smooth quietness—a feature much enhanced by the inclusion of the automatic unit. With the exception of one car (we don't mention the name, but it's synonymous with quality) this is the most refined automobile we have ever driven.

Getting down to the facts, the performance in terms of elapsed time isn't exactly brilliant, particularly after a correction for a rather considerable speedometer error that we just didn't expect in a Rover. Nevertheless, one should note that our test weight exceeded 4000 lb. Also, as is well known, the automatic inhibits performance times and for that reason we have plotted the results of a British test on a similar car equipped with the 4-speed transmission, an overdrive and a 4.3 axle. (See dotted line on acceleration graph.) The automatic transmission version still gets from a standstill to a corrected 60 mph in the respectable time of 17.7 sec, despite the fact that the upshifts occur at 4000 and 4200 rpm respectively, well below the peak power speed of 4500 rpm. (This is done intentionally to eliminate engine noise at full throttle.)

Steering is just about right for such a car as this and we liked its easy, precise feeling. Moderately vigorous cornering produces an extraordinary amount of tire howl, which may have been caused by the nearly new tire treads. There appears to be neither under- nor over-steer and, though there is more roll than we like, the rear end never seems about to let go and the handling qualities can be honestly summarized as good.

Another outstanding feature of the Rover is the Girling

ROAD TEST ROVER 3-LITER

Stately, refined, and elegant,

an altogether superb automobile

Sometimes contemporary mixes with traditional very well indeed.

No glittering band mars the Rover's smooth and uncluttered flanks.

brakes. These are discs in front and drums at the rear, with a diameter of 11 in. The rear shoes are 2.5 in. wide and the rear lining area is 173 sq in., nearly as much area as some similar-weight cars have on all four wheels. A completely innocuous vacuum power booster makes the pedal light but not overly sensitive.

From a technical standpoint, the 3-liter car embodies a host of new and very advanced design features. A unit frame and body is not new, of course, but in the Rover application, extraordinary measures have been incorporated in order to eliminate the last vestige of noise and vibration. For example, in front we find a completely separate sub-frame made of welded steel sections. This carries the engine, transmission, front suspension and steering components, and is attached to the body by 6 rubber insulating mountings. The body hull itself is made entirely of welded steel, including all doors and lids. (The older Rovers used aluminum paneling on all hinged parts.) Fortunately, the indescribable thud of a coach-built door being slammed shut has been retained.

The front suspension is similar to previous Rover practice with Thompson ball joints and rubber-bushed wishbone pivots. However, the coil spring has been replaced by a Salter-type laminated torsion bar, in order to reduce its overall length. Rear springs are conventional variable rate semi-elliptics, but with a very unusual application of rubber at each end to improve shock insulation. Rubber

is also used to insulate the steady-bearing (sealed-ball-type) mounted near the center of the propeller shaft. In short, everything on the car that moves, shakes or vibrates is rubber insulated.

While the 3-liter engine follows previous Rover practice and uses some of the same parts, it is actually a fairly drastic redesign. Thus the ioe valve system (intake over exhaust, or F-head) is unchanged in principle—the block is iron, the head is aluminum and the pistons have the double wedge shaped dome of earlier engines. However, the increased displacement was obtained by a larger cylinder bore (from 2.875 to 3.062) and the cylinder block and crankshaft are entirely new, as a result of a change to 7 main bearings for greater smoothness. There are also many detail changes, including a new roller tappet design to improve camshaft durability as well as to bring the valve gear capability up to the higher speed potential of the new crankshaft (5000 rpm is recommended limit, not attainable on automatic transmission cars).

The big advantage of the ioe arrangement is that it permits very large valves with plenty of room for adequate water cooling passages. However, in the Rover the valve sizes and the valve timing sequence have been selected primarily to give very good low speed torque rather than high output at high speed. Note, for example, that this engine develops its maximum efficiency (torque) at only 1500 rpm, yet the torque figure is equivalent to

Crowded but entirely accessible.

The trunk: spacious and easy to load.

From any angle, a delight to the eye.

0.9 lb/ft per cu in.—very exceptional in view of the peaking speed. What does this mean to the owner/driver? Simply this: in normal driving 1500 rpm is equivalent to 31 mph, and we do a lot more of our everyday driving near this speed than we do at 92 mph (4500).

As for the top end, the 3.9 axle appears to be optimum, for 4900 rpm is only a little past the peak-power point and is equivalent to 100 mph. As a matter of fact, the British test gives the timed top speed as 90.8 mph (mean) in the 4.3 high gear and 96.4 mph in the 3.35 overdrive ratio—which certainly indicates that a ratio somewhere between would give more top speed.

Externally, as shown by our color photo, the Rover is exceptionally clean, accented by a bold grille treatment of traditional Rover shape. The Rover Company had several Italian designers working on this project but no designs were entirely acceptable. The general theme looks (to us), though, as if Farina might have added a touch here and there. In our opinion, the car looks its best in a single color scheme, primarily because the factory dual-color options are separated so low (on the sides) that they make the car look high. The actual height, loaded, is just over 5 ft.

The interior of the Rover is a very nice compromise between the old British school of wood and leather and near-austere contemporary. The seats are leather covered, of course, and wood trim is used sparingly. The front seat is a bench-type, and folding center arm rests are found both front and rear. Very luxurious bucket-type seats can be ordered at extra cost. The instrument panel layout is compact, properly cowled, and one of the neatest and best we have ever seen. There is a glove box and, below this, a full width parcel shelf. Immediately below the shelf, on the passenger's side, a thin drawer-like affair pulls out to disclose a well equipped tool tray. Each tool has its own foam-rubber-lined space. Large tools are clipped into place on the inside of the trunk and covered by a clip-on flap. No imaginable detail has been overlooked and no expense has been spared to make the Rover's interior a study in true luxury. Its safety features are well thought-out and the greatest possible passenger comfort is provided.

Of course, the delivered price of over $5000 is rather steep, and Rover does have an entirely new 2.2-liter 4 cyl model (with the old style body) that sells for much less. This is the model 80 and there is also a model identical with the 80 (externally) to be known as the 100, powered by a 2.6-liter 6 cyl engine with 7 main bearings. However, for our money, we think the Rover 3-liter is an excellent value for those who buy quality rather than price and who do not feel the need to buy a new car every couple of years.

ROAD & TRACK ROAD TEST 228

ROVER 3-LITER

SPECIFICATIONS

List price	$4995
Curb weight	3770
Test weight	4070
distribution, %	54/46
Dimensions, length	187
width	70.0
height	60.3
Wheelbase	110.5
Tread, f and r	55/56
Tire size	6.70-15
Brake lining area	n.a.
Steering, turns	4.3
turning circle, ft	38.5
Engine type	6 cyl, ioe
Bore & stroke	3.06 x 4.14
Displacement, cu in	182.7
cc	2995
Compression ratio	8.75
Bhp @ rpm	115 @ 4500
equivalent mph	91.8
Torque, lb-ft	164 @ 1500
equivalent mph	30.6

PERFORMANCE

Top speed (3rd), mph	100
best timed run	n.a.
3rd ( )	
2nd (4200)	60
1st (4000)	35

FUEL CONSUMPTION

Normal range, mpg	18/22

ACCELERATION

0-30 mph, sec	5.8
0-40 mph	9.1
0-50 mph	13.0
0-60 mph	17.7
0-70 mph	22.7
0-80 mph	35.0
0-90 mph	
0-100 mph	
Standing ¼ mile	21.6
speed at end, mph	64

GEAR RATIOS

O/d ( ), overall	
3rd (1.00)	3.90
2nd (1.43)	5.60
1st (2.31)	9.00
1st (2.3 x 2.1)	18.9

TAPLEY DATA

4th, lb/ton @ mph	@
3rd	220 @ 42
2nd	310 @ 35
1st	500 @ 25
Total drag at 60 mph, lb	162

CALCULATED DATA

Lb/hp (test wt)	35.4
Cu ft/ton mile	76.5
Mph/1000 rpm (3rd)	20.4
Engine revs/mile	2940
Piston travel, ft/mile	2025
Rpm @ 2500 ft/min	3770
equivalent mph	77.0
R&T wear index	59.5

SPEEDOMETER ERROR

30 mph	actual 28.1
40 mph	37.1
50 mph	46.1
60 mph	55.7
70 mph	65.0
80 mph	74.0
90 mph	
100 mph	

ROVER 3-LITER
automatic ———
manual – – – – –
ROAD & TRACK

MPH (corrected) vs ELAPSED TIME IN SECONDS

ROVER

3-litre Mk II Saloon

ENGINE CAPACITY: 183.17 cu in, 2995 cu cm;
FUEL CONSUMPTION: 21 m/imp gal, 17.5 m/US gal, 13.4 l x 100 km;
SEATS: 5 - 6; MAX SPEED: 115.0 mph, 185.1 km/h;
PRICE: list £ 1,358, total £ 1,641.

ENGINE: front, 4 stroke; cylinders: 6, vertical, in line; bore and stroke: 3.06 x 4.13 in, 77.7 x 104.9 mm; engine capacity: 183.17 cu in, 2995 cu cm; compression ratio: 8.75 x 1; max power (SAE): 134 hp at 5000 rpm; max torque (SAE): 169 lb ft, 23.3 kg·m at 1750 rpm; specific power: 44.7 hp/l; cylinder block: cast iron; cylinder head: light alloy; crankshaft bearings: 7; valves: 2 per cylinder, overhead inlet, with push rods and rockers, side exhaust with roller rockers; camshaft: 1, side; lubrication: gear pump, full flow filter; lubricating system capacity: 6.5 imp qt, 7.8 US qt, 7.4 l; carburation: 1 SU

horizontal HD 8 carburettor; fuel feed: electric pump; cooling system: water; cooling system capacity: 13.4 imp qt, 11.2 US qt, 12.7 l.

TRANSMISSION: driving wheels: rear; clutch: single dry plate; gear box: mechanical; gears: 4 + reverse and overdrive; synchromesh gears: II, III, IV; gear box ratios: (I) 3.376, (II) 1.887, (III) 1.274, (IV) 1, (ov.) 0.778, (Rev) 2.968; gear lever: central; final drive: hypoid bevel; ratio: 4.3 : 1.

CHASSIS: box-type long members and cross members; front suspension: independent, wishbones, laminated torsion bars, anti-roll bar, telescopic dampers; rear suspension: rigid axle, semi-elliptic leafsprings, telescopic dampers.

STEERING: recirculating ball; turns of steering wheel lock to lock: 4.75.

BRAKES: front disc, rear drum, servo.

ELECTRICAL EQUIPMENT: voltage: 12 V; battery: 57 Ah; dynamo: 200 W; ignition distributor: Lucas; headlights: 2 front and reversing.

DIMENSIONS AND WEIGHT: wheel base: 110.50 in, 2807 mm; front track: 55.00 in, 1397 mm; rear track: 56.00 in, 1422 mm; overall length: 186.50 in, 4737 mm; overall width: 70 in, 1778 mm; overall height: 59.25 in, 1505 mm; ground clearance: 6.70 in, 170 mm; dry weight: 3589 lb, 1628 kg; distribution of weight: 55 % front axle, 45 % rear axle; turning radius (between walls): 21.0 ft, 6.4 m; tyres: 6.70 - 15; fuel tank capacity: 14 imp gal, 16.8 US gal, 64 l.

BODY: saloon; doors: 4; seats: 5-6; front seat: double.

PERFORMANCE: max speed in 1st gear: 28.0 mph, 45.1 km/h; max speed in 2nd gear: 50.5 mph, 81.3 km/h; max speed in 3rd gear: 76.0 mph, 122.4 km/h; max speed in 4th gear: 96.0 mph, 154.6 km/h; max speed in overdrive: 115.0 mph, 185.1 km/h; power-weight ratio: 26.7 lb/hp, 12.1 kg/hp; useful load: 1058 lb, 480 kg; acceleration: standing ¼ mile 19.6 sec, 0 — 50 mph, (0 — 80 km/h) 11.2 sec; speed in direct drive at 1000 rpm: 18.7 mph, 30.1 km/h.

PRACTICAL INSTRUCTIONS: fuel: petrol, 90 oct; engine sump oil: 5.0 imp qt, 6.0 US qt, 5.7 l, SAE 20W, change every 3000 miles, 4800 km; gearbox oil: 2.3 imp qt, 2.7 US qt, 2.6 l, EP 90, change every 12000 miles, 19300 km; final drive oil: 1.5 imp qt, 1.8 US qt, 1.7 l, EP 90, change every 9000 miles, 14500 km; steering box oil: 0.3 imp qt, 0.4 US qt, 0.4 l, EP 90; greasing: every 6000 miles, 9600 km, 1 point; tappet clearances: inlet 0.006 in, 0.15 mm hot, exhaust 0.010 in, 0.25 mm hot; valve timing: (inlet) opens 13° before tdc and closes 45° after bdc, (exhaust) opens 48° before bdc and closes 16° after tdc; tyre pressure (medium load): front 28 psi, 2.0 atm, rear 28 psi, 2.0 atm.

VARIATIONS AND OPTIONAL ACCESSORIES: Borg-Warner automatic gear box, hydraulic torque convertor and planetary gears with 3 ratios (I 2.308, II 1.435, III 1, Rev 2.009), possible manual selection, max ratio of convertor at stall 2.10, axle ratio 3.9 : 1, speed in direct drive at 1000 rpm 20.5 mph, 33.0 km/h; compression ratio 8.0 : 1; power-assisted steering, 2.5 turns of steering wheel lock to lock.

THE 3 LITRE ROVER

By JIM WHIPPLE

CONTINUED

Solid comfort, long life and staid steering

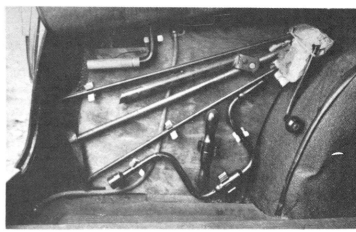

Above: Legendary lifespan of Rover depends on well understressed 7-bearing engine, every one of which is factory tested. Above right: Complete tool kit is standard. Right: Instrument cluster is complete and legible.

ROVER
CONTINUED

Above: Neat, ruggedly finished trunk houses "keep cool" battery. Spare is kept in well underneath.

THE new 3-Litre Rover costs just under $5000 by the time it reaches the East Coast of the U.S. Although it isn't a big car by our standards, its 187 inches is packed with British quality, some 4070 pounds of it to be exact. After a thorough examination I became pretty well convinced that its trim and finish pretty well justified its cost. For me, at least, there's something well nigh intoxicating about the scent of genuine leather, the soft gleam of polished wood and restrained chrome trim. I'm brainwashed before I even touch the ignition key.

In England the Rover has long been a thoroughly "upper-upper" car. It comes in along with the Jaguar and one or two others as "the next best thing to a Rolls Royce or Bentley." At $7000 less than that haughty pair, the new Rover offers a grade of quality and a manner of fitting that is closely approached by only one or two of our very finest cars. The late, and for me definitely lamented, Continental Mark II was the only U.S. car built since the war to top the Rover in quality.

In physical dimension the Rover is a five-passenger sedan, laid out with somewhat the same compromise in width, 70 inches, as the new American compacts. Wheelbase is 110 which puts the Rover squarely in the company of the Falcon-Rambler-Lark contingent. Rover is powered by an in-line six of 182 cubic inches displacement which is rated at ·115 horsepower.

In spite of its compact dimensions there is a massive look about the Rover 3-litre, borne out by its weight of over two tons. Not that there is unnecessary bulk and poundage, because the Rover's weight is well accounted for in heavier gauge body paneling and structural *Continued*

One of world's most reliable cars, Rover persists in providing hand crank.

members than a car of this size would normally call for. Rover's unit body and frame structure is nearly bank-vault solid. Other extra pounds have gone into heavier insulation and extensive sound-proofing materials.

Little effort has been spared to make the Rover's interior as quiet, comfortable and elegant as a London club. There's plenty of room for four on the luxurious bench seats, with broad center arm rests front and rear. Underneath the pleated leather of the cushions there's deep foam rubber over springs. There's also room for a third passenger in the rear seat, if all three are of average size or smaller. A sixth passenger could sit up front for a short trip, but for all intents and purposes the 3-litre Rover is a five-passenger car. The transmission housing up front is fairly broad and the gearshift lever swoops out from under the package shelf in dead center, meaning problems for the center passenger's knees. Of course, with automatic transmission this would be less of a problem.

Leather is used through most of the interior, with high quality leather-cloth (British terminology for plastic) covering the windshield and door pillars above the window sill line. Carpets are deep, soft wool.

A unique and very good idea is the padded roll at the window sill level on each of the four doors. This padding is continued from the rear seatback all the way across the top of the instrument panel. Below it there's a narrow wood panel trimmed with chrome beading. This padding would cushion much of the blow if passengers were thrown violently against the side of the car by a bump or accident.

Rover is full of such practical extras as front arm rests that adjust in a vertical plane at the push of a button, four individual interior lights that turn on with a switch at their location or go on automatically when the nearest door is opened.

Seating position is high and quite comfortable. However, quick adjustment is fore and aft and manual only. The tilt or "rake" or the front seat may be adjusted more or less permanently by fastening and unfastening various nuts and bolts. It's always been a source of wonder to me why makers of European luxury cars don't offer the tremendous practical convenience of the four or six-way power operated front seat. They may think that it's just another toylike

American luxury gadget and sneer at it as such, but I'll bet all the bolts in Birmingham that if one were installed in the personal automobile of the Rover Company's Board Chairman he would not only keep it there but would get the message and make it a stock item. No amount of seat design, no matter how expert, can suit the sizes, postures and contours of so many so well as the power seat. In my opinion it should be standard equipment in any car costing over $4000.

Rover pursues the Citroen theory of ventilation, one which has considerable merit. There are no pivoted glass ventilation wings, the idea being that fresh air, be it outside temperature or heated, should enter the car through damper controlled air ducts, whereupon it will be free from rain, dust and insects. There is also better vision through the unbroken span of glass in the side windows.

Unfortunately, to make any ventilating system efficient, air must not only be brought into the car—it must also be allowed to escape. On the Rover 3-litre such exhaust is provided by lowering the side windows slightly. This can be done even in foul weather because there is a transparent deflection visor on the outside of each window. These visors keep the rain out, as they are intended, but at speeds of 45 mph and up there arises such a bellowing, whistling and roaring as to nullify the painstakingly successful job of soundproofing.

The Rover 3-litre gives a choice of two basic transmissions, the four speed synchromesh manual (with optional overdrive controlled from the steering column) or Borg Warner three speed automatic.

The test car had the standard manual without overdrive, which seemed to be a pretty fair gearbox with synchromesh on the top three speeds. Shifting is easy, quick and quiet up to fourth and back down into third, but a bit sluggish going back down into second. I for one feel that at Rover's price synchromesh should be on all gears.

Steering is manual through recirculating ball gear with 4½ turns lock to lock. There is no optional power steering. I felt that the steering is definitely hard at speeds below 25 mph. Just as all American cars of 4000 plus pounds need power steering, so does the Rover.

The steering picture is further darkened by the fact that out on the

road the steering action is neither adequately precise nor quick. It's not what you would expect on a Jaguar or Humber Super Snipe.

Rover's suspension system is modern in design, with ball joint front spindles and independent laminated torsion bars up front and long leaf springs liberally insulated with rubber in the rear. Shock absorbers are direct acting telescopic all around. In addition, the front suspension and engine are mounted on a separate stub frame a la Mercedes, insulated from the main unit body by six rubber biscuits at the mounting points.

As far as ride is concerned the car is somewhat disappointing. There is a feeling of a great deal of the unsprung weight of the wheels, axles, etc., tossing up, into and through the springs—feeding more judder and vibration back into the body than should be. Springs seem firm in that they inhibit sway, plunge and excessive roll in cornering. There is no problem with excessive pitching (i.e. fore and aft rocking), but when you do hit a sharp bump it's pretty sharply telegraphed back into car motion. The beautifully upholstered seats do a good job of taking the sting out of these occasional jounces, but nevertheless they are there and would not be as bad in, say, a Plymouth or Valiant.

On smooth surfaces Rover corners well, hanging on nicely with only a trace of understeer and tire scrub. However, should you corner on a rippled or bumpy tar surface, rear wheel hop lifts the tires free from the pavement and centrifugal force gets in its licks, pulling the car sideways.

The Rover's overall performance level in brisk touring and traffic work is satisfactory with light or moderate loading. The long stroke engine (3.06" x 4.13") has good high gear torque pulling smoothly up from 15 in high. The engine is smooth and vibration free all the way through the revs.

To sum it all up, Rover is a sedate and solid luxury package almost completely lacking in sporting characteristics. It provides, except for wind noise, smooth, vibration-free travel on good roads and does so at acceptable cruising speeds. Judging from its quality of construction and engineering (it has only two chassis lubrication points) the 3-Litre Rover should provide the same level of smooth, solid transportation for year after year. **END**

The Rover 3-Litre has established itself as a thoroughly outstanding motor car. It has all the grace and comfort required of a town carriage; yet it possesses in full measure the dash—and stamina—necessary for long-distance motoring. A removable division is now available to convert the 3-Litre into a touring limousine. Power steering is an optional extra.

The 80 and 100 complete the Rover range for 1961. The Rover 80 has the new Rover 4 cylinder 2¼-litre engine. The Rover 100 has the new 2.6-litre sloping head engine with 7-bearing crankshaft. Front wheel disc brakes and overdrive are standard equipment on all three Rover models.

The Rover 80 £1,365.7.6d. (inc. P.T.)   The Rover 100 £1,538.4.2d. (inc. P.T.)
The Rover 3-Litre with conventional gearbox £1,783.5.10d. (inc. P.T.); with automatic transmission £1,864.0.10d. (inc. P.T.)

ROVER

THE ROVER COMPANY LIMITED, SOLIHULL, WARWICKSHIRE; ALSO DEVONSHIRE HOUSE, LONDON W.I

A paradise for road-testers, the Autobahn near Dessau in East Germany broadens into six unbroken lanes for the 10-mile *Rennstrecke* of pre-war fame. The Rover wound up to pass 100 m.p.h. on the clock.

GERMAN JOURNEY

By

DAVID

SCOTT

CROSS—

Outside the Chinese exhibition hall at the Leipzig Fair, where the lily ponds and jade carvings of yesteryear have given way to displays of machinery and manufactured goods in keeping with the industrial growth of the mammoth sub-continent.

IT was at an evening reception for businessmen in the stately Chinese exhibition hall at the Leipzig Fair. Hushed strains of exotic music from the mysterious Orient mingled with the gay tinkle of glasses and laughter from Occidental guests as I exchanged pleasantries with one of the Chinese trade officials while surveying the 19-ft. Red Flag rotating majestically on its glazed turntable (news-scooped in *The Motor* of March 9). This massive saloon boasts a 5.65-litre V-8 engine believed to be of local design, and I told my host that I would very much like to look under the bonnet.

He (*through a Chinese-German interpreter*): "But it is moving."
Me: "Perhaps it could be stopped."
He: "The glass would not support your weight."
Me: "We could put down a board or inverted table for me to stand on."
He: "The hall is so crowded with people during the day."
Me: "I could come after 6 p.m. when it is closed."
He (*thinks*): "Capitalist spy."
Me (*thinks*): "Maybe it hasn't got an engine."
He (*smiling*): "Come, let's have a drink."

From an earthenware bottle on a nearby table he decanted a nip of colourless fluid that tasted like radioactive firewater. The subject was dropped.

But viewed soberly in the light of all that is claimed for it, the Red Flag is a significant development indeed. Not only is it the first serious car to enter mass production in China's five-year-old motor industry, but the evolution from idea to manufacture at the Changchun plant was carried out in record time. According to reports, the prototype was made in mid-1958, final designing and tooling-up started in November, and production began in August of last year.

Spurred on by patriotic stimulants like the "Great Leap Forward," the factory workers and their families apparently pitched in with a round-the-clock effort to achieve in little more than one year what more sophisticated motor firms would regard as at least a three-year job. This is typical of the fantastic rate of economic growth of Communist China, which has startled western businessmen making visits to that country. As early as last year it met the Five-year Plan production targets previously set for 1962, and, for example, more than doubled the output of steel in that one year, and increased by 70% that of machine-tools to overtake Britain in this field.

Equally important is the design of this car, which embodies a number of advanced and complex technical features, and is furthermore not a copy of any Russian model. For an infant industry to cut its teeth on a V-8 engine with hydraulic tappets and four-choke carburetter, together with an automatic transmission and power steering and brakes, is no mean

"He decanted a fluid that tasted like radioactive firewater."

CURTAIN ROVING IN A THREE-LITRE AUTOMATIC

accomplishment. No child's play, either, is turning out such a machine on the production line, even though daily output is as yet numbered only in dozens.

And although the Changchun plant, commissioned in early 1956, was built and equipped with Russian help and its first vehicles were replicas of a Russian 4-ton lorry, China has now set off on a new tack with a car of its own conception.

Initially, the country's industries were cast in the Soviet mould in order to telescope the preliminary stages of industrializing a vast, backward nation. Russian finance, equipment and engineers were combined with local labour and materials to produce Russian-designed machine-tools, tractors and many other items.

But the picture is gradually changing, and the shift was reflected in a number of the Chinese exhibits at Leipzig that were proudly indicated as fruits of domestic talent. Why a luxury motorcar intended solely for government officialdom was selected as one of the points of departure is difficult to explain in economic terms. Politically, however, it makes sense. Just as in the West a Rolls-Royce or Cadillac may be a projection of the individual

ego, so in the Communist world a home-built car has become a national status symbol—a rolling testimony to economic maturity.

Judging by other impressions gained at the Fair, China is already chewing more than some of the other Soviet-bloc countries have seen fit to bite off. East Germany, despite its long-standing motor industry, is still producing only a trickle of cars for its 17 million people. While government planners have lavished investment funds on capital equipment, achieving rapid advances in both technology and output, road vehicles have had a low priority.

Target for this year is a mere 67,000 cars, rising to only 115,000 by 1965 at the end of the current Seven-year Plan. As a result, costs are high, and prices are deliberately further inflated for rationing by purse. Thus motoring for pleasure is confined to the few—mainly heroic factory workers laden with overtime cash, and highly paid professional people and politicians.

However, attempts are being made to lower costs in spite of small volumes by narrowing the production programme on the basis of a division of labour among allied Communist states.

East Germany is now making only two different passenger cars, the 500-c.c. Trabant and 900-c.c. Wartburg, bridging the gaps in its domestic range by imports from Czechoslovakia and Russia.

During the past year, decks at the Zwickau works have been cleared entirely for the Trabant, the chosen favourite. Both the 690-c.c. P-70 and the 2.4-litre Sachsenring (ex-Horch) saloon have been dropped, and manufacture of the 4-ton Sachsenring lorries has been transferred to the former bus factory at Werdau (since buses will no longer be made in the country). With undistracted concentration on this model, annual output is expected to increase from the 1959 figure of 20,000 to 65,000 in five years.

A new variant of the baby Trabant (meaning sputnik in Russian, fellow-traveller in English) seen at Leipzig was a tidy-looking "Kombiwagen" à la Hillman Husky. With two on board and the

China's Red Flag progressed from design stage to series production in little more than a year. Powered by a 220 b.h.p. V-8 engine, it boasts advanced features like an automatic transmission, power steering and a station-seeking radio.

The Renaissance Old Town Hall in central Leipzig is now completely restored after damage during the war. It is used as an art gallery and museum.

GERMAN JOURNEY

of reach of East Germany's car-hungry masses. While a good industrial wage is some £550 a year (converting at the official exchange rate), the Trabant costs £630. Absence of hire purchase further raises the financial hurdle to private ownership, and the agony is prolonged by a two-year waiting list. Then there's a big jump to the cheapest Wartburg at £1,250, with a wait of 9 or 10 months even at that figure.

Among Communist imports the Skoda comes to £1,235, the Russian Moskvitch £1,320 and the Volga £1,900. These are the principal foreign makes available in the German Democratic Republic, and during the Fair a contract was signed for delivery of 3,000 Volgas during 1960.

Only a few hundred Western cars were purchased last year, and those currently on sale are the Renault Dauphine (£1,450) and Simca Aronde (£1,570). Yet hope springs eternal among Western motor manufacturers, who are as hungry for new markets as the East Germans are for cars. Merely a shortage of hard currency and political predilections bar the way.

Standard has made a few sales in recent years, and this time its sixth appearance at Leipzig was rewarded with a token order for 19 Heralds under the complicated "Fair Contingency" arrangement. Rootes sold 21 Minxes on the same basis, while Rover saw prospects of breaking the commercial ice with the Land-Rover. Its standing offer to put this go-anywhere machine against the Russian-built GAZ-69 (a pale imitation, bought by East Germany) on any desired course has so far been declined.

Renault, Simca and Daimler-Benz were other outside-world exhibitors. These displays of business enterprise and perseverance in the face of great odds by firms from the "decadent" West should gladden the hearts of loyal citizens at home. At the same time, their domestic customers would undoubtedly be even gladder if they got half the concessions on prices, spare parts and delivery charges offered to foreign importers in the Soviet orbit.

If nothing else, the paucity of cars in East Germany makes motoring in that country a restful experience, even by Continental standards. In fact, this was our easiest cross-Curtain trip yet, the only irritants being on the western approaches.

The new simplification of international travel formalities meant that the British Customs were satisfied with Form 29 (c) Sale (costing 3d.) instead of a carnet and other papers, saving time and bother as well as £3. The Assistant Touring Manager of the R.A.C. took this loss of revenue from me philosophically, saying that this was what the Club had been working for (although he hoped that I might one day go to Spain or Portugal where a carnet is still required!). At the inter-zonal border dividing Germany no documents are needed since theoretically it's all one country.

But after a pleasant Channel crossing on the Dover-Dunkirk night ferry, and with the promise of starting the long eastward trek in the dawn's early light, it was galling to have to wait unattended 30 minutes or so at the port while the local customs and immigration men finished their breakfast (as was reported). Here the boatload of Britons in their chilled cars languished on the bleak quay, like so many phlegmatic camels trying to pass through the needle's eye of French officialdom. To do our Gallic friends justice, however, this dilatoriness may well be calculated retribution for the meticulous scrutiny with which Her Majesty's authorities screen alien visitors, for at France's inland border points motorists are admitted with the utmost casualness.

From Dunkirk the coastal road brought us quickly to Ostend, then 65 miles of motor road provides a swift run to Brussels where

rear seat jack-knifed forward it has a luggage capacity of 460 lb., the cargo area being reached through a full-width rear door.

This model has several points of technical interest. Like the saloon it is of unitized construction, using a steel skeletal frame combined with glass-fibre mouldings for most of the external panels. These reduce weight and noise as well as saving scarce sheet metal and lowering tooling costs. Only the floor, wing interiors, door frames and roof supports are steel, while aluminium is used for bright trim.

The 18-b.h.p. engine, a two-stroke air-cooled twin, is in unit with the transmission and suspension assembly. It is transversely mounted in the frame as a compact front-drive package that can be easily withdrawn for servicing. Aluminium cylinder barrels are cast integral with the iron liners, and fuel mixture is inducted directly into the crankcase via a rotary valve on one of the crankshaft webs, then channelled via transfer ports to the upper cylinders.

Another novel feature is the system for ventilation and heating. Warm air from the shrouded engine is blown through a heat exchanger incorporated in a section of the forward exhaust pipe, then ducted to the car interior. In summer the flexible outlet tube is detached from the exchanger and slipped onto a fresh-air intake on the front of the body.

As for the Wartburg, it continues unchanged except for a few minor improvements to the steering and gearbox. Yearly production at Eisenach of this estranged relative of the West German Auto Union is now about 32,000, with the 1965 target fixed at 50,000. Despite these small numbers it is still made in no fewer than nine body styles in an effort to penetrate western markets. The policy of variations on a theme has had some success, and last year 1,000 Wartburgs were sold in the German Federal Republic, although their price is slightly higher than the similar Auto Union 1000, and well above that of the Volkswagen.

Domestic prices as well as scarcity put these two models out

The new estate car version of the Trabant is a tidy little car. The Trabant's blower-cooled two-cylinder engine incorporates a heat exchanger (just behind the front valance) in the exhaust system to provide warm air for interior heating of the car.

Right: The walled town of Zerbst is more than 1,000 years old, and believed to be one of the earliest settlements in Germany.

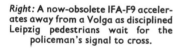

Above: Lawgiver Roland overlooks the market-place at Zerbst, East Germany. This 400-year-old statue was rescued from the bomb-destroyed town hall.

Right: A now-obsolete IFA-F9 accelerates away from a Volga as disciplined Leipzig pedestrians wait for the policeman's signal to cross.

the fine expressway offers transit through that jukebox jungle with gratifying haste. But from here on let the traveller through the Lowlands beware.

Belgian driving and parking habits and that country's secondary roads are a fearful combination, for standard practice among tradesmen is to leave their truck or car blocking half the narrow two-lane stretch outside their port of call in open country, although there is usually ample space in front of the building. When this lethal custom is coupled with Grand Prix weaving and passing by those on the move, one is glad to leave these folks behind for their more methodical Dutch neighbours.

Yet Holland occasionally demands caution on the financial side, for at the border money-changing bureau at Ittervoort we were apparently taken for innocents abroad, and I was initially offered an absurd exchange rate for guilders that was raised only after haggling. Later I was assured that this was exceptional, since most frontier offices are maintained by reputable banks.

Speed and Comfort

Once on the German Autobahn it was plain sailing, and here our Rover 3-litre did much to recapture a relaxed feeling of well-being, for it showed itself to be capable of extremes of speed as well as of comfort. With little effort the 115-b.h.p. engine wound up to beyond an indicated 100 m.p.h., while steady cruising in the upper 80s proved an easy gait.

Even at such a pace the car is one of the quietest I have ever driven, and invites comparison with a Rolls. The inaudible clock is a minor refinement deserving credit, as is the ashtray that is engineered to slide open noiselessly. With the windows closed it is possible to converse in normal tones, and the intricate

system of personalized ventilation directs a controllable wedge of fresh air on your face while warming the feet.

Relaxation must have been in the air, and somehow affected the East German frontier guards at Marienborn on the inter-zonal boundary, scene of many frustrating bureaucratic delays on previous crossings. More likely they were under the influence of the cold thaw in East-West relations; anyhow, they cleared us in a mere 15 minutes, and let us out again in less than five on the homeward journey ten days later.

Dash to Decadency

This border marked the start of a memorable westward run to Dusseldorf, in which the 246 miles were covered in exactly four hours for an average of 61.5 m.p.h. Seventy-five miles went into the first hour, 70 in the second as traffic increased, after which the rate dropped with the build-up of heavy lorries in the Ruhr area and finally the urban conditions off the Autobahn.

Average speeds of this order shortened our travel times substantially, and meant untired arrival at the end of each non-stop leg of the journey. Moreover, switches and controls have been sensibly placed to minimize physical effort. The automatic transmission as a fatigue-limiter was appreciated most during stop-start inching through London congestion, when gentle foot movements were enough to keep the Rover under full control. As an unexpected bonus, it returned an overall fuel consumption of just over 22 m.p.g., a commendable figure for a 3,520-lb. car pushed hard most of the time.

EVERY INCH a Rover. The new 3-litre is lower and wider than previous models and even more luxurious. J.V.B. considered that in spite of the new look the car was every inch a Rover.

JOHN BOLSTER TESTS

The Rover 3-Litre

FOR many years Rovers have made rather a special sort of car. It is difficult to put in a few words the particular characteristics that these machines have possessed, though the faithful band of owners are in no doubt about this. It would perhaps be fair to say that the typical Rover has been a medium-sized car built to the same standards as the largest luxury carriages. Shattering performance and flashy appearance are not expected of this *marque,* but the prospective buyer has always been certain that his cheque will buy an unobtrusive car of exceptional refinement, with a good resale value after many seasons of work.

Therefore, when the rumour began to spread that a 3-litre Rover was on the stocks, we awaited a car of many solid virtues. Sure enough, the new model turned out to be a typical bearer of the name, with even more luxury and refinement than before. There is no spectacular increase in performance. Instead, the extra power of the bigger engine is used to propel a wider and more luxurious body than that of any previous Rover. The car is lower and the noticeably shallow windows give it a rather unusual appearance. Yet, in spite of its new look, the 3-litre is every inch a Rover.

The pressed steel saloon body forms the chassis, but a sub-frame of box section is attached to the front by six rubber mountings. This carries the anchorages for the front suspension and its rear cross-member secures the laminated torsion bars. The engine and gearbox assembly is also supported on this forward extension.

The rear axle is suspended on semi-elliptic springs, which pivot on conventional rubber bushes at their forward ends. Behind there are no shackles, for the springs are secured to prestressed rubber cushions which accommodate the necessary movement. This, coupled with the rubber insulated sub-frame in front, ensures the complete isolation of the body structure from all road and mechanical noises. The few chassis bearings are sealed and require very infrequent lubrication.

Disc brakes are used at the front of all Rover cars and drums at the rear, in conjunction with servo-assisted hydraulic operation. The pistol-grip hand brake operates in the rear drums through a mechanical hook-up. Large by modern standards, the 6.70-15 ins. tubeless tyres are fitted to bolt-on disc wheels.

The six-cylinder engine has a rigid cast-iron cylinder block which carries the seven main bearings. The side cam-shaft is chain driven, and operates the valves through roller cam followers. The exhaust valves are in the block and the pushrod-operated inlet valves are in the light alloy cylinder head. With a single SU carburetter, the unit develops 115 b.h.p. at 4,500 r.p.m. The Borg and Beck clutch has hydraulic operation, and the conventional four-speed gearbox has synchromesh on the upper three ratios. A Laycock-de Normanville overdrive unit is standard, driving the spiral bevel rear axle through a two-piece propeller shaft, of which the central steady bearing is rubber-mounted.

The five/six-seater body is built to typical Rover standards of excellence. Everything about it is unobtrusive but good, and the comfort of the passengers is studied as always. The controls are also similar to those of previous Rovers, the levers on the steering column for lights, overdrive and indicators being a well-remembered feature. The same applies to the electrically operated reserve petrol tap, and the flashing warning light which politely intimates that one should push in the "choke" when the engine is warm.

On taking one's seat, one finds that the new Rover appears to be much wider than its predecessors. At first, the windows do not seem to be as deep as usual, but when this effect has worn off the all-round visibility is found to be satisfactory. The seats are comfortable and the controls well placed, while the instruments are conveniently grouped before the driver.

On moving off the car is found to possess that "silkiness" of a high class production. It picks up speed unobtrusively, and by employing the overdrive one can cruise quite rapidly with the minimum of fuss and mechanical noise. The gears change easily and are commendably silent, except for bottom gear, which is unsynchronized and somewhat audible. Starts on the level can readily be made in second, however.

When pressed, the 3-litre exhibits a useful turn of speed, and approaches

MUCH WIDER: On taking one's seat, one finds that the new Rover appears to be much wider than it predecessors. The windows do not seem as deep as usual but the all-round visibility is found to be satisfactory.

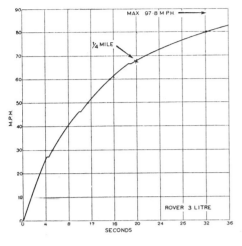

ACCELERATION GRAPH

fairly closely to the "magic hundred". Third gear gives good acceleration and although this is no red hot sports model, it will cruise at 80 m.p.h. without any sign of stress. Towards maximum revolutions, the engine passes through a vibration period, but the average Rover owner will seldom attain such speeds on the gears.

SILKINESS of take-off is one of the pleasures of high-class productions. This 115 b.h.p. unit propels the Rover at speeds approaching the magic hundred with excellent flexibility and power.

The controls are light, especially the steering, which requires much less effort than is usual among cars of comparable weight. At first it feels a little vague at speed, but, in fact, the car is quite controllable during hard driving. The handling characteristic tends towards understeering, especially on wet roads, but while this is not a machine that asks to be "thrown around", it is a safe car which rides well over inferior surfaces.

Once again I can write a hymn of praise on disc brakes. This large car can be driven fast with the knowledge that smooth and oh-so-powerful braking is always available to subdue it. The servo operation gives light pedal pressure, but there is never any doubt about the potency of the retarding force.

There are so many features of the Rover that add to the pleasure of ownership. There is a most elaborate tool kit, of which the small hand tools are in a fitted pull-out tray beneath the front parcel shelf. The heating and ventilation system is a part of the basic design, with special ducts to give face-level ventilation. There are courtesy lights above all four doors and the front door arm rests are instantly adjustable for height—a good point this. The door of the glove locker opens to form a table and the dipping switch for the headlamps is a proper pedal instead of a button. The standard of interior furnishing of this car is equal to that of far more expensive vehicles.

The Rover 3-litre is a car for the man who cannot bear anything cheap and flashy. He buys his car knowing that he will be living with it for a long time, and he chooses it because it will give him smooth, silent travel in an atmosphere that does not affront his good taste. Having regard to the quality and workmanship, the price must be regarded as strictly moderate.

SPECIFICATION AND PERFORMANCE DATA

Car Tested: Rover 3-litre saloon, price £1,783 including P.T.

Engine: Six cylinders 77.8 mm. x 105 mm. (2,995 c.c.). Pushrod-operated overhead inlet valves and side exhaust valves. Compression ratio 8.75 to 1. 115 b.h.p. at 4,500 r.p.m. Single SU carburetter. Lucas coil and distributor.

Transmission: Single dry plate clutch with hydraulic operation. Four-speed gearbox with central lever, ratios 3.01 (O/D), 4.3, 5.92, 8.78, and 14.52 to 1. Divided open propeller shaft with central steady bearing. Spiral bevel rear axle.

Chassis: Pressed steel body with rubber-mounted forward extension to carry engine and front suspension. Independent front suspension by wishbones and laminated torsion bars. Burman recirculating ball steering gear. Rear axle on semi-elliptic springs. Telescopic hydraulic dampers all round. Servo-assisted hydraulic

brakes with discs in front and drums behind. 6.70-15 ins. tubeless tyres on bolt-on steel disc wheels.

Equipment: 12-volt lighting and starting. Speedometer, ammeter, water temperature, fuel and oil level gauges. Clock. Self-parking wipers and washers. Flashing indicators. Heating and demisting. Radio (extra).

Dimensions: Wheelbase, 9 ft. 2½ ins.; track (front), 4 ft. 7⁹⁄₁₆ ins., (rear) 4 ft. 8 ins. Overall length, 15 ft. 6½ ins. Width, 5 ft. 10 ins. Weight, 1 ton 11 cwt.

Performance: Maximum speed 97.8 m.p.h. Speeds in gears: direct top 94 m.p.h.; 3rd 67 m.p.h.; 2nd 46 m.p.h.; 1st 28 m.p.h. Standing quarter-mile 20 secs. Acceleration: 0-30 m.p.h., 5 secs.; 0-50 m.p.h., 11.4 secs.; 0-60 m.p.h., 15.4 secs.; 0-80 m.p.h., 32.2 secs.

Fuel Consumption: 19 m.p.g.

LARGE AND SPACIOUS: The boot is roomy and neatly laid out. The whole car benefits from the extra width—the doors being particularly good.

1961 CARS

ROVER REFINEMENTS

Three photographs on the right show the Harold Radford removable division for the 3-litre. A very simple four-point fixing is used, and the division can accommodate fore-and-aft movements of the front seat.

New Optional Built-in Power Steering and Modified

ALTHOUGH the range of Rover models for the coming season remains as at present, the policy of improving and refining will be in evidence on the cars which will be on view at Earls Court next month. This applies particularly to the 3-litre model, innovations on which include optional power steering, modifications to the Borg Warner automatic transmission system (which is available as an alternative to a synchromesh gearbox with overdrive) and the adoption of sealed universal joints, which reduce the previous four nipples on the two-piece propeller shaft to one—the only one now left on the car.

In addition, a Harold Radford removable limousine conversion is now available and six new exterior colours are offered, making ten colours in all, apart from a number of two-tone combinations which are available at a moderate extra cost.

These new colours are also available on the 2.3-litre, four-cylinder "80" and 2.6-litre, six-cylinder "100" models, which are otherwise continued unchanged, although several minor improvements have, in fact, been quietly brought in during the course of production since these cars first appeared a year ago.

To turn from the overall picture to details, the new power steering, which is offered as an optional extra on the 3-litre model at a cost of £76 10s. (including P.T.), is of the new Hydrosteer type in which the power assistance is built into the cam and lever steering box as opposed to being applied externally to the steering linkage. In consequence, the box is slightly larger but still of compact proportions.

Hydraulic power is supplied by a Hobourn-Eaton roller-type pump capable of delivering 1.8 gallons per minute at a maximum pressure of 750 lb. per sq. in. This is mounted on the back of the dynamo which, on models with power steering, has its own separate ½-in. vee-belt drive from the nose of the crankshaft, a second belt driving the water pump and fan—this arrangement comparing with the normal triangulated drive in which a single ⅜-in. belt serves dynamo, water pump and fan.

The hydraulic pump draws its supply from a reservoir accessibly mounted under the bonnet and delivers fluid under pressure to the steering box via a two-diameter hose, the larger section of which is expansible to damp out noise by eliminating pressure

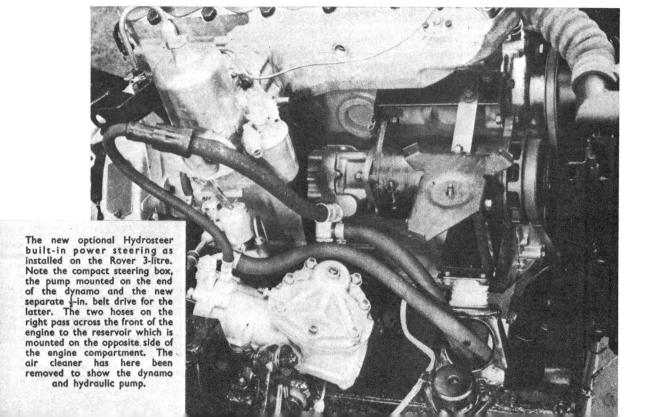

The new optional Hydrosteer built-in power steering as installed on the Rover 3-litre. Note the compact steering box, the pump mounted on the end of the dynamo and the new separate ¼-in. belt drive for the latter. The two hoses on the right pass across the front of the engine to the reservoir which is mounted on the opposite side of the engine compartment. The air cleaner has here been removed to show the dynamo and hydraulic pump.

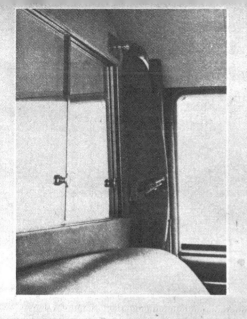

Automatic Transmission on 3-litre Model

pulsations. With no pressure on the steering wheel, fluid circulates freely through the steering box and pressure is equal on both sides of a piston which surrounds the cam and engages with a sleeve surrounding the peg or cam follower. The shaft of the cam, however, is provided with a small degree of end-float and any axial movement is transmitted to a spool-type valve which is maintained in a neutral position by light spring pressure. So soon as any steering pressure is applied, however, the reaction takes up the end float in one or other direction and this progressively closes the valve concerned, so causing pressure to build up on the appropriate side of the piston and thus assist the driver to a degree which is largely proportional to the manual effort. The word "assist" is important because the normal direct mechanical connection is maintained between the steering wheel and the road wheels, so that the only effect of failure in the hydraulic arrangements would be to make the steering heavier.

As applied to the Rover 3-litre, no alterations in steering geometry are involved, but in view of the added loads which can be imposed on the whole front-end layout if, for example, the

steering is turned when the front wheels are against a kerb, new and stiffer steering arms are used, and the front sub-frame which carries the engine and front suspension on this model is suitably stiffened; these modifications, incidentally, apply to all 1961 models, whether fitted with Hydrosteer or not, for simplicity in production. In passing—and to answer a question which owners of existing Rover models may ask—the absence of these modifications makes it impractical to fit power assistance to pre-1961 models.

Other points worth noting are that the bolts securing the steering box to the sub-frame are more widely spaced and that the damper normally fitted to the steering idler is omitted as being unnecessary on Hydrosteer cars.

The turning circle is, of course, unaltered, but power assistance has enabled the number of turns from lock to lock to be reduced from $4\frac{1}{4}$ to $2\frac{1}{2}$, so enabling a skid to be corrected more easily, as well as making the effort required by the driver much less. Care has, however, been taken not to overdo the power assistance and thus destroy the feel of the steering and several miles over streaming wet surfaces both on the road and round the Rover test circuit suggested that this object has been achieved, the impression being more that of handling a car with very light steering than of power assistance. Only when cornering on a considerable lock (when the effect of the variable ratio comes into play) was the power assistance noticeable as such.

Quick or Smooth

The modifications to the Borg Warner automatic transmission have been designed with the dual object of providing a better low-speed get-away under certain conditions and, at the same time, of making general performance more unobtrusive. To this end, the transmission now follows the later Borg Warner system in which a kick-down change is available into bottom gear and normal starts are made in intermediate. On previous Rovers, it will be recalled, the kick-down arrangement was confined to changes from top to intermediate, but no provision was made for kicking down into low and the latter came into action (automatically) only when the car was almost at rest.

With the later plan, normal starts are made unobtrusively in intermediate, but if the driver requires a quick getaway from rest, it is necessary only to employ a three-quarter, or greater, throttle opening. Equally, if rapid acceleration is required for improved pick-up

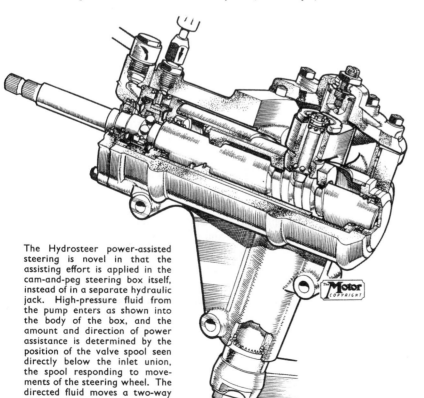

The Hydrosteer power-assisted steering is novel in that the assisting effort is applied in the cam-and-peg steering box itself, instead of in a separate hydraulic jack. High-pressure fluid from the pump enters as shown into the body of the box, and the amount and direction of power assistance is determined by the position of the valve spool seen directly below the inlet union, the spool responding to movements of the steering wheel. The directed fluid moves a two-way piston which operates on the drop-arm.

ROVER
REFINEMENTS

No external changes for 1961 have been made to the Rover 80, 100 (*above, left*) or 3-litre (*above, right*) which now comprise the company's normal passenger-car range.

from a low speed (as, for example, after negotiating a busy roundabout) then low gear can be brought into operation merely by kicking down.

So far as actual changing speeds are concerned, it is now possible to kick down into low gear (through intermediate if top is engaged) at any speed below approximately 25 m.p.h. Below about 18 m.p.h., the transmission will automatically change into low on a wide throttle opening without the need for depressing the accelerator to full kick-down position.

A further point about the new arrangement is that when "Drive" is engaged and the engine is running, the car will not run back on any but the steepest hills, so that, in effect, a "hill-hold" is provided. Even on a very steep gradient the car will merely edge back slowly in these conditions, so that a mere touch of the brake pedal is sufficient to hold it.

Another difference between the latest transmission and the earlier type fitted to the 3-litre is that, apart from the kick-down condition, the range covered by the "Intermediate Hold" is now limited to normal full-throttle change speeds, i.e. the transmission will change from low to intermediate at 20-22 m.p.h. and from intermediate to top at 42-44 m.p.h. despite use of the hold control. All other changes within the speed range take place as before. A small point to note is that the hill-hold effect mentioned above when the control lever is in the "Drive" position does not apply if the "Intermediate Hold" is in use.

A further most interesting development in the 3-litre range is the availability of a Harold Radford limousine conversion for models with the standard bench-type front seat. The division takes the form of a neat framework, including two sliding glass panels, which is designed as a close fit between the roof, fillets on the door pillars and the top of the squab, where a seal is provided by a flange and a flexible flap.

A simple four-point fixing is used. This takes the form of a spring-loaded plunger which fits into a hole in a plate attached to the top of the door pillar on each side, and a thumb screw working in a slotted bracket on each door pillar just above the top of the squab. The beauty of the plan is that, when the thumb screws are slackened off, the whole division is free to pivot about the spring loaded plungers at the top, so that the division accommodates itself to fore-and-aft adjustment of the front seat.

The arrangement is completed by fillers at the sides of the seat squab so that the seal between the front and rear compartments is completed and reasonable privacy is ensured. An excellent feature is that the whole division, which is of quite manageable proportions, is readily detachable, thus permitting a model which is adapted for it to be used as a limousine during the week and as a normal saloon for family purposes at weekends.

Although these are the main innovations in the Rover range for 1961, a number of minor changes have also been incorporated in all models in the course of production during the past twelve months so that the entire range represents an advance on the cars which were exhibited at Earls Court last year. Prices are unchanged.

JOHN BOLSTER TRIES

A ROVER ON THE CONTINENT

THERE is nothing like a long, fast Continental journey, with vital appointments to be kept and no time to waste on servicing, to bring out the virtues and vices of a car. Such a trip is the annual pilgrimage to the Geneva Show, and I have recently completed the journey in a 3-litre Rover.

Personally, I was a great admirer of the Rover 90 and 105S models. Their superb finish, silence and good handling qualities are something unexpected in their price range. Yet, when the 3-litre first came on the scene, I must own to a feeling of disappointment. The steering and roadholding were not up to previous standards and the engine was neither so smooth nor so powerful as I had expected.

Perhaps "my" first 3-litre was a "lemon", for the next one had much more of the feel of the beloved 90 about it. I have driven several since then, and each one was a step forward. Now, I have really thrashed the latest version across England, France and Switzerland, and I can say that the old quality has been fully regained.

The design of the 3-litre is well enough known. It has a six-cylinder, seven-bearing engine, with the inlet valves in the light-alloy head and the exhausts in the cast iron block. It has a long stroke by today's standards, with dimensions of 77.8 mm. x 105 mm., and it develops 117 b.h.p. (s.a.e.) at 4.500 r.p.m. on a compression ratio of 8.75 to 1.

This unit is coupled to a four-speed gearbox with three synchronized ratios and a Laycock-de Normanville overdrive. The propeller shaft is divided, and the hypoid rear axle is on semi-elliptic springs. In front, the whole suspension and engine assembly is carried on a rubber-mounted sub-frame. The test car had a new sub-frame mounting, which has now been standardized, and which greatly improves the front-end rigidity. The front suspension still retains the extra torque arm that is typical of Rover design, and the springing is by laminated torsion bars.

The steering is by a Burman-Douglas box. Power-assisted steering was fitted to the test car and the brakes, with Girling discs in front, also had servo assistance. The whole conception of the car has been worked out on the principle that long life, freedom from maintenance and silent running are the most desirable features.

Of pleasing appearance in a quiet dignified manner, the body has a fairly high waistline, but the windows have adequate depth, and swivelling quarter lights are now fitted to the front doors. Improvements include a new stainless steel wheel trim, and there is a brake warning light for hand brake "on" or low brake fluid level. Twin fuel pumps are now incorporated in the main-reserve switching system.

It was at once apparent on moving off that this is the liveliest of the many Rovers that I have driven. The engine

has more "punch" at low speeds and it also runs more smoothly. The clutch and gear change are light and easy to handle, and though a "plain" first speed is used, it is too low to be required on the move, second sufficing except for uphill starts.

Third gear gives an ideal ratio for pass storming, with an ultimate maximum of 67 m.p.h. This gear was used exclusively for the Col de la Faucille where snow and ice were much in evidence. The direct top gear will give over 90 m.p.h., and the overdrive produces 100 to 105 m.p.h., depending on the length of the straight. Last year's 3-litre would do a timed 100 m.p.h. on M1, but the present car will exceed this speed on ordinary French roads.

The Rover is not intended to be a speed model, but during the whole trip I was never overtaken. This was partly because the new sub-frame mounting gives one much more confidence on 80 to 90 m.p.h. curves. I had to travel at over 100 m.p.h. for 20 miles or so to keep in company with a fast Lancia, but apart from that Citroëns were my only playmates and they dropped astern as the 90 mark was topped. A very "Le Mans" DB Panhard disappointed, running out of "puff" above 85 m.p.h. and appearing none too steady on rough

and steeply cambered roads. Unfortunately, no fast Peugeots did battle on this occasion. Petrol? 16.8 m.p.g. driving "flat", but 18 m.p.g. or more under normal conditions.

The test car was fitted with the optional fully adjustable seats. These are superbly comfortable and any driver, however tall, can find plenty of room for his arms and legs. A passenger who feels sleepy after lunch can ease back the seat and have a "zizz" without disturbing the driver. These seats contributed to the success of the trip in no small way, as one arrived relaxed and ready to start work.

The whole quality of this car reminds one of the ultra-expensive luxury limousines. The way the doors shut, the standard of the interior trim and upholstery—all these things add up to the pleasure of handling a pedigree car. The controls work easily, and the power-assisted steering contributes greatly to the ease of driving on a long day's travel. It took me some time to get the feeling of the steering on ice, and to begin with I wished that I had plain manual operation during the negotiation of the Faucille. Eventually, I got the message, but under all normal conditions the power assistance is definitely an advantage. The servo brakes are smooth and do not fade.

The latest Rover 3-litre is a quality car of exceptional smoothness and silence that yet has a useful performance. The really fastidious owner will enthuse over the luxury and finish, and he would find it hard to tolerate other less perfect carriages even if their performance were greater. At a price, including P.T., of £1,880 (plus extras), the Rover 3-litre gives the same pleasure as some prestige cars of far greater cost.

Road Test

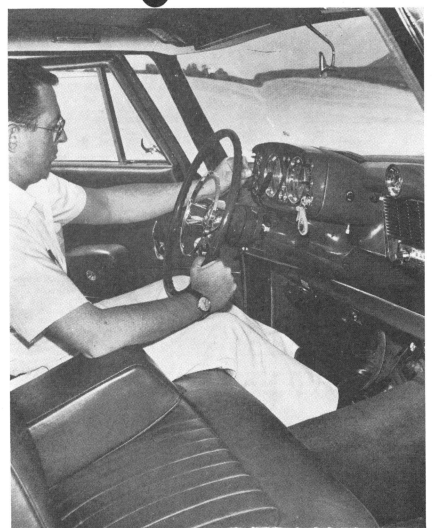

The interior is plush and seems to have been designed primarily with the best interests of the driver in mind. Turret-type instrument panel is efficient and attractive. Two of its features are an oil level indicator and reserve fuel tank control.

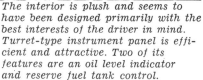

by Jim Wright
Technical Editor

OUR FIRST CONTACT with the Rover was more by word-of-mouth than anything and came from an old friend of ours who happens to be a real car buff. By real, we mean that at least 99 percent of his conversation and thoughts are devoted to the Automobile with the remaining one percent reserved for world affairs, politics, sex, business and other such trivia. And when he talks cars he never fails to bring up the Rover he once owned. To hear him describe it this was the ultimate in fine motoring and nobody should be without at least one of them.

After hearing this for perhaps the hundredth time we decided that we'd better test this wonder for ourselves — if for no other reason than self-defense. And so we did, and as a result we have a new respect for our friend's evaluation. The Rover is indeed a high spot in motoring as well as being just about everything else he said it was.

The MOTOR TREND test car was the Mark 1A model which has been recently introduced as a further development of their well-received 3-litre series that was originally brought out in 1958. Externally the car has undergone no changes and still enjoys the same uncluttered, functional type of styling of its fore runner. We personally go along with the stabilized design theory because it is reassuring to know that after you've parted with

OPEN ROAD CRUISING OR BACK COUNTRY BRUISING MAKE VERY LITTLE DIFFERENCE TO ROVER.

ROVER

3 Litre

Lasting luxury in a compact limousine

Rover 3 Litre
continued

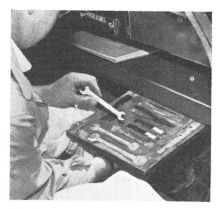

*Handy sponge-rubber lined tray holds
a variety of tools for minor maintenance and adjustments plus a tire
pressure gauge and two tubes of rubbing compound and touch-up paint.
Larger tools are stowed in trunk.*

over $5000 that the factory isn't going to
hand you a psychological set-back by coming out with a totally new design before
you can even get yours broken in. A
Rover owner can be secure in the fact
that the car he bought last year, or this
year, will still be in style when next year's
model is released. The only reason any
motorist should have for selling off or
trading in his car is because it has reached
a point where the cost and frequency of
repairs makes it an unsound investment.
He should never be forced to feel that it
is new car time because of styling dictates.

Technically and mechanically the Rover
embodies some very sound practices and
features that should ensure miles and
years of trouble-free motoring for the
average driver. The 183-cubic-inch, in-
line Six engine is one of the smoothest,
most flexible that we've come across. The
powerplant has several design features
that sets it apart from most other Sixes.
The intake valves are located in the aluminum alloy head while the exhausts are
in the cast-iron block (F-head). Roller-
type cam followers are fitted for longer
cam life. Greater rigidity and reliability
are gained through the use of seven main
bearings. An engine of this type and size
is no doubt capable of putting out more
than 115 hp at 4500 rpm. But the factory
felt that this was an adequate figure and
by limiting it to this they would be as-

*Crank actuated swinging shelf holds
spare tire. Novel arrangement means
neater trunk area with more space.*

sured of longer and smoother engine life.

As a result, performance is on the average side. With two aboard, all our test gear and a full tank of gas the Rover weighed slightly over 4000 lbs. It was also equipped with the optional three-speed automatic transmission (Borg-Warner) and the 3.9 to one rear axle, so one should probably expect to better our figures with the standard four-speed manual gearbox and 4.3 to 1 axle. The 0-to-30, 0-to-45 and 0-to-60 mph times were 6.4, 12.4 and 20.0 seconds respectively. The standing quarter-mile took 23.5 seconds at 65 mph flat. On the top end it felt a little better and the engine wound smoothly and unprotestingly to 5000 rpm which corresponded to an actual 100 mph on our electric speedometer. This run was made on the backstretch at Riverside Raceway which is approximately a mile long.

Fuel consumption was about average considering the weight, automatic transmission, and horsepower. Around town we averaged 14.5, 14.6 and 14.6 mpg on three tanksful. On the open highway the figure went up to 17.3 and would no doubt have been slightly better if we could have kept the Rover under 75 mph — but it felt like that's where it wanted to run — so when traffic allowed, we didn't argue.

The brakes are really something and after you've used them a few times you wonder why can't all cars have their equal. Girling discs are used at the front while big 11-inch drums are used on the rear. These were power assisted but pedal pressure seemed so normal we had to look under the hood to make sure. We used them quite hard while making our acceleration and top speed runs and didn't give them any extra time to cool before trying the braking tests. Even so, the Rover recorded some of the shortest stopping distances we've seen. The distance from 30 mph was 41 feet which is good; from 60 mph it took 147 feet which is excellent for a car of any size. All of the stops were of the straight-line variety and we didn't notice even a slight tendency toward locking. After the braking tests were completed we immediately made several more panic-type stops for the benefit of the photographer and still didn't notice any appreciable fade or pedal hardness. They were hot but they were still ready and able to do their job.

The ride can only be classed as excel-

SMOOTH AND RELIABLE IN-LINE SIX FEATURES ALUMINUM ALLOY "F"-TYPE HEAD, ROLLER TAPPET CAM AND SEVEN MAIN-BEARING CRANKSHAFT.

Rover 3 Litre   *continued*

lent. On all road surfaces and at all speeds the driver (and his passengers) always has that feeling of complete mastery of car and conditions. At speed there is no float or wander and sudden dips produce none of the usual front end oscillations that are apparent in more softly sprung cars. On really rough stretches we had a hard time finding bumps that would cause the suspension to bottom. When we did bottom it, the Rover recovered immediately.

Although the Rover is rather heavy and has slight understeer characteristics it can still be pushed through tight corners with a minimum of driver effort. Body roll isn't at all excessive. The excellent ride and good handling characteristics can be attributed to the well designed suspension: ball-joint control arms with laminated-type torsion bars on the front and conventional, variable-rate leaf springs at the rear. The test car was equipped with power steering which, combined with the automatic transmission, made the Rover easy to handle in heavy traffic. This ease of handling was further enhanced by the flexibility of the engine. Because it pumps out its peak torque (164 lbs-ft) at 1500 rpm it has plenty of pulling power in the mid-speed range where it is needed the most.

The quality of the Rover is best expressed by its sold feel and quietness at cruising speeds. All road shocks, vibrations, and engine noises are either eliminated or reduced to a murmur through the use of effective sound deadening materials and the method of body construction used. The engine and transmission, steering and front suspension components are all mounted on a separate sub-frame that is rubber-mounted and is quickly detachable from the main unit-frame and body.

The high degree of pride of workmanship that exists at the Rover factory is reflected in the excellent detailing of both the interior and exterior of the car. All doors, panels and bits and pieces of trim have evidently been carefully fitted to insure perfect fit and alignment. The doors have a lovely sound and feel when you shut them and this point alone has probably sold a few of them.

The interior is fitted with the same care as the exterior and it is apparent that the factory has spared no expense in providing for the driver's and passenger's comfort. The test car was fitted with a bench-type front seat with pull-down arm rest but individual bucket-type seats are also available. The front seat will sit three persons comfortably and looks as if four will fit without too much crowding. The rear seat is not as large as the front but will also take three average-size adults. Both were upholstered in a very soft pig skin that, with proper care, should last the life of the car. Driving position was very good with the seat offering good support to the back and upper legs and the steering wheel placed just right.

Hip-, leg- and head-room are more than adequate for both driver and passenger. In fact the total interior dimensions belie the short 110½ wheelbase of the car and one gets the idea that it is much bigger.

With the exception of an oil pressure gauge, the instrument panel is one of the nicest we've seen. It seems unthinkable that they would have an idiot light for this one important function. Otherwise the panel is well laid out with all gauges in easy view and all switches and controls in easy reach of the driver. There were also a few extra appointments here that pleased us. By flicking a switch marked oil level we could read the crankcase level on the fuel gauge. Another switch controlled the reserve gas tank (1½ gallons) and came in handy several times. Plenty of storage space was provided by the glove box and by an open tray that runs the full length of the dash board. A sliding tray is fitted under the dash and it contains a tire gauge, assorted wrenches, screw driver and several tubes of rubbing compound and touch-up paint. Larger tools are stored in the large, vinyl upholstered trunk.   /MT

FIRM SUSPENSION HOLDS BODY ROLL TO MINIMUM BUT REVERSE CAMBER TURN AND LOW CAMERA ANGLE TEND TO EXAGGERATE IT IN PHOTO.

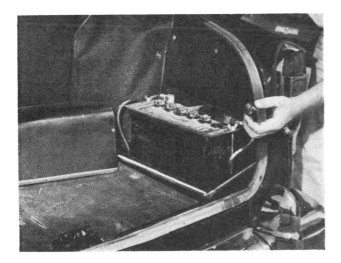

Battery is a long way from the engine but trunk location is a better choice than under the floor or rear seat. Both metal and vinyl battery covers are used.

Braking system is one of the finest used on any production car. With 11 inch drums on the rear and big 9½ inch Girling discs on the front fade is almost non-existent. Stopping distance from 60 mph was one of the shortest we've recorded.

ROVER 3-LITER MARK 1A
4-door, 6-passenger sedan

OPTIONS ON CAR TESTED: Power steering, power brakes, radio, heater, white walls

BASIC PRICE: $4995
PRICE AS TESTED: $5495 (plus tax and license)
ODOMETER READING AT START OF TEST: 770 miles
RECOMMENDED ENGINE RED LINE: 5200 rpm

PERFORMANCE

ACCELERATION (2 aboard)
0-30 mph	6.4 secs.
0-45 mph	12.4
0-60 mph	20.0

Standing start ¼-mile 23.5 secs, and 65 mph
Speeds in gear @ 5000 rpm
1st	40 mph
2nd	68 mph
3rd	100 mph (indicated)

Speedometer Error on Test Car
Car's speedometer reading	30	44	48	58	68	78
Weston electric speedometer	30	45	50	60	70	80

Observed miles per hour per 1000 rpm in top gear................20 mph
Stopping Distances — from 30 mph, 41 ft.; from 60 mph, 147 ft.

SPECIFICATIONS FROM MANUFACTURER

Engine
6 in-line, F-head
Bore: 3.063 ins.
Stroke: 4.134 ins.
Displacement: 183 cubic inches
Compression ratio: 8.75:1
Horsepower: 115 @ 4500 rpm
Horsepower per cubic inch: .628
Torque: 164 lb/ft @ 1500 rpm
Ignition: 12-volt coil

Gearbox
3-speed automatic; column-mounted lever

Body and Frame
Unit frame/body with sub-frame for front suspension
Wheelbase 110½ ins.
Track, front 55 7/16 ins., rear 56 ins.
Overall length 186½ ins.
Curb weight 3640 lbs.
Steering: recirculating ball 4½ turns lock-to-lock
Turning dia. 40 ft.

Wheels and Tires
6.70 x 15, 4-ply
6.75 x 15, 4-ply

Suspension
Front: Independent lateral non-parallel control arms with laminated torsion bars, direct double acting shocks
Rear: Rigid axle semi-elliptic leaf springs, direct double acting shocks

Brakes
Hydraulic with vacuum servo assist
Front and rear: 9½ in. disc and 11 in. x 2½ in. drum, respectively

Differential
Hypoid — semi-floating
Standard ratio 3.9:1

Driveshaft
2-piece open tube with flexibly mounted center bearing

Rover 3-Litre Mark 1a with automatic transmission combines dignity with dash. Power steering and disc brakes contribute to sports car handling and averages. Finish, equipment and trim exceptional for price class. Extensive use of rubber mountings and bushes reduce interior sound level to the minimum

Displaying the dignity and standard of finish which has won the Rover Company world renown over many years, the 3-Litre Mark Ia is a fast car with sporting characteristics, as well as a status symbol. The front turn indicators are blended to the wing curves where they can be seen front and side.

During the test the Rover stood for three days under seven inches of snow. Starting was instantaneous on the third morning, even though temperatures were below freezing.

CARS
ON TEST

ROVER 3-LITRE MARK 1A

Quick check:

PERFORMANCE...	10
ROADHOLDING ...	10
GEARBOX	10
COMFORT	10
FINISH	10
BRAKES	10
VISIBILITY	10
ECONOMY	9
STARTING	10

All assessments commensurate with type of car and price tag. Max.: 10, each category.

LEFT. *A restrained yet eager look characterises the Rover 3-litre Mark Ia. It can be distinguished from earlier models by its quarter ventilating windows in the front doors, and also by the attractive stainless-steel wheel trims.*

A CAR TO BE PROUD OF

With only complimentary intent it is fair to comment that the Rover 3-litre is one of the very few current production cars of any nationality to retain real links with the past. This does not infer that it is "old-fashioned" but rather a car of dignity, quality, and more acrity than would at first seem apparent. Like great touring cars of the past the Rover includes in its specifications every contemporary aid to comfort and fatigue-free motoring, and the quality of its finish and furnishings quite exceptional in this age of "simulation". The Rover 3-litre is a big car (15ft. 6½in. overall) with a weight of well over a ton-and-a-half, yet as tested with power-assisted steering, handled like a small one. Power steering pads the price of the car (with Purchase Tax) by £78 15s. 0d. but the buyer who does not specify it when ordering a new Rover 3-litre is not experiencing the car at its outstanding best.

As tested the 3-litre was equipped with automatic transmission, and besides being completely in keeping with the car, tribute must be paid to its manufacturers Borg-Warner for the tremendous amount of development that they have bestowed on the gearbox, and the high degree of smooth effectiveness that they have extracted from it. The 3-litre is available

less energetic mood, or if the Rover's everyday master (or mistress) demands the ultimate in automatic motoring, the selector lever only needs placing in "D" for smooth travel.

Finish and equipment are taken seriously at the Rover Company. The 3-litre, like all Rover private car models, has lush seats and trim in *real* hide of the softness and texture that recalls the great *marques* of the past. The carpets are of the thickest pile and high quality, and everywhere there is highly polished woodwork in the best possible taste. Equipment is so lavish that the purchase price seems inadequate. The basic price of the "basic" 3-litre is £1,288 and this includes built-in heating, ventilation, servo disc brakes, windscreen washers, hide upholstery, overdrive, and the under-facia kit of small tools set in a sorbo-lined drawer that Rovers' have included in all models since the mid "thirties". Instrumentation is good with instruments and switches mounted above the steering column in a "binnacle" in easy view of the driver's vision. Strangely, for a Rover, the "binnacle" is of plastic but the size and shape of it is such that it blends with the wood and leather.

The long-tongued switches are neatly installed in two horizontal lines, each side of the instruments. Another traditional (and useful)

windscreen washing equipment. There are separate warning lights for ignition, oil pressure headlamp main beam, turn indicators, and an invaluable one for the manually-operated choke which glows when the engine has reached working temperature. The magnificent choke control is shaped for finger-hold and is mounted under the generous, padded, front parcels tray. Yet another warning light, to the right of the not-so-impressive "umbrella-handle" handbrake, informs the driver that either the brake has not been released or that the hydraulic brake fluid level is low.

A key-starter switch is incorporated in the "binnacle" which switches on ignition with a short movement to the right, and operates the starter with a further twist in the same direction. A full twist in the other direction enables "accessories" such as radio, heater, etc., to remain operative with the engine off, and no heating up of ignition coil. To the left of the "binnacle" in the centre of the well-padded windscreen sill is an internally-illuminated electric clock with fast/slow adjustment accessible from the rim. As in most Rover's its tick is audible at most speeds but it is understood that in the near future a different type is to be fitted with "intermittent" electric rewind. Apart from a quick ratchet-

either with four-speed Rover manual gearbox Laycock de Normanville overdrive as standard), in which form it has synchromesh mechanism on all forward ratios except first, or with the Borg-Warner automatic at extra cost. Both transmissions, in the Rover tradition, are subject to factory improvements and refinements.

In the case of the automatic the Rover engineers have incorporated a set of controls which enable the driver to "over-ride" practically any of the automatic sequences—if it is so desired. Under such conditions it is possible to extract the maximum performance from the car, and a great amount of driver enjoyment. If the enthusiastic driver is in a

Rover instrument which has been retained for more than 25 years is the fuel contents gauge which upon operating a switch indicates the contents of the engine sump. The instrument lighting rheostat too is still fitted, but instead of employing a rotary control is ingeniously incorporated in one of the five grouped switches. Thus day or night, the Rover driver can check oil and petrol contents while he drives, and if fuel is running low there is a 1½-gallon reserve which can be brought into play by the movement of another of the grouped switches. Water temperature can be checked on the Centigrade-marked gauge. On the side of the "binnacle" is the press-button for operation of the Lucas electric

like sound approximately every 15 minutes as the clock electrically rewinds itself, the instrument will be silent.

Below the parcel shelf on the passenger's side is an electric "cigar" lighter, and adjacent to it is a pull-out ashtray of impressive proportions. Further left is the splendid Rover tool-tray with spanners, screwdrivers, tyre pressure gauge, etc. There are even two plastic containers of touch-up paint with integral brushes, and separate compartments containing "cleaning" compound! The compound is first used on the paint area to be touched-up, ensuring a workmanlike job.

As standard the Rover 3-litre has two lockable glove boxes with handsome polished drop-

The Viking's Bridge. The automatic model has the selector lever for the Borg-Warner transmission on the left of the steering column. Directly under it and well to hand is the "intermediate hold" switch. On the right of the column is the turn indicator and under it the headlamp flasher switch. All external lights are controlled by the top-right switch on the instrument "binnacle".

From the front passengers' side can be seen the traditional Rover small tools drawer lined with a moulded foam rubber inner. The padded parcels shelf is capacious, and the brake pedal (for either foot) enormous. Windscreen washer button on left of "binnacle". Centre-mounted Pye radio is optional equipment, replaces second glove box.

down lids. If radio equipment is specified the centre locker space can be utilised for the receiver and speaker. On either side of this area is a slim lever working in a vertical plane, the left-hand controlling heat and ventilating air, the right-hand demisting and defrosting. The left-hand lever has a pull-knob which switches the booster motor on or off. The heating arrangements are excellent, rear-seat occupants receiving ample flow of warm air from under the front seats.

The demisting arrangements are also effective but the considerable glass area of the 3-litre demands the full force of the booster motor to keep the windscreen clear under bad weather conditions, particularly if there is more than one person aboard.

When the demisting control is set for any sort of air velocity to the windscreen, it can be set to deliver cold air (with the heater control at "off"). This is a very good feature as high-level warm air has the effect of inducing drowsiness on most people.

The latest Rover 3-litre should prove a most attractive car in hot and dusty climates for not only can the demisting arrangements be set to provide a stream of cool air at face level (lever in the "Defrost" position!) but this is obtainable with all windows closed. In addition there are neat butterfly air valves let into the padded windscreen sill, and a further control knob under the left of the parcels shelf to admit cool air at floor level. The adjustable butterfly valves and floor-level cooling system rely on the forward motion of the car for their operation, but the intakes and ducting have been scientifically designed and the flow and effectiveness are remarkably good —even at relatively low speeds. Thus the 3-litre can be efficiently heated and ventilated with all windows wound up.

As tested the car was fitted with the optional separate front seats (with folding armrests) which afforded great comfort as well as reasonable lateral hold. The separate seats and the standard bench-type can be adjusted for height and rake by repositioning the securing bolts at the seat base. Fore-and-aft

sliding adjustment is generous even for the very long-legged. Front passenger seat on the test car was equipped with a finger-adjusted reclining back, also an optional fitting at extra cost. The driving position was first-class, both wing tips being visible by a six-footer, with available seat height adjustment for shorter drivers. The adjustable diagonal seat belts gave confidence and increased lateral security under fast cornering conditions, but the installation in a quality interior such as the Rover 3-litre's accented the pressing need for integral seats and tidy "built-in" belts in all cars.

The dished two-spoke steering wheel is well positioned and the small diameter horn ring can be reached fairly quickly although required spring pressure was high on the test model. Sitting at the wheel of the 3-litre with the controls so well placed gives the driver the urge to embark on the "Grand Tour".

With the automatic transmission all driving is simplicity itself. As with all Borg-Warner automatics the engine can only be started with the selector lever in "P" (Park) or "N" (Neutral). As soon as the engine is running "D" (Drive) is selected for all normal motoring, and the car draws away with silky smoothness upon depression of the accelerator pedal. With the Rover interpretation of the automatic transmission the 3-litre will take-off in the second gear of the three-speed, the torque convertor coping with the load and the subsequent single gear-change to top making for the smoothest and most fussless motoring possible. If a brisker getaway is required the accelerator is pushed down hard and all three ratios go to work, and under these conditions a 0—60 m.p.h. is possible in 17 seconds. All gear-changing on the Borg-Warner transmission was effected with great smoothness, and with quiet operation.

The transmission will function in its highest (direct) gear down to a road speed of about 22 m.p.h. whereupon "intermediate" is quietly selected. This gear can also be selected from top at any speed below 40 m.p.h. by fully depressing the accelerator pedal, bringing into

play the "kick-down" switch. "Intermediate" can be held by full depression of the accelerator until approximately 65 m.p.h. is reached when top gear is smoothly re-engaged. If "over-run" speed drops in intermediate to below 18 m.p.h., low gear can be engaged by fully depressing the accelerator. If accelerating hard in any gear, top gear can be quickly and smoothly engaged by easing the accelerator.

In addition to the "kick-down" the Rover 3-litre has a neat long-armed toggle switch situated conveniently under the driver's left hand on the steering column. This switch can be used to "hold" intermediate gear for twisty roads, mountain routes, etc., when it is desirable to use a lively gear, and undesirable to have top gear re-engaging itself when the accelerator is eased. The intermediate gear hold is solenoid-operated and can also be used as a very quick means of changing from top to second gear for overtaking etc. Its selections also ensures a first gear "take-off" from a standstill, but intermediate is still automatically engaged according to speed and throttle opening.

When take-offs are made with the selector lever in "D" and the hold switch in the "off" position the Borg-Warner "Hill-Hold" will prevent the car from running backwards when momentarily stopped on an incline. Use of the handbrake is not required. With the intermediate hold in action the "Hill Hold" is inoperative. For descending steep hills, or for "rocking" the car out of mud or snow the selector lever can be placed in position "L" (Low) for this position provides not only the lowest ratio but positive engine braking on the over-run. None of the other gear positions provide engine braking other than at very low road speeds, but the servo-assisted Girling brakes, with $10\frac{3}{4}$ in. discs at the front, effectively illustrate that this is no disadvantage.

With the highly effective transmission and the powerful disc brakes, the expert driver can bend the car to his will, obtaining a high degree of control with the combination of intermediate "hold", "kick-down" switch, and the sensitive accelerator action which will produce

The optionally extra separate front seats can be supplied with reclining squabs which have an excellent range of movement, and easy finger adjustment. The separate front seats each have useful folding centre armrests, and ashtrays as well as map pockets built into both. The folding armrest of the deep and richly upholstered rear seat, and one of the door armrests can be seen.

Typical of Rover attention to detail are the adjustable and well-padded armrests fitted to the front doors. A touch of the countersunk button and the rest can be slid to any one of five positions. The rear doors have similar but fixed rests. The large map pockets are "sprung" towards the door panel, retaining a neat and tidy appearance. The doors are beautifully capped with polished wood and padded leather.

upward or downward changes on demand. By varying accelerator pressure and using the two "switches" the gear changes can be made early at low engine revs, or late with high revs. If full throttle pedal depression is used for maximum acceleration the gear changes are made at the point where the engine is delivering full torque.

When idling in "D" (Drive) there is a slight amount of "creep" but use of the hand or footbrake easily holds the car stationary, the six-cylinder engine continuing to run slowly and sweetly, ready for an immediate take-off. The fluid coupling makes traffic driving a pleasure, it being necessary only to press the double-size brake pedal with either foot to stop the car, and the treadle-type accelerator to draw away with smooth dignity. If the traffic conditions demanded a brisk getaway it was necessary only to click down the "hold" switch to obtain low gear starts. After nights in the open the coupling fluid was inclined to be "lazy", and fairly high revs. were needed to get the car moving, but this state of affairs was purely temporary and as soon as the engine and transmission had gained any sort of warmth the response was instantaneous.

After nights in the open under blizzard conditions the Rover always started at the first twist of the key. Even after three days with seven inches of snow covering the car it started instantly. Warming-up was a fairly slow procedure, and there is no doubt that a radiator blind, or thermostatically-controlled electric cooling fan would improve matters. The 3-litre, like many British cars is "overcooled" for home conditions, and controlled higher coolant temperatures would make for quicker warming-up, improved fuel consumption, higher performance, and hotter air for the heater.

Handling this big 5 ft. 10 in. wide luxury car was an eye-opener. Road view and seating position were good enough to give the feeling of a smaller model even before the engine was started, but the excellence of the handling, roadholding and ride when under way heightened the impression. The power assist-

ance for steering and braking all contributed to a "small car feel".

It took some miles to grow fully used to the power steering as its lightness of operation and relatively high gearing gave an initial impression of above-average understeer. This impression wore off as the driver became more used to the steering, and ultimately the handling characteristics were adjudged as phenomenal for the size, weight and type of car. Although light the Rover power steering never loses road sensitivity, and when the senses are in tune with the fact that only small, effortless movements are required to "will" the car around curves and corners, it becomes obvious that the 3-litre handles better than many sports cars.

There is a slight degree of understeer when fast cornering is indulged in, but as speed and lock are increased this changes gently to oversteer. Under all fast cornering manoeuvres the 3-litre is beautifully neutral with a very low degree of roll for the type of car. Even on greasy roads the Rover can be swerved and cornered with complete confidence, the servo Girling disc/drum brakes bringing down speed with the lightest of pedal pressures and no locking.

At night two little wing-tip "rubies" glow the moment the sidelights are switched on, and these serve not only as a lighting check (from the driver's seat) but also as a width gauge. The gear selector lever and clock are also softly illuminated and are incorporated in the wiring of the rheostat-controlled instrument panel. The headlamps were found to have ample power for ordinary night driving but were certainly not up to the car's high-speed capabilities. An excellent reverse light (incorporated in the rear number plate light) is wired in conjunction with the reverse gear selector, and this and the large curved rear window make backing-up easy.

The Rover 3-litre engine, whilst using a unique valve layout (overhead inlet and angled side exhaust valves) primarily designed to provide sweet and detonation-free running on low-

SPECIFICATION

PERFORMANCE
Using all three ratios of Borg-Warner automatic transmission.

0–30 m.p.h. 6.5 sec.	0–60 m.p.h. 17 sec.
0–40 m.p.h. 9.5 sec.	0–70 m.p.h. 26 sec.
0–50 m.p.h. 13.0 sec.	0–60 m.p.h. 25 sec.
	(using two speeds of automatic transmission)

Car mileage at completion of test: 1,575.
Maximum speeds: Top, 97 m.p.h. Intermediate, 65 m.p.h. Low, 38 m.p.h.

ENGINE
Rover six-cylinder in-line, water-cooled. Overhead inlet valves and angled side exhaust valves operated from single camshaft. Bore: 77.8 mm. Stroke: 105 mm. Cubic capacity: 2,995 c.c. Compression ratio: 8.75 : 1 (7.5 : 1 for certain export territories) Power-output (8.75 : 1 c.r.) 115 b.h.p. (gross) at 4,500 r.p.m. Maximum torque: (8.75 : 1 c.r.) 164 lb/ft. at 1,500 r.p.m. Single S.U. carburetter. Lucas coil and distributor ignition (12-volt). Twin S.U. electric fuel pumps in boot, one main, one reserve.

TRANSMISSION
Borg-Warner three-speed automatic transmission with three-element fluid torque converter incorporating "kick-down", and Rover "intermediate hold". Final drive by spiral bevel, ratio: 3.9 : 1.

SUSPENSION
Independent front by wishbones, links and laminated torsion bars. Rear suspension by live axle, and semi-elliptic leaf springs. Telescopic dampers (hydraulic) all round. Steering by recirculating ball worm and nut (power-assisted on test car).

BRAKES
Girling. Servo-assisted. Front, 10¾ in. discs. Rear, 11 in. by 2¼ in. drums. Pressed steel bolt-on wheels with stainless steel perforated trims.
BRAKING FIGURES. Using Bowmonk Dynometer. From 30 m.p.h., 95 per cent = 31.8 feet.

DIMENSIONS
Wheelbase: 9 ft. 2½ in. Track, front, 4 ft. 7 in. Rear, 4 ft. 8 in. Length, 15 ft. 6½ in. Width, 5 ft. 10 in. Turning circle, 38 ft. 10 in. Kerb weight (with automatic gearbox) 32½ cwt. Fuel capacity: 14 gallons (Imp.) including 1½ gallons reserve. Average fuel consumption: (town and country driving) 18.7 m.p.g. Premium fuel. Tyres: Dunlop 6.70 by 15 Tubeless.

WATER PRESSURE TEST
Slight leakage around top hinge of ventilating window (closed) on driver's door.

BOOT CAPACITY
16 cubic feet approximately.

PRICE IN U.K.
As tested with automatic transmission, individual front seats, (reclining seats extra), power steering, and Pye pushbutton radio, £2,118 2s. 3d. including Purchase Tax. Basic price of 3-litre automatic (without extras) £1,335.

The overhead inlet valve six-cylinder engine, and the comprehensive equipment certainly fill the under-bonnet space. On the left is the large air silencer/cleaner which is connected to the S.U. carburetter by a handsome aluminium casting. The Smiths heater is mounted on the bulkhead where it draws fresh air through the scuttle grille, the Lucas wiper motor is ahead of the heater booster, and in front of that is the Lucas electric windscreen washer. Between the radiator header tank and the washer is the power-steering oil reservoir.

The 3-litre is the first Rover to employ "mono-coque" construction and the Company have retained their reputation for quiet running by mounting the engine, gearbox, and torsion bar suspension on this detachable "wheelbarrow" which is attached to the steel "hull" at six rubber-mounted points. Steering swivel pins require oil reservoirs filling every 12,000 miles. Rear springs have lubrication-free rubber bushes, and there is one grease nipple on the rear propeller-shaft universal joint.

grade fuels, develops the creditable power-output of 115 b.h.p. at 4,500 r.p.m. on a compression ratio of 8.75 : 1. An optional ratio of 7.5 : 1 is available for countries where only low-grade fuels are available. Throughout the 800-mile test the 3-litre was run on premium fuels and no pinking was ever evident. The "in-line" engine always delivered silky smooth power with no suggestion of carburation flat-spots or hesitancy. Using full depression of the accelerator (and all three speeds) the 0—60 m.p.h. figure was 17 seconds —only .4 seconds slower than the manual "five-speed" transmission model tested by our Continental Correspondent some months ago. Under test conditions and giving the gearbox plenty to do most of the time the automatic Rover 3-litre returned 18.7 m.p.g. At the conclusion of the test the car had still covered less than 1,600 miles total, and so under normal motoring conditions and with the engine fully freed off there is no doubt of its ability to better 20 m.p.g. The slow warming-up, and particularly cold time of the year did not assist the fuel consumption figures.

The Rover's ride was exceptionally good. For a car of more than 32 cwt. the use of independent rear suspension is not so important as for small, lightweight models, and the 3-litre demonstrates how refined and effective a well designed live axle will behave. CARS ILLUSTRATED's favoured test road for suspension behaviour, a two-mile country straight with "Colonial" surface could be covered at 90 m.p.h. with the car maintaining a steady smooth course with no shock to the occupants, and a feeling of isolation from the wheels. There were no rattles, and an almost complete absence of pitching even over the small humps on this particular road.

Under these conditions the suspension was first-rate giving a comfortable ride for all occupants, the torsion bar independent front suspension and the well-damped rear axle coping with all normal road irregularities. If however the rear axle struck a series of pot-holes, such as are encountered after a thaw, it would make its presence known noisily. This was not, as was at first thought, due to

ROVER 3-LITRE

rear axle tramp but rather to longitudinal movement of the road springs and casing in the rubber bushes, which connect to the main structure. Never at any time was there any deviation in course, the rubber bushes being incorporated in the suspension to damp out road rumble as well as to eliminate greasing. The 3-litre was the Rover Company's first model to employ *monocoque* construction, and in keeping with their separate chassis models they have achieved remarkable standards of quiet running. By mounting engine and suspension on rubber and by paying careful attention to detail and sound-damping the Rover engineers have produced a model that in its cubic capacity class is as quiet, or quieter than any car in the world—with or without separate chassis frame. At speeds in excess of 70 m.p.h. the engine does become audible, and it is a pity that automatic transmissions aren't available with an overdrive mechanism, particularly for high-speed Continental cruising. Nevertheless a maximum of 97 m.p.h. must be assessed as excellent for a

115 b.h.p. luxury five-seater saloon with a large frontal area, and a loaded weight approaching 2 tons.

Latest modifications to the Rover 3-litre as tested by CARS ILLUSTRATED include heater modifications (for improved circulation to rear passengers), attractive perforated wheel trims, and the adoption of swivelling ventilator windows in the front doors. This last-mentioned "improvement" is of doubtful value as the ventilation arrangements of the 3-litre are so good as to render extra inlets almost unnecessary. In addition, the familiar and highly effective rain deflectors over all four doors have gone. In very hot weather the swivel windows might have some value in that they can be set forward to quickly fill the interior with cool air, but under the CARS ILLUSTRATED pressure test the driver's side ventilator admitted water near the top hinge when fully closed and secured with the excellent locking handles. On the credit side they are good windows of their type as they swivel from their forward edge and not from

CONTINUED ON PAGE 180

A roof line 1½ in. lower and narrow-framed windows distinguish the coupé from the saloon.

NEW ROVERS

High-performance 3-litre engine for saloon* and new four-door coupé. 4-cylinder cars dropped from range.

WHILST Rovers will continue in 1963 to cater for their traditional customer who puts comfort, refinement and good taste above other qualities, they will also move well into the high-performance field with the latest 3-litre P.5 saloon and with a new coupé version of the same car. Both have very much modified cylinder heads and manifolding giving 16% more power and are expected to reach speeds in the region of 110 m.p.h. The 2.6-litre P.4 saloon (hitherto the Rover 100) continues in two different forms which will be known as the Rover 95 and the Rover 110.

The 2.3-litre 4-cylinder Rover 80 is to be dropped altogether and replaced by the Rover 95 which costs only a few pounds more. This 6-cylinder car with its overhead inlet/side exhaust valve engine developing 93 b.h.p. (net) at 4,750 r.p.m. is almost identical with its predecessor, the 100, except for the deletion of the overdrive and the use of a final drive ratio of 3.9 : 1 in place of 4.3 : 1.

The faster 110 will retain the overdrive and 4.3 axle ratio in conjunction with a modified engine giving 115 b.h.p. (net) at 5,000 r.p.m. This increase in power and the very different shape of the torque curve, both of which are shown in the accompanying graphs, are achieved by means of a new cylinder head with modified porting and by inlet manifolding of a most unusual kind. As this head and induction system are essentially similar to that fitted to the new 3-litre engine, which is described in detail below, it will be sufficient to say here that the 24% power increase and extended rev range have made certain other changes necessary.

A Holset crankshaft damper of the unbonded rubber type is used to suppress torsional vibrations at high r.p.m. and the 9-in. Borg and Beck clutch has stronger springs. A kick-down switch on the accelerator pedal has been used hitherto on Rovers so that the overdrive could be cut out in full throttle top gear acceleration. With the considerably higher maximum speed now available, this is no longer safe since it might easily be operated inadvertently at the higher maximum speed, causing engine r.p.m. to rise considerably above the safe limit. Dunlop Road Speed tyres (RS5) will become standard because of the greater sustained cruising speeds which are now possible.

Modifications to the 3-litre P.5 saloon are much more extensive and the coupé is an entirely new addition to the range. Mechanically and in appearance it is very similar to the saloon but a roof line approximately 1½ in. lower has caused some re-arrangement of the seating. The normal bench rear seat is replaced by two separate armchair seats mounted rather further forward in the interests of headroom.

The most interesting part of both cars are the cylinder head and induction tract, details of which are shown in the drawing. Some years ago Harry Weslake was asked to advise on port and valve shapes and these have now been modified to some extent in accordance with his recommendations. Basically the unusual combustion chambers with their overhead inlet and side exhaust valves, the former operated by pushrods and the latter directly from the same camshaft, remain unchanged. The inlet valve still has a head diameter of 1.79 in. and a 30° seat but the port shaping has been modified to give a smoother more streamlined approach to the valve seat. Ideally the profile of the port joining the throat to the seat should be a smooth curve giving a bell mouth. In mass production such a shape

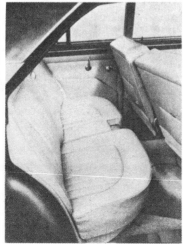

Far right: The 3-litre coupé has a tachometer instead of the combination instrument fitted to the saloon; the thermometer and fuel gauge are underslung. This particular car has the Borg-Warner automatic gearbox.

Right: The rear seat of the coupé is designed specifically to house two people in comfort rather than three.

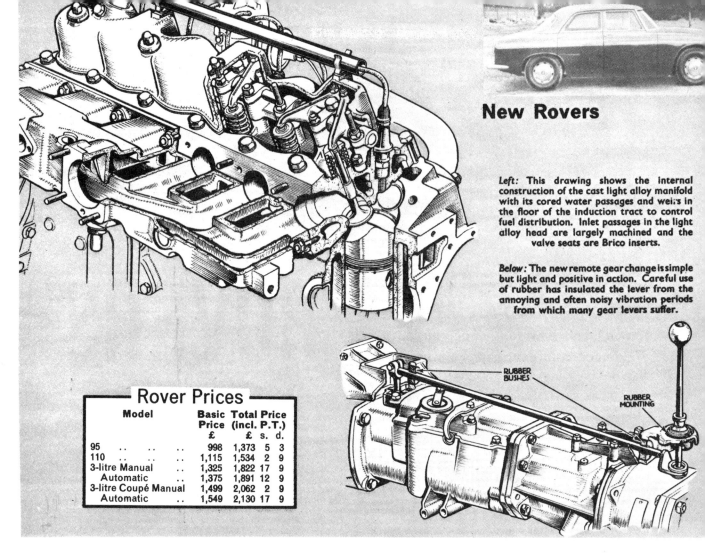

New Rovers

Left: This drawing shows the internal construction of the cast light alloy manifold with its cored water passages and weirs in the floor of the induction tract to control fuel distribution. Inlet passages in the light alloy head are largely machined and the valve seats are Brico inserts.

Below: The new remote gear change is simple but light and positive in action. Careful use of rubber has insulated the lever from the annoying and often noisy vibration periods from which many gear levers suffer.

RUBBER BUSHES

RUBBER MOUNTING

Rover Prices

Model	Basic Price £	Total Price (incl. P.T.) £ s. d.
95	998	1,373 5 3
110	1,115	1,534 2 9
3-litre Manual ..	1,325	1,822 17 9
Automatic ..	1,375	1,891 12 9
3-litre Coupé Manual	1,499	2,062 2 9
Automatic ..	1,549	2,130 17 9

cannot be reproduced but Rover come near it by machining with successive cutters of different taper angles to produce a profile with three "flats."

A single 2-in. bore S.U. carburetter feeds a water-heated manifold which gives very long separated tracts to the 6-port head. From the inlet flange to the valve seat these passages measure some 12-13 in. (differing for different cylinders) and whilst this is not enough for the optimum ramming effect it gives a degree of inertia charging at high speeds which increases the torque very considerably in the middle and upper ranges. At 4,750 r.p.m., for example, torque is increased from 114 lb. ft. to 134 lb. ft. Available space under the bonnet sets a practical limit to the induction lengths which might otherwise have been even greater; the narrower bonnet of the 110 demands a further reduction of about 1 in. in the manifold length.

The manifold is formed from light alloy castings and is dowelled to the head for accurate matching of the machined ports. Six-cylinder engines with single carburetters and long inlet tracts can be a nightmare from the point of view of petrol deposition and bad distribution but since the exhaust is on the opposite side of the engine very rapid empirical development proved possible in this case by using wooden manifolds and by visual examination of the conditions inside through clear plastic windows. It was found that liquid petrol deposited on the vertical wall of the manifold furthest from the head and flowed along it into the two end cylinders. Petrol also deposits on the vertical wall immediately facing the carburetter inlet hole and flows round into the two middle cylinders although this action is discouraged to some extent by a projecting water heated buffer-plate which is designed to bounce neat petrol back into the airstream.

This tendency for cylinders 1 and 6 and 3 and 4 to run rich, and for 2 and 5 to be starved is overcome by the use of weirs in the floor of the passages, which can be seen clearly in the drawing. These divert part of the wall petrol flow and all the stream running along the floor of the manifold into the two cylinders which would otherwise run weak. A different camshaft has now been adopted which gives better idling and low speed torque with this new cylinder head although the new

camshaft gives 3-4 b.h.p. less at the top end than the old one. Inlet and exhaust valve lifts are 0.357 in. and 0.418 in. respectively.

The 3-litre car is available either with a manual gearbox and overdrive or with Borg-Warner automatic transmission and some changes have been made to both. With the manual box, 2nd and 3rd speed gearing has been raised to give closer ratios and an entirely new floor gear lever linkage gives much more positive operation than before. A drawing shows the arrangement of this remote control in which the use of rubber at three points has eliminated noise and vibration transmission without giving a spongy feel. As on the 110, the kick-down switch of the Laycock-de Normanville overdrive has been eliminated. A new "high K" hydraulic torque-converter in the optional Borg-Warner transmission gives a higher torque multiplication at the stalling point. With a 3.9 : 1 final drive ratio, the automatic car reaches 5,000 r.p.m. at 101 m.p.h. and it is expected that drivers who intend to use appreciably higher speeds than this will choose the manual change model.

Suspension remains basically unchanged; the spring rates have not been altered but the springs have been re-set to lower the whole car by 1 in. and smaller bump rubbers are used to recover about half of the resulting loss of free bump travel. The rear semi-elliptic leaf springs have nylon "Berry" buttons to separate the five longest plates, giving reduced wear and friction; these are expected to last at least 100,000 miles in England.

95 and 110 models retain the P.4 body which was used previously for the Rover 80 and 100.

Woodhead-Monroe 1 in. bore telescopic dampers are used in front and behind. Their compression valves are now controlled by coil springs which allow a wider valve opening and it has been found that this stops the build-up of fine dirt on the valve seat which can otherwise seriously impair efficiency after a few thousand miles. The settings have been modified to give less orifice control and more bleed restriction—in other words there is less damping at high rates of suspension movement and more at low velocities. It has been found that this helps to reduce road noise from the rather harsher Dunlop Road Speed tyres, which are now standard and which allow continuous cruising at speeds up to 105 m.p.h. (or spurts at higher speed) without the need to raise the standard tyre pressures of 26 lb. all round.

The higher cornering power of these RS5 tyres and the use of a new Burman F.3 recirculating ball steering box, which is sturdier and more rigid than its predecessor, has improved steering response so much that it has been possible to lower the overall ratio to 20.6 : 1 at the straight ahead position instead of 17.6 : 1, the friction damper has been replaced by a telescopic hydraulic shock absorber (Telaflo TFM) connecting the front suspension sub-frame and the track rod. On the coupé model power assistance from a "Hydrosteer" strut is standard and the ratio is raised to give about 2½ turns from lock to lock instead of four. This power steering can be specified at extra cost on the saloon.

Modifications to the Girling braking system include a change to a pad material which does not need to be used hard in order to retain a high coefficient of friction and the elimination of the vacuum servo reservoir. There is still sufficient vacuum capacity in the system to give about five stops with a dead engine (instead of ten).

There are a number of modifications to the interior trim, electrical equipment and instruments which include the provision of a headlamp flasher controlled by the direction indicator switch, a two-speed heater fan, and a switch to give parking lights on one side of the car only. The coupé has a rev counter and frame-top doors which help to restore most of the side window area lost through the lower roof line. It also has exceptionally comfortable bucket seats which not only have reclining backrests and 7 in. of fore and aft adjustment but also 1½ in. of vertical movement controlled by a small winding handle at the front. These are an optional extra on the 3-litre and 110 saloons.

Finally there are two special export versions of the P.5 saloon which have smaller engines to suit the taxation classes of the countries for which they are intended. For France this capacity will be 2.6 litres and for Austria 2.49 litres; otherwise these cars will be identical with the 3-litre saloon except for the retention of last year's wider gear ratios.

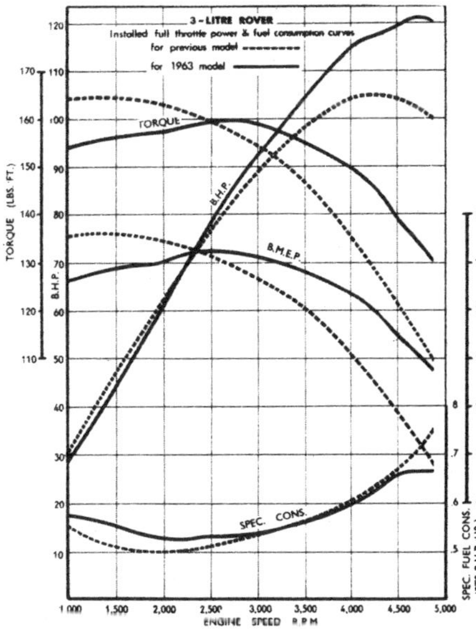

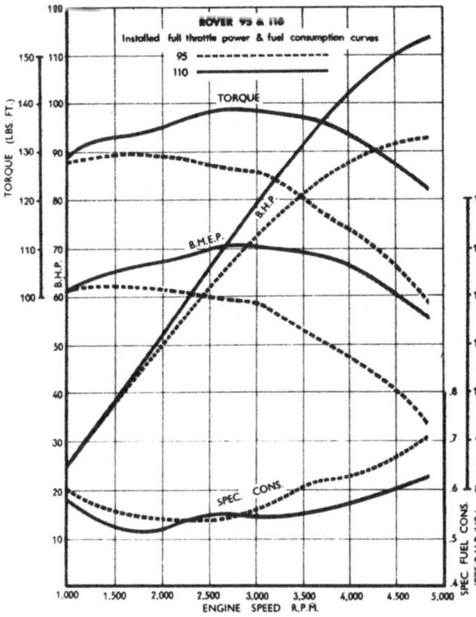

Specification (Rover 3-litre Saloon and Coupé)

ENGINE

Cylinders	6 in-line with 7-bearing crankshaft.
Bore and stroke	77.79 mm. × 104.77 mm. (3$\frac{1}{16}$ in. × 4⅛ in.).
Cubic capacity	2,995 cc. (183 cu. in.).
Piston area	44.1 sq. in.
Compression ratio	8.75/1.
Valvegear	Overhead inlet valves (pushrod operated), side exhaust valves. Single camshaft.
Carburation	1 SU HD8 carburetter (with economiser), fed by rear-mounted SU dual electric pump, from 14-gallon tank.
Ignition	12-volt coil, centrifugal and vacuum timing control, 14 mm. Champion N5 sparking plugs.
Lubrication	AC-Delco full flow filter and 11-pint sump.
Cooling	Water cooling with pump, fan and thermostat; 24-pint water capacity.
Electrical system	57 amp. hour 12-volt battery charged by 22 amp. Lucas C.42 generator.
Maximum power (net)	121 b.h.p. at 4,800 r.p.m., equivalent to 110 lb./sq. in. b.m.e.p. at 3,300 ft./min. piston and 2.74 b.h.p. per sq. in. of piston area.
Maximum torque (net)	160 lb. ft. at 2,650 r.p.m., equivalent to 132 lb./sq. in. b.m.e.p. at 1,820 ft./min. piston speed.

TRANSMISSION (Manual)

Clutch	10 in. dia. Borg and Beck, hydraulically operated.
Gearbox	4-speed and reverse with direct top, synchromesh on upper 3 gears and Laycock-de Normanville overdrive.
Overall ratios	14.52, 8.12, 5.48, 4.3, o/d 3.34; rev. 14.52.

TRANSMISSION (Automatic)

	Borg-Warner Torque converter and automatic 3-speed gearbox with ratios 3.9, 5.6 and 9.0; rev. 7.84.
Propeller shaft	Hardy Spicer divided shaft with centre bearing.
Final Drive	Hypoid bevel.

CHASSIS

Brakes	Girling hydraulic, disc front, drum rear with vacuum servo.
Brake dimensions	Front discs 10¾ in. dia.; rear drums 11 in. dia. × 2¼ in. wide.
Brake areas	122.7 sq. in. of lining (27.7 sq. in. front plus 95 sq. in. rear) working on 404 sq. in. rubbed area of discs and drums.
Front suspension	Independent by transverse wishbones, laminated torsion bars and anti-roll bar. Woodhead-Monroe 1 in. telescopic dampers.
Rear suspension	Semi-elliptic leaf springs and live axle. Woodhead-Monroe 1 in. telescopic dampers.
Wheels and tyres	5-stud pressed steel wheels with 5K rims and 6.70-15 Dunlop RS5 tyres.
Steering	Burman F3 recirculating ball steering box and hydraulic damper.

DIMENSIONS

Length	Overall 15 ft. 7 in.; wheelbase 9 ft. 3 in.
Width	Overall 5 ft. 9¾ in.; track 4 ft. 7½ in. at front and 4 ft. 7¾in. at rear.
Height	Saloon, 5 ft. 1½ in.; Coupé, 5 ft.; ground clearance 6¼ in.
Turning circle	40 ft.
Kerb weight	32¼ cwt. (without fuel but with oil, water, tools, spare wheel etc.).

EFFECTIVE GEARING

Top gear ratio (manual)	18.3 m.p.h. at 1,000 r.p.m. and 35.8 m.p.h. at 1,000 ft./min. piston speed (overdrive, 23.5 m.p.h. and 46 m.p.h.). Automatic: 20.2 m.p.h. and 39.5 m.p.h.
Maximum torque	2,650 r.p.m. corresponds to approx. 48.5 m.p.h. in top gear (62 m.p.h. in overdrive).
Maximum power	4,800 r.p.m. corresponds to approx. 88 m.p.h. in top gear (113 m.p.h. in overdrive).
Probable direct top gear pulling power	See Road Test on pages 318—321.

FOR ROVER BUYERS...
A HIGH PERFORMANCE COUPE

A shapely addition to the Rover range, the 3-litre coupe has performance to match its looks and quality

From
GORDON WILKINS

ROVERS seem to become younger as the years go by. The appearance of works entries in major International competitions typifies the new atmosphere at the works. Rovers did well in the East African Safari and the Liege-Sofia-Liege. Now comes a new high performance 3-litre coupe as proof that the manufacturer is intent on attracting other buyers besides the elderly lovers of quality cars who have hitherto been its main supporters.

The 1963 range consists entirely of six-cylinder cars. Star performer is the new 3-litre four door coupe with a roof line 2½ in lower than that of the sedan. The six-cylinder engine has been modified with a new gas-flowed cylinder head and high efficiency induction manifold to produce 134 bhp at 5000 rpm — an increase of 17 percent. Maximum torque is now raised to 169 lb/ft at 1750 rpm.

The 3-litre coupe uses the same basic structure as the sedan but it has a new lower roof of slim lines which are emphasised by narrow bright metal window frames in the doors. It is set off by modernistic Viking ship emblems against a brushed metal background on the quarter panels.

It is solely a four-seater. Front seats are outstandingly comfortable with adjustment for height and reach and full reclining backrest adjustment by the new Widney regulators. In view of the low roof line, rear seats have been moved slightly forward of the position used in the sedan. They are two very comfortable seats with an armrest, ashtray and lighter in between. Rear headroom is not as great as on the sedan but the rear part of the roof is well padded.

The coupe has an entirely new instrument panel of very modern appearance with speedometer and tachometer grouped under a cowl in front of the driver and four separate instruments in streamlined housings below it — oil pressure gauge, ammeter, thermometer, and fuel gauge. All instruments are finished in matt black; so is the padding across the top of the facia, which includes two adjustable fresh air outlets for the face.

Tops of the door garnish rails are also padded and below the pads is a band of African cherry wood running round the sides and front of the body. In a drawer under the front parcel shelf is a high grade tool kit in moulded rubber. There is a big glove box and a tray for gloves or sun glasses is now moulded into the top of the centre tunnel.

Manual gearbox cars have a new and much more precise remote control gear lever. The coupe has the lowered suspension also found on the sedans. Sedans without power steering have a telescopic hydraulic damper on the steering. The old friction type damper imposed a resistance as high as 26 lb on the steering linkage. The hydraulic damper adds only 1 lb to the effort required at the steering wheel. Another contribution to lighter and more accurate steering is a new steering box with more balls in circulation which is more robust and permits less wind up in the system. Power assisted steering is standard on the coupe. Buyers of the sedan have the option of manual or assisted steering and the difference between the two is rather startling for a driver switching suddenly from one car to the other, for the manual steering requires about four and a half turns from lock to lock whereas the power assisted system needs only about two and a quarter.

The improved 3-litre engine in both sedan and coupe has an air flowed head for which Weslake acted as consultant. There has been no basic change in the head during the years when the engine was enlarged by stages from 2.1 to 3 litres, but now the inlet valves have been repositioned (the exhausts are in the cylinder block) and the passage leading to the valve has been made smoother, and the exhaust cams have been changed.

There is also a new six branch water jacketed inlet manifold cast in light alloy with a hot spot and built-in ridges to control the flow of wet petrol after cold starts.

Stronger valve springs prevent inlet valve bounce below 5200 rpm and a new crankshaft damper im-

Rover coupe actually has four doors and retains the general shape of the sedan. However, roof line is much lower, interior completely new and the engine upped in power.

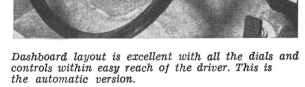

Dashboard layout is excellent with all the dials and controls within easy reach of the driver. This is the automatic version.

The coupe is strictly a four seater and a very luxurious one at that. Front seats recline and there is a large amount of fore and aft adjustment.

proves engine smoothness at high cruising speeds.

The exhaust is now a straight through system with absorption type silencer. There have also been changes in the camshaft to combine higher power output with better idling. The power unit has the new four point mounting which was introduced a short time ago. To obtain full benefit from the engine modifications second and third gear ratios have been raised by 10 percent (lower numerically) which gives about 80 mph in third gear. The gear box has a larger front lay-shaft bearing and the de Normanville overdrive, which is a standard fitting on the sedan and coupe, has been given its own separate lubrication system to prevent oil draining from overdrive to gearbox when the car is parked on a steep hill. The only greasing points on the car are the joints on the propeller shaft which rarely need attention.

Manual transmission cars have an axle ratio of 4.3 to 1 but, of course, high speed cruising is done in overdrive top which gives an effective ratio of 3.345 to 1. Cars fitted with the Borg Warner automatic transmission have an axle ratio of 3.9 to 1 to give the best results in acceleration and hill climbing and in order to discourage over-revving with the new more powerful engine there is a red sector on the speedometer starting at 105 mph

The latest 3-litre sedan has a similar interior to that of the coupe but does not have the four separate instruments below the main group.

The Rover 110 has a water jacketed inlet manifold similar to that of the 3-litre but with shorter branch pipes because of the more limited space under the bonnet. It has the air flowed cylinder head and gives 20 hp more than last year's Rover 100. The exterior is unchanged except for different badges and new wheel discs but there are detail changes to the interior and fully adjusted front seats with reclining back-rests are now available as optional equipment.

Like the 3-litre, the 110 has a 4.3 axle ratio with de Normanville overdrive and Dunlop RS5 or Avon Turbo Speed tyres for safe high-speed cruising. On all cars the overdrive kick down switch has been omitted to prevent inadvertent changes from overdrive into direct top at high speed.

The Rover 95 is similar but does not have the new

wheel discs. It has the unmodified 2.6 litre engine used in last year's 100, giving 102 bhp and is supplied with a four-speed manual transmission using a 3.9 axle ratio and no overdrive. All Rovers have servo assisted brakes, disc at the front and drums at the rear.

ROAD IMPRESSIONS 3-LITRE COUPE

I tried the coupe with both manual and automatic transmissions and it is obviously going to appeal to a lot of performance conscious quality car buyers who have previously thought of Rovers in terms of comfort rather than speed.

It rushes up to 100 mph in a most satisfactory way and holds it quietly and smoothly with no sign of strain. The new remote control gear shift is excellent and the steering is much improved — lighter, more accurate and far less prone to shake. In fact, the only time I encountered a trace of the old front end shake was on an indifferent road at about 30 mph. Fast cornering is good, with little roll and the tyres don't squeal. There is no less than 7 in of sliding adjustment on the front seats and this coupled with 1½ in of height adjustment and a full range of adjustments on the backrest should enable any driver to find a comfortable position. The two rear seats on the coupe are generously proportioned. Knee room and head room are limited, but for anyone who wants to carry large rear passengers regularly there is always the sedan.

Automatic transmission cars have a steering column selector lever and beside it a small trigger which allows the intermediate gear to be held. On the opposite side of the column is an indicator switch which will also flash the headlamps and a hand dipper switch. Longer wiper blades cover a large area of screen.

Rover 110. Anyone who is not discouraged by its rather elderly appearance will find the 110 a splendidly developed car with a lively performance. The new engine gives it a comfortable 100 mph and is flexible enough to pull smoothly from 20 mph in top.

The manual steering is not particularly light but there is less understeer which makes these Rovers easier to handle on winding roads than they used to be. The improved interior trim and instrument panel are in the best Rover tradition and the seats are particularly comfortable. #

Rover with a bite

RALLY coverage for journalists becomes more specialized as rallies themselves b e c o m e specialist operations. In the old days, even the classic events tended to be something of a *tour gastronomique*, with a little hard motoring between repasts. Today, things are different, rally schedules are fierce and on-the-spot reporting is essential. Reporting crews must be prepared to keep up with the rally, and get ahead of it at times. Hard motoring is the order of the day—and night—while meals become a secondary consideration.

On a rally assignment, the car is as much a working tool as a typewriter or a camera, and must be chosen as carefully. This year *Autocar* sent out four teams to cover the Monte Carlo Rally; our narrative concerns the experiences of one of them, mounted in

a Rover 3-litre. This covered the core of the rally, from Paris to The Hague and Boulogne, thereafter from Rheims to Chambéry and all the special tests between Chambéry and Pont Charles Albert; 2,000 miles of coverage and another 1,000 miles to be in the right places at the right times.

In its latest form, with revised suspension and Westlake head, the Rover seemed ideal for the job. It has the weight and the power to burst through snowdrifts, the speed and handling to keep up with the rally and bags of room for a complete set of spare wheels and bulky photographic equipment—funny how a Leica outfit takes up as much room as the old plate outfits. The reclining seats give the off-duty watch the chance to rest, while the optional Hydrosteer power steering, with just over two turns between locks,

makes for quick recovery from slides when things get interesting.

The gimmicks you leave off a rally car don't go wrong. Preparation of the Rover was minimal; a routine check in the works, a couple of spotlights (for fog) and replacement of the standard tyres with Dunlop SPs. Dick Jeffries and Oliver Speight of Dunlop organized studded SP tyres at short notice and four of these—on wheels—were distributed about the car. We prefer to slumber with our tyres rather than suffer the encumbrance of a roof rack. Sleeping bags and a folding spade completed the equipment.

Taking the car to Paris for the start revealed the wisdom of the choice of steering. Recent snowstorms had left a couple of inches of slush in the fast lane of M1 and we were able to prove a private theory that power steering is the antidote to the "pull-in" effect when putting right- or left-hand wheels into snow at speed. Leaving the Midlands at 11.00 and making a brief call at our London office to pick up photographer Ron Easton, we still caught a late afternoon Silver City flight and were snug in our hotel in the Avenue Montaigne by 8 p.m. that evening.

At scrutineering the following morning, an icy blast blowing through the *Centre de Sécurité* in the Bois de Boulogne, with chilly forecasts of snow on the Belgian border, decided us to move northwards and intercept the Paris column there the next day.

Comfortable quarters were found in the Hotel de France at Urcel, a hostelry not unnoticed by M. Bibendum. Here, after an excellent supper of onion soup, followed by *marcassin, sauce poirade* (wild boar with pear sauce) we tumbled into bed for our first and last full night's sleep of the rally.

Study of the map suggested possible difficulties for competitors on the 30km or so before the first control at Etreaupont. Hereabouts we did find one decent snowdrift, but with only a police jeep and a Renault van stuck in it. While Ron Easton took photographs of competitors bursting through the snow, I helped shoulder the jeep out of the ditch with loud cries of "*doucement!*" to the heavy-footed *gendarme* driver.

An uneventful but snowy drive across the Ardennes into Belgium, to Liège and across to Holland gave us an insight into the amazing grip offered by unstudded SP tyres. The Dutch motorways alternated between hard-packed snow with rapidly forming drifts, and hard-rutted black ice. The Rover took the former in bursts of snow crystals; on the ice we sped towards The Hague at 70 m.p.h., thinking we were great guys. . . until Pat Moss stormed past in her Anglia . . . flashing her lights and blowing her horn in recognition—or was it derision?

At the control I talked to drivers and wrote copy, warmed by great bowls of soup laced with *wurst* and potatoes, while an icy gale blew people in and out through the revolving doors of the hotel. Many crews were changing to studded tyres here after lurid slides on the *autoweg*. We opted to keep ours in the boot for use later.

At 3.0 a.m., in Antwerp, we found a café open and ate *steak tartare* sandwiches, washed down with black coffee, before taking to minor roads across the battlefields of Flanders. In the eerie wee hours, with snow threatening to blot out the featureless landscape, one almost expected to come face to face with marching ghosts of our fathers as we passed signposts bearing the names Ypres, Menin and Passendale.

On the steep descent out of Cassel we had a moment when hard, rutted snow threw the Rover into a wild slide, but the high-geared steering saved the day. Later, approaching Boulogne, we came upon our first road block and deviated through narrow lanes deep in

Above: Deep freeze in Gérardmer; setting out for Chambéry after breakfast in the modern Hotel Viry. Right: You are in for chilly motoring when this happens in winter on the Continent. It is best to knock the fragmented glass out and carry on without a screen, with all side windows closed. The heading picture opposite shows the car with its temporary screen.
Below: Typical continental winter going; deep ruts are worn in the hard packed snow. The culprits are usually lorries or snow ploughs

BY EDWARD EVES

Plunging down into Morez. Probably the only snow free patch of road we saw for 400 miles on the return trip

ROVER WITH A BITE...

snow. Then freezing rain began to fall, blotting out the windscreen and turning the streets of the town into a skating rink. Here we snatched a few hours sleep, the last for 56 hours, before cutting across to Rheims to rejoin the rally.

We came back to a Rover encased in a ¼in. layer of ice. With the roads similarly covered, here was an excuse to fit the studded tyres. Even thus equipped one must take it easy; but with fresh studs it is quite possible to maintain 50 m.p.h. or so on the slipperiest roads, but braking demands care. The best method is to use short, hard dabs.

After midnight we followed the cars over dry roads for the first 100 km with a huge crescent moon hanging low over the Forêt d'Argonne. The column of cars spaced out ahead of us, rear lights twinkling, clattering through the decrepit villages of this rural area. At Gérardmer, one can always be sure of snow in winter. The temperature at the top of the Col de la Schluct was such that a film of ice formed over my Leica when I popped into a café for a warm drink. Down in Gérardmer we breakfasted with Sam Croft-Pearson, who was leading a Ford-America service crew in a Ford Futura, decked up like a pathetic Man Friday. It even had VHF radio and a 100-gallon bag-type petrol tank on the roof rack.

Windscreen Shattered

After lunch at St. Loup we had our first and only setback. Following close behind a competing Reliant near Dôle, a stone picked out of the road by studded tyres exploded our toughened windscreen like a pistol shot. Progress was impossible, and knocking out the remains of the screen we hastened off course to Besançon to phone Geneva for a replacement. The Swiss agent had no screen (nor had his colleague in Monaco at the finish) and we cast around quickly for a substitute. Fortunately the excellent Garage Daclin was at hand. The "chef" quickly sized up the situation and, impressed by our rally press plates, dispatched us into the nether regions of Besançon in the wake of a small, old man driving a Fiat

500. This old man must surely have been the father of Phillipe Etancelin, we thought, as we slithered round the back streets of Besançon in a vain attempt to stay with him.

Fortunately our destination was not far; it proved to be a small plastics factory on the outskirts; here our wizened benefactor proudly ushered us into the office and left us in the good hands of the foreman. Again the rally plates were an open sesame. Within minutes, large sheets of cardboard were found to make templates for a new screen. Meanwhile, Perspex sheet thick enough to withstand wind pressures and thin enough to bend round the corners of the screen aperture was chosen from piles of stock and taken to be cut to size. The manager appeared with a large roll of wide sticky tape, another man cut a stick to make a vertical support across the middle of the screen aperture. Within 40 minutes we had a complete screen of clear Perspex.

All of one street in Chambéry was given over to the rally. It seemed fractionally warmer, but the ground was still hard frozen and those worthy souls, the mechanics, scarcely noticed it as they chipped recesses in the frozen snow to give room to work beneath their charges. Tyres were the focus of interest and were here in wide variety and profusion, piled high at the roadside beneath the glare of makeshift floodlights, or spilling from the boots of service cars. Many works cars had been checked at garages on the entrance to the town, but Ford-America had taken over the only service station in the control area, and serviced their cars with smooth efficiency. Other crews worked on the pavement alongside the control. Eric Carlsson's diminutive Saab service van was eclipsed by this imposing array; it was significant that his car needed only the briefest of mechanical checks and a tyre change before going on.

The excitement was electrifying and there was no thought of sleep as we clattered off down the main road to Chamrousse. At this point we began to see the form at last and, after the Chamrousse test, what times were available gave Toivenen, Carlsson and

Aaltonen as likely winners. A surprising prognosis, but we recalled that Stuart Turner had laid down, before the rally, that the Chamrousse and the Granier tests would decide the winner.

From Chamrousse our next interception point was La Mure, where we picked up the route to take a look at the interesting new section, for a winter rally, over the Col de Sautet and the Lautaret. Here many less hardened competitors lost time. It was easy to see why, as we wound through the multiple bends of the Sautet, the icy road often barely wide enough for a car, with steep drops over unguarded edges. Wheel tracks on these edges betrayed hectic moments. We came upon Hazard's Facelia nose down in a steep gully, while farther on there was a Fiat 500 to be shouldered out of a ditch. Descending the Lautaret, deep in snow with a blizzard raging, we made our one and only contact with the scenery. Fortunately, the scenery was a soft snowbank and the Rover was unmarked.

Fuel Line Repairs

The control at Montmaur was our last sight of the rally until it reached Castellane. While the column struggled eastward across Les Baronnies to Ventoux, we cut along the snow-covered Route Napoleon by way of Digne and Sisteron. Entering Barrème, a rock, hidden in the soft snow, neatly snipped the main petrol line where it passed under a cross member. Fortunately, the carburettor-to-air cleaner balance pipe bridged the break nicely—we replaced the balance pipe with a piece cut from the radiator overflow—and were on our way in minutes.

The rest of the tale is one of deep snow and marginal traction across the Clue de Tallouse between Barrème and Castellane and again over the Col de Luens before Grasse. So deep was the snow that we were glad of the marker poles which defined the verges. High on the Luens we found Fraser's Rapier being hitched to a breakdown crane after a severe off-the-road excursion, the crew sorrowfully packing their rally plates into the boot. Hard luck within 100 miles of the finish. It was almost our last real contact with the rally until Monte Carlo, another crew taking over at the Pont Charles Albert.

The 1963 Monte Carlo Rally will stand out as one of the hardest and fairest of the series. In our minds it will also stand out as the one that went most smoothly; for that we had in large part to thank our car. Completely reliable, in the 3,000 miles it needed no mechanical attention save for that after mishaps. Two litres of oil were consumed and petrol consumption worked out at a little over 18 miles per gallon, good considering the high rolling resistance on the snow-covered roads which made up half the mileage. In the past we have regarded the Rover as a Labrador of a motorcar, sleek, reliable and with the best of breeding . . . but no racer. This latest of the line made us revise this last opinion.

CAR and DRIVER
ROAD TEST

Rover
3-Liter

*Rover's luxurious
3-Liter is for those
who demand quality
in the family car*

Rover's factory entries in the recent Liège-Sofia-Liège rally raised a few eyebrows in Mayfair, and we were impressed to see that two three-liter Rovers completed this grueling event among 18 finishers out of 82 cars started. Who would have thought in 1958, when the 3-Liter was introduced, that four years later the car would prove itself as a successful rally car of extreme ruggedness and reliability? Probably the factory did not even have such plans at the time.

Such outstanding performances serve to change the image of Rover as a sedate car for senior citizens to one of a competitive and agile car for discerning drivers of any age.

The current three-liter is an exceptional car in spite of its lack of radical design features. Many enthusiasts feel that it stands alone in displaying eminently satisfactory qualities in so many respects: comfort, silence, economy, performance and reliability.

The excellence of the Rover is not immediately apparent—it takes a few hundred miles to reach the full appreciation of this automobile. Four members of the editorial staff drove the Rover during our test, and reactions varied from favorable comment to very high praise. No one had any serious complaints.

Although the three-liter has been changed very slightly in appearance in its four years of production, chas-

CONTINUED

ROVER CONTINUED

sis development has been constant.

As the first-ever unitized-construction Rover, it offers greater space with a lower floor and lighter weight than the Rover 80 and 100 models. The engine is carried in a subframe attached to the body shell by means of six Metalastik rubber cushions. Earlier models had some vibration from the engine at very high speeds or on slightly rough surfaces, but new rear engine mountings have now eliminated this.

The 117 bhp of the seven-main-bearing F-head engine works in almost uncanny silence. If its performance is not breathtaking, it is steady rather than sluggish. It never seems stressed, and accelerates freely to 5,000 rpm.

We noted with pleasure the good accessibility under the hood, which may seem an unnecessary luxury in a car which demands so little maintenance. The only lubrication recommendations (beyond engine oil changes) are greasing four points for the propeller-shaft universal joints at intervals of 3,000 miles and simultaneous inspection of the steering-box oil level.

The 3-Liter now has a lever below the steering wheel to hold the automatic transmission in intermediate range. This is much easier

to operate than the T-handle below the parcel shelf under the dashboard, which served as a "hold" switch on earlier three-liters. This switch can keep you in intermediate on a slight throttle opening, where the Borg-Warner transmission would normally upchange itself into direct drive. It thus provides the driver with better control for smooth driving in traffic or on give-and-take roads, while saving brakes.

On leisurely starts the car will move off in intermediate, but if you are in a hurry low range can take you up to 33 mph.

Another feature of the Rover which is not usually associated with rally cars is the power steering but, as with the Daimler-Benz unit (*January C/D*), there is enough feedback to give the driver good road feel under all circumstances. The Rover system is called "Hydro-steer" and employs a pump at the rear of the generator shaft. It has been used to quicken the steering much more than is common on American cars—and to good advantage. Rovers without power steering require a full four turns of the wheel lock to lock, but the power steering reduces the figure to 2.6, thus appreciably increasing the safety of the car for competitive motoring.

With springs of sufficient softness to remain in keeping with the plush

A well-poised and elegant car in city traffic, the 3-Liter is in its element here.

interior, the three-liter also has some body roll on hard cornering. There is a medium-diameter anti-roll bar at front, and the rear suspension with semi-elliptic leaf springs provides reasonable roll stiffness. The

---

ROVER 3-LITER

Price as tested: $5,595 POE N.Y.

Importer: Rover Motor Company of North America, Inc.
405 Lexington Avenue
New York, New York

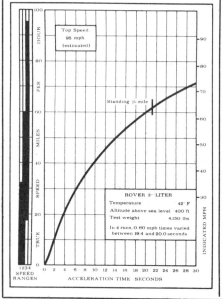

ENGINE:

Displacement	183 cu in, 2,995 cc
Dimensions	6 cyl, 3.06-in bore, 4.13-in stroke
Valve gear: Pushrod-operated overhead inlet valves, side exhaust valves	
Compression ratio	8.75 to one
Power (SAE)	117 bhp @ 4,500 rpm
Torque	164 lb-ft @ 1,500 rpm
Usable range of engine speeds	1,000-5,000 rpm
Carburetion	Single horizontal SU HD 8 carburetor
Fuel recommended	Premium
Mileage	18-26 mpg
Range on 17.5-gallon tank	315-455 miles

CHASSIS:

Wheelbase	110.5 in
Tread	F 55.3 in, R 56 in
Length	186.5 in
Ground clearance	8 in
Suspension: F: Ind., wishbones and laminated torsion bars, anti-roll bar. R: Rigid axle, semi-elliptic leaf springs.	
Steering	Recirculating ball worm and nut
Turns, lock to lock	2.6
Turning circle diameter between curbs	42 ft
Tire size	6.70 x 15
Pressures recommended Normal. F 24, R 22 psi High-speed F 30, R 28 psi	
Brakes	Girling 11-in discs front, 11-in drums rear, 416 sq in swept area.
Curb weight (full tank)	3,850 lbs
Percentage on the driving wheels	45.5

DRIVE TRAIN:

Clutch.........Borg-Warner hydraulic torque converter

Gear	Ratio	Over-all	Mph per 1,000 rpm
Rev	2.30-4.82	9.00-18.90	-4.2-8.7
Low	2.30-4.82	9.00-18.90	4.2-8.7
Intermediate	1.44-2.98	5.60-11.80	6.8-14.0
Drive	1.00	3.90	20.1
Final drive ratio		3.9 to one	

ROVER 3-LITER
Temperature 42° F
Altitude above sea level 400 ft
Test weight 4,150 lbs
In 4 runs, 0-60 mph times varied between 19.4 and 20.0 seconds

Top Speed 95 mph (estimated)

Standing ¼ mile

leaf springs have no rear shackles but are suspended in pre-stressed rubber cushions, and the front eye is hinged eccentrically. This combination provides enough movement for all normal spring deflections.

Many of the luxury items in the Rover are for the benefit of the passengers. There are courtesy lights over all doors and four separate ashtrays. But the driver has not been neglected. He has an oil-level gauge, and a warning light that comes on if the choke is in use after suitable operating temperature has been reached. There is a warning tween front and rear is based on a full complement of passengers and luggage. This provides highly balanced braking on a basically understeering car such as the Rover 3-Liter. A nice feature of the brake pedal is its great width, enabling you to use either foot as on most American cars. The handbrake has an umbrella-type handle and does not give the impression of being able to hold the car on a steep hill, but looks are deceptive. The parking brake worked perfectly on the worst gradients we could find.

Road noise would be reduced and

The intake manifold is placed at a sharp angle to the light-alloy cylinder head.

Although the transmission tunnel is both high and wide, it is possible to seat three in front without discomfort. Padded armrests on the doors are adjustable.

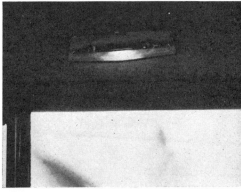
Each of the doors has its own courtesy light, with an overriding manual switch.

An unusually generous trunk has been made at cost of bends in fuel filler neck.

light for the hand-brake which also lights up if the brake-fluid level gets too low. The instruments are grouped in a separate panel, projecting from the dashboard. In view of the distance between the front seats and the windshield, this is a very logical solution which has also been taken advantage of to raise the main instruments closer to the driver's eye level.

Brakes are Girling (incorporating a vacuum servo) and with large discs on the front wheels there is adequate stopping power even for such a relatively heavy car. Wet roads did not reduce their effectiveness as much as expected, since the distribution of braking power be- road-holding improved with an increase in tire pressures, and we would recommend the factory's high-speed figures for normal use and a still higher inflation for competition. Both mechanical noise and wind noise are so low at all speeds that no improvement can be envisaged in these fields.

Very few cars so typically British blend so well into the American scene. The Rover has a lot to offer, and although the price is high it should find a ready market. In preparation for growing demand, Land-Rover assembly has been transferred to a new plant at Cardiff to leave the entire Solihull factory for passenger-car production. **C/D**

With the central armrest down, the two rear passengers have exceptional comfort.

ROVER COUPE

*A 4-door, 4-passenger model with
no bark and considerably more bite*

ROVER CARS LTD. of Solihull, England is world renowned for producing good cars. They have even been accused of building a poor man's Rolls-Royce—an expression that may have a modicum of truth in it but one which hardly seems appropriate for a car which sells in the U.S. for well over $5000. Nevertheless the Rover is a very exceptional automobile; designed for the connoisseur, built to standards of quality and detail which are truly extraordinary—at the price.

The "trouble" with the Rover is that it is so plain, so conservative, so ordinary. It simply has no outstanding features which attract attention. The styling is simple and conservative, the performance is so-so, the overall feel (if there is such a thing) is not at all sensational in any respect. The ride is excellent, the engine is smooth and quiet; the durability, longevity and overall quality are there—unquestionably. But a Rover doesn't have the prestige of a Rolls-Royce; it doesn't have the performance of a Jaguar. Simply stated, the Rover 3-liter is an extremely well balanced package—and beautifully put together by people who take pride in their work.

In an effort to put a little more glamour into the Rover image the latest model is a cut-down, 4-door sedan, officially designated as "coupe." And so we come to our own special complaint with Rover Ltd—how can a 4-door sedan be called

a coupe? *Webster's New International Dictionary (Second Edition)* says as follows:

"Coú pé′ (kōō pā′; often incorrectly Anglicized kōōp), n. 1. The front or after compartment of a Continental diligence; also a half compartment on British Railway cars. 2. A four-wheeled close carriage for two persons inside, with an outside seat for the driver;—so called because giving the appearance of a large carriage cut off. 3. A two-door automobile having an enclosed body of one compartment, usually seating two to five persons."

Considering the fact that the English language, as distinct from Americana, is usually so concise and even precise we can only hope that hardtop "convertibles" will not (ultimately) be called roadsters in our own country.

However, this is a road test report on the Rover 3-liter Mark II coupe (sic), a car ostensibly designed for the American market and (apparently) supposed to put more glamour and sales appeal into a machine which, in its normal sedan form, is far more practical and useful, in our opinion.

Previous tests of the 3-liter sedan by R&T have established a high degree of respect for the make. For this test we elected to try the more sporting 4-speed plus overdrive transmission option; primarily to see if the latest improvements (including coupe body) might offer something a little more exciting.

The answer to this question is a qualified yes. The 1963 3-liter models have detail changes in carburetion and manifolding which boost the peak horsepower from 115 to 134. The test weights of the sedan and coupe are virtually identical and the performance is nearly the same if both cars are equipped with the same transmission option, axle ratio, etc.

Thanks primarily to a very efficient 4-speed and Laycock

de Normanville overdrive, but not forgetting the increased bhp, our test coupe performed in a manner much more acceptable to American demands. Our previous test of a sedan (June 1962) gave rather unsatisfactory acceleration times, primarily because of the very slow initial starting characteristics of the Borg-Warner automatic transmission.

The Rover with manual transmission is much more lively; the 0 to 60 mph time is 3.1 sec quicker, for example. Although 1st gear is somewhat noisy the "jump" when moving off from a standing start is tremendously improved and no longer gives the feel of being a sitting duck—in an emergency. In brief, the manual gears convert the Rover from a staid "old-man's car" to one with a little more interest and enough performance to be at least acceptable though still not worthy of the term "sports sedan."

As for general road feel, the Rover 3-liter is definitely among the best of the expensive imports. The engine in particular is one of the smoothest and quietest in the world, better than any 6-cyl unit we can remember and virtually equal to the best of the V-8s. Riding qualities are first rate and the handling and roadability have not been sacrificed to accomplish this. Sports car enthusiasts can really object in this department only to the inordinate amount of tire squeal which we felt inexcusable—primarily because American cars don't do it under the same conditions. At any rate the Rover unit chassis/body rates special praise because, unlike certain American designs of similar size, this car is absolutely impeccable when it comes to insulation from road noise, rumble, or ride harshness. Also, unlike too many American cars, the Rover's disc/drum brake system will survive more than one crash stop from 80 mph and the power steering is so perfect that it's difficult to be sure it's there.

As mentioned earlier, we fail to see any real benefit in the so-called coupe vs. sedan body style. The sedan, even though rather perpendicular, is at least a well balanced and pleasing design. The coupe roof is lower by 2.5-in. and our frank opinion is that it looks like a California Chop Job and would

have come off much better if the 2.5-in. had been removed from the body section rather than the glass area. At least a part of this opinion is influenced by the fact that headroom in the coupe is minimal; two of our 6-foot members proved that one's head tends to rub the headlining when sitting erect in either the front or rear seat.

On the credit side the Rover detailing, inside and outside, borders on the fantastic. There are no file marks under the paint, the doors fit, trim is in alignment, the interior is every bit as elegant as any Rover that preceded it and sincerely upholds the company's tradition of luxurious comfort and fine craftsmanship. The instrument panel layout is a good case in

Luxury fit for a queen: the finish and fit are superb in every respect. Some windshield distortion can be noticed at corner.

ROVER COUPE

point: the coupe features a large diameter tachometer which matches the speedometer. This entails a relocation of other instruments but the layout is neat, readable and complete. Essential items included in the grouping under the driver's eyes are an ammeter, water temperature, oil pressure and a unique fuel/oil level gauge. Solid, toggle-type switches are conveniently located on the panel and the usual warning lights are also contained in the overall layout.

Standard equipment on all 3-liter Rovers includes power brakes, genuine leather upholstery, vinyl headlining, adjustable front door arm rests, dash panel and window moldings of African cherry wood, heater and defroster with 2-speed fan control, padded sun visors, clock, seat belt anchorages, four inside courtesy lights, full width front parcel shelf under the dash panel, fitted tray of handtools below parcel shelf on passenger's side, heavy pile carpeting and felt underlay, bumper guards, back-up light, dual electric fuel pumps, electric oil gauge for sump level, warning lights for engine temperature (on cold starting) and for brake fluid reservoir level, and lights in both engine and trunk compartments. In addition the coupe model has 2 cigarette lighters and front seats with manual four-way adjustment (up and down, fore and aft) plus an adjustment for seat-back rake.

While we recommend the older 4-door sedan model over the new, lower coupe model, our reasons are based purely on practical considerations; we are sure that there are those who disagree with us and the acceptance of the coupe model in England has been excellent. 🐂

Jack, crank, lug wrench and tire pump are conveniently stored.

Engine compartment is illuminated by twin trouble lights.

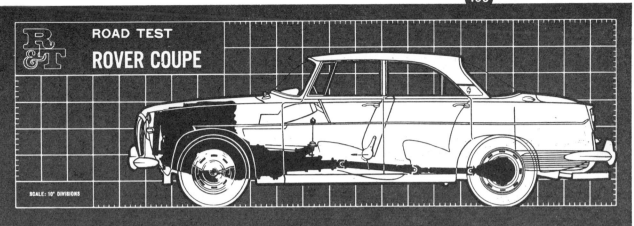

R&T ROAD TEST
ROVER COUPE

SCALE: 10" DIVISIONS

DIMENSIONS

Wheelbase, in	110.5
Tread, f and r	55.3/56.0
Over-all length, in	186.5
width	70.0
height	57.2
equivalent vol, cu ft	432
Frontal area, sq ft	22.2
Ground clearance, in	7.8
Steering ratio, o/a	n.a.
turns, lock to lock	2.5
turning circle, ft	40.0
Hip room, front	2 x 24.3
Hip room, rear	58.5
Pedal to seat back, max	39.0
Floor to ground	10.0

CALCULATED DATA

Lb/hp (test wt)	29.9
Cu ft/ton mile	67.6
Mph/1000 rpm (o/d)	24.4
Engine revs/mile	2560
Piston travel, ft/mile	1765
Rpm @ 2500 ft/min	3630
equivalent mph	85
R&T wear index	45.2

SPECIFICATIONS

List price	$5896
Curb weight, lb	3640
Test weight	4005
distribution, %	55/45
Tire size	6.70-15
Brake swept area	419
Engine type	6-cyl, F-head
Bore & stroke	3.06 x 4.13
Displacement, cc	2995
cu in	182.7
Compression ratio	8.75
Bhp @ rpm	134 @ 5000
equivalent mph	117
Torque, lb-ft	169 @ 1750
equivalent mph	41

GEAR RATIOS

O/d (0.78)	3.35
4th (1.00)	4.30
3rd (1.28)	5.48
2nd (1.89)	8.11
1st (3.38)	14.5

SPEEDOMETER ERROR

30 mph	actual, 28.1
60 mph	58.0

PERFORMANCE

Top speed (o/d), mph	105
Shifts, rpm-mph	
3rd (5000)	72
2nd (5000)	48
1st (5000)	27

FUEL CONSUMPTION

Normal range, mpg	17-20

ACCELERATION

0-30 mph, sec	5.3
0-40	7.9
0-50	11.6
0-60	15.5
0-70	20.2
0-80	27.4
0-100	
Standing ¼ mile	19.7
speed at end	69

TAPLEY DATA

4th, maximum gradient, %	10.0
3rd	12.6
2nd	20.2
Total drag at 60 mph, lb	125

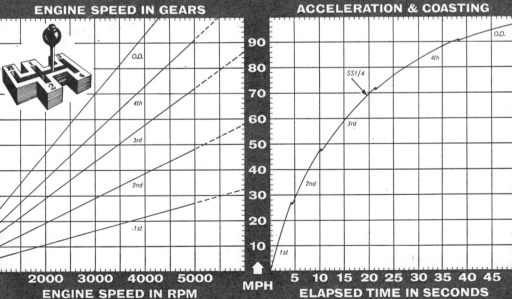

ENGINE SPEED IN GEARS

ACCELERATION & COASTING

ENGINE SPEED IN RPM — MPH — ELAPSED TIME IN SECONDS

USED CARS ON TEST

PRICES

Car for sale at Victoria at	£775
Typical trade advertised price for same age and model in average condition	£755
Total cost of car when new including tax	£1,772
Depreciation over 3½ years	£1,017

DATA

Date first registered	6 June 1962	Fuel consumption	18-22 m.p.g.
No. of owners	2	Oil consumption	130 m.p. pint
Tax expires	31 March 1966	Mileometer reading	34,486

No. 250: *1962 Rover 3-litre*

Above:
A cigarette lighter and clock are among the comprehensive standard equipment, nearly every item of which is still working perfectly. This car has a bench seat, but bucket seats were a listed extra

Above left:
Quarter vents in the front doors, and the deletion of window-louvres, identify this as a Mark IA 3-litre, on which the improved engine mountings and incorporation of overdrive as standard were the most significant changes

Left:
The engine compartment is extremely clean—always a good sign for the man who is looking for a car that has been cared-for and well maintained

OFTEN the bigger used cars—usually anything much over 1½ litres—seem such outstanding value that one wonders why more people do not turn a blind eye to fuel costs and always go for a big one when buying secondhand. Yet referring back to our last test in the series, dealing with a Hillman Super Minx at much the same age as this Rover, it is interesting to note that used car values have kept much in proportion. The extra cost of a Rover 3-litre compared with a Hillman Super Minx when new is about 110 per cent; and with these secondhand examples it is 95 per cent, the slight difference being compensated by the fact that the Rover, at 3½ years, is five months older than was our late 1962 Hillman.

Heavy oil consumption has been a feature of nearly all our tests of used Rovers, and it by no means suggests that anything is amiss; in fact many such engines are designed for fairly liberal passage of oil past the piston rings as part of the long-life factor, ensuring high mileages between over-hauls. At 130 miles per pint, this engine's oil thirst is acceptable, and the power unit is considered to be in

thoroughly good condition, confirmed by the performance check. It is an admirable engine all round, and from the first touch of the starter when cold it fires and pulls strongly at once, and the choke can soon be pushed home. Its smoothness, with really vigorous torque at low revs, quiet, vibration-free tickover after prolonged hard driving, and seemingly tireless performance, all on mixture grade fuel at nearly 20 m.p.g., are all most impressive on a long run.

Rather long travel before the clutch pedal is released enough for the drive to take up suggests need for adjust-ment, but the clutch is extremely smooth and the car will pull away without protest in second gear if needed. In bottom gear there is the characteristic whine familiar to owners of 6-cylinder Rovers and, of course, there is no synchromesh on first gear. In second gear, also, the syn-chromesh is a little too weak for hurried changes. The gear change is the now-discontinued type with long lever and slightly notchy action, though age and mileage have not made it any less precise. Overdrive on top gear was stand-ard, and both engages and disengages smoothly. The

PERFORMANCE CHECK

(Figures in brackets are those of the original Road Test,
21 August, 1959)

		In top gear:	
0 to 30 m.p.h.	5·8 sec (5·0)		
0 to 40 m.p.h.	9·9 sec (7·5)	10 to 30 m.p.h.	8·6 sec (—)
0 to 50 m.p.h.	13·5 sec (11·7)	20 to 40 m.p.h.	8·8 sec (8·8)
0 to 60 m.p.h.	19·6 sec (16·2)	30 to 50 m.p.h.	8·6 sec (9·2)
0 to 70 m.p.h.	25·5 sec (22·7)	40 to 60 m.p.h.	10·2 sec (10·3)
0 to 80 m.p.h.	32·8 sec (31·5)	50 to 70 m.p.h.	11·7 sec (12·4)
0 to 90 m.p.h.	45·1 sec (46·8)	60 to 80 m.p.h.	11·9 sec (15·7)

Standing quarter-mile 21·3 sec (20·3)

TYRES

Size: 6·70-15in. Approx. cost per replacement cover £10 13s 6d
Depth of original tread, 10mm. Remaining tread depth, approx. 5mm on each, except spare, 7mm. Avon Turbospeed on road, standard Avon on spare.

TOOLS

Most of the hand tools in tray under facia still in place. Main tools in boot scarcely used. Handbook with car.

CAR FOR SALE AT:

C. G. Norman (Victoria) Ltd., 50 Vauxhall Bridge Road, London, S.W.1. Telephone: VICtoria 2211.

CONDITION SUMMARY

Bodywork

Checking with care, one is able to spot signs which show that not all of the glistening black paintwork is original, though it is evidently skilled coachbuilder's finish, not just a used car spray job. There are no blemishes anywhere, nor any signs of rust. In contrast, the chromium plate is poor for the quality and relative youth of the car, and there are pimples of corrosion on door handles and lamp surrounds. Underbody examination of the Rover is a used car buyer's delight, and as the entire subframe, wheel arches and all other parts revealed have been sealed, corrosion is entirely absent. This protection is applied at the factory to all new Rovers. Inside the car, the maroon leather seats show a lot of creasing both front and rear, but have not sagged at all and the seats give good support even though perhaps not quite up to the standard one might hope for in this class of car. They are bench seats both front and rear, with huge centre armrests. There are also adjustable armrests on each door, and that on the driver's door is now rather loose. The maroon carpets show little wear, but there are one or two marks on the p.v.c. roof lining, and weathering of the wooden trim around the driver's side window suggests that this has usually been open.

Equipment

When the car was first taken over, the battery lacked punch, but improved with use although the ammeter never showed a high rate of charge; we think the battery may prove an early casualty. Although well cleaned for sale, the car had not been checked over thoroughly, and the windscreen washer was not working properly, nor were the windscreen wiper arms on the correct splines. The passenger's windscreen wiper blade disintegrated in the first 50 miles of driving in rain, and the driver's wiper blade also had to be renewed. The foglamp is not working, and the heater has lost the knob from its temperature and fan lever. It is a vigorous and controllable heater—part of the car's original standard equipment, and there is a clock, keeping good time. The headlamps are adequate, but no more. All instruments are working correctly, including the switch for indicating sump oil level on the fuel gauge, and the speedometer exaggerates to 8 m.p.h. at 80 m.p.h.

Accessories

Two quite useless flat-glass wing mirrors, and fog and spot lamps, are the only extras added to the car, but of course the Rover specification includes many items like the clock, heater, cigarette lighter, and trip mileometer.

ABOUT THE ROVER

ONLY the engine of the 3-litre Rover was directly related to any previous Solihull product when the new car was introduced in September 1958. Overdrive or Borg-Warner automatic transmission were optional extras. Brakes were 11in. Girling drums all round. The latest, 7-bearing, 3-litre engine produced 115 b.h.p.

At the 1959 London Show, Girling front wheel disc brakes had been adopted, and overdrive had become standard with manual transmission. Optional high-geared Hydrosteer power steering was offered as optional equipment at the 1960 Show, using only 2·5 turns from lock to lock (4·3 without).

In September 1961, changes to the automatic transmission, engine mountings, and the provision of quarter vents in the front doors (to assist the dashboard ventilation) led to the car being renamed the "New Series," or Series 1A. A smart low-roof Coupé was added to the range; the cylinder head and inlet manifolding was revised to give 134 b.h.p. (gross) at 5,000 r.p.m., with close ratio gearbox and remote control gearchange. The suspension was lowered by about 1in. The range became the 3-litre Mk. II.

The Mark II models continue basically unchanged today but, in October 1965, even more luxuriously trimmed and furnished versions of the saloon and Coupé were named the Mark III.

amount of throttle needed to overcome the inhibitor switch is sometimes a nuisance and makes it difficult to take advantage of the overdrive in gentle running, but it ensures that disengagement never occurs with a jolt when the car is on the overrun.

In direct top the engine begins to sound as though it is revving rather hard above about 75 m.p.h., but in overdrive there is no limit to the car's cruising, right up to the maximum speed of about 100 m.p.h., and at 85 it is particularly effortless.

Rover's 3-litre is still one of few cars to use laminated torsion bars for the front suspension; there is an occasional dull thump over a particularly bad bump or pothole, but on most surfaces the ride is outstandingly comfortable and "dignified" for both front and rear occupants. On corners there is a lot of roll, especially when the car is being hurried along, and the pull on the steering is tremendous; there is no power assistance on this car, and even at more than 4 turns lock to lock, a lot of effort is needed at the wheel. There is only slight play in the control, and

in any case the directional stability is so good that the car holds true to course at speed regardless of wind or camber.

With its great weight, and little engine braking in overdrive when the driver releases the accelerator, the Rover feels like a car which will take a lot of stopping, but this is not true at all. The brakes respond reassuringly even in pouring rain, without any need to press hard on the pedal or fear of skidding. The pull-out handbrake beneath the facia is also good, and holds securely on steep gradients. Brakes are by Girling, disc at the front and drums at rear, with strong servo assistance.

For all its size and weight, the Rover 3-litre is not a particularly spacious car inside, and even the luggage locker is not as large as with some more recent cars. Yet a long journey in it leaves one quite delighted at its refinement and comfort. As a used car, also, it impresses with its excellent solidity and the feeling of robustness in its construction; purchase would be an investment in its long potential life. ∎

In its finished form one would never guess that this two-door coupé was once a four-door saloon

Panelcraft Rover 3-litre

MOST potential buyers of new cars know what they want and can usually find at least one model that meets their needs. The others can come to a compromise between their wives, bank managers and childhood dreams and at least feel satisfied with their choice. There must be, however, a small fraction that cannot find just what they want, whatever the cost. One of these recently took a bold step in his quest for a luxury class convertible and commissioned a firm of specialist coachbuilders literally to saw up a Rover 3-litre saloon.

Apart from cutting off the roof, the four doors were removed and two new wide aluminium ones substituted. This operation meant moving the central door pillar back by seven inches and welding in part of the rear doors flush with the rear quarter panels, transforming the car into a two-door model.

The next task was to replace as much of the original rigidity as possible by bracing struts and stiffening plates. Under each door sill a U-section channel was welded from the main cross member supporting the rear of the engine to the front of the rear spring mounting points. Across the car, under the rear seat and the scuttle, there is much strengthening and filleting of corners. The boot hinges are reinforced around their mounting points, and there are tie-bars across the corners of the engine compartment to brace the tops of the wheel arches.

Inside the car new trimming was made to match the existing hide and woodwork, in addition to special front quarter-lights and side windows. The hood is made from p.v.c. and fully lined with cloth. It folds down into a well behind the rear seats and can then be hidden under a small tonneau cover.

F.L.M. (Panelcraft) Ltd., Arches 33-34 Broughton Street, London, S.W.8, carried out the work for the owner, George Hansson of Purley, at a cost of £700. This puts the price of the complete car at about £2,441—some £574 less than its nearest competitor, the Alvis TE 21 convertible.

The roof is removed across a straight line between the windscreen pillars, leaving a broad metal capping

Armchair luxury

*'. . . quality is ingrained,
not superficial.'*

ROVERS have been described as among the seven best-made cars in the World. We won't start an argument here about which are the other six qualifiers or exactly what position the Rover holds. Who is to judge such a nebulous contest? But it is certainly true that Rover build cars with a thoroughness and philosophy matched by few other manufacturers. Quality is ingrained, not superficial. Rovers are made to last. We cannot verify this objectively in a 1,500-mile road test but you can look elsewhere for confirmation. Try spotting an early 3-litre from its condition: generally you cannot because most of the Mk. I cars (identified by the anti-draught glass strip above the side windows) look and sound just as healthy as the models now leaving Solihull.

Although the 3-litre is now eight years old, it is still one of the most refined saloons in the world for comfort and quietness; few cars provide better insulation from the traffic commotion outside. Four contoured armchair seats (adapted from the successful Rover 2000 formula) and a separate heating system at the back have raised the standard of comfort on the Mk. III to such a high level that you can forgive the slightly turbulent ride on bad roads—one of the few things that betray the design's age.

The 2000 conquered the traditional Rover image of a car for elderly gentlemen but you could hardly describe the 3-litre, with a price of £2,000, as a young man's car; young tycoons would probably prefer something more lively and responsive, even though the 3-litre will top 100 m.p.h. and handles a lot better than might

be expected for such a stately carriage. It is a car for relaxation, not exhilaration. Hence the optional automatic transmission, perhaps the smoothest Borg Warner 35 installation we have yet tried, and power steering that did not get such unanimous praise although it makes the car very easy and light to drive.

Performance and economy

Most people who drove our test car said that it felt sluggish. For half the price you can certainly buy other saloons with more performance but we suspect that 3-litre owners will be satisfied with what they have. Moreover, the stop-watch shows the acceleration to be better than it feels—the smooth serenity of it all is deceptive. Over-riding automatic drive manually, the acceleration to 50 m.p.h. is equal to that of a Triumph Spitfire, Citroen ID19 or Simca 1500 Estate though it is generally inferior to competitive automatics shown in the comparison charts. The Rover is at its best when cruising quietly and effortlessly at up to 90 m.p.h. on fast main roads or motorways.

After pulling a T-handle choke control under the dashboard, the engine starts instantly from cold: the choke can then be set to give a fast idle until a thermostatically controlled yellow light shines from the facia indicating that normal running temperature has been reached and that the choke should be in. During the warming up period, the engine pulls smoothly from low revs but on full throttle will occasionally miss a beat with a muffled cough.

By *Motor's* standards, the overall petrol consumption of 17.4 m.p.g. is not too bad for such a heavy car; it is 2 m.p.g. better than that of the 3-litre automatic coupé we tested in 1963, though the

Continued on the next page

PRICE £1,571 10s. plus £328 19s. 2d. purchase tax equals £1,900 9s. 2d. (*including automatic transmission*).

Clubland: deep, contoured armchairs (adjustable for reach, height and rake at the front) provide sumptuous comfort for four people. The central arm-rest at the back—which conceals a trinket box—can be folded away to make room for a fifth person. The passenger's headrest shown here is an extra.

The grille badge is now like the Rover 2000's and the side strip is new. Rare novelty: you can start the 3-litre with a handle.

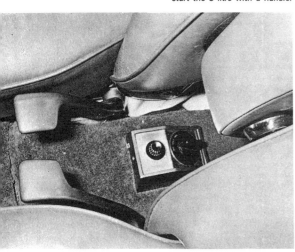

Pulling up on the lever releases the friction lock that holds the squab angle. Very fine adjustment is possible. The panel behind—operated by either front-or back-seat passengers—houses a two-speed rear heater and a radio control.

Parcel accommodation is good but the facia and its controls—even those on the instruments nascelle —are rather distant. Uninterrupted crash padding extends along the top and bottom of the facia.

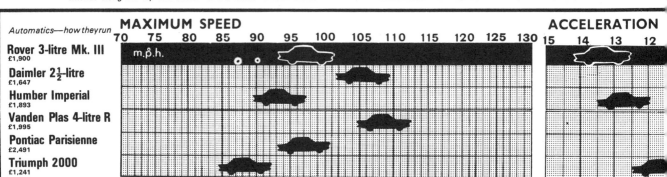

Automatics—how they run

MAXIMUM SPEED — m.p.h. — 70 75 80 85 90 95 100 105 110 115 120 125 130

ACCELERATION — 15 14 13 12

Rover 3-litre Mk. III £1,900
Daimler 2½-litre £1,647
Humber Imperial £1,893
Vanden Plas 4-litre R £1,995
Pontiac Parisienne £2,491
Triumph 2000 £1,241

Rover 3-litre automatic
Continued

figures are not strictly comparable. The saloon's consumption has also benefited from the 70 m.p.h. speed limit: normally, we would have cruised at 90 m.p.h. when the consumption falls to less than 16 m.p.g. compared with 21½ m.p.g. at 70 m.p.h. There is no pinking on 98 octane Premium petrol.

Transmission

On Mk. III automatics, a Borg Warner 35 gearbox replaces the older DG model. Gearbox ratios are slightly lower than before but the 3.54:1 final drive raises the overall gearing so that top gear now gives 22.4 m.p.h. per 1,000 engine r.p.m. compared with the 20.6 m.p.h. of the earlier 119 b.h.p. car. The effect on performance

is negligible but there are gains in quietness and economy at high speeds.

Undoubtedly the cushioning effect of a heavy car has helped to smooth the gearchanges but the transmission has also been carefully matched to the engine, even to the extent of having a special torque converter. There is a slight but definite judder when accelerating hard in first and we would prefer a more progressive throttle linkage to give finer starting and manoeuvring control; otherwise, the transmission is free from jerks and surging and even the kick-down operates smoothly. Apart from a curious hissing noise when moving off, it is also very quiet.

The short steering column selector is easy to use for downward lever movements, a little less so for moving up and it is sometimes hard to see the indicator if a steering wheel spoke is in the way. Automatic drive gives full-throttle maximum speeds in the two lower gears of 38 and 69 m.p.h.; by using the selector, these can be raised to 45 and 75 m.p.h. respectively—both of them clearly marked on the speedometer. Far more important than these academic facts is that the transmission, apart from being very

Continued on the next page

Performance

Test Data: World copyright reserved; no unauthorized reproduction in whole or in part.

Conditions:

Weather: Cool, damp and breezy.
Temperature 42°–46°F, 10-20 m.p.h. wind.
Barometer 29.50 in. Hg.
Surface: Tarmacadam and concrete.
Fuel: Premium 98 octane (R.M.).

Maximum speeds

	m.p.h.
Mean lap speed banked circuit	101.2
Best one-way ¼-mile	104.5
2nd gear ⎱ max. in auto	69
1st gear ⎰	38
"Maximile" speed: (Timed quarter mile after 1 mile accelerating from rest)	
Mean	93.9
Best	94.9

Acceleration times

	auto sec.	manual sec.
m.p.h.		
0-30	5.6	5.6
0-40	8.4	8.1
0-50	12.5	11.4
0-60	17.0	15.8
0-70	22.4	21.4
0-80	33.0	29.2
0-90	50.2	45.2

Standing quarter mile 20.8

	kick down sec.
m.p.h.	
20-40	5.0
30-50	6.9
40-60	8.6
50-70	9.9
60-80	16.0
70-90	27.8

Fuel consumption

Touring (consumption midway between 30 m.p.h. and maximum less 5% allowance for acceleration) . . . . 20.9 m.p.g.
Overall . . . . 17.4 m.p.g.
= 16.2 litres/100 km.
Total test distance . . . . 1,300 miles

Tank capacity (maker's figure) 14 gal.

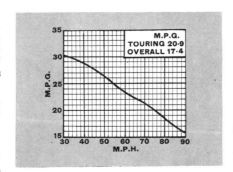

M.P.G.
TOURING 20·9
OVERALL 17·4

Weight

Kerb weight (unladen with fuel for approximately 50 miles) . . . . . . 33.7 cwt.
Front/rear distribution 53/47
Weight laden as tested . . . . . . 37.4 cwt.

Steering

Turning circle between kerbs: ft.
Left 37
Right 36.5
Turns of steering wheel from lock to lock . . 3.2
Steering wheel deflection for 50 ft. diameter circle
. . . . 1.3 turns

Brakes

Pedal pressure, deceleration and equivalent stopping distance from 30 m.p.h.

lb.	g	ft.
25	0.33	91
50	0.70	43
75	0.85	85
100	0.98	30½
Handbrake	0.42	71

Fade test

20 stops at ½g deceleration at 1 min. intervals from a speed midway between 30 m.p.h. and maximum speed (= 66 m.p.h.)

	lb.
Pedal force at beginning	45
Pedal force at 10th stop	45
Pedal force at 20th stop	45

Speedometer

Indicated	10	20	30	40	50	60	70	80	90	100
True	12½	19½	29	38	48	58	67	76½	86½	96
Distance recorder										2% slow

Parkability

Gap needed to clear a 6 ft. wide obstruction parked in front.

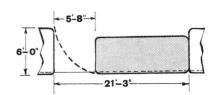

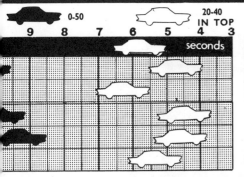

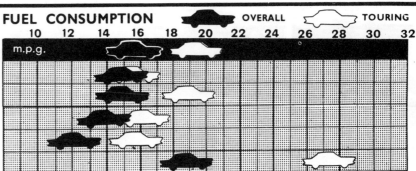

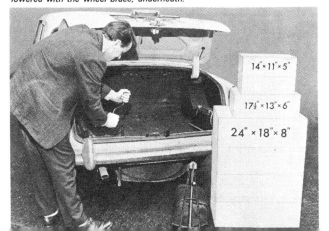

The bright-metal strip running down the side distinguishes Mk. III versions of the 3-litre. Pronounced "tuck-in" at the bottom of the body prevents scuffing against high kerbs.

smooth, is apparently foolproof: it is not confused by sudden open/shut throttle movements and never leaps uncertainly from one gear to another. Apart from the occasional use of intermediate hold for hill-climbing or slow, twisty roads, you tend to retain the lever at the fully automatic setting and leave the rest to science.

Handling and brakes

This big, unsporting car can be hurled through corners with great whooshing noises coming from the tyres but little fear of unsticking them unless you try a great deal harder than was ever intended. On wet or dry roads, consistent understeer dictates big, indelicate steering wheel movements for fast cornering and, predictably, it is the front wheels that will ultimately break away first. At this improbable stage, tyre scrub is so acute that the car slows down quickly when you lift off and adhesion is restored. We did not have a chance to drive on snow or ice but on a particularly greasy country road—splattered with mud from a tractor convoy—the Rover changed its character and slid the tail first with little provocation from the throttle. Again, a minor slide is virtually self-correcting when you lift off.

The Hydrosteer power assistance fitted as standard to all 3-litre Rovers takes most of the effort out of steering without displaying that featherweight, unconnected feel so typical of most American cars. To reduce rapid wheel turning on sharp, slow corners the variable ratio linkage gets progressively quicker as you wind on lock: relatively large movements are needed for gentle bends, which gives the impression of little or no road feel around the straight-ahead position. Probably because of this, some of our drivers did not like the steering very much until they had done a considerable mileage.

As the figures show, the servo-assisted disc/drum brakes worked impressively well at only moderate pedal pressures, though the brake pedal on our test car had a rather long, spongy travel and did not feel very reassuring at first. The handbrake provides quite a good emergency stop but needed a pull beyond the strength of most women to hold the car on a 1 in 3 hill.

Comfort and controls

Comfort depends on a great many things—ride, seats, quietness, ventilation, heating, fittings. . . . In all these respects except the ride, the 3-litre sets very high standards. Both front and back seats are very deep, fairly firm and expertly contoured to support the thighs, spine and shoulders in the right places. You would not fit these big, heavy seats in a competition car—side support is not *that* good—but they would make splendid armchairs in anyone's living room. Other manufacturers must soon copy Rover's lead of providing infinitely fine squab movements with a friction lock operated simply by releasing a handy lever; the usual notched adjusters seldom provide exactly the right angle. You can raise yourself above other motorists by winding on a handle at the front of the seat and there is the usual wide adjustment for reach so the 3-litre caters for people of all shapes and sizes. Even the arm-rests can be adjusted. Although the back seat has been contoured for only two people, a third can sit less comfortably in the centre between them; because he sits further forward, there is no battle for shoulder space. Rear-seat legroom has been increased by a useful 2½ inches and is now sufficient to be able to stretch and relax in great comfort. The suspension is harder than currently fashionable for a luxury saloon and on bad roads it can be heard and felt beating a relatively smooth passage for the heavy body. The 2000 does the job very much better and gives an insight of what to expect from the next generation of big Rovers.

The 3-litre makes very little noise. Only when accelerating hard in the lower gears are you really conscious of the muffled hum from the engine: at 70 m.p.h. it is scarcely audible and wind and tyre roar have also been well isolated. Two distant heater controls working vertically in the centre of the facia regulate the temperature and distribution of incoming air which seems to seep through the car—taking some time to do it after a cold start—without causing any uncomfortable blasts or hot spots. There is a completely separate recirculatory heater at the back with a two-speed fan control between the front seats on the transmission tunnel. Outlets beneath the back seat keep your feet comfortably warm without making the air at head height too stuffy. In addition to the front

These two handy adjusters move the seat up or down (the handle foreground) and back and forth.

Sensible novelty: the door arm-rests are adjustable for height and there is a wide pocket for maps and books.

The battery on the right steals a little boot space but there is still room for 9.8 cu. ft. of our test boxes. The spare wheel has its own carrier, lowered with the wheel brace, underneath.

Specification

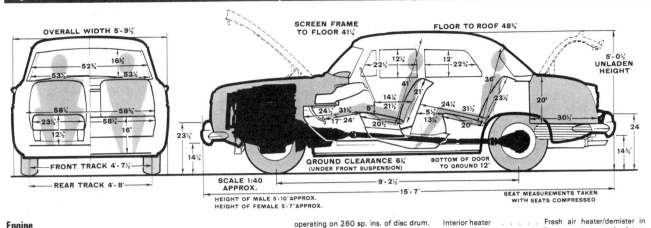

OVERALL WIDTH 5'-9¼"

SCREEN FRAME TO FLOOR 41¼"   FLOOR TO ROOF 48¾"

5'-0½" UNLADEN HEIGHT

FRONT TRACK 4'-7½"
REAR TRACK 4'-8"

GROUND CLEARANCE 6¼" (UNDER FRONT SUSPENSION)   BOTTOM OF DOOR TO GROUND 12"

SCALE 1:40 APPROX.   9'-2½"   15'-7"

HEIGHT OF MALE 5'-10" APPROX.
HEIGHT OF FEMALE 5'-7" APPROX.

SEAT MEASUREMENTS TAKEN WITH SEATS COMPRESSED

Engine

Cylinders	6
Bore and stroke	77.8 mm. x 105 mm.
Cubic capacity	2,995 c.c.
Valves	overhead inlet, side exhaust
Compression ratio	8.75 : 1
Carburetter	S.U. HD8 2in. horizontal
Fuel pump	S.U. electric
Oil filter	AC Delco full flow
Max. power (net)	121 b.h.p. at 4,800 r.p.m.
Max. torque (net)	160 lb. ft. at 2,650 r.p.m.

Transmission

Gearbox	Borg Warner 35 automatic with fluid torque converter driving a 3-speed planetary gear train
Top gear	1.00 : 1
2nd gear	1.45 : 1
1st gear	2.39 : 1
Reverse	2.09 : 1
Final drive	Spiral bevel 3.54 : 1

M.p.h. at 1,000 r.p.m. in:—

Top gear	22.4
2nd gear	15.2
1st gear	9.4

Chassis

Construction	Unitary steel body attached to a welded steel chassis unit at the front

Brakes

Type	Girling vacuum-servo assisted
Dimensions	10.75 in. front discs; 11 in. rear drums, 2.25 in. wide
Friction areas	Front: 20.35 sp. ins. of lining operating on 260 sp. ins. of disc drum. Rear: 106.35 sq. ins. of lining operating on 154.4 sq. ins. of disc/drum

Suspension and steering

Front	Independent by wishbones and laminated torsion bars, telescopic dampers and an anti-roll bar.
Rear	Live rear axle with semi-elliptic leaf springs and telescopic dampers.
Shock absorbers: Front and rear	Woodromatic telescopic
Steering gear	"Hydrosteer" power-assisted worm and peg.
Tyres	6.70 x 15 (Dunlop Roadspeed tubeless or Avon Turbospeed Mr. IV tubed)
Rim size	5K x 15 in.

Coachwork and equipment

Starting handle	Yes
Jack	Screw pillar
Jacking points	2 each side under body sills
Battery	12 volt, 57 amp. hrs. capacity
Number of electrical fuses	11
Indicators	Self cancelling flashers
Screen wipers	Variable speed self parking electric
Screen washers	Press button electric
Sun visors	2
Locks: With ignition key	Front doors and petrol filler cap
With other keys	Boot and facia glove box

Interior heater	Fresh air heater/demister in front, separate recirculatory heater in rear compartment
Major extras on test car	Automatic transmission, Heated back window, laminated windscreen, passenger head rest
Upholstery	Leather
Floor covering	Carpet with felt underlay
Alternative body styles	Coupé

Maintenance

Sump	10 pints S.A.E. 20
Gearbox	15 pints ATF
Rear axle	3 pints 90 EP
Steering gear	ATF
Cooling system	26 pints (drain taps 2)
Chassis lubrication	Every 6,000 miles to 1 point
Minimum service interval	3,000 miles
Ignition timing	3° b.t.d.c.
Contact breaker gap	0.014-0.016 in.
Sparking plug gap	0.028-0.033 in.
Sparking plug type	Champion N5
Tappet clearances (hot)	Inlet 0.006 in.; Exhaust 0.010 in.
Valve timing: inlet opens	13° b.t.d.c.
inlet closes	45° a.b.d.c.
exhaust opens	48° b.b.d.c.
exhaust closes	16° a.t.d.c.
Front wheel toe-in	Zero ± 1/16 in.
Camber angle	1.5°
Castor angle	0.25° positive
Kingpin inclination	4.5°
Tyre pressures	26 p.s.i. front and rear

1, glove box. 2, temperature control. 3, radio. 4, picnic tray concealing tool kit. 5, gear selector. 6, wipers. 7, wiper rheostat. 8, panel lights. 9, speedometer. 10, trip mileage recorder. 11, total mileage recorder. 12, main beam tell tale. 13, petrol reserve. 14, ignition light. 15, water temperature. 16, petrol gauge. 17, ammeter. 18, lights. 19, heater fan speed. 20, ignition/starter. 21, air vent. 22, horn. 23, choke. 24, oil pressure low. 25, cold start tell-tale. 26, rear screen demister. 27, headlights. 28, direction indicator and headlight flasher. 29, bonnet release. 30, handbrake. 31, cold air vent. 32, handbrake warning light.

Fittings and furniture

Time alone will measure the quality and workmanship behind the 3-litre's engineering; it takes only a few minutes to see and assess the quality of the fittings and furniture inside. The decor is traditional British, which is traditional Rover: leather upholstery, African Cherry wood cappings (a nice change from walnut), thick carpets, and black fittings and controls. It is all very tasteful, unembellished and expensive. We have never particularly liked the 3-litre's instruments nacelle. The clear, round, white-on-black instruments are easy to see and read. But the minor toggle switches, all working in a horizontal plane, cannot be operated without taking a hand off the wheel and although the positions are logical it takes some time to memorize them all. The windscreen washer, tucked away on the side of the nacelle, the two heater controls in the centre and several

quarter lights (which disturb the quietness when open) the inside can be ventilated with small butterfly-valve vents, one each end of the facia, or bigger inlets under the scuttle that are controlled by push-pull knobs. Our test car also had a heated back window which quickly dispersed any misting.

The windows are shallower than normal though the high waist-line is not a handicap when the seats are adjustable for height. All-round visibility is reasonable but you do not get quite such a panoramic or skywards view as in some modern saloons.

Continued on the next page

under-scuttle knobs are all particularly awkward to reach if you are strapped in.

There are a number of unusual luxury fittings. The electric clock, which used to be in the centre of the facia where parallax made it difficult to read, has been moved to the passenger's end of the curved wrap-round facia. This leaves a safer unobstructed padded roll right round the top of the scuttle. Apart from individual reading lights for each passenger, there is a light in the front passenger's headrest (an option) which can be adjusted to a position just above your lap in the back seat. There are stow-away central picnic trays —the back one with cut-outs to hold glasses, the front one concealing a splendid tool-set embedded in a foam rubber cradle. Little touches like this will delight the connoisseur. The deep full-width parcel shelf in front will swallow more oddments than that of most cars but it is well forward of the seats and not within easy reach. However, it does emphasize the spacious feeling inside the car. There is also a lockable facia glove box and the back-seat arm-rest conceals a "trinket" compartment. The battery steals a useful corner in the boot, but not the spare wheel which has its own cradle underneath, leaving room for plenty of luggage.

Full-width padding on the top and bottom of the facia provides a soft landing for passengers thrown forward in a crash or sudden braking but there are a few hard projections in between. Our test cars had lap-and-diagonal seat belts which were easy to clip together and tension but, as so often happens, they tended to get trapped beneath the front seats: with a distant facia and controls, inertia lock safety belts which provide more freedom of movement would be better.

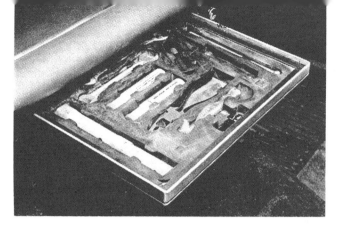

A slide-out picnic tray beneath the facia conceals this nest of tools.

Servicing and accessibility

Very few new-car owners are going to maintain a 3-litre Rover themselves; for those who do, the servicing schedule is summarized below. Service intervals have been extended to once every 5,000 miles so most people will only lose their car to the garage two or three times a year. There is no fixed price for each service and the handbook says "where a high standard of work is looked for the higher price of labour charges is inevitable". So competent servicing is not likely to be cheap.

Although the bonnet is pretty well filled with machinery, those ancillaries that are likely to involve the owner are mostly accessible —the coil, windscreen washer bottle, filler caps for the radiator, oil, powersteering and hydraulic reservoir, two dipsticks, distributor and starter solenoid.

Maintenance summary

A Engine. Every 5,000 miles: change oil, renew external filter, check slow running, clean spark plugs, check distributor points, water level. Every 10,000 miles: clean and re-oil engine breather filter, check oil in carb, damper, renew spark plugs, clean and oil distributor, check tappets, fan belt. Every 20,000 miles: replace air cleaner, clean sediment bowl.

B Gearbox. Every 5,000 miles: check fluid level. Every 10,000 miles: drain and re-fill.

C Back axle and prop shaft. Every 5,000 miles: check oil level, lubricate prop shaft sliding joint. Every 10,000 miles: drain and re-fill back axle.

D Power steering. Every 5,000 miles: check fluid level. Every 10,000 miles: check rubber boots on steering joints.

E Brakes and wheels. Every 5,000 miles: check brake reservoir level, level safety switch, thickness of front pads (min. 3 mm), adjust rear wheel brakes, change and wash road wheels, check tyre pressures. Every 10,000 miles: check front hubs for leaks. Every 20,000 miles: check front wheel alignment, renew air filter element on servo.

Every 40,000 miles: renew all rubber seals in brake system.

F Electrical. Every 5,000 miles: check battery acid level. Every 10,000 miles: clean, grease and tighten terminals, check headlamps setting.

Miscellaneous; check water level in screen washer periodically, oil linkages, doors, etc., every 10,000 miles.

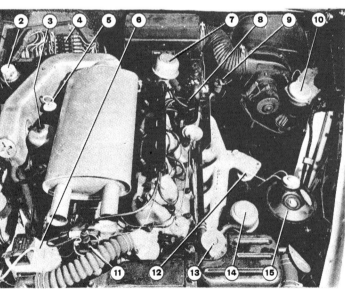

1, petrol filter. 2, hydraulic reservoir. 3, SU carburetter. 4, fuses. 5, automatic gearbox oil dipstick. 6, screen washer bottle. 7, oil filler. 8, distributor. 9, starter solenoid. 10, windscreen wiper motor. 11, coil. 12, engine oil dipstick. 13, radiator filler cap. 14, oil filler cap. 15, power steering reservoir.

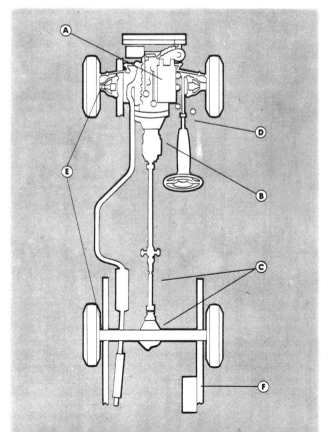

V FOR THE ROVER

Chromium plated Rostyle wheels, and the longer chrome rubbing strip, with painted flash beneath it, are identifying features of the new 3·5-litre models; this is the Coupé. The fog lamps and rubber faced bumper over-riders are standard

In the limited but profitable field of high quality executive cars, production quantities are not big enough to allow quick recovery of body tooling costs, but cars can be transformed mechanically. The Rover Company have given their very successful P5 3-litre model a new lease of life and completely changed its character and performance by fitting a light-alloy 3·5-litre vee-8 engine built by them to American designs. A weight saving of 200lb at the front of the car helps to improve handling and the 160 b.h.p. (net) engine gives a 108 m.p.h. maximum speed. All cars are fitted with Borg-Warner type 35 automatic transmission.

THE idea of taking an American engine design and manufacturing it in the United Kingdom is not new. William Morris did just this thing when he bought the manufacturing rights of the American Continental engine and had it manufactured in the old Hotchkiss works in Coventry, using it as a power plant for his Morris Cowleys.

William Martin-Hurst, managing director of the Rover Company, and his engineers showed great perception when they saw an ideal unit in the advanced light-alloy General Motors engine, developed for the Buick Special compact. General Motors had only abandoned this engine because of a general change to cast-iron engines when the mass production of thin-section iron castings became technically feasible. Since modern engine development is mainly a story of better and better materials, the design of the unit is quite up to date and it is really more suitable for European manufacturing methods than for American.

To install the smaller vee-8 engine in the P5 it has been necessary to add extra members inside the front subframe, which carries the engine, transmission and front suspension. These members originate at the middle of the forward transverse member and terminate at each rear corner of the frame. Although their main function is to support the engine, they also impart considerable extra stiffness. The engine is mounted at two points alongside the crankcase and at a single point at the back of the gearbox.

To reduce noise a single exhaust system is used, the pipes from each bank of cylinders joining at the back of the sump, the gases then passing through a main silencer and a tailpipe silencer with twin outlets.

The Borg-Warner type 35 automatic transmission, which is standard equipment without the alternative of manual change, has been considerably strengthened structurally to deal with the increased torque loading. It is controlled by a quadrant lever on the central console and has positions for starting in first (D1) or second (D2) gear; there is a lock-up provision for holding lower gears. It drives the 3·54-to-1 back axle through a two-piece propeller shaft. As an aid to appearance Rostyle pressed steel, chromium plated wheels with 5J rims have been adopted; they are fitted with 6·70×15 Dunlop RS5 or Avon Turbospeed tyres.

To cope with the increased speed of the car Ferodo 2424F pads are fitted to the front brakes in conjunction with a larger

capacity, Lockheed type 7 servo. With a greater proportion of the total weight on the rear wheels—although the car is lighter overall—the rear drum brakes will have more work to do. They have therefore been given larger wheel cylinders and the rubbing surfaces are now fine turned instead of ground.

To give the 3·5 litre a distinctive appearance there have been a number of changes to the exterior brightwork. Plated body side mouldings, in line with repeater flashers, stainless steel sill mouldings and matt black painted sills are new. The latter on lighter coloured cars help to slim the lines. New wing valance pressings have been made to raise the head-lamps and to make room for raised "craters" below the head-lamps which accommodate twin spotlamps. The centre bar of the radiator has also been thinned down and the marque name is gilded. In the rear view the car is identified by a 3·5 litre motif on the boot lid.

Internally a new console has been designed to accommodate the gear quadrant and the traditional Rover large ashtray. There is a shallow depression on which small objects could lie without rolling off and a small, leather-covered panel at the front of the console houses the cigar lighter and spotlamp switches. The interior is trimmed in the usual luxurious Rover style, with best quality hide seats and pile carpets.

The 3,528 c.c. vee-8 power plant of the Rover 3·5 litre saloon and coupé is completely new. Although it is derived from the engine of the Buick Special of 1960 it would be wrong to assume that the design is that old. In taking over the manufacturing rights, the Rover Company were free to develop the design and they had a free hand so far as machining was concerned, for none of the Buick tooling was purchased. Apart from practical considerations it would have been against Rover policy to machine a new line of engines on second-hand tools. Thus they were able to change the design in detail to allow for possible stretch and to bring it into line with 1967 practice and with European manufacturing methods.

Whereas Buick produced their cylinder blocks as gravity castings in metal dies with sand cores for the water jackets, Rover will produce this unit as a sand casting. In redesigning the block for this method of manufacture, the opportunity was taken to put more metal in the main bearing diaphragms and in the main bearing bosses to provide for the eventual possibility of larger crankshaft main journals. The crankshaft runs on five main bearings with cast-iron caps. By mixing the materials in this way adequate cold clearance can be allowed without the bearings becoming too sloppy a fit when the engine heats up. In its general features of crankcase skirts extending well below the crankshaft centre line and cylinder studs spaced equally round the bores, this is a classic high-performance design and it is easy to see why it appealed not only to Rover engineers but to Jack Brabham, who used a standard Buick block for his championship-winning car last season.

The cylinder liners are simple cylindrical centrifugal castings pressed into place and located axially by stops at the bottom of the housings rather than by flanges on the tops of the liners. This design was chosen instead of the American ▶

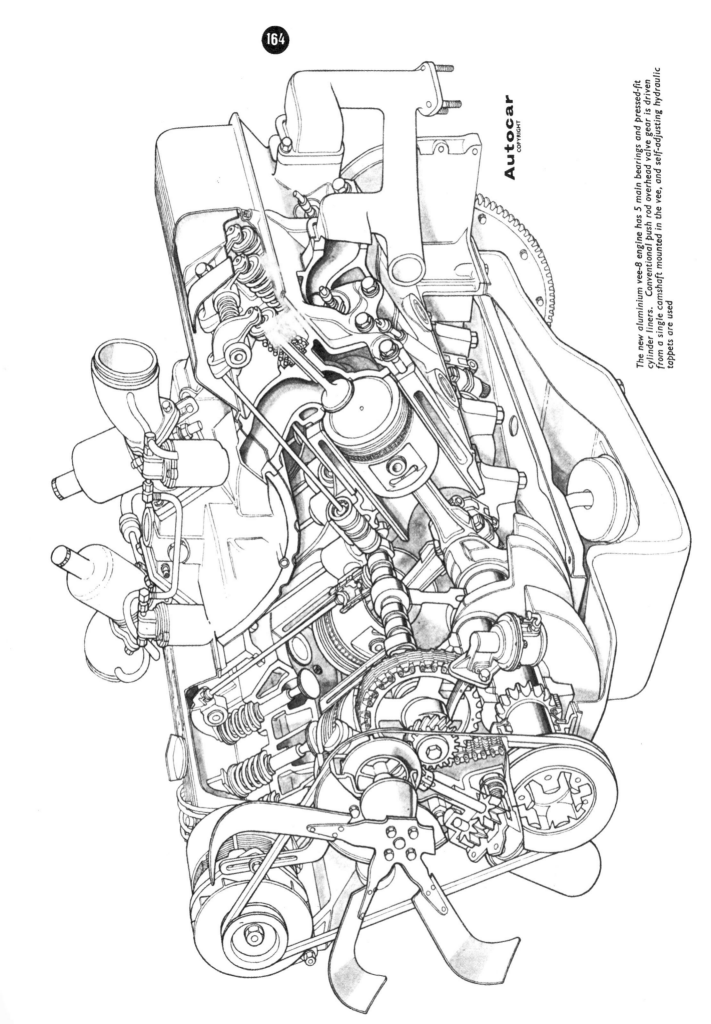

Autocar
COPYRIGHT

The new aluminium vee-8 engine has 5 main bearings and pressed-fit cylinder liners. Conventional push rod overhead valve gear is driven from a single camshaft mounted in the vee, and self-adjusting hydraulic tappets are used

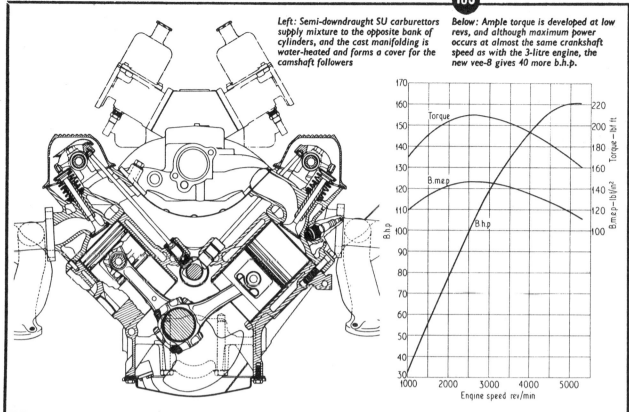

Left: Semi-downdraught SU carburettors supply mixture to the opposite bank of cylinders, and the cast manifolding is water-heated and forms a cover for the camshaft followers

Below: Ample torque is developed at low revs, and although maximum power occurs at almost the same crankshaft speed as with the 3-litre engine, the new vee-8 gives 40 more b.h.p.

V FOR THE ROVER

method of casting the liners in place because of the difficulty of "wetting" them prior to casting. It has been found repeatedly by a number of engine designers that pressed-in liners with an interference fit give just as good heat transfer to the block as the cast-in type. Good gas sealing is obtained by fitting the liners slightly proud of the block so that they take the cylinder head clamping loads when the engine is cold.

The two-plane, spheroidal-cast-iron crankshaft is fully balanced against reciprocating forces, the balance weights being cut away to clear the pistons when they are at the bottom of the stroke. Connecting rods are to the original American design; they appear unusual to British eyes because of balance bulges formed on the flanks of the rod above the big end eyes. These balance weights are machined during manufacture to standardize the reciprocating and rotating weight of each connecting rod. Otherwise the rods are conventional, the big end eyes being split at right angles to the centreline and the caps retained by dowel bolts and stiffnuts. A rubber-bonded crankshaft damper mounted on the back of the crankshaft pulley absorbs residual vibrations.

An overhung skew gear on the end of the camshaft drives an inclined distributor shaft which is supported in the timing case. The lower end of this shaft drives the Hobourn-Eaton oil pump which has a short-circuit oil-relief valve and has the filter casing mounted on its lower cover, making it a very compact unit. An interesting point about the camshaft drive, typical of American economy of means, is that thrust is taken only in the direction in which it is pushed by the thrust of the skew gear. A small pip on the timing cover is the only safeguard in case the engine backfires.

No change has been made in the design of the combustion chambers of the cross-flow heads. The shape of the chamber is in effect a segment of a sphere deformed in the valve area to take the seats of two parallel valves inclined at 20 deg. to the cylinder axis. Hollow piston crowns combine to give the combustion chamber a lenticular form. It is interesting to recall that the first prototype of the Buick Special engine had Heron-type combustion chambers in the pistons, although the spheroid head was chosen for production.

General Motors machined their combustion chambers, but the Rover heads are diecast with sand cores, the combustion chambers being left as cast and the cylinder head face machined relative to small registers cast in the combustion chambers. A small but important detail is that the centre-pop hole in the bowl-top American pistons was found to harbour residual burning and does not appear on the Rover pistons. Separate inlet ports are employed, the section being rectangular, and "door-shaped" to clear the push rod tubes. Compression ratio is 10.5 to 1, the engine producing 160.5 b.h.p. net at 5,200 r.p.m. Maximum torque is 210 lb. ft. at the quite low speed of 2,600 r.p.m., making the engine very suitable for use with automatic transmission.

To obtain reasonably quiet valve gear with a light-alloy push-rod engine it is essential to use self-adjusting tappets. Because of the experience required to produce hydraulic tappets, Rover have gone to America for this vital item, which is produced by the Diesel Equipment Company of Grand Rapids. This is the only item of American manufacture in the whole unit. The valves are closed by double coil springs and operated by short, small-diameter push-rods and rockers from a single camshaft mounted in the vee of the cylinder block. A sintered crankshaft gear with nylon-coated teeth drives the camshaft through a single link-belt chain.

Mixture is supplied by two 1¾in. SU HS6 carburettors mounted on a one-piece, water-heated manifold between the cylinder banks, a novelty being that the steel manifold joint is extended to form a cover which spans the vee of the blocks and encloses the camshaft and tappet blocks. The possibility of using a single four-barrel fixed jet carburettor of American manufacture was considered, but was discarded because of this type's susceptibility to flooding and surge under the high cornering forces which are found in European motoring and also because of Rover's familiarity with the British made SU instrument. A twin-volute impeller, partly formed in the diecast timing cover and driven by a vee-belt off the crankshaft pulley pumps water from the front to back of the blocks and then through transfer passages into the head. The water is biased towards the exhaust ports inside the head before passing into the inlet manifold and on to the thermostat and radiator. The same belt also drives a Lucas alternator.

Tooling for the Rover vee-8 engine has cost £3 million, the main bulk of the equipment being British or German. In view of the investment it would not be logical to restrict it to the comparatively low-volume production P5. We shall look forward to future applications of this very interesting engine.

Make: Rover
Type: 3·5-Litre

TEST CONDITIONS
Weather: Cloudy, bright. Wind 10-15 m.p.h.
Temperature: 18 deg. C. (65 deg. F.)
Barometer: 29·6in. Hg.
Humidity: 50 per cent
Surfaces: Dry concrete and asphalt

Test distance 3,404 miles. Figures taken at 2,500 miles by our own staff at the Motor Industry Research Association proving ground at Nuneaton.

WEIGHT
Kerb weight: 31·4 cwt (3,514lb-1,593kg) (with oil, water and half-full fuel tank)
Distribution, per cent: F, 50·0; R, 49·0
Laden as tested: 34·8 cwt (3,899lb-1,770kg)

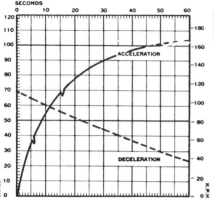

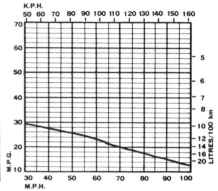

MAXIMUM SPEEDS

Gear	m.p.h.	k.p.h.	r.p.m.
Top (mean)	108	174	4,750
(best)	109	175	4,800
Intermediate	77	124	4,900
Low	47	79	4,900

Standing ¼-Mile 18·3 sec 74 m.p.h.
Standing Kilometre 34·1 sec 92 m.p.h.

TIME IN SECONDS	4·8	6·6	8·9	12·4	16·3	21·8	31·5	45·0	
TRUE SPEED M.P.H.	30	40	50	60	70	80	90	100	110
INDICATED SPEED	31	42	53	64	76	87	97	106	116

Speed range, gear ratios and time in seconds

m.p.h.	Top (3·45-7·43)	Intermediate (5·13-10·78)	Low (8·46-17·77)
10— 30	—	4·2	3·3
20— 40	6·8	5·1	3·6
30— 50	7·6	5·8	—
40— 60	8·5	6·6	—
50— 70	9·6	—	—
60— 80	11·8	—	—
70— 90	15·5	—	—
80—100	19·8	—	—

FUEL CONSUMPTION
(At constant speeds—m.p.g.)

30 m.p.h.	28·5
40	27·6
50	25·7
60	23·0
70	20·3
80	17·7
90	15·4
100	13·7

Typical m.p.g. 20 (14·1 litres/100km)
Calculated (DIN) m.p.g. 18·5 (15·3 litres/100km)
Overall m.p.g. 19·2 (14·7 litres/100km)
Grade of fuel, Super Premium, 5-star (min. 100RM)

OIL CONSUMPTION
Miles per pint (SAE 10W/40) .. 2,000

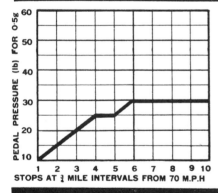

BRAKES (from 30 m.p.h. in neutral)

Load	g	Distance
25 lb	0·60	50ft
50 „	1·05	28·7 „
Handbrake	0·45	67 „

Max. Gradient, 1 in 3

TURNING CIRCLES
Between kerbs L, 38ft 5in.; R, 39ft 5in.
Between walls L, 40ft 2in.; R, 41ft 2in.
Steering wheel turns, lock to lock .. 3·2

HOW THE CAR COMPARES:

MAXIMUM SPEED (mean) M.P.H.
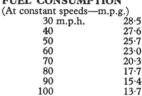
Rover 3·5 Litre Auto
Jaguar 420
Mercedes Benz 300 SE Auto
Vanden Plas R Auto
Vauxhall Viscount Auto

0-60 M.P.H. (sec)
Rover 3·5 Litre Auto
Jaguar 420
Mercedes Benz 300 SE Auto
Vanden Plas R Auto
Vauxhall Viscount Auto

STANDING START ¼-MILE (sec)
Rover 3·5 Litre Auto
Jaguar 420
Mercedes Benz 300 SE Auto
Vanden Plas R Auto
Vauxhall Viscount Auto

M.P.G. OVERALL
Rover 3·5 Litre Auto
Jaguar 420
Mercedes Benz 300 SE Auto
Vanden Plas R Auto
Vauxhall Viscount Auto

PRICES

Rover 3·5 Litre (Auto.)	£1,999
Jaguar 420	£1,930
Mercedes-Benz 300SE (Auto)	£4,159
Vanden Plas R (Auto.)	£2,030
Vauxhall Viscount (Auto.)	£1,483

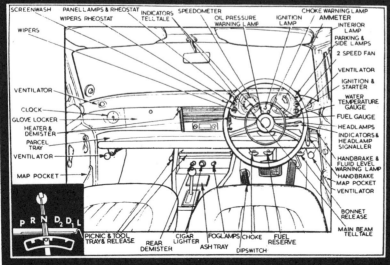

Rover 3·5-Litre   3,528 c.c.

AT A GLANCE: Familiar Rover with unfamiliar performance; acceleration, top speed and fuel economy all improved. Still a very quiet and refined car, now capable of cruising at over 100 m.p.h. Reduced understeer gives better handling, but slight loss of directional stability; steering a little woolly. Ride comfort and brakes excellent.

MANUFACTURER
The Rover Co. Ltd.,
Solihull, Warwickshire

PRICES

Basic	£1,625	0s	0d
Purchase Tax ..	£374	3s	4d
Seat belts (approx.)..	£10	0s	0d
Total (in G.B.) ..	£2,009	3s	4d

EXTRAS (inc. P.T.)

Heated rear window..	£21	10s	3d
Radio	£38	10s	8d

PERFORMANCE SUMMARY

Mean maximum speed	108 m.p.h.
Standing-start ¼-mile	18·3 sec
0-60 m.p.h.	12·4 sec
30-70 m.p.h. (through gears)	17·0 sec
Fuel consumption ..	20 m.p.g.
Miles per tankful ..	280

WITH its new vee-8 engine, the latest version of the Rover P5 model is a tremendously improved car, without being transformed. The old characteristics of quietness, refinement and solid quality are still there and similarly the car has not moved up into the "tiger" bracket of performance. However, acceleration times have been reduced very considerably, high speeds call for much less effort than before, and the maximum and cruising speeds are a lot higher. Big improvements in fuel economy, handling and braking have also resulted from the better efficiency and the 200 lb weight saving of the new aluminium engine.

All acceleration figures are a lot better, including that for picking up from low speeds in top gear, avoiding kickdown, but it is at the higher speeds that the improvement is most pronounced. Where the 6-cylinder car's acceleration used to tail off at about 80 m.p.h., the 3·5-litre continues accelerating strongly to 100 m.p.h., which it will reach in 45 sec from rest. Overtaking is much easier, particularly if the kickdown or lock-up is used and intermediate held to about 65 m.p.h. The 18·3 sec time

for a standing start quarter-mile is still quite good by sports car standards, and shows the really vigorous getaway now available.

Rover's previous engine was exceptionally quiet so although the new power unit is almost inaudible all the time in top gear, and remains quiet even when worked hard in low or indirect, the gain here is not so marked. There is much bigger improvement in the smoothness and free-revving potential of the vee-8, which develops its maximum power at 5,200 r.p.m.—600 r.p.m. higher than did the six. Having more revs available and appreciably higher final drive gearing, the maximum speed in intermediate has been raised by no less than 20 m.p.h.—from 57 to 77 m.p.h., and the car's top speed is also up by fully 6 m.p.h.—from a mean of 102 to 108 m.p.h. A red segment on the speedometer starts at 115 m.p.h., but in practice this speed cannot be exceeded on the level; in fact, on one long, downhill stretch of straight road the speed did not rise above 116 m.p.h. on the speedometer. This instrument proved the only source of trouble in a road test which, by the time we had included a trip ▶

through Denmark to Sweden and back *via* Germany and Holland, totalled more than 3,000 miles. When working the speedometer is a very steady instrument; it exaggerates by 6 m.p.h. at top speed.

For smooth and accurate throttle control, Rover use unusually long accelerator travel, and one tends to forget sometimes just how much more throttle opening is still available. There is even a good bit left when the car is cruising at 100 m.p.h., a speed which it maintains with ease, and it is not very difficult to put 85 or 90 miles into an hour when the roads and conditions are right. At high speeds the engine is still very quiet but it seems a pity that Rover were persuaded by buyers to reintroduce swivelling quarter vents after the initial 3-litre model, as they give rise to a lot of wind whistle even when tightly closed.

Sometimes we are worried about the unduly high proportion of town driving which has been included in a car's test mileage, but with this Rover, if anything, it is the other way round. This car had the benefit of a long Continental trip followed by the failure of the distance recorder before London traffic and performance testing had their effect on consumption. But this does not wholly account for the overall fuel consumption figure of 19 m.p.g.; even with fast cruising and liberal use of the performance, the 3·5-litre frequently returned over 20 m.p.g., excellent for a car of this size with automatic transmission. Oil consumption is also very light—we had covered 2,000 miles before the engine was ready to accept its first pint for topping up. Little more than two pints will usually be needed in the 5,000 miles between recommended oil changes.

In addition to a 12½-gallon main capacity, the fuel tank has a 1½-gallon reserve, brought in by pulling a T-handle matching the cold starting mixture control, beneath the parcels shelf. The fuel gauge goes very definitely on to the " E " mark before the main tank is emptied. The total 14-gallon capacity gives a good range and, provided one remembers not to rely on the performance in the last few miles before the main tank runs dry, as much as 250 miles are possible without refuelling. The filler blows back if a pump's delivery is fast, and the engine requires 100-octane fuel.

Cold starting calls for full travel of the mixture control, and needs one or two quick turns on the starter before the engine will fire. The transmission selector can then be moved into Drive almost at once without fear of stalling, and the engine pulls strongly without any protracted warming up. Starting when hot is much better, and it is seldom necessary to use the starter more than once. Although so smooth when pulling, the engine is a little lumpy at tickover, often giving noticeable tremor and shake in prolonged traffic

Even the Rover's engine compartment looks packed to capacity. The neat and clearly marked wiring panel is a very good service feature, and the quality of finish on the engine is most impressive

holdups, and making it worthwhile to slip the gear selector into neutral.

Borg-Warner 35 transmission is standard, and Rover use the same floor-mounted transmission selector for the 3·5-litre as for the 2000 automatic, working in a straight, to-and-fro plane, with a push button in the top of the gear knob. The lever moves freely between the D2 and D1 positions, or from Lockup back to D1; for all other movements the push button must be depressed—usually done easily with the ball of the first finger. Down changes, whether with kickdown or the Lockup control, go in very smoothly, but if a lot of acceleration is used in intermediate, there is a mild jolt when the accelerator is released to allow the transmission to change back into top. Position D2, which eliminates bottom gear, may be of occasional use in town, to make the take-up even smoother, but we are rather doubtful of the need for it.

The change in weight distribution compared with the 3-litre, reducing the 59 per cent nose heaviness to near-neutral front-rear balance, has naturally affected the handling, mainly with substantial benefit; but in one respect the new car is not as good as before. There is now some wander when running straight. Previously the very heavy engine gave the car such good directional stability that any free movement in the steering was disguised. At first the wander is a little disconcerting, and one feels that better steering response in the straight-ahead position is needed; however, it is soon appreciated that the car does not drift far

off course, and correction is easy. In one stage of the test, speeds of up to 100 m.p.h. were being held in very high winds, and this experience showed that the stability of the Rover is still very good indeed.

Hydrosteer power-assisted steering is standard, and it is of varying ratio —15·6 to 1 in the straight ahead position, reducing to a ratio of 10·2 on full lock, so that there are only 3·2 turns of the wheel from lock to lock. Control is extremely light, even at manœuvring speeds, which helps to make it a fairly easy car to park, in spite of its size and nearly 40ft wide turning circle.

Where the reduced front-end weight has assisted is in the much improved cornering, although the very light steering is inclined to make a driver fresh to the car " over corner." Previous tendencies to tyre scrub and excessive understeer have given way to much more balanced handling. The car still understeers but can now be cornered fast and confidently without having the feeling all the time that the nose wants to go straight. On the initial movement of the springs the ride is fairly soft, and until some of the spring resistance has been taken up there is appreciable roll on corners. This tends to become a sway if one corner is followed swiftly by another in the opposite direction. However, once the car has settled into its line for a corner, the roll angle does not increase much, and the car can be controlled very easily, with the power assistance absorbing most of the extra pull on the steering.

A very comfortable and quiet ride ▶

Centre armrest and others on the doors, with three-way seat adjustment, all make for relaxed comfort. Right: Rear cushions are designed for two, but a third passenger could manage in the middle

ROVER 3·5-LITRE

accounts for much of the feeling of refinement and the effortless long-distance travel in which the Rover excels. It is a fairly soft suspension, with ample range of wheel movement to absorb big undulations or humps at speed, yet it is excellently damped, and there is no float or wallow on any surface. Road roar is completely insulated, as are vibration and wheel patter when sections of cobbled road or broken up patches of *autobahn* are taken at relatively high speed.

Although good before, the brakes, too, are better as a result of the weight reduction. They are 10·75 in. dia discs at the front and 11 in. drums at rear, as with the 3-litre, but they now give greater response. Very light pedal loads are needed in ordinary driving, and the response is in direct proportion to the load. At 30 m.p.h. only 50 lb load on the pedal sent our Mintex brake efficiency meter right off its scale, at 1·05g. Fade tests had little effect on the brakes, though the front pads were

smoking by the time the ten 70 m.p.h. stops were completed, and the handbrake at 30 m.p.h. gave one of the highest efficiencies ever obtained with rear wheel brakes only. Pulled on really firmly, it holds the car securely on 1 in 3.

Two generous armchairs at the front, and a rear seat shaped for two, with wide central division which could take an occasional fifth passenger in the centre, give promise of sumptuous comfort. Reclining backrests, with the Rover-patented adjusters which lock the backrest in any desired position, are standard, as also is the rare feature of a winding handle at the front of the seat to give vertical adjustment through a range of 1½ in. One can certainly obtain exactly the right driving position for individual taste, but it would be helpful if the steering column were also adjustable. On a long journey the seats remain very comfortable, but they are apparently designed for the heavyweight; light bodies tend to sit on the seats rather than in them, and could do with a little more rounding of the backrests for lateral location.

Buyers are strongly advised to insist on inertia reel safety belts for

this car. With standard belts, as on the test car, all sorts of switches and controls, including the handbrake, are out of reach.

The rather narrow windscreen gives an impression of restricted forward visibility, but the ability to adjust seat height largely compensates for this. If the driver leans forward both front corners—with their practical red tell-tales for the sidelamps at night—are in view. The screen is well cleared by wipers which have a variable speed control; the difference between fastest and slowest wiping frequencies is fairly small, so they are normally used simply as two-speed wipers, with the unusual complication that the speed control is separate from the on-off switch. We certainly feel that the Rover needs a better mirror than the tiny diminishing one fitted as standard.

With a few shillings to spare, Rover have managed to keep the price of the new 3·5-litre just under £2,000, a creditable figure for the amount of performance and quality provided. The console arrangement looks neater than before, and the pull-out tray beneath the parcels shelf is typical of the refinement and attention to detail

Covered sides and a rubber floor mat protect the contents of the uncluttered, but not very capacious, boot. Right: The wheels and the neat emblem on the boot lid are distinctive. Front and rear indicator repeaters are included in the side flash

in the whole car. It does not move, even under fierce acceleration, yet simply pulls out when required. A small catch at the side is pressed in to release it completely and the lid then comes away to reveal a toolkit, with each item nestling in shaped rubber moulding.

Beneath the tray are switches for the standard fog lamps (wired through the side lamps), rear window demister, and the cigarette lighter.

Opening any door automatically switches on the appropriate courtesy light. A very efficient and controllable heater, with separate fresh air inlets is, of course, standard.

The new arrangement for the gear selector is more convenient for regular use of the lock-up; the quadrant is illuminated when the side lamps are switched on, but surprisingly the pointer is not.

In its previous form, the Rover

3-litre was justifiably praised for its comfort and luxury, but was generally considered—particularly in its automatic form—to be rather staid and stodgy. Now with the vee-8 under the bonnet it has made such gains in performance and economy that it has gone ahead of most of its competitors, and has taken on a different image by being so much faster and more manageable. It is also exceptionally good value for money. ∎

SPECIFICATION: ROVER 3·5-LITRE (FRONT ENGINE, REAR-WHEEL DRIVE)

ENGINE
Cylinders .. .. 8, in 90 deg. vee
Cooling system .. Water; pump, fan and thermostat
Bore .. .. 88·90mm (3·50in.)
Stroke .. .. 71·12mm (2·80in.)
Displacement .. 3,528 c.c. (215 cu. in,)
Valve gear .. Overhead, pushrods and rockers
Compression ratio 10·5-to-1: Min. octane rating 100RM
Carburettors .. Two SU HS6
Fuel pump .. AC mechanical
Oil filter .. .. Full flow, renewable element
Max. power .. 160·5 b.h.p. (net) at 5,200 r.p.m.
Max torque .. 210 lb. ft. (net) at 2,600 r.p.m.

TRANSMISSION
Gearbox .. .. Borg-Warner Type 35 three-speed automatic
Gear ratios .. With torque converter 1·0-2·1.
Top
Inter. 1·45-3·04.
Low 2·39-5·02
Reverse 2·09-4·39
Final drive .. Hypoid bevel, 3·54-to-1

CHASSIS and BODY
Construction .. Integral with steel body

SUSPENSION
Front .. .. Independent, wishbones with laminated torsion bars, anti-roll bar, telescopic dampers

Rear .. .. Live axle, half-elliptic leaf springs, telescopic dampers

STEERING
Type .. .. Hydrosteer, power assisted worm and peg
Wheel dia. 17in.

BRAKES
Make and type .. Girling disc front, drum rear
Servo .. .. Lockheed vacuum
Dimensions .. F, 10·75in. dia.; R, 11·0in. dia. 2·25in. wide shoes.
Swept area .. F, 260 sq. in.; R, 155 sq. in. Total 415 sq. in. (257 sq. in.) ton laden)

WHEELS
Type .. .. Pressed steel disc, 5-stud fixing; 5in. wide rim
Tyres make .. Dunlop
type .. RS5 cross-ply/tubeless
size .. 670-15 in

EQUIPMENT
Battery .. .. 12-volt, 57 amp.hr.
Alternator .. Lucas 11AC 45-amp
Headlamps .. Lucas sealed filament 150/90-watt (total)
Reversing lamp .. One standard
Electric fuses .. 12
Screen wipers .. Variable speed, self-parking
Screen washer .. Standard, Lucas electric
Interior heater .. Standard, air-blending
Heated backlight Extra

Safety belts .. Extra, anchorages built-in
Interior trim .. Leather seats, pvc headlining
Floor covering .. Carpet
Starting handle .. No provision
Jack .. .. Mechanical Bevelift
Jacking points .. 4, near wheels
Windscreen .. Zone toughened
Underbody protection .. Bitumastic on surfaces exposed to road

MAINTENANCE
Fuel tank .. 14 Imp. gallons (1·5 reserve) (63·7 litres)
Cooling system .. 16 pints (including heater) (9 litres)
Engine sump .. 10 pints (5·7 litres) SAE 10W/40. Change oil every 5,000 miles; Change filter element every 5,000 miles
Automatic gearbox 14·5 pints ATF. No change; torque converter Check level every 5,000 and oil cooler .. miles
Final drive .. 3 pints SAE90 EP. Change oil every 5,000 miles
Grease .. .. 1 point every 5,000 miles
Tyre pressures .. F, 26; R, 26 p.s.i. (normal driving).

PERFORMANCE DATA
Top gear m.p.h. per 1,000 r.p.m. .. .. .. 22·7
Mean piston speed at max. power 2,435 ft/min
B.h.p. per ton laden .. .. 92·2

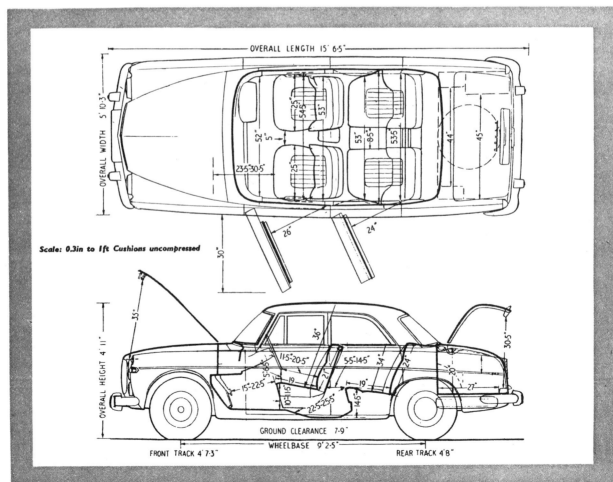

OVERALL LENGTH 15' 6·5"
OVERALL WIDTH 5' 10·3"
Scale: 0·3in to 1ft Cushions uncompressed
OVERALL HEIGHT 4' 11"
GROUND CLEARANCE 7·9"
WHEELBASE 9' 2·5"
FRONT TRACK 4' 7·3"
REAR TRACK 4' 8"

The 3.5 coupé has distinguishing flashes on the sides: the full road test starts on page 75

Rover go V

3.5 litre V8 engines replace inline sixes in saloon and coupé

THE introduction of a V-8 engine by Rover is a big step in the company's history—and for several reasons. One is that it ends a continuous history of in-line, six-cylinder cars which (war years apart) goes back to the late 1920's; another is that this move seems to confirm that Rover engineers have definitely abandoned all thoughts of a V-6 layout, which might seem a logical step from in-line sixes; and the third point is that the basic design is of American origin, although a great deal of development work and modification have gone into it at Solihull.

The new engine is of light alloy and weighs some 200 lb. less than the six it replaces, although the power output is 32% greater and the maximum torque up by 31%. As the pair of cars, saloon and coupé, in which it is used, are basically the former 3-litre models (although considerably improved in detail) both performance and handling are very substantially improved—by just how much can be gathered from the road test report elsewhere in this issue.

For a company so traditionally British in its policy and engineering as Rover to turn to the U.S. for a new engine design may

seem strange and, for that reason alone, called for a courageous decision; in the light of hard commercial expediency, it makes very sound sense.

The need was for a new engine to replace the six-cylinder overhead-inlet/side-exhaust-valve engine which, with modifications, has served Rover for their larger and more expensive models for nearly 20 years. The replacement obviously had to be more powerful, but it was equally desirable that it should be both lighter and more compact. With their long tradition of sixes, the first thoughts of Rover engineers were for a V-6 and, as anyone(!) with access to the Rover Experimental Department will know, a lot of work was done on this type of engine; but for various reasons, the type was rejected and attention turned to eight cylinders in the same formation.

To start completely from scratch on an eight-cylinder design calls for the expenditure of a great deal of time and money and even when the prototypes have been made, there is still a great deal of development work to do.

By a fortunate coincidence the General Motors Corporation of America had already developed an engine which, although

not an exact replica of what Rover engineers would have produced, met all the requirements. It was a V-8 of 3.5-litre capacity, it offered around 30 per cent more power and torque, it was of light-alloy, which meant a big weight saving and the design lent itself to manufacture in the factories of Rover and their suppliers. It appeared at the end of 1960 in two GM "compact" cars, the Buick Special and Oldsmobile F-85, but later went out of production because the American compacts became far less compact, thus eliminating the need for a relatively expensive light-alloy design.

Thanks to the enterprise of Mr. Martin-Hurst, the Rover managing director, the company had the opportunity to acquire the design rights of this GM engine, and although this represented a break with tradition, the advantages were great. All basic development work was done and it remained only to modify the design for its new role and the production facilities available.

The outcome of some three years' work at Solihull is the engine illustrated in the

Continued on next page

Saloon version has the "sporty" wheels of the coupé, and more headroom.

special drawing by *Motor* artist Sidney Porter, reproduced on these pages.

The 90-degree cylinder blocks and deep crankcase are now a single light-alloy sand casting into which dry cylinder liners are pressed; the original had liners cast directly into a pressure die-cast block. The head and valve covers are, of course, also of light alloy and a pleasing feature is the high finish of all the castings.

The crankshaft runs in five copper-lead, steel-shell bearings and is fitted with a torsional vibration damper combined with the pulleys for the auxiliary drives. Big ends of opposite con. rods share a single journal in the normal way; the gudgeon pins are a press fit in the little ends.

A shallow depression characterizes the piston crowns but, apart from its beneficial effect on the quench area, does not form a very significant part of the combustion chambers which are wedge-shaped and formed primarily in the head; this depression does, however, provide a ready means of varying the compression ratio to suit particular markets.

The in-line valves are inclined at an angle of 10 degrees to the cylinder axes and are operated by push-rods and rockers from a single camshaft centrally placed in the base of the V. An unusual refinement for British cars is the use of self-adjusting hydraulic tappets while the rockers are also notable, being of light-alloy with sintered iron insets for the push-rod sockets and steel insets for the valve stem contact pads. Another interesting detail is the use of a composite chain wheel for the camshaft drive, the wheel itself being of light-alloy and the teeth of nylon for quiet running. A sintered crankshaft sprocket is used.

As will be seen from the drawing, two inclined SU carburetters are bolted to a common water-heated distribution block, the passages of which are arranged so that each carburetter feeds the two inner

cylinders of the block opposite to it and the outer pair of the block on its own side, thereby largely equalizing the lengths of the induction tracts. Crankcase breathing is via pipes connecting the valve covers to the engine side of the carburetter throttles, each pipe incorporated a small flame trap.

The lubrication system is conventional with a gear-type oil pump delivering lubricant to galleries whence it is led to the main bearings, big ends, camshaft bearings and hydraulic tappets. A full-flow oil filter is fitted, and the pump has short-circuit, pressure-relief arrangements which minimize the amount of oil in circulation.

A feature of the cooling system is the use of a five-bladed fan with bent-over ends rather reminiscent of the propeller of a plane which has made a wheels-up landing. This unusual shape is designed to lower the level of fan noise by reducing the breakaway of air at the blade tips. In other respects, the cooling system is conventional, with a cross-flow radiator and a breather cap designed to maintain the system at 15 lb./sq. in.

Automatic transmission has been standardized, the system chosen being the Borg-Warner Type 35 with D1 and D2 ranges for normal and leisurely traffic conditions respectively. Operation in D2 also has advantages on icy roads in minimizing the kick-down effect and limiting starting torque. The control lever is centrally mounted and works in an illuminated quadrant in a central console in the front compartment. As an insurance against overheating an oil radiator for the transmission lubricant is provided and is arranged neatly at the base of the normal engine-cooling radiator.

Other mechanical features mainly follow the 3-litre design, but notable improvements include the use of a larger-capacity servo for the brakes in conjunction with larger wheel cylinders, an improved linkage for the handbrake, the use of chromium-plated pressed-steel wheels with black recesses similar in appearance to those introduced for North American versions of the Rover 2000 TC together, of course, with minor modifications to such things as the front subframe to accept the new engine and modified damper settings to suit the new weight and performance characteristics.

As before, saloon and so-called coupé bodies are available, the roof lines and window arrangements of the latter giving a more sleek appearance at the cost of some sacrifice in rear headroom. Features which distinguish the new models (apart from "3.5-litre" motifs on the front wings and boot) include a painted coach line under the body side mouldings, matt black painted body sills (which also add to the sleeker appearance of the latest models) full-length side mouldings with apertures for repeater flashers, fog-lamp depressions formed in the front wings, and a modified radiator grille with a slimmer centre spine and the Rover motif now in gilded metal.

Although prices are slightly higher the differences are very modest in view of the new engine and other improvements. The new recommended total prices including PT, with the old 3-litre equivalent in brackets, are: saloon £1,999 (£1,933); coupé, £2,097 (£2,032). **M**

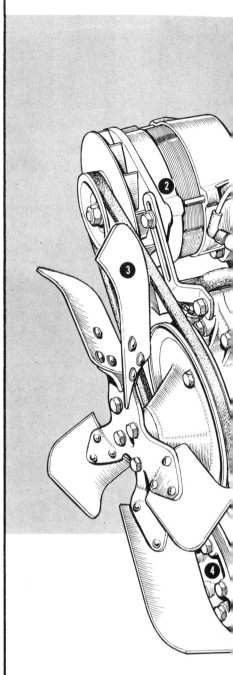

KEY

1 *Inclined SU carburetters.*
2 *Alternator.*
3 *Fan (with noise-reducing blade contours).*
4 *Crankshaft damper.*
5 *Fuel pump operating cam.*
6 *Distributor and oil pump drive gear.*
7 *Inverted tooth camshaft drive chain.*
8 *Petrol pump.*
9 *Power steering pump.*
10 *Pressed steel sump.*
11 *Hydraulic self-adjusting tappets.*
12 *Water heated inlet manifold.*
13 *Crankcase ventilation.*
14 *Flame trap.*
15 *Press fit gudgeon pins.*
16 *Light-alloy rockers.*
17 *Double valve springs.*
18 *Dry cylinder liners.*
19 *Light-alloy cylinder block.*
20 *Light-alloy cylinder heads.*
21 *Cast light-alloy valve covers.*

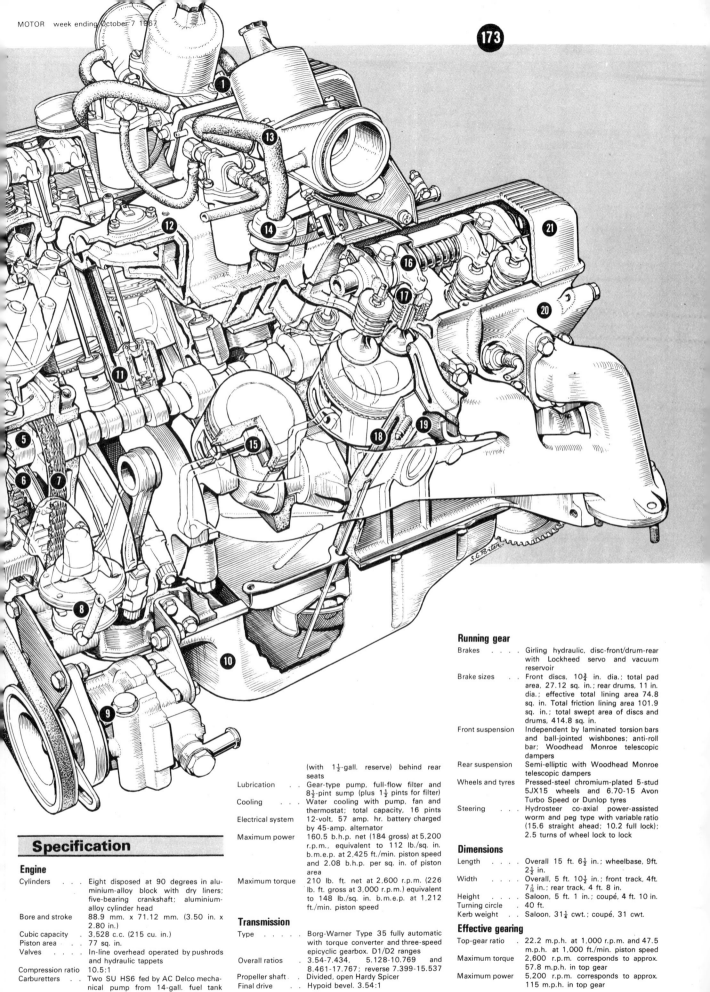

S. G. Porter

Specification

Engine

Cylinders . . .	Eight disposed at 90 degrees in aluminium-alloy block with dry liners; five-bearing crankshaft; aluminium-alloy cylinder head
Bore and stroke	88.9 mm. x 71.12 mm. (3.50 in. x 2.80 in.)
Cubic capacity .	3,528 c.c. (215 cu. in.)
Piston area . .	77 sq. in.
Valves . . .	In-line overhead operated by pushrods and hydraulic tappets
Compression ratio	10.5:1
Carburetters .	Two SU HS6 fed by AC Delco mechanical pump from 14-gall. fuel tank

	(with 1½-gall. reserve) behind rear seats
Lubrication . .	Gear-type pump, full-flow filter and 8½-pint sump (plus 1½ pints for filter)
Cooling . . .	Water cooling with pump, fan and thermostat; total capacity, 16 pints
Electrical system	12-volt, 57 amp. hr. battery charged by 45-amp. alternator
Maximum power	160.5 b.h.p. net (184 gross) at 5,200 r.p.m., equivalent to 112 lb./sq. in. b.m.e.p. at 2,425 ft./min. piston speed and 2.08 b.h.p. per sq. in. of piston area
Maximum torque	210 lb. ft. net at 2,600 r.p.m. (226 lb. ft. gross at 3,000 r.p.m.) equivalent to 148 lb./sq. in. b.m.e.p. at 1,212 ft./min. piston speed

Transmission

Type . . .	Borg-Warner Type 35 fully automatic with torque converter and three-speed epicyclic gearbox. D1/D2 ranges
Overall ratios .	3.54-7.434, 5.128-10.769 and 8.461-17.767; reverse 7.399-15.537
Propeller shaft .	Divided, open Hardy Spicer
Final drive . .	Hypoid bevel. 3.54:1

Running gear

Brakes	Girling hydraulic, disc-front/drum-rear with Lockheed servo and vacuum reservoir
Brake sizes .	Front discs, 10¾ in. dia.; total pad area, 27.12 sq. in.; rear drums, 11 in. dia.; effective total lining area 74.8 sq. in. Total friction lining area 101.9 sq. in.; total swept area of discs and drums, 414.8 sq. in.
Front suspension	Independent by laminated torsion bars and ball-jointed wishbones; anti-roll bar; Woodhead Monroe telescopic dampers
Rear suspension	Semi-elliptic with Woodhead Monroe telescopic dampers
Wheels and tyres	Pressed-steel chromium-plated 5-stud 5JX15 wheels and 6.70-15 Avon Turbo Speed or Dunlop tyres
Steering . . .	Hydrosteer co-axial power-assisted worm and peg type with variable ratio (15.6 straight ahead; 10.2 full lock); 2.5 turns of wheel lock to lock

Dimensions

Length	Overall 15 ft. 6½ in.; wheelbase, 9ft. 2½ in.
Width	Overall, 5 ft. 10½ in.; front track, 4ft. 7⅝ in.; rear track, 4 ft. 8 in.
Height	Saloon, 5 ft. 1 in.; coupé, 4 ft. 10 in.
Turning circle .	40 ft.
Kerb weight . .	Saloon, 31¼ cwt.; coupé, 31 cwt.

Effective gearing

Top-gear ratio .	22.2 m.p.h. at 1,000 r.p.m. and 47.5 m.p.h. at 1,000 ft./min. piston speed
Maximum torque	2,600 r.p.m. corresponds to approx. 57.8 m.p.h. in top gear
Maximum power	5,200 r.p.m. corresponds to approx. 115 m.p.h. in top gear

CARS TO KEEP
Rover 3½-litre saloon, coupé

Rover's Return

Now is the time to buy a Rover V8 saloon or coupé as interest in these large, luxurious yet fairly quick cars is growing steadily, and pristine examples are now becoming quite valuable

The massive and dignified Rover P5s and P5Bs of the 1958/1973 period could not really have been developed by any other British company. Rover had been building cars of this type — with a subtle blend of high-quality construction, solid middle-class appeal, surprisingly acceptable road behaviour and remarkable value for money for many years before they revealed the P5 in 1958. The P5 was quite different from the P4s which it supplemented, but was precisely the same in its intentions.

Any P5 might be chosen as a 'Car to Keep', because it is an ideal subject for attention from the lover of 'classic' cars. P5s were distinctive, were in relatively limited supply, built themselves a remarkable reputation, and it now seems that good examples show all the signs of being likely to last indefinitely. There are, however, two basic types — those with six-cylinder engines, and those with V8 engines — and this survey concentrates on the later models, which were fitted with 3½-litre V8 engines.

First, however, a few words about model history, and about the engine in particular. Way back in the early 1930s, Rover had been rescued from the very edge of bankruptcy by the efforts of Spencer Wilks. He was a middle-class gentleman in every way, and

believed in building cars for his sort of people. For the next quarter of a century, therefore, his policy was to build limited numbers of Rovers to a high quality standard of specification and engineering. The miracle, however, was not that Spencer Wilks turned the company round in this way, but that the new type of quality cars could be sold at such reasonable prices. The major new post-war Rover was the legendary P4 ('Auntie' to its friends), and the P5 followed on to supplement it, as a larger, faster and rather more prestigious machine.

Faster and more prestigious

Apart from its basic engine and transmission designs, the P5 of 1958 was largely new — the power train being developed from that of the long-established six-cylinder P4. Styling was by a new recruit to Rover, a young man called David Bache, whose intention was always that one basic style should be built in normal saloon and lowered-roof coupé forms. The bodies themselves were built by the Pressed Steel Company, originally at their factory at Linwood, in Scotland.

The engine ran out of development potential by the early 1960s so for this, and other applications, Rover cast around for another power unit. The story of how managing

director William Martin-Hurst found out about the light-alloy General Motors (Buick) design by accident has often been told. Basically, Buick had developed a V8 engine, with light alloy cylinder block and cylinder heads, for their 'compact' cars of the early 1960s, but it was costly to build, and was rapidly made obsolete for their needs by the advances in 'thin-wall' casting technology of cast-iron blocks and heads in North America. General Motors, therefore, were eventually persuaded to licence the design to Rover in 1965, who re-engineered it in detail to suit British production methods, and launched it, in the Rover 3.5-litre of September 1967.

Since then, of course, the light (if not very powerful) 3528cc Rover engine has found its way into several important cars, including the small-body Rover 3500 (P6B), the modern 'SD1' Rover 3500s, Triumph TR8s, MGB GT V8s, Range Rovers, Land-Rover V8s, and Morgan Plus 8s. Have I forgotten anything? I'm sure I have.

What was effectively the rejuvenation of the big Rover P5, therefore, took place in 1967. P5 became P5B (B = Buick, obvious, isn't it?), and the Rover 3-litre with its six-cylinder engine was instantly rendered obsolete by the V8 engined Rover 3.5-litre.

Much of the 3.5-litre's engineering was that of the old 3-litre, which meant that much of the car had a very long and worthy reputation to back its new performance image. Effectively, only the V8 engine was new, and even that had sold to the tune of 750,000 examples in the United States, and had already been used as the basis for the power units of the World Championship-winning Repco-Brabham Grand Prix cars of 1966 and 1967.

This low, rear quarter view of a V8 coupé emphasises the car's general size and overall bulk

A six-cylinder, P5 saloon, top, and coupé below. Like the P5B, both are becoming collectable

Right from the start, the big Rover had the unique combination of a massive four-door steel body shell allied to a front 'half-chassis' which carried the engine, gearbox and front suspension. Not only did the half-chassis allow Rover to carry on building structures which they knew all about (the Rover P5 of 1958, let's not forget, was the first Rover monocoque, all previous Rovers having had complete separate chassis frames), but it also allowed them to insulate the passengers from much of the commotion and disturbance of the power unit, and the front suspension, for the half-chassis was securely rubber-mounted to the rest of the body shell.

The P5B, therefore, rode on a dignified 9ft 2.5in wheelbase, had an overall length of 15ft 6.5in, and in normal saloon form had nearly 8in of ground clearance. Overall height was 5ft 1in. No stuck-to-the-ground road hugger, this one, but a car designed for sensible people to step into sensibly, having spacious seating, and what old-time testers used to call 'a commanding view of the road'.

Like the obsolete P5 3-litre, it came in two subtly different body types. Interestingly enough, David Bache once told Rover historian Graham Robson that he designed both the saloon and coupé styles at the same time, yet the coupé derivative was not launched until the saloon had been on the market for four whole years.

Saloons and coupés share precisely the same chassis engineering, engines, transmissions, and basic equipment, and up to the cars' waistline all the panels are the same too. Saloons, however, have an overall height of 5ft 1in, front-seat headroom of 36in, and what the motor industry calls 'full-frame' doors with pressed steel all the way up and around the top of the window glasses. The coupés were lower, with an overall height of 4ft 10in, almost all of this reduction coming from the head room (though the seats were slightly modified), especially in the rear seat area. The doors had 'half-frames', which is to say that door pressings ended at waist height, with the drop glasses surrounded by thin brass castings. In this way, the reduction of the coupé's roof height was not allowed to result in a major reduction of glass area.

'Coupé', in fact, was rather a strange name for a car which was still effectively a four-door saloon, which had no more performance than the saloon and which, at a glance, was not visually all that different. The author's opinion, if it is worth anything, is that the coupé's styling was rather less well balanced than that of the saloon, and by the looks of the sales figures, the majority of P5B customers seemed to agree. When the V8 engined cars were announced, incidentally, you could have bought a saloon for £1999 and a coupé for £2098. At the end of the production run, in 1973, those prices had risen to £2699 and £2812 respectively.

Coupés more popular

In recent years, if you were to believe Glass's Guide to second-hand car values, saloons and coupés were worth about the same, but we suspect that the 'classic car' enthusiast will be marginally more attracted to a P5B coupé, and be willing to pay more for it.

Compared with the obsolete P5, not only did the P5B have V8 power and automatic transmission (without the choice of a manual box), but it had a stiffer front half-chassis, a bigger brake servo, special Rostyle road wheels, a new radiator grille, built-in auxiliary lamps, a centre console between the front seats, and extra decorative details. In terms of 'body sheet metal', as the Americans would have it, the P5B was precisely like the P5 which it replaced.

Earlier I said that the 3528cc engine wasn't very efficient, by which I mean that its output of 160.5bhp (net) — a figure subsequently re-calibrated to 150bhp (Din) in the early 1970s — only represented 45.5bhp/litre. Its main attraction to P5B customers (and to Rover, incidentally) was that it produced

The luxurious interior of a P5B. Renovation of the leather upholstery will be expensive

yonks of torque at low engine speeds with almost turbine smoothness and a total lack of temperament. You can make it *much* more powerful, of course, but somehow that wouldn't be right for a big Rover, would it?

There was no sinister marketing reason why you couldn't buy a manual-transmission P5B, (though, in fairness, we have to admit that most people would prefer to use such cars in this guise). The fact was that Rover had no manual transmission really capable of dealing with the torque produced by the V8 engine, and couldn't afford to design one just at this time. The P5 gearbox would quickly have wilted under the strain. Even when the smaller-bodied and lighter P6B was launched, there wasn't a manual box to do that job either, and the box subsequently made available for the P6B 3500S was marginal. So don't try a 'private' conversion, we beseech you — not, that is, unless you intend slotting an SD1's five-speed box under that patrician body shell, but that would be cheating in any case, wouldn't it?

With a specification including three-way front seat adjustment, fold down centre arm rests front *and* rear, a full tool kit in a tray under the facia, and a full range of instruments, you wouldn't expect to see many extras. Even so, you had to pay £10 for seat belts, £21.50 for a heated rear window, and £38.55 for a radio at first. Neither, in those days, did you get radial ply tyres, for Rover still had to be convinced that they could make quiet, refined P5Bs with big fat radials. Normal equipment were Dunlop RS5 Roadspeeds, 6.70-15in section, or equivalent cross-ply treads from Avon.

Radial ply tyres work well on this car (the rims are 5in wide, which doesn't sound much by 1981 standards, but was considered quite enough in 1967), but if you worry about originality, don't fit them.

Was it all worth it? And once you know, will this still be a Car to Keep? The Bad News — let's get it right out of the way at once — is that the P5B wasn't a very economical car, for it weighed up to 3900lb with two people on board, and the inefficiencies of the Borg Warner automatic transmission didn't help either. In day-to-day use, you'll get about

The wonderfully dated facia of a P5B with its preponderence of dials, switches and levers

Snug fit: the 160bhp Rover V8 engine and its radiator fills up most of the P5B engine bay

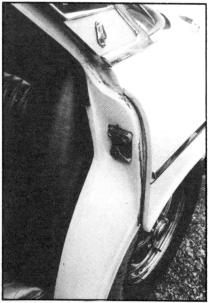
A P5 danger sign. If the rear door shut faces have rusted, the rest of the car could be in bad shape

20mpg from a well-maintained example, but if you like to use all the performance something like 17mpg is more likely. Cruise it at an illegal 80mph on motoways and 18mpg is the best you'll get at steady speeds — ear'ole it and you'll do even worse.

A P5B is a big barge, but it goes very well. No doubt if you can afford the fuel you could cruise at 100mph all day, but it's flat out at about 110mph. The weight and the automatic transmission mean that you need 18.5sec or thereabouts to reach a quarter mile from rest, which isn't going to trouble many latter-day Rovers and Granadas, but then the P5B is an entirely different type of car.

Large, ponderous and dignified

The important thing to remember about this car is not how fast it goes, or how much fuel it uses, by *how* it carries out its duties. A P5B is, in all respects, a very large, ponderous and dignified car. The fact that the power steering takes all the effort out of manoeuvring the car, and the big Lockheed servo sorts out the pedal pressures can't disguise the bulk of the machine. On twisty roads there is still considerable roll on corners, understeer in abundance, and an understandable reluctance to change direction in a hurry. You'll need to wear safety belts to stay securely in place on

those shiny leather seat cushions, and after a time you'll probably attune your driving methods to the more stately progress that this Rover encourages.

Our bet is that most of the asking prices for these cars are subject to a good deal of negotiation before the deal is done — not only because most sellers of 'classic cars' have an inflated idea of the value of their machines, but because the big, heavy, fuel-burning 'classics' have suffered more than sports cars in the recession in this market.

Be prepared to have to do quite some work on the car of your choice to bring it back to 'as new' standards for the all-steel body shell was, after all, no more than a quantity-production Pressed Steel Co. product, and rusts no less quickly than other cars of its type. It should be possible to find most mechanical (and some body) spares from Rover-Triumph, even if your BL dealer may not be very helpful, and it will help enormously if you know the part number required, so that the spares stockists can't plead ignorance for not helping.

Be prepared for your driving style, and the way you dress, to be affected by a P5B, for they seem to demand a certain standard of proficiency and behaviour. In the 1950s and 1960s, after all, a Rover was that type of car.

Jonathan Edwards

Brief specification

Engine	90-degree V8
Capacity	3528cc
Bore/stroke	88.9mm x 71.1mm
Valves	Overhead, pushrod operation
Compression	10.5:1
Power	160.5bhp (net) at 5200rpm
Torque	210lb.ft (net) at 2600rpm
Transmission	Borg Warner automatic (standard)
Top gear	22.7mph per 1000rpm
Brakes	Front discs, rear drums, with servo
Front sus.	Independent by torsion bars and wishbones
Rear sus.	Live axle, half-elliptics
Steering	Worm and peg, power assisted
Tyres	6.70-15in cross-ply
Length	15ft 6.5in
Width	5ft 10.3in
Weight	3479lb (coupé), 3498lb (saloon)

Performance

Max speed	108mph
0-60mph	12.4sec
30-50mph	4.1sec
(through gears)	
Fuel con.	17/22mpg

Production History

The models surveyed — the P5B models, in Rover parlance — were launched in the autumn of 1967. Effectively, these were the old P5 structures and chassis engineering, with the new light-alloy (ex-Buick) V8 engine mated to a Borg Warner Type 35 automatic transmission. At first the cars were advertised as 3.5-litres, and badged as such, but from the autumn of 1968 they were officially called 3½-litres (this was so that they should not be confused with the small-body P6B 3500s, which had been launched by then).

Chassis sequences for saloons started at 8400, and for coupés they started at 8450. This sequence was carried on without break until May 1973, when the models were phased out, at which point the final saloon chassis number was 84010341, and the final coupé number was 84508195. As you would infer from these numbers, it meant that 10,341 saloons and 8195 coupés were built in rather less than six years.

In all that time, virtually no important changes were made to the specification of the cars, as Rover were completely bound up with the development of other new cars including the Range Rover and the first of the P8/SD1 prototypes.

Buyers' spot check

'Chassis' engineering on these cars is good and durable, but rust may become a nuisance on the sills under the doors, (don't forget the sill boxes are structural, so this is an MoT 'fail' point), on the front wheel arches near the toeboard, and rear wheel arches near the door shut faces. Look especially at the rear spring hangers, which are obviously important to back axle location.

There are no light-alloy skin panels on these cars (unlike the dear old P4s), so look for surface rust on the top of the front wings, and on their edges near the door hinges, and on the rear wings along their crowns, and near their front edges (but front *and* rear wings are bolt-on items which can easily be renewed).

Rostyle wheels rust, but this isn't structurally dangerous, but springs and dampers shouldn't have deteriorated with age. Damper settings always were soft, incidentally, so expect a very supple ride with lots of body roll; don't expect too much 'feel' from the power steering, which was extremely light.

Engines are big, lazy, and sturdy, and the light-alloy construction holds no terrors if the right type of inhibited coolant has always been used. Everything points to the engines having an easy time — with revs limited by hydraulic tappets, and by the automatic transmission. A pointer here is to look at the tappets to see that they are not sludged up and working improperly; keep the oil clean, and change it regularly.

The Type 35 Borg Warner transmission is at the limit of its torque capabilities, so it may be showing signs of wear when you test a P5B. If the changes, upwards or downward, are rough, rather than silky smooth, you may have badly worn brake bands. Whining noises from the intermediates, too, may spell trouble. But it's not the end of the world — spares and rebuilds for this transmission are freely available.

The inside of a P5B can be in superb condition, if it has been well-looked-after. Restoring the seats and carpets to their former glory can be very costly (those seats are real leather, of course), but it is still possible.

Rivals then and now

When they were new, these big-engined Rovers were mainly 'home-market' cars, and faced up directly to cars like the Austin 3-litre (which was much cheaper), the 4.2-litre Jaguar/Daimler XJ6/Sovereign models and the ageing 420G, 3-litre Volvo 164, and even to the more prestigious of Ford's Zodiacs and Granadas.

In effect, therefore, the Rover was battling in the prestige/directors' bracket, where the *class* competition came only from Daimler-Jaguar, and where the new XJ6 design offered such a refined specification. It was probably the incredible value for money offered by the Sovereigns which tended to hold down sales of P5Bs, especially as prices were so very similar.

Clubs, specialists and books

Rover owners and enthusiasts are catered for most ably by the Rover Sports Register.

The Register is divided into two halves with 1950 the watershed year. Adrian Mitchell of 42 Cecil Road, Ilford, Essex IG1 2EW is the current secretary of the post 1950 section of the RSR but the Register is shortly to undergo a reshuffle whereupon *three* membership secretaries will be appointed! In the meantime, Adrian Mitchell is the man to contact if you drive or simply admire P5s and would like to join the Sports Register.

Six editions of the RSR's bulletin *Freewheel* are published each year and Register membership subscriptions stand at £6.50 with a £1 joining fee. A national Rover P5 day is held annually, this event usually attracting some 70/80 cars.

Your local Jaguar-Rover-Triumph agent will almost certainly hold a selection of P5 parts but of course very few of these will be replenished as the stock runs down. Herongate (the Rover people) specialise in new and used parts for P5s as well as other examples of the marque and they can be reached on Brentwood 810098. Servicing and repairs for pre SD1 Rovers are also on offer. Roverpoint, meanwhile, of Fifth Avenue, Romford Road, Manor Park, London E12 (tel: 01-478 2756) are noted Rover specialists of 18 years standing. In a recent letter they state 'we are a small company but pride ourselves on personal, fast service; we also know what we are doing!'

Chris George of TS Motors in Watford (tel: Watford 29228) is a RSR-recommended specialist, his forte being expert mechanical work while Richard Stenning of 'Masquerade', 22/24 Silver Street, Wiveliscombe, Somerset and John Mann (5 Nevis Close, Loundsley Green, Chesterfield) are both useful sources of P5 spares.

P5 and P5B reading material is rather thin on the ground at present as *Rover Memories* and *The Rover* titles are now very much out of print. All is not lost, however, since Graham Robson's *The Rover Story* is soon to be republished in an updated second edition by Patrick Stephens, the price being £9.95.

Prices

According to Adrian Mitchell of the Rover Sports Register, the price differential for P5s and P5Bs ranges from £40 to £4000!

The first price obviously applies to a rust-ridden scrap car, fit only for spares and *not* the road and a P5 derivative would obviously have to be in outstanding condition to be worth £4000 or more. In the vast majority of cases, an 'average' P5/P5B model can be bought for between £800 and £1000 and for that kind of money you can expect a basically sound, roadworthy car with an MoT, which probably needs some tidying.

Bargain basement prices apply to mid-1960s Rover-engined saloons which (say Adrian Mitchell) are very underrated while late-model V8 coupés in good condition are understandably the most sought-after P5s. Clean, original examples of the latter breed currently fetch between £1000 and £1500 while excellent (but not concours) P5B coupés are usually pegged at around £2000.

Owner view

Colin Whiteside acquired his smart, 69,000 mile Rover V8 coupé some 15 months ago, for what seems like the proverbial song.

"I bought the car from a bloke who runs a pub in London," he recalls. "The engine was seized and the car had been standing outside the pub for about a year, waiting for someone to buy it. The owner wanted £600 but we agreed on £450.

A rebuilt, secondhand engine with new pistons, main bearings, cams and so on was fitted by Colin and to date he reckons he has spent around £800 on the Rover, £160 of this going towards the engine rebuild. He's also changed the automatic gearbox and had the body resprayed although the latter work will have to be carried out again as a few bubbles are reappearing around the rear wings.

The bonnet, too, is new since a week after the initial respray someone thoughtfully bounced a Party Four can of beer across the front of the Rover. Inside the car, the wood trim and leather upholstery will need attention at some point as will the coupé's rear exhaust and steering box.

"It's surprising the attention this car causes" he concludes, "people are always asking me where I bought it and how much I paid for it. I don't often tell them, though!" □

Colin's loyal coupé: bought for a song

One might be forgiven for thinking that designing and testing such sober cars as Rovers produced in the Fifties and Sixties was a straight-faced, serious business. Serious indeed it was, but straight-faced only on occasion! These extracts from an interview with Brian Terry, a former Rover test engineer, show how much fun went on behind the scenes of that outwardly most strait-laced of motor car manufacturers.

Brian joined Rover as an apprentice in 1955, and by 1958 had become assistant to Philip Wilson, the chief test engineer. Although his job was really engine testing, it spilled over into other areas of the engineering department's work. In his own words: "If you're driving cars on their door handles, trying to wear them out or blow them up, or find the limits of their performance, you can't do it without being able to make some suitable comments about the handling or the fact that the wheels didn't stay on the ground, or the doors fell open, or somethng of that sort!" To an enthusiast such as Brian, this job was "just like having a hobby as full-time occupation!"

The car which was under development at Rover's Solihull works in the mid-Fifties was the stately 3.0-litre P5, renowned for its comfort and appointments rather than its performance. In those days before speed limits, Rover did much of its testing on public roads, and Brian recalls an outing with one of the two 3.0-litre prototypes:

BT: "It had drum brakes all round, which was very exciting when we were doing maximum speed testing! I can remember seeing the island on the Coleshill by-pass coming up at an alarming rate, and having absolutely no brakes left at all! I had to go round the island at 40mph because there was no way I could get it to go any slower! Mind you, I had got the car to do something like an indicated 98 before I got there, and it was only about a mile long, so it wasn't bad going. Downhill, mind you."

JT: "Was that the manual car?"

BT: "No, that was the automatic! It was on valve-bounce! That was the trouble: you couldn't even

Behind the scenes

change down a gear when you got to low speed — there was nothing left. It had a funny gearstick on it as well, where you only had in fact D and L, and if you put it into L it selected bottom gear. So in D you got 1-2-3; if you put it into L you got 1 and that was the end of that, which was all very well as long as you weren't going too fast, but it would blow the whole thing up if you put it in at too high a speed. I hadn't been in the company that long, and I didn't want to make that sort of a name for myself at the time, so I didn't risk it!"

Rover was, in fact, acutely conscious of the barely adequate performance which the original 3.0-litre offered, but the only performance increase in the production models was brought about when the MkIII cars for 1963 were fitted with a revised cylinder head and inlet manifold which incorporated some improvements suggested by Harry Weslake. Significant performance increases had to wait until the V8 engine replaced the old 3.0-litre straight-six and the rejuvenated car became a 3.5-litre, although tests had been done at Solihull with uprated one, two, and three-carburettor engines. One idea, to provide a bolt-on 'go-faster' kit, however, came from outside Solihull:

BT: "In fact, Raymond Mays spent vast sums of his money, well mostly the Rover Company's money, I think, in doing all sorts of phenomenal development work, and turned up a proper road-

James Taylor interviews Brian Terry, former Rover test engineer, and reveals the lighter side of Solihull life

Above, Pressed Steel's official photograph of the 3.0-litre estate prototype. Left, the youthful and serious-looking pairing of Roger Clark and Jim Porter at the start of the 1965 Acropolis. The car, 4 KUE, was later owned by Brian Terry. Clark came sixth on the Monte with it — does it still exist? Below and right, tester's remains! William Martin-Hurst's 3.0-litre

converted road-trim three-carburettor set, which he was going to market, and which had got the most beautiful idling on it. My pride and joy in those days, before we went all silly and metric . . . I could stand threepenny bits on top of the carburettors when they were running properly, any way, pointing in any direction, and they didn't fall over. Now he had got this three-carburettor set which would idle at 400 revs with a threepenny bit standing on top! And it was magnificent! The bottom end performance was excellent, but we thought it rather strange that it didn't seem to go any faster. We put it on the test-bed and in fact it turned out 1½bhp more than the single-carburettor which we'd done!''

There were, of course, limits on what could be achieved in the way of performance increases anyway:

BT: ''There was always a limiting factor with any of those vehicles, you see . . . the limiting factor on putting extra performance into them was that the gearbox wouldn't stand it. It was basically a 1934 design, and it wouldn't stand the extra power through it. Generally, P4s used to hold together, but, you know, I've stripped first gears and cracked gearboxes in 3.0-litres more times than I care to think about. If you got the wheels to bite properly, as opposed to getting them to spin hard, the chances were you would damage something. On the original 3.0-litre, perhaps not, but certainly with the Weslake-head engine you did. But I mean, there's all sorts of tales like that. We used to split gearboxes in half . . . I've done one right in the middle of the Coventry Road. We literally lost all the gears out of the bottom, all over the road! This was with a 3.0-litre straight-six while doing a performance-test type standing start — you know, 3500 revs and foot sideways off the clutch pedal. It just went bang and stood still. And the gearbox cracked straight down the centre where the sump plug was, it fell open, and all the gears fell out. It was rather fun!''

Fortunately, most Rover customers treated their cars rather more gently, and it is doubtful whether any 3.0-litres were returned to Solihull under warranty with wrecked gearboxes. Nevertheless, when *Motor*'s testers road tested a MkII Saloon in October 1962, they observed, discreetly, that under the unnatural conditions of a fierce standing-start test, first gear had 'failed'. What that meant can perhaps be imagined from the foregoing! Generally speaking, though, gearboxes were long-lived and reliable units, and the same applied to the engines, the forerunners of which had appeared as early as 1948. They seemed to go on for ever, and there was therefore no real cause for major development work.

BT: ''There wasn't any *real* work done on the original 3.0-litre engine. The first development was the addition of roller cam-followers in place of the 'flat feet' ones, and there was a rather hilarious exercise when we decided — somebody decided, I wasn't involved at that stage — on putting nylon rollers in to cut down the noise, which was a beautiful idea, in fact. We put them in an engine on the test-bed and warmed it up, and it was all purring away ever so nicely and quietly when all of a sudden it started misfiring and popping and banging and all sorts of things — and the followers had melted! They weren't terribly successful.''

Even so, the engine test people were given their head when it came to helping out in the preparation of the works rally 3.0-litres, which first went into action in 1962. Within the constraints imposed by the rally regulations, and the Rover Company's unwillingness to increase the competitions department's budget, they did their best to help things along:

BT: ''We didn't *really* cheat, but when we blueprinted the engine we went through an awful lot of valve springs to find the stiffest production ones we could get! They really were production batches, but a lot of them should have been rejected as they were too stiff. The life of the camshaft didn't matter too much, of course, nor that of the cam-followers, but it did put the valve-bounce up. I think they all used to bounce a bit at about 6000 on those, but it didn't seem to matter. I've driven them for, oh, ages and ages with the valves bouncing, and they never had any notice. Shakes the loose carbon off them! In fact, eventually it used to make the valves go like tulips, you know; the stems pulled through and left the heads sticking up round the edge! This only happened on the inlets, though, so it didn't matter too much. You just adjusted it out and that was the end of that.''

Throughout the late Forties and the Fifties, Rover had built up a large export organisation, but relatively few concessions were made to local requirements in the company's overseas markets. At the beginning of the Sixties, however, it became clear that better market penetration might be achieved if special export models were made available. The first such saloons were smaller-engined versions of the 3.0-litre, never sold in this country, and one of them was powered by the 2.6-litre engine of the P4 110.

BT: ''Now I only saw one of those, which we had in the experimental department. It was a blue one, and I think the registration number was 8396 AC. In fact, that particular engine was relatively famous, because I could not make it bounce its valves, and we never found out why. I found out originally because I was doing some distributor tests — we were trying to decide whether it wanted a 3.0-litre or a 2.6 distributor in it. I was doing some tests with this on the test track at Solihull, and I found for some reason one day I overshot the mark. I was given to chasing somebody around the track, which was my wont on occasions — particularly at lunch-time when nobody was looking(!) — and I realised that it was, in fact, doing 6000 revs, and not bouncing its valves. Eventually I went and told Jack Swaine, and he said that couldn't be right. He went and thrashed the hell out of it, and decided I might have a valid point somewhere, and as long as I didn't blow it up I could find out what the valve bounce point was. I got that thing up to 6400 in second gear and it still didn't bounce its valves, but I wasn't brave enough to blow it up and go back and tell him!''

Not all the engines with which Brian had to deal were this good, although some were equally memorable. One which stands out was the detuned 3.0-litre unit tried out in some Land-Rover prototypes.

BT: ''These were the 129-inch Land-Rovers — the one-ton Land-Rovers which never went into production. They were just like trucks, very high, with big square wings and a big open back to them. They had a 3.0-litre engine . . . initially the early 3.0-litre engine. Then they had the long-manifold engine, the 110 manifold on a 3.0-litre engine. They ran low-compression versions as well because the engineers reckoned the high-compression one was using exotic fuel when they'd rather it used rubbish fuel. The one big joke about those was that they used to run on like things possessed. I've gone round the Rover test track in one of those, done three quick laps — I've

Main picture, one of the rallying 3.0-litres in action on the 1964 Spa-Sofia-Liege Rally. The cars were almost standard production models. **Inset**, sales catalogue shot of the MkIII 3.0-litre engine installation

Behind the scenes

actually timed it — turned the thing off, got out of the cab and timed it for 30 seconds still running on, got back in, turned the key back on and driven away again without using the starter! They were unbelievable! They knocked and knocked and clattered and rattled and they just would not stop. They were just self-igniting and they carried on — they were that bad! Which is funny, because they didn't suffer from it in the car.''

Another prototype which passed through the experimental department in the early Sixties was the 3.0-litre estate car, which had difficulties of a different kind.

BT: ''There were problems with it: shake, body-shake, was the big one. I can remember doing some testing — not very strenuous, mind you, I must admit, because it wasn't our car. It belonged to whoever put the body on.''

JT: ''It was a conversion by Pressed Steel, I believe.''

BT: ''Yes. It was converted from an existing saloon, but it did have fairly bad shake. I think that was the reason it wasn't continued, apart from the fact that, if I remember rightly, it was going to cost a lot more than the saloon. I've got a feeling it was going to be about £3000. The standard car was about £1700, wasn't it?. No, I can remember that car had a top-hinged door in it, and the top-hinged door used to wag like fury, and in fact if you went on a fairly rough-surfaced road it would pop open, it was that bad. The whole thing shook at the back. We had at the same time a Humber Super Snipe estate for test purposes, which didn't do it. But the Humber weighed a hell of a lot more than the Rover did, and I presume that's how they'd done it. They'd just put damn great RSJs across the back or something, to hold it together! I would guess that the combination of those two problems was why it wasn't produced: the price was a bit on the high side compared with that of the Humber which it would have been competing with, and, certainly, torsionally it was bad. There's no question about it.''

Far more successful was Rover's adoption of the lightweight 3½-litre V8 engine originally developed during the Fifties by General Motors in America for use in the 'compact' Buicks, Oldsmobiles and Pontiacs. Once the engine had arrived in Britain in early 1965, Solihull's engineers lost no time in getting to grips with it. Brian

Above, former Rover test driver, Brian Terry, seen this year with his uncle's 3½-litre coupé, one of the many Rover models he tested when new

remembers a problem with the very first V8-engined Rover development car:

BT: ''The original one we had in a P6 was a straightforward Buick engine, straight in, with standard carburettor, a Rochester four-barrel, and we couldn't make out why the damn thing wouldn't go round corners! Every time you put it round an island reasonably quickly it used to die on one bank. We left the bonnet off one day and did it, and you could see the petrol pouring straight out of the overflow of the flat chamber on one side! The Americans obviously had got this beautiful engine — which was a very nice piece of work — but it would not go other than in a straight line, perhaps because their cornering was so bad, or because they didn't have many corners! It was a disaster. We tried Rochester, Holley and Carter carburettors, and they were all exactly the same, which is why they had to be SUs when we got down to it. It's a pity they were too small but that was somebody else's silly choice, I suppose! Anyway, that's that. But the original P5 had a Rochester carburettor on as well, and even that wouldn't go round corners very well.''

JT: ''Do you remember testing the V8-engined P5 cars?''

BT: ''I spent many hours flying up and down the M6 when it was first opened, from Birmingham to Morecambe. We used to go up as far as they'd done. We'd reckon to leave after we'd started work in the morning, get to Morecambe, have a snack at coffee-time and get back by lunch-time. The highest average speed we ever got? We did 19 miles up at the North end of the M6 at an

average speed of 117.4mph, if I remember correctly. That was a barmy set-up: we had a battery of instruments made up for engine speed, engine oil temperature — at two points, one actually in the middle of the oil pump and one in the sump — water temperature in the radiator and in the cylinder head, oil pressure, gearbox input oil temperature, output oil temperature, exhaust manifold temperature, first silencer temperature . . . and several others. I think there were eight gauges all mounted on a panel in front of the passenger seat, and we set up a cine-camera in the back seat photographing these intruments. This was the point in going up there. We hammered up and down this blasted road, which made me feel sick, as I had to sit in the back keeping an eye on the camera, turning it on and off as we got held up with traffic delays. Philip insisted on doing the driving as it made *him* feel sick if he had to sit in the back . . . We were taking one shot every second initially, and eventually it drove me spare . . . then he relented and I think we had one shot every *two* seconds for the whole journey! And we did this every day for three weeks . . . four weeks, something like that. Drove me absolutely spare. I very nearly went home and said: ''That's it, I'm leaving!'' I didn't, but oh, dear, talk about soul-destroying! In fact it showed up all sorts of problems with the engine, the cooling system, the oil pump, all sorts of things. That engine is very much changed from the American engine, far more than people realise, I think.''

With a decade of close familiarity with Rover's engines behind him, it was scarcely surprising that, in 1968, Brian should find himself seconded · to a special team formed to deal with adapting these engines to meet the new American exhaust emission control requirements. He soon found, however, that he ''quite honestly couldn't stand it. Having spent years trying to make them go properly and drive properly . . . I was down there losing performance hand over fist for the sake of a gang of Americans that had got a kink! It just wasn't my idea at all.''

So, with many regrets, Brian left Solihull for pastures new. But old habits die hard. When his new employers bought him an SD1 3500, he was unable to resist the temptation to have David Price Racing tweak the engine. Just a *little* bit, of course.

CONTINUED FROM PAGE 138

the centre. This means that rain cannot blow in forward of the window when it is in the open position, and water drips do not run down the forward extremity of the frame and into the interior.

In keeping with a "Grand Tourer", stowage space on the 3-litre has received great attention. As well as the already-mentioned dash locker and parcels tray there are really large pockets in the front doors with spring-loaded flaps, and smaller ones in the rear of the front seats. There is another large parcels shelf under the rear window.

Boot capacity is vast. The upward-opening lid is counter-balanced and is internally illuminated when sidelights are switched on. The spare wheel is mounted in a separate compartment below the floor, and can be wound down with the wheelbrace from a socket in the boot. This feature frees the entire boot for luggage but the 12-volt battery and large tools (jack, wheelbrace, starting handle, tyre pump, and nave plate removal lever) are neatly stowed

under trimmed flaps. The whole of the boot interior is trimmed, and the lid is lockable.

Door locks are of the press-button type and on front doors the key has to be inserted into the press-buttons to lock or unlock. These locks were not a pleasing feature of the car as the buttons were lacking in rigidity, the task of inserting the key into a rather "sloppy" lock being something that could never be accomplished easily. Separate locks in the door panels would be an undoubted improvement. The interior door handles were excellent, the rear doors incorporating foolproof "child" locks. The bonnet lock was operated from under the right-hand side of the parcels shelf by another well-shaped pull-lever.

With finish, equipment, and engineering to such very high standards the Rover 3-litre is indeed a British car to be proud of. Although a luxury car in every sense of the word it has performance and controllability in unusually high measure, and must be assessed as great value for money.